THE JEWISH
UNDERGROUND
OF SAMARKAND

THE JEWISH UNDERGROUND OF SAMARKAND

HOW FAITH DEFIED SOVIET RULE

A Memoir and a History

RABBI HILLEL ZALTZMAN

[M]

MANDEL VILAR PRESS

This book is based on the author's memoir, *Samarkand, The Underground with a Far-Reaching Impact*, published privately in 2016.

This book is typeset in Minion Pro 11.5/14.5. The paper used in this book meets the minimum requirements of ANSI/NISO Z39.48- 1992 (R1997) ∞

Cover and text designed by Sophie Appel

PUBLISHERS CATALOGUING-IN-PUBLICATION DATA

Name: Zaltzman, Rabbi Hillel
Title: The Jewish Underground of Samarkand: How Faith Defied Soviet Rule (2023)
Description: Simsbury, Connecticut, Mandel Vilar Press
Identifiers: ISBN: 9781942134923 (pbk.)
E-ISBN: 9781942134930 (ebook)

Subjects: Zaltzman, Hillel—Memoir and History—World War Two—Ukrainian Chassidic Chabad Jewish Community—Nazi invasion of Ukraine—The Chabad Community emigration to Samarkand, Uzbekistan—Jews Under Soviet Communism—Jews, the KGB, and the struggles for religious liberty—The survival of Jewish rituals, practices, and education in the USSR—*Chamah*, Underground Jewish Organization—Clandestine schools and Jewish religious education—The survival of Jewish life and practices in the Soviet Union—Soviet Jewish emigration—*Chamah's* continued support for Jews living in Russia and Jewish immigrants to Israel and America

Classification LCC DS134.85 Z73

Printed in the United States of America

23 24 25 26 27 28 29 / 9 8 7 6 5 4 3 2 1

Mandel Vilar Press
Simsbury, Connecticut

www.americasforconservation.org / www.mvpublishers.org

CONTENTS

PUBLISHER'S NOTE

This note refers to spellings used in the book. In accordance with the practice of Orthodox and Chassidic Jews, the Almighty is always referred to in writing as G-d, or Hashem (which, in Hebrew, means "The Name"). The name of G-d is treated with respect; therefore it is customary not to spell out G-d's name in any language on any document that could be destroyed or erased.

Most of the Hebrew terms are transliterated according to the Ashkenazi pronunciation used by Chassidic Jews, for example, Shabbos (the Sabbath), *mitzvos* (the commandments), and Kosel (the Western Wall).

"R." before a name stands for "Reb," a standard prefix for adult Jewish men, a respectful way of calling them by their first names, similar to "Mister."

PREFACE

Oh Samarkand!

The Chabad-Lubavitch association with Samarkand came to pass during the Second World War. As the Nazis pressed into Russia, throngs of Jews fled eastward to the Soviet provinces of Central Asia. Members of the Chabad stream of Chassidic Jewry, along with other religiously observant Jews, settled primarily in the cities of Samarkand and Tashkent, both located in present-day Uzbekistan. My family was among them. During the war years and after, the Chabad chassidim of Samarkand focused on their Jewish survival, forming secret prayer groups, Hebrew schools, and yeshivas for older students.

The sublime, impassioned style of religious devotion that set the Chabad chassidim apart—their Torah study, prayers, and their inspirational, song-filled Chassidic get-togethers (*farbrengens* in Yiddish)—made a strong impression upon the youth there. They would often declare of the place, *S'gist zich elokus mamash.* "It overflows with G-dliness!"

In that era, the Chabad community in Samarkand was known among the chassidim of the Soviet Union as the "Israel of the USSR," or in the Chassidic idiom, Samarkand is the "*shpitz*—the height of Chabad."

Even outside Russia, the Chabad community in Samarkand was regarded with great admiration, and R. Yosef Yitzchak Schneersohn, the sixth Lubavitcher Rebbe, expressed special affection towards the chassidim there. This was evidenced by the Rebbe's 1950 directive to a group of yeshiva students, newly arrived in New York from Russia by way of Brunoy, France: "See to it that the good customs of Samarkand are instituted here," he told them.

A year after the war, in 1946–47, there was a great flight of Chabad chassidim from the Soviet Union, with only a few scattered chassidim remaining in Samarkand. Divine Providence placed upon them—that is, upon us—the mission of nurturing Judaism and the Chassidic spirit there.

Although all of our Jewish-related activities, especially those associated with the yeshiva, were clandestine and guarded with the utmost secrecy, the Chassidic spirit penetrated all veils of secrecy. Whether we liked it or not, the spirit of Samarkand was felt far and wide.

Religious Jews throughout the Soviet Union longed to be in the presence of the chassidim of Samarkand, to join in their *farbrengens* and experience their warm, spiritual atmosphere. Whoever visited Samarkand would secretly transmit his impressions of the place to his own community and to other Jews in his surroundings, in turn inspiring them.

I have always felt that the atmosphere of Samarkand had a spiritually uplifting effect on those who lived there. Once, soon after the legendary Chabad mentor and personality R. Mendel Futerfas arrived in Samarkand, I shared my sentiments with him. *"Nu, nu,"* he shrugged, "everyone is uplifted in your Samarkand."

When R. Mendel finally received his long-awaited exit visa, I sensed that it was difficult for him to leave us. At that time, he turned to me and said, "Hil'ke, do you remember you told me that just by being in Samarkand, one is uplifted. Now I see there's some truth in your words."

I am sure that certain people who lived in Samarkand or elsewhere in the Soviet Union at the time will raise protest: "What are you fantasizing about? A flourishing Chassidic community in Samarkand? I lived there myself, and I never saw or heard anything about it!"

They won't be the only ones. Many Russian Jews cannot believe that religious Jews, let alone entire communities, existed in Russia at the time. For them I have but one reply: "If you would have indeed known about us then, I wouldn't be here today. This book would then indeed be a work of fiction!"

In 1968, R. Yehuda Leib Levin, then the official chief rabbi of the Soviet Union, went on a special visit to the United States, accompanied by the cantor of Leningrad's Grand Choral Synagogue. This cantor, it was commonly known, was a KGB informant, sent to keep a close eye on Rabbi Levin's movements. Even when Rabbi Levin went to New York for a private audience with the Rebbe, he couldn't leave his minder outside.

At the beginning of their meeting, when the Rebbe asked if there had been positive development for Russian Jewry of late, Rabbi Levin replied, "You want to hear the good? Let me tell you about Samarkand! There's a group of young men there doing wonderful—"

The Rebbe interrupted the chief rabbi with a smile. "Why are you sending me to Samarkand? I want to hear what's happening in Moscow! As the rabbi of Moscow, why think about other places?"

When word of this audience eventually made it back to us, some people speculated that the Rebbe didn't want Rabbi Levin to speak too much about us, out of concern that there would be negative repercussions for us.

Sometime around the High Holidays of 1971, a group of emigrants fresh from the community in Samarkand arrived in New York and visited the great Torah scholar R. Moshe Feinstein. During their conversation about the difficult conditions of life in the USSR and the continual risks they took there to maintain Jewish life, Rabbi Feinstein asked them: "How could you survive under these conditions?"

"Did we have a choice?" they answered, and the sage burst into tears.

I am not a professional writer or journalist. I never once imagined that I would one day record my memories of Samarkand, let alone write an entire book. How, then, did this book come to be?

In early 2000, my son, Efraim Fishel Zaltzman, asked me to tell him about my activities in the former Soviet Union with Chamah (acronym for *Chaburas Mezakei Ha'Rabim*—Society for the Promotion of Public Merit), the organization we had founded to preserve and promote Judaism, to provide economic assistance for Jews in Samarkand, and to maintain the relationship we had with the Lubavitcher Rebbe at that time.

My son's request touched my heart, and wanting to give a precise accounting of those times, I decided to put those experiences into writing and fax them to my friend R. Moshe Nissilevitch. Rabbi Nissilevitch founded Chamah sixty years ago in Russia as an underground Jewish activist movement and headed the organization until his death in 2011. I had worked with him for decades and intended that he review the manuscript and make notations. As I was writing, I remembered more and more details about the activities of Chamah in Samarkand and about the events that transpired in those years and the "fax" just grew and grew. Without realizing, I had written more than twenty pages. Obviously, I had no intention of faxing something of that size.

Writing these memories was a tremendously enjoyable experience for me. I felt as though I had gone back in time to the places and events of which I wrote. Truth be told, despite my experience of writing these memoirs, after rereading them some time later, I considered throwing them away. The information was interesting, but the narrative was poor. I myself had difficulty reading the words, having hastily included many notes and corrections throughout the manuscript, with arrows and lines indicating details to be included before or after, or removed altogether. In short: it was a mess.

In a telephone conversation with a colleague in Israel, R. Shmuel Levin, I mentioned all of this, as well as my intentions to discard the entire manuscript. R. Shmuel convinced me to hold on to it and promised to send me someone who would type out the stories in a clear, organized fashion. I figured that no one would be able to make sense of the manuscript, but I agreed nonetheless.

After a while, R. Shmuel recommended that I approach R. Avrohom Yeshaya Reinitz, who had helped edit the memoirs of a number of chassidim. As he reviewed what I had written, he was deeply touched by the Chassidic wealth found within those memories. To him, the book formed a vivid narrative that transported the reader back to those times. He edited those memoirs and published them in a Chabad periodical published in New York. The first installment appeared before Passover in 2000 and over the next several years dozens of articles followed and became quite popular with the readers.

In order to facilitate the writing of the manuscript, I purchased a new laptop. Many of my friends were skeptical, thinking that it was too late for a man of my age to learn to type, but I always replied with the familiar refrain, "It's never too late." Before long, I had learned to type in both Hebrew and English and this removed a burden from my shoulders.

Thus did Hil'ke—as they called me in Samarkand—become a writer.

As the articles started to become more widely read, there were those who questioned why I had not written about them, seeing as they also lived through those same adventures and risked their lives for Judaism in those years. I can answer all of those complaints with one reply: I am no historian. My intention was merely to put my personal memories into writing. Nor do I presume that I can make a complete accounting of the history of Chabad in Samarkand—it's only because Divine Providence thrust me into the Jewish underground that I became involved with affairs that impacted the broader community. Therefore, no one should take offense if they are not mentioned in these pages: their omission does not suggest that they did not fight for and accomplish things for their Jewish brethren.

This memoir is a new revised and shortened edition of my original book, which was published by Chamah in Hebrew in 2013, and in English translation in 2016 under the title *Samarkand: The Underground with a Far-Reaching Impact,* translated from the Hebrew by Boruch Werdiger and Naomi Raksin and edited by Yakov Gershon. (There were also editions in Russian and Yiddish.)

The English edition of the book was so well-received by readers, it occurred to me that this story could reach a wider audience in addition to the Chabad community. Towards that end, I shortened my 800-page book by almost half, resulting in this new, abridged version. I am grateful to Robert Mandel of Mandel Vilar Press, for taking it on and helping me bring this project to fruition. I want to acknowledge my agent, Regina Ryan, who believed in the value of this story and helped me find a publisher who believed in it too. I also wish to thank Bonny V. Fetterman, who edited this abridged edition of my book, and Yakov Gershon for his assistance.

I would also like to acknowledge R. Avrohom Reinitz, who edited the original Hebrew manuscript, and R. Shlomo Galperin, who read the Hebrew manuscript and made edits and notations. I am also grateful to R. Betzalel Schiff for graciously giving me access to the impressive photo archives in his possession. Although I already had a number of photos, I found so many pictures in his collection that have truly enriched this memoir, I owe him an enormous debt of gratitude.

Last, but certainly not least, I am eternally thankful and indebted to my dear wife, Shoshana, may she live and be well, whose constant encouragement has allowed me to reach this point. The writing of this book took place mainly in my home after work hours. Allowing me to immerse myself in the writing of this book at the expense of family time was a tremendous sacrifice on her part.

To my dear friends and to the many students who learned in the Samarkand underground, I beg you: Write down your memoirs, as the Rebbe desired, "in order that the next generation shall know."

Rabbi Hillel Zaltzman
February 2023

THE JEWISH
UNDERGROUND
OF SAMARKAND

INTRODUCTION

The book before you focuses on the story of the Jewish underground that operated in Samarkand under the Communists from 1946 until the early 1970s. In order to better understand the historical background of the events described within these pages, I will begin with a brief accounting of the formation of the Communist regime. I will try to explain how it was possible for such a vicious and evil entity to arise, and in particular, how and why some Jews took part in its founding.

Until the Revolution of 1917, the Russian Empire was ruled by the czars of the Romanov dynasty. The empire was divided into districts, called *gubernias*. Each *gubernia* was comprised of estates containing numerous plots of land. The squire of the estate, the *pomeschik*, or the *poritz* in Yiddish, was a kind of "minor king," whose authority was distinct from that of the central government. The serfs who lived and worked on the estate were literally slaves to their squire. The residents of the estate, Jewish and gentile, constantly sought to find favor in the eyes of the *poritz*. Many of the classic Jewish folk tales from this time period involve unfortunate Jews enduring horrible punishments by the *poritz* when they were unable to keep up with the rent they owed him. In addition, the Jews of these estates were often subject to persecution at the hands of Russian Orthodox priests, who would incite their congregations to violence against their Jewish neighbors. Under the czarist regime, hundreds of thousands of Jews were murdered or expelled from their homes and had their possessions plundered. The czars did nothing to prevent these pogroms or to protect their Jewish subjects.

From 1791 until the Revolution in 1917, Jewish settlement was confined to a specific region in the western part of the Russian Empire known as the "Pale of Settlement." Czarist Russia had annexed these areas after the partitions of Poland in 1772 and 1795, bringing a large population of Jews under Russian control. During this period, it was illegal for Jews to live in areas that were designated for ethnic Russians only. Jews comprised about 10 percent of the total population of the Pale. Some, mostly professionals and businessmen, lived in big cities, but most of them lived in *shtetls,* small villages and towns. They made their living as peddlers and craftsmen, storekeepers and innkeepers, and dealers in timber and grain; university study was restricted for Jews by quotas.

Against this background, we can easily understand why, as the winds of change started to blow in Russia, people were inspired by all sorts of rousing slogans—*A Government of Workers and Peasants; Equality for All; Tear down the old and build the new; From each according to his ability and to each according to his need.* Many Jews stood on the front lines to support the revolution. Obviously, the "enlightened" Jews who sought to assimilate into society and become "like all the other nations" were the most involved, but there were instances where even religious Jews joined the revolution. They were tired of persecution at every turn, and they saw the revolution as an opportunity to change the government's approach to dealing with the Jews. They had the purest of ideological intentions and thus fought for the cause with great devotion.

Relative to their population, a great number of Jews took part in the revolution, and many of them became leaders among the revolutionaries. Some notable figures were Trotsky, Kamenev, Zinoviev, and Sverdlov, among others. The most dynamic of these characters was Leon "Leibel" Trotsky, a fiery orator and a natural leader. He founded and commanded the Communist's revolutionary army and was a confidante of revolutionary leader Vladimir Lenin, with whom he worked hand in hand. Seeing so many of their brethren among the revolution's leaders, many Jews were drawn in.

Whether this is truth or a joke, I don't know, but the following story illustrates how strongly Russian Jewry was attracted to the revolution: Trotsky's father pays a visit to Communist headquarters, and sees all of his son's Jewish friends there. Suddenly, Lenin arrives. The elder Trotsky asks his son, "Leibel, what's this *goy* doing here?" "Lenin?" Leibel says. "We need him to keep up appearances." Another such anecdote goes: Trotsky's father came by the headquarters, and cried out, "Leibel! What are you doing here? Today is your mother's *yahrzeit*! You should be in shul to say *Kaddish!*" Trotsky calmed his father. "Don't worry. As soon as the *goy* leaves," he said, pointing to Lenin, "we'll make a minyan here."

In 1917, the Communists declared that they had established a new government for the nation, which would henceforth be referred to as the Soviet Union. The revolutionaries wanted to emphasize that the government would not be run by one person, as in the past, but by a council. In reality, this newly minted nation would eventually be ruled by tyranny. After Lenin's death in 1924, the dictator Josef Stalin moved to seize power over the Soviet Union. He was a very simple, uneducated man, with a terrible temper and cruel nature. Immediately grasping the potential of the political climate created by Lenin's demise, he rapidly capitalized upon it. In the 1930s, to completely consolidate his power, he set about purging the political landscape of anyone suspected of "anti-revolutionary" activities.

Under this pretext, millions of Communists were arrested, tortured, and sent to forced labor camps in Siberia. Among them were those who had fought most valiantly for the Communist cause. Stalin was fearful of his colleagues in the Party, and especially the Jews, who were accomplished and effective leaders. He conspired to quickly rid himself of the other party leaders and become the sole head of state. Citizens were arrested in unprecedented numbers and shooting squads worked around the clock. Leon Trotsky, the renowned colleague of Lenin, was exiled and wound up in faraway

Mexico. Yet the long arm of Soviet intrigue reached him even there and in 1940 he was found dead in Mexico City after being attacked with a pick-axe in his home.

Even while his purges were raging, Stalin wanted his name engraved in the hearts of the masses as the savior of all humanity. Through an unprecedented propaganda campaign, Stalin succeeded in bringing the citizens of the Soviet Union to believe that he was the most humane and dedicated leader in the world. So successful was this campaign that even prisoners condemned to death at Stalin's own command were convinced that had Stalin only known of their plight, he would surely save them! And so they went to their deaths, still professing their fervent allegiance to Stalin.

The purges, or "repressions," as they were known in Russia, extended far beyond the Party elite, reaching down into every local Party cell and nearly all of the intellectual professions, since anyone with a higher education was suspected of being a potential counter-revolutionary. This depleted the Soviet Union of its brainpower and left Stalin as the sole intellectual force in the country—the expert on virtually every human endeavor.

In the early days of the regime, and especially during Stalin's reign, the Communists had started carrying out their plans for the transferal of economic power, ostensibly to the workers and peasants, under the slogan "Equality for All." Wealthy landowners and others who had enjoyed affluence during the previous regime were arrested and sent to labor camps and many were executed. These prisoners were literally slaves to the government. They built cities, roads, and railroads throughout the Soviet Union. When the prisons could not possibly hold any more prisoners, the prisoners themselves would be used to build new prison camps. They were worked to near death, receiving little more than a day's bread and water for their labor. Private stores were closed, their proprietors were imprisoned and their goods expropriated. Thus were yesterday's wealthy reduced to paupers, and yesterday's slaves to masters.

The Communists waged a relentless propaganda war to change the definitions of "wealth" and "equality." The greatest wealth was to

work for the benefit of the Motherland, while equality simply referred to equality of pay. Therefore, a professor and the janitor at the
university would earn the same salary. After all, were they not both
working for the good of the country? Furthermore, the doctrine of
"From each according to his ability, to each according to his need,"
introduced a new factor: If this professor had one child, and the
janitor had five, the janitor would have to earn more in order to
support his family. Within a few years, the Communists succeeded
in fulfilling their promise to "destroy the old," but they never succeeded in "building the new." Equal distribution of wealth destroyed
the incentive to work and the economy fell into ruin.

Perhaps most catastrophic was Stalin's policy of forced collec-
tivization of agriculture—the replacement of individual peasant
farms by collective ones—which led directly to the famine of the
early 1930s. Millions of people died of starvation when the government appropriated food supplies and failed to distribute them.

In spite of the economic collapse of their nation, the Soviet Union
conducted a huge campaign to publicize the success of Communism
to the world. As the citizens of their country suffered from bread
shortages, the Communists filled trainloads of wheat as foreign aid
for the French people, whose wheat crops had suffered blight. These
trains would be parked at the border, where foreign trains would
frequently pass. Thousands of foreign passengers saw the Soviet freight
cars inscribed with massive letters reading: "Wheat for France from
Soviet surplus." It was a campaign of deception.

For a period during the early 1920s, Lenin had introduced a
different approach, referred to as the NEP, an acronym for New
Economic Plan (Novaya Ekonomicheskaya Politika). This plan allowed citizens to engage in nominal private commerce. Those who
were allowed began to devote themselves to doing business, and
before long, many of them started to build wealth. When the Communists saw this new crop of affluent businesspeople, they decried
the ways of capitalism and ended the program. They set certain
standards for how much someone could earn at any given profession and structured the economy in such a way that the citizens

would earn the bare minimum to provide for their needs, but no more. In order to survive, everyone sought out underhanded ways to earn a living without having to report the income to the government. People would jokingly ask: How could you steal from the state? The answer: We're only getting back a fraction of what the government steals from us!

At the same time that the government introduced their economic policy, the Communists embraced an atheist ideology, and they fought against anything that smelled of religion. A special bureau was created for the sole purpose of stamping out Judaism, the Yevreskaya Sektzia, or Yevsektzia for short. This bureau was staffed by young Jewish men and women who had dedicated their lives to fighting religion and harassing religious Jews and closing down their institutions.

The Communists called religion the "opiate of the masses," claiming that it poisoned the mind and should be totally uprooted. Any Jew who sought to adhere to Torah and *mitzvos* was marked for incessant persecution.

The harassment began, in fact, from the day a child was born. By performing the circumcision rite on his son, a father risked his livelihood, since his government-appointed employers would fire him as soon as the matter became known. Therefore, the mother and father would leave home on the day of the ceremony and leave their child in the care of the grandparents. Thus, the parents would have an alibi should the authorities discover that a *bris* (circumcision) had been performed by their child's old-fashioned grandparents.

As the children got older, they would have to be enrolled in a government school where they would be educated to embrace atheism and forced to desecrate Shabbos and the Jewish holidays. Parents who wanted to raise their children in the ways of Torah had no choice but to hide their children, or send them to the public schools and hope they could manage to undo the damage at home.

When it came time to marry off one's children, it was extremely difficult to find a young woman to make a suitable match for a young man—let alone one of a truly Chassidic religious character. If, in the end, a couple did succeed in building a Chassidic home, they would have to struggle to observe Shabbos, since all employment was through the government and everyone was expected to work on Shabbos.

Maintaining Jewish family life was incredibly difficult, as the nearest kosher *mikvah*—the women's ritual bath essential for any observant Jewish community—was usually several hours' journey. Public Jewish community life was, for all purposes, extinct. In large cities, the Communists allowed one synagogue to operate, but whoever attended was certain to be dismissed from his job, so underground prayer groups formed in their stead.

In this atmosphere of unending dread, we lived for decades. It was only through the power of faith, along with the intense idealism and spirit of sacrifice instilled within us by the Chabad rebbes, that we succeeded in raising a generation of chassidim.

CHAPTER 1

A Chassidic Education in Communist Russia

When reminiscing about the past, most people will only recall a few vague memories from early childhood. Not so those who grew up under the shadow of Soviet rule. Our parents' struggle to provide us with an authentically Jewish education and their efforts to prevent us from being exposed to the heresies of Communism made a profound impression on us as children that affects us to this day. To illustrate the setting of my childhood years, I will begin with some historical background.

After the Russian Revolution in 1917, the new Communist regime began a ruthless battle to eradicate religion. According to law, citizens were granted the freedom of religion, but in actuality, anyone who failed to follow the government program was in serious peril. In the 1930s, when the Communist rage was at its peak, thousands of people were exiled to labor camps in the Arctic wilderness of Siberia, and numerous Jews were shot dead in the cellars of the NKVD, the Soviet secret police. The NKVD, a forerunner of the KGB, was only one of a few dreaded Soviet acronyms, as the names of the Soviet internal security apparatus changed over the years. At first they were the "Cheka" and later the GPU, MVD, KGB, and so on. Chassidim would refer to the secret police as *di [drai] osiyos*— the [three] letters, or simply, the *knepl* (button), after the brass buttons on their uniforms.

The same fate was meted out to anyone who dared to educate his children in the spirit of Judaism. He was marked as an enemy of the state for poisoning his children with religious propaganda. Since Mother Russia was so concerned for the welfare of her citizens, the law stated that the right of such a parent to educate his or her children was rescinded and the children were sent to special institutions for orphans where they were "re-educated."

The words of the prophet, "Your demolishers and destroyers will emerge from you," were born to fruition in Communist Russia. The notorious Yevsektzia, the Jewish Section of the Communist Party, composed of party zealots, took the lead in the propaganda war against Jewish religion from 1918, until the section was disbanded in 1930. Its members included Jews who had turned their backs on Judaism, even including, unfortunately, the children of religious Jews. In his account of his 1927 imprisonment at the hands of the Soviet authorities, R. Yosef Yitzchak Schneersohn—the Lubavitcher Rebbe of the day—makes it clear that it was the Yevsektzia who initiated the war against him. His arrest was a direct result of their work.

Working hand in hand with governmental agencies and the secret police, this propaganda agency went after all the institutions of Jewish life. The Jewish schools and yeshivas were the Yevsektzia's first target. Within a short time, all religious schools in the Soviet Union were closed. The newly opened public schools taught a curriculum based on the Marxist-Leninist ideology. In the early years after the Revolution, the Communists invested great effort to uproot belief in G-d from the hearts of the children. Public school teachers dedicated many lessons to this subject and they brought up their heretical dogma at every opportunity. Parents were legally obligated to register their children in these schools.

In Samarkand, there was a local Jew named Daniel. His surname—Borisovitch—was simply a derivative of his father's first name, as was traditional in Russia. Daniel Borisovitch was a cultural Jew, firmly irreligious, though deeply appreciative of the Yiddish language and culture, or a Yiddishist, as they were known. After the Revolution, he was one of the early members of the

Yevsektzia, but once he saw through the lies of the Communists, he became disillusioned and left. Later, he would achingly tell us of the methods the Yevsektzia used to promote their agenda:

"We had to approach religious parents to persuade them to send their children to government schools, where the children would be taught—in Yiddish—outright heresy. But once his superiors received reports that the Jews were standing firm and refusing outright to send their children to the schools, they had a new idea. The children would go to the schools, but the parents would be able to choose whomever they wanted for the teaching staff.

"The Jews accepted the offer," Daniel continued, "and after some time had passed, and the children grew comfortable at school and amongst their classmates, the school discreetly switched a teacher with one of their own. Some time later, they did the same with another teacher, and eventually, they were all replaced."

With a pained heart, he recalled their orders to try and force-feed Jewish children non-kosher food or bread on Pesach. The children held their mouths tightly shut and desperately fought back. "I'll never forget," he said, "how cruelly we acted towards those innocent children."

But the Yevsektzia did not stop there. They wanted to ensure that the children would be completely severed from religious life, so they closed down the shuls—the synagogues—as well. Anyone who organized a prayer service would be accused of involvement in illegal underground activity. In the big cities, the government permitted one or two shuls to be active, so as to demonstrate to the world that Mother Russia allowed freedom of religion. In many towns, however, not even one remained. Minsk, to name one, had ninety-six synagogues in operation before the Communist Revolution. Afterwards, there remained only one small, secret prayer group, denied of its own quarters at that: they were forced to hold services in a rented room.

In order to receive government approval, these few remaining shuls were required to have a committee of twenty people, most of whom were loyal to the secret police and would report to them the names of the individuals that prayed there. Most importantly, these committee members ensured that parents did not bring their children along. Whoever violated the law in this way was accused of contaminating their children with anti-Communist values. This accusation would endanger the shul's existence, since it often served as an excuse for the authorities to shut it down completely.

There was one Jew in Samarkand by the name of Chaim Chernovitzer. He was an active presence in the shul and a proud member of its committee. Whenever a tourist would arrive from abroad he would approach him, talk to him, and not give anyone else a chance to welcome the newcomer. He would proclaim proudly that he is an appointee of the KGB, and if not for him the shul would be closed down. If the tourist had the idea of offering any support to the other members of the community, Chaim Chernovitzer's little chat was intimidating enough to make him think again.

Naturally, most of the people who prayed in the official shuls were elderly retirees: they hadn't much to lose. Working people, however, were afraid to attend since their names would be recorded on a black list and they were liable to lose their jobs.

The Hebrew term for education is *chinuch*, but it means so much more. *Chinuch* refers to one's academic, emotional, spiritual, and religious upbringing; it is the cornerstone of Jewish tradition and continuity. You can understand how difficult it was to give children a *chinuch* without a Jewish school, or a yeshiva, without any formal prayer, and worst of all—while sending them to a public school where heresy was instilled in every possible way.

Every parent was saddled with the burden of their own child's education. If one wanted his child to receive a religious education, he had to sit down and teach the child himself or hire someone to do so, several times a week, and be ever vigilant that neighbors wouldn't notice. As the fifth Lubavitcher Rebbe, Sholom Dovber Schneersohn, once declared, just as the practice of donning *tefillin* daily is a commandment incumbent upon every man, so too it is obligatory for every Jew to dedicate half an hour of thought each day to his children's *chinuch*. In those days, we felt the immediacy of this directive.

The Chabad chassidim were taught by the previous Lubavitcher Rebbe to risk their lives for their beliefs. Summoning the innermost depths of their souls, they fought against a cruel regime with courage and remarkable strength. Against all odds, they managed to instill a kosher education in their children. Some of these children learned at home and some in secret yeshivas. Other religious non-Lubavitchers also brought their children to the secret Chabad yeshivas, pleading for them to be accepted, knowing that this was the only way to maintain the continuity of their Jewish upbringing.

First Mission:
Hide the Children from the Neighbors

The war for Jewish education was both offensive and defensive: Parents struggled to keep their children from attending the Soviet schools, or at the very least to keep them home on Shabbos and holidays, if they were forced to attend at all. At the same time, they tried to provide their children with an authentic Jewish education at home. These were the two battlefronts my parents fought on as I was growing up.

I was born in Kharkov and lived there until I was about three years of age, when in 1941 the Nazis invaded the city. Like the other families of the community, we fled from the front and traveled east until we reached Samarkand, in Central Asia.

Shortly after we arrived in Samarkand, my older brother and sister became old enough for school. That was when my parents, R. Avrohom and Bracha Zaltzman, began their prolonged battle over the *chinuch* of their children. It is hard to describe the suffering my parents endured. In addition to the heresy in the schools mentioned earlier, going to school also meant regularly desecrating Shabbos and the festivals. It was a poisonous environment for a young Jewish child and my father did all that he could to prevent us from going to public school.

The courage of the young mothers of these children avoiding school was especially noteworthy. Generally, they were the ones who were left alone with their children while their husbands went to work and every knock on the door brought with it a rush of fear and anxiety. Unfortunately, the tremendous stress had a detrimental effect on the health of many of these heroic women.

Throughout the years that we were afraid of the KGB, we had special codes for communicating, for how to knock on a door or ring a bell. Each of us was very careful not to make a mistake, G-d forbid, so as not to cause fear or panic to the families in our neighborhood. Our code is still etched in my memory: two knocks on the door or ringing the bell, pause; three knocks, pause; and then two more knocks.

Using this code helped us to ensure that the whereabouts of any children not in school wouldn't be revealed to the authorities. The same code was employed when Jewish studies were held underground. Before anyone started to knock, he or she would concentrate and go through the steps in his or her mind so as not to make any mistakes.

The first stage in the battle, then, was to hide the children from the neighbors, so they wouldn't be aware that there were school-aged children in the house. The government had set up a centralized educational system that required every local principal to register all the school-aged children in his district with the school. The principal would send out his teachers during the day to trek from house to house, courtyard to courtyard, and innocently inquire of the neighbors whether there were any school-aged children around. When the neighbors knew of children who were the right age for school, they wouldn't hesitate to say so.

Registration generally took place in the summer, before the school year began. When it was over, my parents, as well as we children, would breathe a sigh of relief. Beforehand, we couldn't be seen on the street or even in the courtyard of our house. If the teachers received information about school-aged children not registered in school, they would hurriedly report them to the principal. According to law, the principal was obligated to go to the parents' home and find out why their children did not attend school. Refusing to register one's children for religious reasons was considered a serious crime, one that often reached the offices of the KGB.

It is impossible to judge those parents who did not stand up to the Communist government and sent their children to the public schools. Some parents claimed that keeping their child at home twenty-four hours a day would have had an adverse effect on their physical and emotional health.

There were a small number of parents who were not satisfied with sending their children to elementary school, but advocated advancing their education by sending them to university as well. They claimed that as long as they were in Russia without a hope on the horizon for receiving permission to emigrate, studying for a profession in university was a necessity. Some justified sending their children to university on the grounds that students were exempt from the army for the duration of their studies. Everyone had their reasons.

Many G-d-fearing individuals found it difficult to fight to such a degree, especially considering the risk that their children could be forcibly removed from their care and sent for "re-education" in government homes. A child educated in this way would be completely alienated from his parents and from anything Jewish.

So in the event that the authorities did receive word that children of school age were still at home, the parents often had no choice but to send a child to school. Historically, it was the boys who bore primary responsibility for studying Torah and attending yeshiva; the girls, on the other hand, for whom there was little precedent for providing a Jewish education in a formal setting, would receive their Jewish education at home. Consequently, in instances like these, many chassidim "sacrificed" their daughters and sent them to public school and were thus able to continue hiding their sons. Of course, they did not abandon their daughters to their spiritual fate, but spent hours at home on their Jewish education to minimize the damage caused to their souls in school. Still, as discussed elsewhere in this book, the Soviet education system would ultimately take an especially heavy toll on the girls.

My father tried to hide us and was successful for some years. But it soon became impossible to hide all of the children from the neighbors, so he decided to send my sister to school to minimize the pressure on the boys. My sister was representing the family, allowing my father to hide my older brother until he was past school age and the danger had dissipated.

For over two years after I reached school age, my father managed to hide me as well. However, my respite did not last, and at the age of nine, our neighbors discovered my existence and passed the information on to the principal of the local school. After refusing to send me to school, my father began receiving threats from the principal. If my father did not send me to school, warned the principal, his rights as a parent would be revoked. I would then be sent to a government orphanage. He had no choice and was forced to register me in public school; however, he was determined that I would not attend school on Shabbos.

My father registered me in a school in a neighborhood of non-Jews, in this case, a predominantly Muslim district, in the hope that the teachers and staff would be unfamiliar with Jewish law. This way, they wouldn't notice that I was only missing from school on Shabbos and other holidays.

Because of my advanced age, I was registered for second grade. My father spoke to the teacher—Ms. Nina Semyanova was her name—and after presenting her with a nice gift, he explained that until now I hadn't attended school because I was a weak child and the doctors said that I needed a lot of rest. For this reason, I had to rest two days a week: in addition to Sundays, when the entire school was out of session, I would not be attending on Saturdays either. The teacher, who was unaware of the sanctity of Shabbos in the Jewish religion, accepted his explanation and allowed me to stay home on Shabbos.

Since the school was in a non-Jewish, Muslim district, most of the children were gentiles. I remember how as a child, I would constantly tell myself that I was different from my peers. In time, I instilled myself with a distinct sense of my own identity and viewed my classmates, their holidays, customs, and way of life, with a sense of distance.

My father's family was artistically and musically inclined, and as a child, I also loved art, drawing, and music. I can remember my classmates enthusiastically declaring me an artist after seeing some pictures I had drawn in art class. However, I generally tried to hide my talents and not attract attention.

Every song in music class praised Mother Russia, Father Stalin, Lenin, and the Communist Party. Although I knew how to sing well, I despised singing these songs. The teacher once asked me, "Zaltzman, why don't you ever sing?" Without thinking, I blurted out, "I don't like your songs."

In the immediate second that followed my response, I realized this comment of mine had placed me in jeopardy. I broke out in a cold sweat. The teacher's brow shot up and looking at me in amazement, she asked, "What do you mean by 'your songs'? Which songs are 'ours' and which songs are 'yours'? Go over to the blackboard and sing one of 'your' songs!"

With Hashem's help, I managed to extricate myself from the predicament I had brought upon myself. Our landlord's son, a university student by the name of Pinchas Pinchasov, lived in our housing district and enjoyed listening to records of Rashid Baibutov, a popular Azerbaijani singer. He would play his music loudly and I knew many of his songs by heart. As I walked to the blackboard, my heart skipping a beat, I decided to sing one of his songs.

As I began to sing, the teacher opened her mouth wide in surprise. She had not imagined that I was able to sing so nicely! She enjoyed it so much that she completely forgot my faux pas, or perhaps she thought that I had been referring to Azerbaijani music all along.

In those days, due to the shortage of classrooms, lessons took place in shifts: one shift in the morning, and one in the afternoon. The music class took place in the final hour of the morning session, and at the precise time that I was singing, the teachers of the afternoon session arrived. Entering the hallway outside our classroom, they heard me singing. Noticing the afternoon teachers, my teacher invited them to quietly enter the classroom. She took pride in her student who sang so well.

Once my talent for singing was discovered, the school began asking me to perform on all sorts of holidays, such as May 1st, International Workers' Day; November 7th, anniversary of the Communist Revolution; and New Year's Day. Every time I was asked, a tumultuous battle waged within me. On the one hand, like any child, I loved to perform and to demonstrate my abilities, to prove that I could perform and sing as well if not better than anyone else. On the other hand, I still had a deep-seated aversion towards the non-Jewish atmosphere and Soviet holidays. In the end, I never performed for their celebrations and I didn't even attend them. When I think about it today, I realize how powerful my upbringing—my *chinuch*—must have been, and how much courage an eleven-year-old boy needed to not be drawn after the ways of his gentile classmates.

Remaining observant while attending a Communist school demanded much creativity on my part. When I would go to school on Monday, after my two-day absence, I was afraid that the other kids would openly tease me when they saw me again. I tried to arrive earlier and to walk around the block so my classmates would catch sight of me earlier and become accustomed to my presence.

Apart from being noticed for my irregular attendance, there was also the issue of my dress; namely my *yarmulke* and the *tzitzis*, the fringed garment, I wore beneath my shirt.

I did not remove the Uzbek cap I used as a *yarmulke* when I entered the classroom. The black and white caps were commonly worn in that region, so there was nothing obviously Jewish about them. However, sometimes the teacher would tell me to remove the head-covering, as a sign of respect. I didn't try to defy her and cause trouble, but I would place my hand on my head to appear as though I was scratching my head, so as not to walk around bareheaded. I would keep my hand in this position until seated in my chair.

Occasionally, we would receive medical exams or vaccinations at school, administered by the government. Once, our teacher announced that a nurse would soon enter our classroom to inject us with a vaccine. Generally, the shots were given in the arm or shoulder, and I became terrified, wondering how I would hide my *tzitzis*. If I took them off, the entire class would notice, and who knows what would happen.

At the last minute, instead of waiting for the nurse, I decided to lift my own shirt for the injection and tried to hide the *tzitzis* underneath. It didn't quite work. The nurse, who was a Bukharian Jewess, noticed the strings of the *tzitzis* protruding from under my shirt and whispered to me in Russian, "You are a good boy, a *chachamchik* (little rabbi)."

After that incident, I was afraid to wear *tzitzis* to school. From then on, I would wear them until I arrived at school. Before I entered the classroom, I would go to the bathroom, remove them, and hide them in my briefcase. At the end of the day, before leaving school, I went to the bathroom again and put the *tzitzis* back on.

Another disguise I put on in the bathroom before entering the classroom was a red tie, or as we referred to it, "the red rag." In those days, every child registered in the Pioneers, the Communist youth group, would receive a red tie to wear to school. Since the registration for the Pioneers was done automatically, I too was signed up and received my tie. Every morning I went into the bathroom, removed my *tzitzis,* and put on the red tie. In the afternoon I took off the tie and put on the *tzitzis*.

A Summons to the Principal's Office

At the beginning of my second year in public school, my father was also able to arrange things with the third grade teacher so that she too would turn a blind eye to my regular Shabbos absences. Since this was working well, my father hoped to leave me in third grade for another year: fourth grade offered additional subjects, with more teachers, and he was worried that he wouldn't be able to come to an arrangement with all of them.

Again, my father claimed that I was a weak child and would have a hard time acclimating to the pressures of fourth grade, so he requested that I stay in third grade. I remember R. Yaakov Notik, himself an esteemed member of our community, being surprised by my father's degree of sacrifice for Jewish education: "Everybody wants his child to be skipped a grade, while R. Avrohom is trying to keep his son back!"

However, at the end of the year, my secret was discovered when the principal found out that my regular absences were connected with religion. I arrived early at school one Monday, as usual, and when I entered the classroom I noticed that the teacher hadn't yet showed up. A few minutes later, I received orders to go immediately to the principal's office.

I fearfully made my way to the principal's office, where the principal, assistant principal, and teacher were waiting—by law, my teacher also had direct responsibility for her students. The three of them gazed at me intently, and then the principal asked in a firm voice: "Tell us Zaltzman, why don't you attend school on Saturday? Who forbids you to do so?"

I said that I was weak and the doctor said I should rest two days a week. Despite my young age, I knew the game I was supposed to play and I knew to insist that my absences had nothing to do with Judaism. The principal and assistant principal, as well as my teacher, yelled at me and berated me for my fanaticism. They said that if I insisted on resting two days a week, I could pick another day of the week—but not Saturday. They finally told me that my father was being summoned to come down to the school.

When my father appeared in school, they warned him that if he continued to prevent his son from going to school on Shabbos for religious reasons, he would be in trouble. They threatened that his parental rights could be rescinded and I would be re-educated in a state school where I would be forced to stay in a dormitory. My father denied responsibility for my absences and maintained that it was only a matter of my health. They demanded that if it was so, I had better appear in school the following Saturday.

After that menacing meeting, my father began to look for a school in another district. Once again, he hoped to enroll me in a school in a non-Jewish area so that the real reason for my absence on Shabbos would remain unknown. In the meantime, my father tried to convince me to go to school the next Shabbos. He told me he would hide my briefcase in school on Friday so that I could go to school on Shabbos without having to carry it. He would speak to the teacher to arrange permission to abstain from writing or any other desecration of Shabbos.

Still, I was nervous that I would be compelled to write and I refused to go to school. My father, afraid that they would carry out their threat of sending me to a government orphanage, pleaded with me:

"You are not yet a bar mitzvah," he said—technically, I was not fully obligated to observe the Shabbos. "But," he continued, "if you don't go to school for just this one Shabbos to placate the principal, it poses a big danger for all of us. They can arrest me and send you to a state orphanage where they will certainly force you to write on Shabbos!"

Despite my father's exhortations, I was still scared by the thought of being forced to write. So, the next Shabbos morning I got up early, and while my father and the family were still sleeping, I quietly left the house and went over to my friend Michoel Mishulovin's for a while. By the time I came back, it was already too late to go to school.

Although my father fully accepted my decision, after this incident, he began searching feverishly for a new school, hoping they wouldn't learn of what had happened at the school I had left. Indeed, after a short while, my father found a new school for me in another district of the city, almost an hour's walk from the Jewish neighborhood. They hadn't heard about Shabbos over there and I would be able to be absent without arousing suspicion. My father explained to the principal of my present school that he wanted to transfer me to a different school because my aunt lived in that area and she would care for me.

The administration, uninterested in problems with a religiously observant child, happily agreed to get rid of me and quickly transferred the appropriate documents to the new school.

My father spoke to my new teacher, Ms. Fedosya Archipovna, and arranged that I would not attend school on Saturdays due to my poor health. As such, my staying home on Shabbos was not an issue. However, the great distance to the new school made things very difficult for me. There was no transportation to school and I had to walk about fifty minutes on foot each way. During the winter months, whether it was raining or snowing, I had to leave early in the morning while it was still dark outside. The streets weren't lit up at night and I was afraid to walk alone. Still, I was happy that this sacrifice granted me the ability to sanctify Shabbos.

After some months went by, the new school began asking me why I didn't show up on Shabbos. This time, my father decided that perhaps we should deploy the opposite tactic: transfer me to a school in the Jewish neighborhood close to home, where the staff was Jewish, and hope that as a favor, they would allow me to be absent on Shabbos.

According to the law, when a student moved to another school, the principal had to transfer all of his papers, thus transferring the responsibility of the child to the new school. When my father went to my school and said he was switching me to a new school, he suggested that they avoid the bother of transferring the documents and that he would take care of it. The principal, happy to avoid the paperwork, agreed to his suggestion and handed my father the stack of papers.

As it happened, my father forgot to promptly proceed with the next step and took his time getting to the new school where he'd decided to register me. Two weeks elapsed and my father noted that neither school had taken any further interest in his son. He decided to wait a bit longer and see what would happen. After another few weeks went by, he realized that nobody had information about where I was supposed to be going to school and nobody cared.

So I remained at home and my public school tribulations came to a close.

Preparation for Prayer

Even before having to deal with the Communist schools, my parents made great effort, at tremendous personal danger, to give us a proper Chassidic upbringing and set us on the path of religious observance. Aside from learning Torah with us themselves, our parents also took the risk of sending us to a strictly illegal traditional Jewish school, a *cheder*.

My first teacher, with whom I learned in 1944, was R. Zushe Paz, who was known by all as R. Zushe *der shamash* (the sexton). He was a short man with a flowing white beard and he was tough. He didn't use a leather strap to hit us, as teachers of the previous generation were accustomed, but he would punish students with a slap of his *gartel*, the soft fabric belt worn during prayer. The children were still deathly afraid of him.

I remember that I had to go to the doctor later in the day, so my sister, Sarah, accompanied me to school and sat next to me on the bench until the time for my appointment. I was five years old and we were learning the *alef-beis,* the Hebrew letters and vowels. R. Zushe, toying with his silk *gartel* between his fingers, asked me how to pronounce the letter *lamed* with the *segol* vowel. Although I knew the answer, I was afraid to say it in case I was mistaken. My sister wanted to whisper the answer to me because she heard that he hit the boys if they didn't know something, but she was afraid lest R. Zushe notice her whispering and hit her. That's how afraid we were of him.

I heard that one time a child was sick at home and R. Zushe went to visit him. When the child, who was somewhat emotionally fragile, heard that his teacher had come to visit him, his whole body began to tremble and R. Zushe was not allowed to approach him.

But even though his tough persona made him come across to us children as a somewhat terrifying figure, it was clear that he was a deeply devoted educator, with a genuine concern for his students.

I later heard that R. Zushe took no personal remuneration for teaching us: he did his work solely for the sake of Heaven. With the money he did receive, he would prepare bread and butter for the boys every morning. In those days of famine, there wasn't much and you could barely discern the little dabs of butter in the cracks of the dark bread, but for our malnourished bodies, starting the day with some buttered bread was revitalizing. His rigorous approach also made him an effective teacher. He taught his students to pray with a singsong tune, and ensured that every letter received its proper enunciation and emphasis. Years later, when I was leading a minyan, R. Chaim Zalman Kozliner approached me afterwards and said, "From hearing the way you read the words, I think you must have learned to read and pray with R. Zushe *der shamash*."

When he grew older, R. Zushe relocated to Moscow. I heard that every Shabbos morning he would walk two hours each way to immerse in the *mikvah,* so as to properly prepare for his prayers, as per the Chassidic custom.

For a few months, I also learned with a non-Chassidic Lithuanian Jew by the name of R. Moshe Vinarski, who taught us the weekly Torah reading along with the Aramaic translation every Friday. Another teacher we had for a few months was R. Berel Gurevich, and for nearly a year I learned with R. Avrohom Yosef Entin, a former student and secretary of one of the greatest rabbis to come out of Lithuania, R. Yisroel Meir Kagan, popularly known as the Chofetz Chaim (Seeker of Life). R. Avrohom Yosef supplied the Jewish community of Samarkand with yearly Jewish calendars that he would calculate and write himself, a difficult but vital service. Those were relatively short periods of my life, but with my child's sense of time, they seemed like a long while.

The Teacher Who Taught Us Sacrifice

I recall the years between 1946 and 1949 as the best of my *cheder* years. I learned with a group of my friends: Michoel Mishulovin, Yaakov Lerner, Mottel Goldschmidt, Binyamin Malachovsky, Zalman Friedman, and others. Our teacher was R. Benzion Maroz, fondly known as Bentcha Maroz. When I meet my former classmates today and talk about those old bittersweet days, it is clear to us that the fact that we remained religious Jews is largely to his credit.

R. Bentcha was not just a teacher; he was a *mechanech*, an educator, interested in far more than the transmission of information. As a chassid of the Rebbe Rashab and a student of Tomchei Temimim—the Chabad yeshiva at the center of the movement (founded in 1897 in the town of Lubavitch)—he tried with all his might to spread his vibrant Chassidic zeal to his students. He taught us that for the fulfillment of the Torah and its directives, one must be prepared to sacrifice every ounce of one's being.

Desperate to be exempted from the Russian army draft and the enormous challenges to religious life that came along with it, many young men of the day made various physical deformities on their bodies to render themselves unfit to serve. R. Bentcha, or so we heard, had sliced the tendons in the middle of his right fingers and then tied the fingers down for some time until they were left permanently crooked. When he went to the draft board and the doctors saw the fingers of his right hand, they immediately exempted him: with those fingers, he'd never able to shoot a rifle straight.

Later on, we learned the full story: When he received the summons for a medical examination in order to assess whether he was fit for the draft, R. Bentcha promptly sought advice and a blessing from the Rebbe Rashab.

The Rebbe's response to the request, however, was somewhat curious. The Rebbe told him that when he was supposed to disrobe for his examination, he should make sure to leave on his set of *tzitzis*, as well as the *yarmulke* on his head. That was all.

Though a devout chassid and an ardent student of Chassidus, R. Bentcha thought to himself that along with the Rebbe's advice he'd best take some extra precautions, perhaps something that made a little more worldly sense, and left him a little less reliant on a miracle. He had heard of some kind of injection that, when administered in the right place, would cause his finger to temporarily curl in and stiffen up. After a few months, the effect was supposed to wear off and his fingers would be back in perfect working order. As a backup plan, he decided to take the shot.

When he entered the doctor's rooms as the Rebbe had instructed—almost entirely undressed, with exception of his *yarmulke* and *tallis katan*—the presiding gentile military official gawked at him for a moment. It was obvious that he'd never come across this variety of odd bird before, with its even odder clothes, and was quite convinced that the fellow standing before him was not entirely right in the head. "Get this lunatic out of here!" he called out accordingly.

Some of the Jewish doctors present quickly rushed over to explain what the strange striped, four-cornered garment was, why the fellow had it on, and that he might not necessarily be insane, in spite of his clothing choices. But the commissar would have none of their apologetics and stood by his initial assessment. "Just throw the madman out and be done with him," he ordered.

With no other choice, the doctors handed R. Bentcha the precious white card: Exempt!

So it was that the measures he'd taken on the Rebbe's instructions had saved him, and whatever he thought he'd do to his finger had been for nothing; they hadn't so much as glanced at his hands. Still, R. Bentcha's own story instilled in us the notion that it was far better to be maimed for life than to be in a situation where you could not observe the Torah, as was the case in the Russian army.

There was another striking story R. Bentcha would tell to illustrate this spirit of utter devotion to a cause—*mesiras nefesh* in the Chassidic lexicon. "An army was once marching out to conquer a city," he would begin. "To reach the city, they would have to cross a river, but as they reached the river bank, they could not see any bridges or ferries and they had no time to make one."

"Still, the commander of the army sent out the order: Forward march!"

"Unquestioning, the soldiers pressed onwards into the river. One after another, the soldiers at the front of the formation were covered by the waters and drowned, may G-d spare us, until eventually their bodies began to pile up and form a human bridge. The rest of the soldiers continued forward, marching over their comrades' corpses, crossed the river, and captured the city."

"The question is," he would say fervently, "Who conquered the city? Was it the soldiers who crossed the river, fought in battle, and seized control of the city? No! The true conquerors of the city are the soldiers who went into the river and drowned in order to pave the way for their comrades to remain alive, fight, and take the city."

"Those heroes represent the chassidim who became holy martyrs for a higher cause, shot dead in the NKVD cellars, or sent into Siberian exile, never to even receive a proper Jewish burial. These chassidim are the true heroes."

R. Bentcha taught two classes: one for us children before our bar mitzvah and another for older boys. We learned in an apartment that sat in an enclosed courtyard occupied only by the Mishulovin family. R. Bentcha had rented it specifically for our classes, as it was a relatively secure place to have an underground *cheder*. There weren't any other neighbors to notice what was taking place in the apartment, and furthermore, the windows of the apartment faced the courtyard entrance, granting R. Bentcha a perfect view of anyone entering.

R. Bentcha was especially fond of the elder two Mishulovin boys, Dovid and Eliyahu, who were often nearby, even though they were too old for our class. He had nicknames for them and greatly enjoyed conversing with them. After he had completed the lesson, we would review the material we had just learned while he would chat with them. It was clear that he delighted in these conversations. He spoke to them at length about various topics in Chassidic philosophy and stories of the Rebbes. We children knew that when he was talking to them it would take a long while until he was finished, so in addition to reviewing the material he had taught us, we had some extra time to play around and get into mischief.

As an educator, his approach was always to avoid hitting his students in response to misbehavior, preferring instead to help us understand what it was we had done wrong. As it happened, he had an incredible knack for describing the severity of our crimes. If the misconduct was more severe, he would put the child in a corner. On rare occasions, when a child did something seriously wrong, he would punish him in his own unique way, by slapping the child's hand against the table.

R. Bentcha had us review our studies and understand them well. One time, when he heard how I reviewed a Talmudic passage, he stopped me and said, "You don't understand its meaning!"

We reviewed it again but he insisted: "You don't understand it." When he saw that I didn't understand what he meant, he said: "*Gemara*—the Talmud—has to be learned with a certain tune. From the way you're chanting the passage, I can tell that you don't properly understand it."

He once explained the importance of learning Talmud with the proper melody as follows: "Reuven was once insulted because Shimon had called him a thief, and he demanded that Shimon publicly announce that Reuven was in fact not a thief. Shimon did as he had asked—almost. He went up onto the podium in the center of the synagogue and declared rhetorically: 'Reuven, whom I had called a thief, is not a thief?'"

He once said to me: "I want you to go home and explain the *Gemara* that you learned to your mother. If she tells you that she understands it, then I will know that you understand it too!"

Tragically, R. Bentcha suffered a great deal in his time and it was clear to us that he had a troubled family life. The time he spent in school with us and with the Mishulovin brothers was near therapeutic, a respite from his problems at home.

Still, it seemed as though he managed to keep his sense of humor about him. Entering the courtyard our *cheder* was located in, he sometimes would declare with a smile, "Ah! It's like America here! No wife and no children—I'm a free man!"

When the Elder Chassidim Played Soccer

R. Bentcha was blessed with a wonderful ability to depict things in a way that made them come alive, an ability he would put to use for educational purposes. One time, he entered the yard while we were in the middle of a lively game of soccer. We were children, aged eight to ten, and were so involved in the sport that we didn't notice his entrance. For a man of R. Bentcha's character, who lives by such lofty ideals, it is difficult to overstate how petty a thing like a soccer game must appear. He simply couldn't bear to see how invested we were in the sport. He stood in the center of the yard, grasping his head with his hands, until we noticed him. We suspected that the incident would not go by unaddressed. Embarrassed, we sat down to learn, but he said that before we started to learn he wanted to tell us something interesting. We were curious and paid close attention to his story:

"On my way here I saw a strange sight. R. Eliyahu Paritcher, Yerachmiel *der alter* (the Elder), and R. Boruch the *shochet* (ritual slaughterer) were all playing soccer."

These three ballplayers, namely, R. Eliyahu Levin (called "Paritcher" after his hometown of Paritch), Yerachmiel Chodosh, and Boruch Duchman, were three of the most senior and revered chassidim living in Samarkand at the time. The thought of these venerable personages kicking a soccer ball around was clearly absurd, and as we began to understand what he was getting at, we started to giggle. But R. Bentcha said sternly, "What are you laughing about? Listen to what I am telling you! Boruch the *shochet* kicked the ball and Yerachmiel ran to catch it, but the ball hit Eliyahu Paritcher on the head…"

He told the story with such enthusiasm that we couldn't help it and started laughing. He said to us, "Why are you laughing? Just a few minutes ago I saw you playing in the same manner. What's the difference between elder chassidim and you? You are also boys who sit and learn Torah. If it's not appropriate for them, it's not appropriate for you either!"

Chased by an Armed Soldier

As I related earlier, the room we learned in was opposite the courtyard gate, and R. Bentcha would always sit near the window with view of the gate and glance at it periodically. When he noticed a stranger entering, he would motion to us to quickly run out of the room. Many such occurrences took place over my years in *cheder*. One such time, perhaps because I didn't move quickly enough, I was unable to run outside before the stranger entered. R. Bentcha opened the door for the unexpected guest and I managed to quickly hide behind the door itself. The few minutes that I stood behind the door until R. Bentcha succeeded in getting rid of the intruder seemed like days.

We once had a really frightening situation at our school and it turned out to be nothing short of a miracle that I remained unscathed. The government was constructing a large building near our yard and the construction workers were prisoners serving their terms. In order that the prisoners would not escape, their overseers put up a barbed-wire fence all around the construction site with four watchtowers placed around the yard, each one manned by an armed guard.

One day, one of the prisoners escaped and chaos ensued. The guards ran with rifles as they scoured the area for him and naturally the first places they searched were the neighboring yards.

When R. Bentcha saw the commotion, he instructed us to go home immediately and to walk slowly, so as not to arouse the suspicion of the guards and endanger ourselves. I went out to the yard slowly, but when I walked out of the gate, I saw a guard with a rifle running after me. Terrified, I began to run.

I was nine years old but tall for my age and the guard, spotting a young person running, apparently thought that I had something to do with the runaway prisoner. He shouted at me to stop, but I became even more frightened and ran faster, without thinking that this would endanger me even more.

The guard began shooting into the air while shouting for me to stop. I ran even faster until I managed to turn a corner and hide until the guard passed.

Afterwards, it was explained to me what a terrible mistake it had been to run and what could have happened to me, G-d forbid, had the bullets struck me. It was by a miracle alone that I remained alive.

How to Keep a Secret

After a few more unpleasant incidents in which strangers from various government agencies entered the yard, R. Bentcha thought of a better location for us during the summer: the cellar of the house that we learned in.

The cellar was neglected, and it was full of garbage, dust, and manure, previously having been used as a stable for horses and donkeys. But it was an excellent place for our studies, with many advantages over the room we had been using. First of all, nobody would suspect that anyone was down in the dark, dingy cellar. Additionally, one side of the cellar had two windows, one of which faced the gate of the yard, letting in a broad stream of sunlight that enabled us to read, and allowing us to see any intruder approaching the yard. The second window faced the parallel street. This was of great benefit, because if it was necessary to flee, we could easily climb out the window onto the street. And finally, the two opposite windows created a draft that cooled the cellar.

It happened more than once that we used the second window as a means of escape. In doing so, we would scratch our hands on the nails and metal in the window frame, making our fingers bleed. But we children were very satisfied with the new place. It was cool and pleasant for us and our new underground hideaway exuded a certain mystique.

To prepare the cellar for learning, R. Bentcha hired someone to clean it up. Out of concern that the intended purpose of the cellar would be discovered, R. Bentcha warned us that he was not to be approached or asked any questions while the cleaner was there. In the midst of the cleanup operation, I forgot his warning and went over to R. Bentcha, and, addressing him with the traditional title for teachers of *cheder,* asked in a whisper, "*Rebbi,* we'll learn here?" R. Bentcha became very angry and he yelled at me to leave.

I immediately realized my mistake, and in particular the fact I referred to him as *Rebbi,* but R. Bentcha decided to make sure that I would never make a similar mistake. When the fellow had left and we sat down to learn, he scolded me firmly and said, "I warned you not to mention our learning and you kept asking: '*Rebbi,* we'll learn here? *Rebbi,* we'll play here? *Rebbi,* we'll eat here?'" That was enough of a lesson for me and from then on, I learned how to keep a secret.

One Jew Against Eight Million Soldiers

In addition to the subjects that R. Bentcha taught us, we absorbed a wealth of Chassidic values during his *farbrengens.* One time, during one of these community gatherings, R. Berel Itkin, one of the local chassidim, spoke harshly of another Jew who was forced to join the Communist party and whose religious observance had since cooled off. He referred to him as a *basiak*—an outcast.

R. Bentcha, as sharp and impassioned as ever, immediately retorted, "What do you want from him? When eight million soldiers—referring to the Russian army—stand facing him with drawn rifles and don't allow him to put on *tefillin,* and he still perseveres and puts them on, is he not a *tzaddik,* a truly righteous man?" R. Bentcha viewed this Jew virtuously, out of his consideration for the situation at the time.

Often, the discussion at these *farbrengens* would turn to profound issues, exploring the Chassidic perspective on life, and its sense of priority. When R. Bentcha would try to describe the futility of getting too invested in the more temporal, material aspects of life, he would say, "I was once in Moscow, in the Red Square, and saw thousands of people rushing here and there. In my mind, I asked them: 'What are you so enthusiastic about? One hundred years ago none of you were here, and in another hundred years none of you will be here, so why the emphasis and excitement about matters of this world?" For R. Bentcha, there was far more than the life of this physical world.

When he would hear people engage in idle chatter, or when he would want to demonstrate the unimportance of some issue people were droning on about, he would approach them and begin searching for something on the table or floor. Finally, he would locate some scrap of paper and he would ask them, "Does this have any value? Your words are worth even less."

"Know that life is like a fair," he would repeat to the youngsters. "At a fair, one buys, sells, and engages in business. Life is full of all sorts of so-called achievements and goals. When young men such as yourselves are setting out for the fair; they think, 'I can do this and I can accomplish that; my life is ahead of me. I will be successful and show everyone what I've got!' My dear friends, believe me, when I was young, I was also full of similar notions. I am now older and I'm getting ready to come back from the fair. I've realized that these thoughts lead absolutely nowhere; all these wild ambitions and dreams are merely fantasies. The main thing is to be a loyal Jew who follows the ways of the Torah. Everything else in life is trivial."

After saying *l'chaim* on a few shots of vodka, he loved to sing a Russian lullaby in which a Jewish mother tells her son to remain a faithful Jew in all of life's circumstances. He loved emphasizing the part of the song in which the son is told that even when great sorrows befall him, he should still remain loyal to G-d. He would sing it with gusto as he knocked on the table with his finger.

Years later, my brother, Berel, sang this song before the Rebbe, at a public *farbrengen*. To his surprise, however, the Rebbe didn't encourage the singing as he often would. My brother soon understood that the Rebbe didn't want to dwell on the words of the mother describing the calamities that would befall her son.

R. Bentcha was a close friend of R. Boruch Duchman and R. Eliyahu Paritcher—those "soccer-playing" community elders—and would address them with the informal Yiddish *du*. To us boys, their casual friendship seemed a little odd because while R. Boruch and R. Eliyahu were older, stately chassidim, R. Bentcha always struck us as being somewhat younger. He was a classy fellow, sporting a neat beard, a tie, and a stylish walking stick, and the way he strolled around with his boots and his erect posture made him seem to be of another generation. R. Bentcha noticed our surprise and commented, "We learned together back in Lubavitch!"

During one *farbrengen*, after R. Bentcha had drunk a little, he spoke about R. Eliyahu Paritcher with characteristic vigor. It turned out that R. Eliyahu had been one of the select few students the Rebbe Rashab appointed to memorize the Rebbe's teachings delivered on Shabbos. Since this was the only way the teachings could be recorded and transmitted, this was an enormously important role. "You see him as a short man, but you should know that after R. Shilem, the main Chassidic mentor in the early days of Tomchei Temimim, he was the chief reviewer for the Rebbe Rashab! As the Rebbe was delivering a lecture, each of them would focus in his own way; R. Shilem would sway back and forth, while R. Eliyahu would stand quietly in his place and listen.

"Just picture it!" R. Bentcha urged us. "On Shabbos morning, the Lubavitcher Rebbe would come to shul for prayers after immersing himself in the *mikvah*, and R. Eliyahu here would jump on the table and review the lecture for the Rebbe from the night before! Can you imagine such an amazing scene? And did you ever hear what the Rebbe Rashab once said about R. Eliyahu's balding head? That his hair fell out because of how deeply he would meditate on Chassidic concepts before prayer!"

This was how R. Bentcha would constantly share with us the Chassidic warmth he was blessed with, as well as a proper Chassidic mindset and outlook on life.

Skating in Line with the Elder Chassidim

R. Bentcha also taught my brother Berel in a separate class for older boys. One time, when my brother was a young boy, he wanted my parents to buy him a pair of ice skates. My mother felt that skating around outside in the icy streets was something that only the local gentile children did and felt it was inappropriate for a boy who learned Torah, but Berel longed for them.

At that time, for whatever reason, our *cheder* was unable to hold regular classes and R. Bentcha would study with each student privately at home. My mother finally said to Berel, "You know what? We'll wait for R. Bentcha. When he comes to teach you, we'll ask him. If he agrees, then I'll buy them for you."

My brother knew that R. Bentcha would oppose the idea and he did not want my mother to ask him, so as to not be embarrassed. But one day, when R. Bentcha came to our house, my mother asked him, "My Berele wants me to buy him a pair of skates. What is your opinion?"

R. Bentcha wrinkled his forehead and with a show of seriousness he said, "Berele wants skates? Why don't you buy them? It's definitely a good idea to buy them."

My brother looked on in delighted surprise, while my mother was disappointed with his reply. But then, after a short contemplative pause, R. Bentcha went on: "Of course you should buy skates. But on one condition: If R. Boruch the *shochet* and R. Eliyahu Paritcher, followed by R. Yerachmiel the Elder skate in front of him, why shouldn't Berele skate fourth in line?"

An Education Engraved Forever

In the Soviet Union of those days, as I mentioned, most people simply thought in terms of how they could best live a normal life. Every patriotic Soviet parent wanted his child to receive an advanced education in the Soviet system; to attend school and then university, thereby acquiring a profession.

But for a religious Jew, this presented tremendous problems. In university, the student was among a mix of young men and women from various nationalities. The heretical ideology of Marxism and Leninism was emphasized, with strict tests administered on this material. The student, after graduating with a degree, strove to find a prestigious position, which made it much more difficult to observe Shabbos and Yom Tov than if he had a simple job. Moreover, his profession would complicate his prospect of emigrating from Russia—the goal of every Jew. I knew an individual with a prestigious job and as soon as he submitted immigration papers he was fired, creating a political stain on his file for the rest of his life. He was left without income and he had to look for a menial job to be able to support his family.

Now, my father didn't have his head in the sky. He had both feet planted firmly on the ground and he was known to be practical and down to earth. R. Mendel Futerfas once said of him, "A clever man is not one that *speaks* in a clever manner. A clever man is one who *acts* in a clever manner. And such a man is your father."

Nevertheless, my father would insist that at such a time, when winds of heresy blew through the streets and the public schools, it was absolutely forbidden to send a child to school. He maintained that a child can acquire basic skills such as reading, writing, and arithmetic at home. The rest of his intellectual development can be achieved from the study of the Talmud, its commentaries, and Chassidic philosophy far more effectively than it can be from secular studies.

"As for livelihood, one need not worry," he would say, and then, quoting the Talmudic dictum, "'The One who provides life will provide sustenance.' It's not necessary for my child to become an engineer or a doctor. Better that he earn a livelihood in a simpler trade, so long as he remains a loyal, observant Jew of noble character. He should carry on our forefather Avrohom's golden chain of tradition and ensure that it continues for all future generations!"

When my brother Berel grew older, my father found him a job in a factory that manufactured commercial signs, with the eventual plan that my father would be able to open a factory of his own. Berel learned the trade quickly and adeptly. My father then opened his own factory and we all earned a livelihood from this trade. Many of our community in Samarkand and Tashkent followed suit and sustained themselves from commercial sign-making as well. Among them were many graduates of prominent universities.

My parents and people like R. Bentcha tried to give us children a proper sense of priority in regard to school degrees and jobs.

One day, one of our friends came to school and boasted that his mother had registered him for public school and that he would now grow up to be an educated person. "What will become of you?" he asked of us derisively.

Just then R. Bentcha walked in and he overheard this comment. We were learning the Book of Deuteronomy at the time, and were up to the verse, "Go after Hashem your G-d, fear Him... worship Him, and cleave to Him."

R. Bentcha, who would often test the skills of each student, turned to the boy who had boasted about going to public school and told him to explain the verse. The boy explained the simple meaning, but R. Bentcha made an angry face and told him to repeat the verse and say the correct meaning.

He went back and explained the verse, but R. Bentcha wasn't satisfied with his explanation and told him to say it a third time. By this time we could hear a distinctly angry tone ringing in his voice and he extended the bent fingers of his right hand in front of the boy, pointing firmly at the book. We shrank in our places in fear, not understanding what R. Bentcha wanted, seeing as our friend was providing the correct translation.

We all sat there trembling and R. Bentcha exclaimed loudly in his typical fashion, "What is the meaning of the verse? I will tell you the meaning." Then, with a melody and his characteristic vigor, he said:

"*Go after Hashem your G-d*—means to go *only* after Hashem your G-d; *fear Him*—don't go to the Communist school; *worship Him*—despise the Communist school." At this point he used a slew of derisive expressions to describe the school that I cannot bring myself to transcribe. Then he said: "You understand the meaning, eh? *Nu*, repeat after me."

After a lesson like that, the boy understood that he shouldn't have boasted about being registered in school. Fortunately, the

Chassidic atmosphere in which the boy lived had a positive influence on him—enough to counteract his experiences at school—and he grew up to be a G-d-fearing young man, bringing up devout children and grandchildren of his own.

I myself once experienced a similar story. Once, during a Hebrew writing lesson, my friend Mordechai Goldschmidt forgot his inkwell. I didn't want to let him dip his pen into my inkwell and told him that he should have brought his own. R. Bentcha noticed this, but said nothing.

After a while he asked me, "Hil'ke, did you say *Modeh Ani* today?" *Modeh Ani* is the first prayer of the day, an acknowledgment of G-d recited immediately upon waking up each morning. I said that I had.

R. Bentcha asked me to explain the *Modeh Ani*, which I did to the best of my ability: "I give thanks before You..." R. Bentcha stopped me and, in the manner he reserved for chastising someone, said disapprovingly, "That's not what it means," and he went on to explain it:

"*Modeh* means *bittul*—selflessness. This means that when a friend asks for ink, you give it to him. *Ani* means that when your friend asks you for a pen, you must give him a pen," and so he went on to explain the rest of the words in a similar fashion. "Now do you know the meaning of *Modeh Ani*?" he concluded.

These scenes typified his method of education and they have remained etched in our souls for life.

CHAPTER 2

My Father's Youth in Lubavitch

My father, R. Avrohom Zaltzman, was, as R. Yosef Yitzchak Schneersohn, the previous Rebbe of Chabad-Lubavitch, once described him, a *penimi*: An "inward" person, who lived by his own internal considerations alone. This does not mean that he was an introvert or socially awkward; on the contrary, as all those who knew him can testify, he was friendly and socially adept. However, for the most part, his true character was not readily on display. He was a businessman his entire life and gave off the impression of an ordinary person. The truth is that he was a chassid in the fullest sense of the word, although it was only on rare occasions that his innermost essence came to the fore and one could see what was really important to him.

In Soviet Russia there were numerous rabbis and Torah scholars; however, when put to the test, they were unable to come up with the tenacity and sacrifice that the times demanded. Instead, they used their Torah knowledge to find what loopholes they could, using the halachic recognition of civil law and the flexibility of rabbinic law to endorse their lenient views. This was not the case for my father: He did not surrender an iota to the pressures of the Communist culture. Incredibly, throughout all those dangerous times in Soviet Russia, he never even so much as trimmed his beard, a remarkable testament to his deep, resolute faith and fear of G-d. It was this same spirit that enabled him to fight with all he had to raise his children as he saw fit and in all other matters of Judaism. I am sure he got this strength from his early years studying in the Lubavitch yeshiva.

Off to Lubavitch

My father was born on October 6, 1899, in the city of Smargon in Belarus. His parents, Dovber and Shaina Zaltzman, had eleven children.

One day, a funds collector from Lubavitch by the name of R. Tuvia Skolnik came to the city of Smargon. While making his rounds, he visited the Zaltzman family and upon seeing the poverty they endured, he convinced my grandfather to send his then eleven-year-old son Avrohom to the Tomchei Temimim yeshiva in Lubavitch. Avrohom was excited about the prospect of learning in yeshiva. Also, R. Tuvia said that there would be food to eat in the yeshiva, since he saw the poverty and scarcity of food in the home.

The yeshiva had a reputation as a place of Torah study imbued with the fear of Heaven, where the students were educated to acquire fine character traits and love for their fellow Jews. My grandparents, despite their qualms about sending such a young child away from home, were glad for the opportunity to send their son to Lubavitch.

My father joined R. Tuvia and after a long journey they eventually reached their destination. He was tested in chapter *Eilu Metzios* of the Talmud and was then called in for an interview with the principal. The principal of the yeshiva was R. Yosef Yitzchak Schneersohn, who would, of course, later become the sixth Lubavitcher Rebbe. R. Yosef Yitzchak asked him why he had come to Lubavitch and why he preferred this yeshiva over other Lithuanian yeshivas. R. Yosef Yitzchak also asked him detailed questions regarding the material and spiritual situation in his home.

When he left R. Yosef Yitzchak's office, he did not know whether or not he had been accepted and he was very nervous. It was a week before Rosh Hashana and the upcoming High Holidays would prove to be days of judgment in more ways than one. On Rosh Hashana, he begged Hashem to help him be accepted into the yeshiva. He was thrilled when, after the holidays, he was told that he was accepted and would learn with the teacher R. Leib from Viyatke.

Yeshiva life was not easy for a young boy like my father. My father related that during his initial stay in Lubavitch, he slept in the shul adjacent to the cemetery. The older fourteen-year-old boys warned him that he must make sure to go to sleep right away, since at midnight the dead rise from their graves, dressed in white, and peer through the windows to see who was still awake. "You can just imagine," my father concluded, "how little I slept those nights!"

Later my father slept in the former home of the Rebbe Maharash, which was then being used to house some of the students. This presented a rare opportunity to see the Rebbe's dining room, the study he had used for private audiences, and so on. My father also related that his room was located next to the main study hall and every Thursday night he was able to hear the students in the hall singing melodies at Chassidic gatherings, or listen to them discussing Talmud or Chassidus all through the night.

For one period of time, my father ate the Shabbos meals at the home of R. Hirsch, the butcher of Lubavitch. One Friday night during the month of Cheshvan, he arrived at the butcher's house at a late hour and found the door locked and the family asleep. Dejected and very hungry, he trudged back to the yeshiva on Shilava Street. When he returned, his friends advised him to go to the home of R. Michoel Bliner (R. Michoel the Elder) who was known to be a chassid with a heart of gold. My father recalled how, in the previous month, on Yom Kippur night, R. Michoel was so ill that he had to have his bed brought to shul so that he could pray there while lying down. My father felt very uncomfortable about bothering this old, frail chassid, but due to his hunger, he listened to their suggestion and hurried to R. Michoel's house. He knocked lightly and within a few moments R. Michoel opened the door. His frailty was apparent and it was quite obvious that he had been asleep for a while and got

up especially for the young boy. R. Michoel went to the kitchen and
served my father some *lokshen,* leftover egg noodles.

On the very next evening following Shabbos, R. Michoel passed
away. My father joined the rotation that sat in his house before the
funeral to recite Psalms at his bedside. The funeral took place on
Sunday, with the participation of the Rebbe Rashab and his son, the
Rebbe Rayatz.

My father's young age, coupled with the distance from home, made
it difficult for him to adjust to his new surroundings. As a result, he
sometimes found it hard to learn properly, and at times he even
joined some older students in pranks, like trying to get a goat in the
courtyard drunk on Purim. At one point, the student supervisor, or
mashgiach, of the yeshiva, R. Yechezkel (Chatche) Himelstein, decided to send my father, along with another boy, away from the yeshiva. The reason for his decision was recorded on a note: "The
child needs his mother."

The two boys visited the *mashgiach* and pleaded with him to
reconsider. He didn't even answer their pleas and just sat there silently. They then decided to entreat R. Chatche's wife, known to
possess a gentle disposition, to intercede on their behalf. She promised to speak to her husband, but this too produced no results.

They consulted with their friends in the yeshiva and were told
that since the Rebbe Rayatz, as dean of the yeshiva, had agreed to R.
Chatche's decision, the only one that could prevent the verdict from
being carried out was his father, the Rebbe Rashab himself. But how
were two small boys to secure a private audience with the Rebbe
Rashab? To amplify the problem, overseeing private meetings with
the Rebbe was R. Nachman the attendant, a strict, rigid individual,
who would doubtless refuse them entry to the Rebbe's room.

My father thought of an original idea. A second attendant, R.
Mendel, assisted the Rebbe in his house. Among other duties, he was
responsible for serving supper to the Rebbe. My father knew he was
a kindhearted fellow who wouldn't chase them. Nervous and with a
trembling heart, my father crept into the Rebbe's house and waited in

the hallway that separated the kitchen from the dining room. As soon as R. Mendel turned into the kitchen, my father ran down the hall, and with quivering steps he entered the dining room where the Rebbe sat. He then burst into uncontrollable tears, unable to utter a word.

The Rebbe Rashab was sitting at the table eating a dairy meal. Rebbetzin Shterna Sarah sat at the table as well, while the renowned chassid R. Shlomo Leib Eliezerov sat to the side, conversing with the Rebbe.

The Rebbe noticed my father, and he turned to him and asked gently, "*Yingele*—little boy—why are you crying?"

"R. Yechezkel Himelstein wants to send me away from the school," my father answered in a tear-choked voice.

"And why would he send you away?"

"I don't know."

The Rebbe chuckled. "*Nu,* so go learn in the yeshiva in Radin!"

My father's cries intensified. "No! I want to learn in Lubavitch!"

The Rebbe smiled and continued, "So learn in Slabodka, Mir..." The Rebbe continued enumerating all the famous Lithuanian yeshivas of the time as my father continued crying and refusing each proposal: "I only want to learn in Lubavitch!"

The Rebbetzin then interceded on my father's behalf. She said to the Rebbe: "What do you want from the boy? Promise him!"

She then turned to my father and said: "Go, *yingele.* I'll speak to my husband."

My father was happy to hear that the Rebbetzin was willing to intercede, but he said that he wanted to hear from the Rebbe himself. The Rebbe then turned to him and said he'd speak to his son, R. Rayatz. However, my father continued standing and didn't budge. Seeing this, the Rebbe asked him, "What else?"

"I have a friend who was also sent home and he also wants to stay here and learn."

"Where is he?"

"He is standing behind the door."

"Why doesn't he want to come in?"

"Because he's embarrassed."

Indeed, a short while later, my father was summoned and informed that he had been reaccepted. However, he wouldn't learn in the actual yeshiva but on the second floor of the building, with the teacher R. Mendel Liadier.

The significance of my father's steadfast resolution to remain in Lubavitch is clearly apparent now. From all of the eleven Zaltzman siblings, my father was the only one that merited to build a true Jewish home with children, grandchildren, and great-grandchildren. The majority of his brothers and sisters succumbed to the pressures of the time, leaving the path of Torah and becoming staunch Communists.

Many years later, my father sat at a *farbrengen* together with R. Mendel Futerfas in Eretz Yisrael and repeated this story. In his characteristic style, R. Mendel explained the episode as follows: "Do you think that the Rebbe Rashab acceded to your request because of your cries and entreaties? No! The Rebbe saw that you had love for your fellow Jew. You weren't concerned only about yourself, but you remembered to mention your friend as well. That's what enabled you to remain in Tomchei Temimim!"

I once heard a story that took place on the 19th of Kislev, a Chassidic holiday held every year to commemorate the release of R. Schneur Zalman of Liadi (the founder of Chabad Chassidism), from czarist imprisonment in 1798. Once, when all of the students attended the central *farbrengen* held in honor of the great day, my father preferred to stay near the bed of a sick friend so he wouldn't remain alone. They say that at one point in that *farbrengen*, the Rebbe Rashab said, "Who knows who has greater merit, the boys who came to the *farbrengen*, or the boy who stayed with his sick friend?"

Memories of Lubavitch

My father recounted many more of his memories of Lubavitch in a letter he penned to his grandson, my nephew R. Yosef Yitzchak Zaltzman, an emissary of the seventh Lubavitcher Rebbe in Toronto.

He wrote how on the day before Rosh Hashana, before the After-noon Prayers, all of the yeshiva students, young and old, would come to recite *Tehillim* (Psalms), along with the Rebbe Rashab. The Rebbe would read aloud, with devout concentration and heartfelt emotion.

On Erev Rosh Hashana, the Rebbe Rashab spent about two hours immersed in the silent *Shmoneh Esrei* prayer, his brow creased in concentration as he softly hummed the words of the prayer. My father would nostalgically recount how he was fortunate to stand together with the other *bochurim*—yeshiva boys—near the Rebbe Rashab, and from time to time the Rebbe's sweet voice in prayer would reach their ears.

One year, before his bar mitzvah, my father participated in the Yom Kippur prayers in Lubavitch in the small shul next to the Ohel, the resting place of the previous rebbes. The leader of the services was an old chassid of the Rebbe Maharash who claimed that the Rebbe Maharash had appeared to him in a dream and requested that he pray in the shul next to the Ohel. That Yom Kippur, my father slept on the floor of the shul in a corner covered with some straw. It was a Yom Kippur that remained engraved in his memory, and every Yom Kippur thereafter he would picture himself standing in prayer in that holy shul.

The night of the Seder in Lubavitch held a place of honor in my father's memories of Tomchei Temimim. A small table was set up in the center of the study hall upon which a beautiful handcrafted wooden candelabrum was placed. This candelabrum had been made by the Rebbe Maharash after doctors told him that working with his hands would benefit his health. It was fashioned out of 613 pieces of wood, and comprised thirteen arms, for the 613 com-mandments, and the numerical value of the Hebrew word *echad*, "One." There was one central candle-holder and two rings of hold-ers encompassing it. The outer ring had eight holders and the inner ring had four.

Surrounding the table with the candelabrum were another eighteen tables that seated about three hundred students. When the Seder began, they would announce: "Table One: *Kiddush!*" and so on. At every table, when it was their turn, the students would recite *Kiddush* simultaneously, and when they drank in a traditional reclining position they would lean on the person beside them. My father said that it looked like a falling set of dominoes: an entire table of people dropping to the shoulder of the person to their left. On the final day of Pesach there was a large *farbrengen,* known as the "Feast of *Moshiach*," which was graced with the Rebbe Rashab's presence.

When my father spoke of Lubavitch, he would describe the dilapidated houses of the town, made of flimsy wooden panels. These small houses were so frail looking that it seemed a single gust of wind could topple them. Once, while making his way to the *mikvah* near the small synagogue known as Binyomin's shtiebel, he saw a tiny, decaying house in a corner that was said to be the house of Yossel, the uncle of the Tzemach Tzedek (Rabbi Menachem Mendel of Lubavitch, the third Rebbe of Chabad). He was a man of great spiritual stature, for whom the Tzemach Tzedek had great respect. My father always recalled how the poor appearance of the town's dwellings contrasted with the spiritual richness within.

"Please Give Me a Jewish Burial"

One day, a stranger came to Lubavitch. He entered the study hall, and my father observed him praying the Afternoon Prayer with great concentration and sobbing profusely. In those days, new faces were a common sight in Lubavitch, and this person did not attract undue attention. Sometime later, my father went out to the yard and suddenly heard the sound of choking. He tried to locate the source of the sound, until he realized that it was coming from the outhouse. He rushed over and found the stranger lying on the ground with his eyes closed, completely unconscious. There was a distinctly toxic smell emanating from his mouth. On his chest lay a note, which read: *Nobody is culpable for my death; please give me a Jewish burial.*

My father ran to his friends. Together, they carried the man to the yard and tried to resuscitate him, forcing him to retch until he threw up the poison he had swallowed.

When he recovered, he told my father his story. He came from a wealthy family and was on his way from Austria to his relatives in the Land of Israel. On the way, he had been robbed of all his money and was left without a penny. For a few days he had nothing to eat and was too ashamed to ask for a handout. That day he couldn't take it anymore, and after his heartfelt *Mincha*, tried to commit suicide.

My father raised money for the man's trip, prepared a bag laden with food and sent him on his way. Before he departed, the man told my father his last name, "Brawerfon-Meisel-Gibori," an unusual composite of an Austrian and a Hebrew name. He begged my father that if he ever went to Eretz Yisrael, he should locate his family who would pay him back for his efforts.

Over fifty years later, once we had arrived in Eretz Yisrael, I asked my father whether he had located the man's family. He said that he had heard about a family with a similar name who once resided in the Gadera area, but he had not succeeded in locating them.

Trying His Hand at Producing Vodka

During the time he learned in Lubavitch, in the years from 1912 to 1918, my father would travel on rare occasions to visit his parents and relatives in his hometown of Smargon. During one of these visits, he heard about a local man who was preparing to marry off his daughter but was having a hard time raising the necessary funds. My father felt sorry for him and decided to try to help by saving him some of the wedding expenses. He went over to the father of the bride and confided that he knew how to make vodka out of potatoes and could produce the amount needed for the wedding. In those days, alcohol was expensive, so his offer made for significant savings.

The truth was that my father had never tried producing alcohol before. His "experience" was limited to the one time he had watched someone produce vodka out of potatoes. But he commiserated with this man and decided to try his luck. My father was quite skilled with his hands and he believed it would turn out well.

He ground the potatoes and mixed them with sugar as he had once observed, and he put the mixture in a warm place to ferment. Once a day he would mix the combination. Days went by and nothing happened. My father felt terrible, thinking that because of him there would be nothing to drink at the wedding. The man, as well, regretted having agreed to this young man's suggestion. My father was all of fifteen at the time.

But in the end, with Hashem's help the mixture fermented over time, and by the time the wedding day arrived, his efforts had yielded a fine batch of vodka. My father was ecstatic, happy to have merited helping another Jew.

Miraculous Rescue on the Train

In the aftermath of the Bolshevik Revolution of 1917, Russia was beset by chaos and disorder. Civil war ravaged the country for the next few years, and various gangs sprouted throughout Russia, vying for power and influence. One of the most infamous bandit armies, notorious for its viciousness, was the Makhnovites, under the leadership of the anti-Semite Nestor Makhno, a Ukrainian anarchist revolutionary who believed in the total abolition of government and the state.

In those terrifying times, a train ride was a treacherous undertaking for a Jew. If a Jewish passenger fell into the hands of one of the Makhnovites, he could be taunted and eventually hurled to his death from the rapidly moving train. None of the other passengers would interfere or attempt to prevent the catastrophe.

It once happened that my father had to travel by train. He was then in his twenties, and his recently grown beard served as an obvious indication of his Jewish identity. He tried to sit quietly in a corner of the compartment so as not to attract undue attention.

Not far from his seat sat a Makhnovite who noticed my father and began to mock and degrade him. My father was terrified and pretended that he didn't realize that he was the target of the stinging remarks. The hoodlum increased the volume of his vile words until, overcome with a spasm of hate, he approached my father, grabbed him by the neck and started to drag him to the door at the end of the train.

My father began to plead with him, saying, "Let me be, I am still young! What do you want from me? I also want to live!" But the thug continued to spit out a slew of curses and dragged him along the compartment.

Suddenly, from a corner of the compartment rose a huge man, of even larger physical build than the Makhnovite. He lunged forward and started bellowing: "What are you doing? Leave him alone!"

As he said this, he approached the Makhnovite and grabbed him by the neck. The Makhnovite dropped my father and began to argue with the giant, saying, "He's a filthy Jew!" The giant ignored him, and clutching him firmly by the neck, he dragged him to the end of the train, opened the door, and shoved him out as the train lurched forward at high speed. My father, overwhelmed by the turn of events, fearfully returned to his place and sat down quietly.

Looking calmer, the giant returned to the compartment and gently motioned for my father to approach him. My father, still un-comprehending what had just occurred, or who this towering man was, was afraid to refuse and approached him with trembling steps. The enormous man calmed him, saying, "Do not fear. Come with me; I want to show you something."

Needless to say, my father was still afraid. He followed the man to the small entrance located at the front of the train compartment. The man bent down and whispered into his ear, "You should know that I am a *ger tzedek*—a convert."

My father gawked at him incredulously. To prove himself, the man recited the first paragraph of the *Shema* and then lifted his shirt to display the *tzitzis* that he wore underneath. He parted from my father with a smile and said smugly, "I taught that despicable anti-Semite a lesson. If he remained alive after I tossed him off the train, he will remember this until the end of his days."

Learning to Play the Violin

As a young man, my father suffered severely from asthma and the doctors ordered him to relocate to a warmer climate. My father traveled to the Caucasus Mountains in Georgia, and he rented an apartment from a Jewish landlord. After living there for a year and drinking the local warm spring water, he was completely healed.

My father had always been good with his hands, and that year his landlord gave him a plot of land upon which my father mastered the skill of gardening. He loved gardening because in this work one can see Hashem's blessings in action, in how a simple seed can produce an entire plant. It was also healthy for him to be out in the fresh air doing physical activity.

The landlord played the violin and during that year, after asking for lessons, my father also learned to play. Later on, he bought himself a violin that would go on to accompany him for many years thereafter. At weddings that took place in Samarkand during the war years and afterwards, when there was no possibility to hire a band or musicians, he would happily volunteer to bring his violin and enliven the atmosphere. He would perform the *kazatzke* dance as if he were still a youngster, and after having a bit to drink, he would stand on his head and dance on the tables, and continued to do so into his old age.

On special occasions marked by a Chassidic *farbrengen*, he would bring along his violin and play in honor of the auspicious day. This continued for many years, even after his emigration from Russia and eventual settlement at Nachalas Har Chabad in Israel.

Having a talent in music was not unusual for my father's family; many of his siblings were likewise involved in music and art, some of them professionally.

During the late 1920s, Shlomo (Solomon) Mikhoels, a famous Jewish actor of international repute, was encouraged by the Soviet regime to organize a Jewish theater. He announced that every young Jew with talent in the arts should come to audition, and whoever would pass his evaluation would be guaranteed a considerable salary. During those years of hunger, many young Jews went to audition: perhaps they would be accepted to the theater and would have some kind of income. About five hundred people arrived from many locations within the Soviet Union, and among them were my uncle, Shimon Zaltzman, and my aunt, Nechama Zaltzman. From the hundreds of applicants, only eighteen candidates were accepted, including my uncle and aunt.

After World War II, Stalin decided to liquidate the Jewish theater and arrest the actors. On the night of January 12, 1948, Stalin's angels of death and terror killed Shlomo Mikhoels in a dark alley in Minsk.

Artistic talent also ran in the family. My uncle Zalman, who was killed during the war, was a student in an art academy. For his degree, he submitted a rendition of the famous painting *The Last Day of Pompeii* by the Russian artist Karl Bryullov. It was considered the best piece of art among all those submitted by the graduating students.

Surprising Instructions from the Rebbe

When my father came of age, a match was suggested for him with my mother, Bracha Pevzner. Her older brother, R. Avrohom Boruch Pevzner, the *mashpia* (Chassidic mentor) of the Chabad community in Minsk, went to ask for approval of the Rebbe Rayatz, as is customary amongst chassidim. "Avremel Smargoner?" asked the Rebbe, referring to my father by his hometown of Smargon. "*Nu…* he's a *penimi!*" The reply was brief, but the Rebbe's approval was clear: Avremel Smargoner is a man of integrity, a genuine "inward" person. Indeed, those few words of approval made for an apt summary of my father's character.

A short time after the wedding, in the year 1927, my father heard that the kosher slaughterer in the town of Cherepovets, Siberia, had passed away. Since the town was left bereft of a *shochet,* many had resorted to eating non-kosher meat, and members of the community were looking for someone to take his place.

My father traveled to his brother-in-law, R. Boruch Duchman (another Boruch, they were married to sisters) in Medved, near Leningrad, and studied kosher slaughtering with him for three months. The people of Cherepovets were still waiting, so he rushed his studies and learned the laws of *shechita* as condensed in the work *Simla Chadasha,* along with the commentary of the *Levushei Serad.* He spent most of his time at the town slaughterhouse, where they slaughtered the numerous chickens and cows that arrived from the merchants in Leningrad. This was in the regime's early days, at a time when limited private enterprise was still allowed under the New Economic Policy, so such activity at the slaughterhouse was not yet the major risk it would become in a few years.

After he completed his studies, and before traveling to Cherepovets, he went to the Rebbe Rayatz. When he entered the room for his private audience and told the Rebbe that he had learned *shechita,* the Rebbe asked him, "What have you studied?"

My father, somewhat diffidently, told him the truth, that he had only managed to learn the relevant laws from the *Simla Chadasha* with the commentary of the *Levushei Serad.* The Rebbe smiled and said, "A *tendetner*—standard—*shochet.*" The condensed laws, in other words, is what a typical *shochet* knows.

Then the Rebbe asked my father from whom he was planning on receiving his certification, and my father said that he wanted to ask R. Shimon Lazarov, the Lubavitcher rabbi in Leningrad. The Rebbe said that he should also receive certification from Rabbi Katzenelenbogen, the official chief rabbi of Leningrad.

At that precise time, a difference of opinion had developed between the Rebbe Rayatz and Rabbi Katzenelenbogen over a prospective meeting of rabbis proposed by the Leningrad Jewish community, ostensibly to strengthen the practice of Judaism. Rabbi Katzenelenbogen, the official rabbi of Leningrad, was in favor of the meeting. But Rebbe Rayatz was opposed to the meeting, because he suspected that members of the Yevsektzia (the Jewish section of the Communist Party) were behind it and intended to use the meeting to advance their own agenda.

The Rebbe's request, therefore, came as a surprise to my father, but he didn't dare say so to the Rebbe directly. Instead, being that his study of the laws of *shechita* had been limited, he said that he was afraid that Rabbi Katzenelenbogen would test him on source material that he hadn't studied, and he would not know the answers.

"You will know," the Rebbe replied.

Still, my father struggled to understand why he was being asked to seek out Rabbi Katzenelenbogen's endorsement. "But Rabbi Katzenelenbogen is a *misnaged,* an opponent," he said, referring to the rabbi's opposition to the Chassidic lifestyle and its teachings.

The Rebbe said, "Indeed, but he is an *erlicher Yid*; a pious and upstanding Jew."

My father accepted the undertaking, but then, seizing the opportunity, confided to the Rebbe that he had been married for two years and had not yet been blessed with children. The Rebbe raised his hands and said, "You will have children, you will have children."

After this audience, my father went to Rabbi Katzenelenbogen and managed to impress him with his knowledge when they turned to discuss his learning. Rabbi Katzenelenbogen examined his knife three times and upon finding it flawless, he wrote him an approving endorsement. Before he left, the rabbi warned him not to learn any Chassidus…

My father later received certification from R. Shlomo Yosef Zevin as well, who was a rabbi in the city of Kalintzy, Ukraine, at that time. And, as he had initially intended, he was also certified by Rabbi Lazarov. (The NKVD later confiscated these certificates when they came to our house to conduct a search.)

Kosher slaughterers often dislike having their knives inspected by others and the questioning of their honesty or proficiency that it implies; my father, however, had the opposite attitude. When he encountered someone who knew how to check a knife, he would happily proffer his knife for inspection.

My father would often encourage the yeshiva students and young men in Samarkand to master *shechita;* at the very least, the ability to slaughter chickens. "One can never know where one will end up," he would explain. "Who knows, you might eventually find yourself residing in a location without a *shochet.* If you know what to do, you will be able to slaughter for yourself as well as assist others in eating kosher meat."

My parents lived in Cherepovets for a number of years. My father told us that on the outskirts of the city, located high on the Siberian steppe, he found many wild deer that he was able to slaughter under the laws of *kashrus,* thus providing kosher meat for the Jews of that area.

Settling in Kharkov

My father worked as the local *shochet* in Cherepovets until religious persecution forced him to discontinue the practice. My parents then chose to settle in Kharkov, Ukraine, where there was a large community of religious Jews and many Chabad chassidim.

Upon his arrival, my father opened a kosher restaurant, but in 1931 the newly passed Passportizatzya law offered a new opportunity. This law stated that every person from the age of sixteen and older needed an identity card that would serve as a residency permit and which, importantly, required a photograph. Photography became a popular new profession and a number of community members quickly learned the trade, my father among them. Many Lubavitchers had their pictures for this card taken by my father, and he snapped many of their personal photos as well. Indeed, many pictures that Lubavitchers have from their years in Kharkov were taken by my father.

I heard that the legendary chassid R. Berke Chein adopted this profession as well, after a fashion. He would arrive to work only after his lengthy morning prayers and their attendant preparations, such as immersing in the *mikvah* and studying Chassidus. Despite the late hour, he would find a long line of customers waiting for him!

A Wedding Ring for *Maamad*

We always wondered why we never saw my mother wearing her wedding ring. It was when I heard the following story that the mystery was solved.

For chassidim, the annual tradition of providing financial support to the Rebbe's household, known as *maamad,* is a cherished, deeply held one, and an expression of devotion to their rebbe. But, while preparing for a trip to the Rebbe Rayatz to request a blessing for children, my father once found he had no money to bring, on account of his dire financial situation. My father could not bear to forego giving something, and spoke with my mother about this painful prospect: "How can I go to the Rebbe without *maamad?*"

It seemed to my mother at that moment as though my father was glancing at the wedding ring on her finger. She didn't hesitate for a moment. She took off the ring and gave it to my father.

When my father entered his audience with the Rebbe, he presented the Rebbe with the ring, saying, "My wife sent this for *maamad.*"

At the time, the Tomchei Temimim yeshiva found itself in dire financial straits of its own. The Rebbe appreciated my mother's devotion tremendously and decided to use the ring to ease the yeshiva's state. He instructed that a public auction be held to sell off the ring. However, unlike a regular auction, whoever bid an amount would have to pay that amount toward the yeshiva, even if he was outbid. The winner of the actual ring would be the highest bidder. In this manner, a substantial sum of money was raised for the yeshiva.

The Rebbe's Promise Is Fulfilled

Several years had passed since my parents' marriage, and they had not yet been blessed with a child. My parents visited professional doctors and the prognosis was that my mother would never bear children. My mother once cried to my father, "If ten years pass since our marriage and we do not have children, we will have to divorce. Why should you continue to suffer? You can get married to someone else who will bear you children!"

My father said that if in Heaven it was decreed that he should have children, they would come from her, since the Rebbe had promised that *they* would have children. He also pointed out that the Rebbe had said *children*, in plural.

Still, after hearing what my mother had said, my father decided to write of the doctors' bleak predictions to the Rebbe. The Rebbe's response was that my mother should go to an even more prominent specialist. I believe the Rebbe mentioned the city of Kiev.

My parents went to Kiev and made an appointment with a specialist. After examining my mother, he said in surprise, "Who told you that she can't bear children?"

When my mother heard this, she nearly fainted. After she recovered, the doctor gave her some medication, and within a short time she was pregnant with my older sister, Fruma Sarah.

My parents told the Rebbe the good news, and the Rebbe wrote back that they would have a healthy child.

When my mother went to the hospital in Kharkov to give birth, R. Itche *der Masmid*, the much revered chassid and community stalwart, suggested that she take the Rebbe's letter with her to the hospital to put under her pillow. When R. Itche heard the happy news that my mother had given birth to a healthy baby girl, he was overcome with joy over the open miracle my parents had experienced. He had understood from the Rebbe's response that they would have a girl, he said, since the Rebbe had not mentioned that they would have a healthy "son." R. Itche *farbrenged* in their home all week, and when my mother returned from the hospital, she found the house in a state of total disarray.

My mother enjoyed relating that when the baby would cry, my father would jokingly say, "Who is crying? The daughter of Bracha the *akara,* the barren woman?"

She also related that when my father first saw the baby, he said, "Are you sure this is our child and they didn't exchange ours for another baby? It doesn't matter to me whether she resembles her father or her mother more; all I want to make sure is that she's ours!"

CHAPTER 3

The War Years
in Samarkand

By 1941, my parents had two more children—first my brother Berel, followed by myself—and in the summer of that year, Germany invaded Russia in the enormous Operation Barbarossa, breaking the non-aggression pact the two countries had signed two years earlier. Stalin trusted the Germans and the Russian army was caught unprepared. The Germans were thus able to advance rapidly through Ukraine and along the entire Russian front.

The Germans were very close to Kharkov by the fall of 1941. Radio reports broadcast the atrocities that the Nazis had perpetrated against Jewish civilians in conquered territory and encouraged the Jews to leave Kharkov for safer regions.

The Jews, who had grown accustomed to ignoring the generally exaggerated or false Soviet propaganda, were inclined to believe that these reports were, once again, baseless. After all, the Germans had been noteworthy for their civilized treatment of refugees during the First World War. Many Jews, my father included, remembered the German merchants who came to their city to sell their merchandise and how they treated the Jews with respect and propriety. Many Jews, after paying the ten golden ruble crossing fee, would likewise travel to Germany for business purposes.

It was only when letters from family members began to arrive describing German cruelty that nearly all of the Jews decided to flee. Most Lubavitcher chassidim crossed over the Soviet border and subsequently traveled on to Tashkent or Samarkand in Central Asia. These cities were far away from the battlefields and in a region with a more moderate climate. For chassidim, there was another incentive to travel to these cities in particular. They knew that they contained large Jewish communities of local Jews who held warm regard for the Chabad chassidim. This high regard was thanks to the work of Rabbis Shlomo Leib Eliezerov, Chaim Noeh, and Simcha Gorodetzky, who had been sent to the region years earlier as emissaries of the Rebbe Rashab and Rebbe Rayatz, and about whom there is more to be said.

Our family was one of the last to flee Kharkov. The train tracks were in bad shape due to the frenzied bombing of the German air force and the freight train that we traveled on moved slowly. It was surely a miracle that we made it out without a bomb striking the train.

The lack of room on the train out of Kharkov forced the passengers to crowd together, and in those tumultuous times, when it had become impossible to keep proper standards of hygiene, most people had not washed for days. There was an increase in the spread of dangerous diseases and an abundance of lice which, in addition to the unbearable itching they caused, further assisted the spread of disease. Understandably, we were wary of coming close to anyone unfamiliar to us.

At one point, Berel noticed a non-Jewish woman nearby whose hair seemed to be moving about on its own! My brother did not understand this phenomenon, but when my mother took notice, she quickly distanced him from the lady; her hair was teeming with lice.

For my mother, maintaining our dignity meant more than just staying disease free. I was a young child then, not yet three years of age, and as the train ride wore on, I later heard from my mother, I began to cry from hunger. A gentile woman offered to give me some non-kosher food to eat, but my mother politely refused.

Our long journey to Samarkand brought us to the city Makhachkala on the shore of the Caspian Sea for a brief stay. At that time, a general draft was announced and everyone was summoned. Officials combed the streets of Makhachkala and they stopped my father and directed him to appear at the draft office. He was not sure how to respond. On the one hand, most of the soldiers sent to the front were killed. On the other, avoiding a draft during wartime came with a guaranteed death sentence.

My father told us that he recalled the story of the arrest of the Alter Rebbe, the first Chabad Rebbe. When the Alter Rebbe heard that he was being sought after by czarist authorities, he first fled and hid for a short while before deciding to go with the soldiers who had been sent for him. The Alter Rebbe explained that this is what our patriarch Yaakov [Jacob] did when he fled from his brother, Eisav [Esau]. According to the midrash, he first hid in the study hall of Shem and only then did he go on his way. My father decided to remain at home and leave for the draft office one hour later than the time written on his order.

When he left the house, we were playing outside in the yard. My father kissed each one of us, sobbing softly, his tears cascading down onto our small heads. We did not understand what was happening and we asked him where he was going and why he was crying. He whispered tearfully that he would soon return.

Miraculously, this is precisely what happened. When he arrived at the draft office, only the local authorities were there. "Why are you late?" they yelled at him. "All the draftees have already been sent to the front! Next time, come at the time we tell you!"

My father joyfully returned home and was thus saved from almost certain death.

At that time, another miracle occurred: A directive from Stalin declared that family members en route to safety should not be drafted so as not to break up the family. Instead, they were to be drafted upon reaching their destination.

Refugees in Samarkand

During World War II, the physical conditions in Samarkand were exceedingly harsh. In addition to the Chabad chassidim, literally thousands of refugees had arrived from all over Europe, and Poland in particular—among them many distinguished rabbinic and Chassidic leaders—who now swarmed the streets, starving and bereft of the most basic necessities. The lack of food and resulting malnourishment was so severe that people would simply languish and drop dead in the street. It was not unusual to awake in the morning and discover the skeletal bodies of Jews strewn on the road or in the local hospital. The valiant R. Aharon Yosef Bilinitzky would identify the Jewish dead, pile them onto a wheelbarrow he had prepared for the purpose, and ensure that they had proper Jewish burials.

R. Aharon Yosef was an incredibly courageous individual, not to mention a sincere and devout chassid. It is considered inauspicious to leave a grave vacant overnight, so on many occasions, R. Aharon Yosef would spend the night in a freshly dug grave as they awaited the arrival of a corpse. A similar law prohibits leaving a dead body alone overnight. So, at other times, when corpses were brought to the cemetery in the evening before enough graves had been prepared, R. Aharon Yosef did not think twice before spending the night beside the body, so as to guard it until the morning.

During the cold winter nights, he would sometimes be forced to remove the sheet covering the dead body and use it to cover himself. He once noted at a *farbrengen* that he learned an invaluable lesson from his morbid experiences: "I have come to recognize the difference between the living and the dead: The dead don't have the capacity to care for another. When a Jew lacks care and concern for his fellow, he may as well be a corpse!"

For the most part, the refugees inhabited the old sections of the cities of Samarkand and Tashkent, where the local Bukharian communities lived. The Bukharian Jews were religious and traditionally observant Jews, while the few Ashkenazic Jews who lived in the new part of the city were largely unobservant. When we arrived in Samarkand, we too joined the Bukharian community in the Old City.

Our meeting with the Jews of Samarkand reminds me of a talk of the Rebbe, in which he spoke of the Torah as a force for unity. Jewish people scattered over the globe do not have a shared language or culture, nor a common look. There is only one thing that unites us all: the holy Torah.

When our group of refugees first arrived in Samarkand, we kept a certain distance from the local Jews, who in their dress and appearance resembled Uzbeks—the local gentile population, some of whom were not very friendly toward the Jews. Their language was Tajik, and their culture was completely different from what we were accustomed to. However, when we went to their shul and saw their Torah scrolls, observed their prayers and listened to their Torah study, all barriers fell away. We felt that, although we might be spread out among the nations, we are essentially a single people.

These Jews of Bukharian descent, particularly those who had been students of R. Simcha Gorodetzky, did all they could and more to care for the Jewish refugees. I was told that one Shabbos, a Bukharian Jew by the name of R. Dzura Niyazov, whom R. Simcha had sent many years earlier to learn in Tomchei Temimim, made his way from house to house and yelled: "How is it that we can sit and eat the Shabbos meal while other Jews have no bread? I demand that every individual take some challah bread and bring it to them: saving a life overrides the prohibition of carrying on Shabbos!" He explained the responsibility of the community to feed and nurture their brethren spared from the Nazi massacre, and the tremendous merit involved in doing so, thus inspiring many of the local Jews to take part in helping the refugees.

We arrived in Samarkand in time to spend the High Holidays there. Being that my father was known to have a gift for music and a soulful singing voice, the fledgling Chabad community asked him to lead the prayers for the upcoming holidays. I have a sweet childhood memory, from when I was about three years of age, of my father preparing the prayers. Beyond simply practicing the relevant melodies and tunes, he would intently study the prayers themselves, and delve into the meaning of the *piyutim*, the liturgical poems. At one point, he was so overcome by their power that he began to cry. I was taking an afternoon nap, and when I awoke to my father crying, I began to wail too. Calming me down he explained, in a way that the small child I was could understand, that he was only crying from emotion as he read the prayers of the High Holidays.

Hunger and the Search for Work

All the refugees who had come to Samarkand set themselves to looking for some work so as to earn a few morsels of food for their families. Bread had been rationed and was distributed solely in exchange for government issued coupons. Only the lucky ones managed to receive additional coupons by bribing the officials. My mother tried to save her own portion of bread for us, and when we awoke at night from severe hunger pangs, she would give us a small piece of bread to quiet our hunger so we could fall back asleep.

I remember how my mother would rise at four o'clock in the morning—and sometimes even earlier—take the coupons, and hurry to stand in line for bread. On some days, she still returned empty-handed. Generally, soldiers who had returned from the front wounded or decorated, and women with babies, were given preferential treatment at the breadline. If enough of them came on a given day, there would be nothing left for "regular" people like my mother. Then there were the ruffians who pushed everybody aside. Those not considered privileged would often return home empty-handed, and there were those who did not return at all. They had been crushed to death in the pushing.

We children roamed the streets, searching for seeds to eat. I recall my brother Berel returning from his classes smiling happily with a few dozen seeds he had gathered in the marketplace on his way home.

One morning, we woke up early, our stomachs growling hungrily. My mother had already gone to stand on line for bread, and we children remained home alone. Berel and Sarah looked for pieces of dry bread in the kitchen, and after not finding any, we went to forage for seeds outside.

Suddenly, I heard the voice of a woman behind me calling, "Look, *yingele*, there's another seed for you."

I recognized my mother's voice, and I turned around and ran towards her while asking plaintively, "Mother, did you get a little bread?"

She answered with tears flowing down her cheeks, "No, Hilinke, there was no bread left for me."

It is impossible to describe the pain of a mother unable to provide her children with even the most basic provisions. For much of the Chabad community in Samarkand and Tashkent, this is how things were in those early days.

As the war continued, my father kept looking for a source of income until he found some more work in the photography business and became a photo salesman of sorts. He would travel to villages and towns around Samarkand where the Uzbeks lived, and offered to take any small pictures they had of themselves or relatives and enlarge them in a photo lab in Samarkand. It was a novel service and a number of community members made a livelihood of it.

On one of my father's trips, he entered the home of a Uzbek lawyer who served as a prosecutor and asked whether he was interested in having any pictures enlarged. Unfortunately for him, the lawyer decided to make trouble for my father. He asked to see the permits for his business and all his receipts. When my father could not provide them to his satisfaction, he called the police and told them that my father was working illegally. He also claimed that my father was collecting photos of citizens for purposes of espionage, making my father a tasty catch for the war years.

The police arrested my father and placed him in jail, where he spent four months, including the High Holidays, Sukkos, and Simchas Torah. Afterwards, he told us how on Simchas Torah, he had explained to the non-Jews in the cell, "Today is a holiday of rejoicing for the Jews. I would like to ask you to stand in a circle as I sing and dance merrily." That was how he celebrated Simchas Torah.

While he was in prison, the jailors forcefully cut his beard. He tried to protest, and they punched him on the face so hard that he lost two teeth. I remember being afraid of him when he returned home; I didn't recognize him with only a part of his beard intact.

After my father left prison, he couldn't continue with the photo business. One day, he met with his friend R. Asher Batomer (Sossonkin), who asked him, "Avremel, what are you working at now?" My father told him that he didn't want to deal in pictures anymore and that he didn't know what to do. R. Asher suggested that he sell bread.

At first my father refused, saying that he had no idea how to go about the business. But R. Asher insisted: "You have young children! Sell bread and make a living for your family!" Although R. Asher worked in the same field and had good reason to be concerned about competition, he revealed the "secrets of the trade" to my father and encouraged him to begin the venture. This story is a wonderful example of how we helped each other out in times of need, and of R. Asher's tremendous love for his fellow Jew.

R. Asher proceeded to explain to my father how the business worked. First, you bribed the officials at the office so they would give you a permit to sell bread. Then you bribed the people at the government bakery to set aside a certain amount of bread for you daily, and so they wouldn't say they had run out. Finally, after bribing everyone, you were able to receive the bread and sell it in the marketplace. R. Asher told my father the exact names of the people and locations he needed to know.

My father accepted his idea, and after bribing the right people, he hired a non-Jew with a donkey and an enclosed wagon and equipped it with shelves to carry the bread. Every morning he would go to the government bakery, load the shelves with loaves of bread, and sell the bread in the market. My father was able to support our family in this way for some time, and we were thus saved from starvation, for every night he would come home with some loaves of bread for us.

One day, a Polish Jew came to my father and told him that he was a professional baker, with a specialty in cream cakes. Since he was a stranger without a penny in his pocket, he suggested that my father become his partner and start a bakery, promising him that it would produce a substantial profit.

My father borrowed money from his friends, the Pole bought the ingredients, and promptly began baking delicious cakes. The baking was done in our house, and we children found ourselves the main beneficiaries of this new enterprise. But in addition to us children sneaking bits of cake, other problems arose. Since the house had no proper space to store the cakes, they were kept on the table instead. One time, after a beautiful batch of cakes decorated with red cream flowers was left to cool out on the table overnight, a cat got into the house and licked off nearly every flower!

A few weeks later, when the Pole saw that he had gained my father's trust, he told my father that he needed to buy a large quantity of merchandise that required a large sum of money. My father borrowed the money and gave it to him, and the man disappeared with the cash. That was the end of both the money and the cake venture.

Discovering a Yiddish Songwriter

During one of my father's trips to the surrounding villages for his photography business, he met a Polish Jewish family in a forsaken Uzbek communal farm, or *kolkhoz*. My father asked them who they were and what they were doing there, alone among non-Jews. The family explained that after the Germans had divided Poland with Russia, they found themselves in Russian territory. Fearing the Nazi onslaught nonetheless, their mother had pressed them to escape further into the Russian interior, which is how they ended up in this far-flung *kolkhoz*. My father told them about the thriving Jewish community in Samarkand and invited them to visit.

Indeed, not long after the Ehrlich family relocated to Samarkand; the mother, two sisters, and a son, who would in time become the well-known and much-loved Yiddish singer and songwriter R. Yom Tov Ehrlich.

My father immediately recognized Yom Tov's musical talents and his unique gift for composition. He offered him his violin and suggested that he go to weddings to sing his songs, which would also earn him some money. R. Yom Tov took up my father's advice, and out of appreciation, would often come by our house to visit my father.

As with others who had come from Poland, R. Yom Tov always thought the way of life in Uzbekistan endlessly strange. The rough Uzbek mentality was very different from his own more European lifestyle. The Uzbeks used donkeys for transportation, and the floors of their houses were constructed from clay, or at best from bricks, covered with cotton blankets or mats.

The Uzbeks had an extremely primitive way of warming themselves in the winter. First, they would dig a pit in the center of the room, some two meters in diameter and a half-meter deep. They would then dig another cavity in the center of the pit, a half meter in both diameter and depth, into which they would insert burning coals. The inner cavity was then covered by a wooden grid, upon which a table was placed, and then covered by a large tablecloth that hung to the floor.

After all this had been prepared, the family members would sit on the floor surrounding the table, sticking their feet underneath to keep warm. The meals would be eaten in this position, and at night they would sleep near the table as well, with their feet positioned in a similar fashion.

R. Yom Tov, always one to express his experiences through song, wrote lyrics full of his characteristic sharp wit, with lighthearted depictions of the Uzbeks and their peculiar-seeming way of life. Before long, he had become the preferred *badchan*, the entertainer, at the many weddings that took place in Samarkand during those years.

Once, R. Yisrael Noach Belinitzky said to R. Yom Tov, "Yom Tov, is that all you found in Samarkand? What about the Chassidic Jewish community?!"

R. Yom Tov accepted his words, and for the next wedding he composed a special song about Jewish Samarkand. He sang of his amazement at the remarkable Jewish communities that had formed, their shuls and yeshivas, and their unique weddings.

R. Yom Tov left Russia in 1946. While most Lubavitcher chassidim were basically trapped by that point, as a Polish citizen, he had little problem leaving the country once the war was over. After traveling about, he reached America and settled in Williamsburg.

In the 1960s, when the Iron Curtain opened a crack and Jews began leaving Russia, he inquired among Lubavitcher chassidim whether my father had been able to leave as well. When my father arrived in New York in 1969, R. Yom Tov located him and they had a warm, heartfelt reunion, during which he presented my father with a set of his records.

Three years later, when I arrived in New York, I traveled to Williamsburg to meet with R. Yom Tov, who still remembered me, although as a little boy. Although I had been a young child when R. Yom Tov had left Samarkand, I had heard the songs he had composed in Samarkand from my father and other individuals, and I knew them well. He was overjoyed to see me and we had a long conversation about our memories of those times.

Avoiding the Black Market

In the Soviet Union of those days, it was extremely hard to support a family relying on the frugal legally-approved salary, and many citizens supplemented their income with work in the black market. Still, it was criminal activity, so despite his difficult financial situation, my father kept a distance from the black market. He would say, "It's enough that we are religious and Chabad chassidim. We don't need to add anything more to our criminal record."

Many people who were wary about doing business on the black market made small profits on the "gray" market. There was a big difference between a citizen whose business was, say, dealing in foreign currency or gold and one with a government-approved job who occasionally strayed over the legal line. One way many citizens did just that was by trading in "obligations," the tickets in the government's biannual lottery.

Citizens received these obligation notes as part of their salary, which enabled the government to reduce its expenses. No one was really interested in the tickets, as it was known that the government claimed 80 percent of them anyway and only gave 20 percent to the citizens, so the chances of winning were very slim. For this reason, all of the poor laborers were willing to sell their tickets for much less than their advertised worth.

Some people bought these notes from the poor workers in large quantities for half their original price. Some invested tens of thousands, and others invested millions. As in every business, there were also middlemen who purchased large quantities from various people and sold them to the big dealers at a profit. Twice a year, when the lottery took place, these dealers would sit to check their papers and see how much they'd won. Those who bought large amounts of notes had a large chance of winning almost every time.

I recall reading an article in the *Ogonyok* weekly about a certain individual who purchased obligation notes worth millions of rubles for a tiny fraction of their cost, and once every six months, when the lottery was drawn, the entire family would join together to examine the notes. Almost each time he would win thousands of rubles, if not tens of thousands. They were afraid to cash the money in one city, so they would spread out to different cities and claim a portion of the money in each location.

Of course, this business wasn't legal, and whoever was caught could be sent to jail for many years. One time, a Polish Jew by the name of Max approached my father. He wasn't religious, but he hung around our community in Samarkand during the war. He suggested that my father buy some obligation notes, and in order to convince him, he named other Lubavitchers who had bought from him as well. My father agreed to buy several notes.

That night my father was so worried that he couldn't sleep. He was afraid that the Polish Jew would now include my father's name in his list of buyers, just as he had named the other people who had bought from him. Who knows who would eventually hear that he was involved in these activities?

In the morning he returned to Max and told him that he was afraid to be involved in this activity and wanted to sell the notes back to him. He was willing to receive less money than what he had paid, just so that Max would know that he had rid himself of them.

My father tried his hand over the years at various fields of work that wouldn't force him to desecrate the Shabbos. Although he was a talented individual with expertise in many areas, his luck didn't always shine through and he was constantly making his way from one endeavor to the next.

During the postwar years, most houses did not have access to electricity, and kerosene lamps were used for light instead. Each lamp contained a wick and, attached to the side, had a knob to control the light's intensity. The flame was covered with a thin glass lampshade, protecting it from the wind as well as dispersing the light evenly throughout the room.

These fragile lampshades broke easily and were in constant demand. When a lampshade factory opened in Samarkand, my father seized the opportunity and opened a store to sell lampshades.

This endeavor didn't last that long, for soon after, most houses were set up with electrical wiring and the need for these lampshades diminished. Instead, my father opened a store to sell the colored fabrics favored by the Uzbeks. At around the same time, to earn a little more on the side, my mother also found some work with a community member with a similar business. On Sundays—market day in those parts—this Jewish fellow would travel to a neighboring hamlet, where he would do as much business in a single day as he would in an entire week back in the city. Every so often, my brother Berel would go along to help out selling the fabrics, and was paid well for his work.

Ordinarily, they would set out early in the morning, well before it was light, in order to arrive by daybreak. Berel would have to do his morning prayers on board the truck, en route to the village. Once, an Uzbek laborer also came along on board. Left with no choice, Berel began donning his *tefillin* and preparing to *daven* in full view.

"What's this?" cried the worker, as soon as he noticed. He sidled over to Berel, and tried tugging the *tefillin* off—he wanted to try them too!

Now in the middle of his prayers and unable to talk, Berel shrugged the excitable Uzbek off. Calming down, the latter spoke up again. "I know what those are. The Jews use them for healing," he said. He wasn't quite done yet, either. Still next to Berel, he unwrapped the turban he had been wearing from his head, in typical Muslim-Uzbek fashion, and then wound the long strip of fabric around his arm, and sat in silent solidarity, as Berel finished up his prayers.

On another occasion, my father decided that since there were few photographers in Samarkand, it would be worthwhile to revisit the profession he had held in Kharkov. He opened a photography shop, and it indeed brought in some income. However, this by itself was insufficient, and he needed to be occupied simultaneously in a number of other projects.

Among other ventures, my father made *coda,* a delicacy made from sheep tail fat. Producing *coda* that was guaranteed to last and not spoil was a complicated procedure. My father would sell the finished product to families in our local community. He also produced sausages, as well as wine for Pesach, and for a time he manufactured candles for Shabbos and the festivals.

Finding a Stable Livelihood

In Samarkand, there lived a Jew by the name of Constantine Yakovlevitch Tchachnovitzer, or Kostya for short, who dealt in sign manufacturing. Ostensibly to ease his acclimation to the Soviet lifestyle, he adopted a Russian identity after the Revolution and even married a non-Jewish woman. The only thing he was unsuccessful in transforming was his stereotypical Jewish appearance, testifying to all that he was, indeed, a Jew.

My father once heard that Kostya was looking for an assistant in his factory. Since my father was of the opinion that a young man who was not sitting and learning should work to fill up his time, he decided to send my brother Berel to Kostya's factory. Berel had a talent for design and was thus suitable for the position. Furthermore, the job would enable him to keep Shabbos, as well as earn a higher salary: designing was considered a professional career, and Soviet law allowed professionals to earn a higher salary than that earned by regular workers. Ultimately, my father's intent was that Berel would be able to open up his own business in this field.

Kostya assigned Berel with simple tasks, but Berel was perceptive and soon mastered the art of designing the signs. Berel observed Kostya preparing the stencils for the letters, but the actual painting of the signs was done out of sight, in a side room. The signs always came out beautifully painted, but Kostya made sure that no one saw his technique.

Once, officials from the central office visited the factory precisely at the time when Kostya was painting the signs. Kostya kept his cool and didn't allow them to enter the room, calling out from behind the closed door, "I'm taking a shower!"

Berel was extremely curious to discover Kostya's secret, and eventually succeeded in uncovering the mystery. The standard procedure used by sign manufacturers was to paint the letters in the stencils using a hairbrush. This would inevitably leave traces of paint around the border of each letter that would have to be removed manually when the paint was still wet. Kostya devised a simple solution: he used a sponge instead of a hairbrush to paint the letters, yielding a clean, professional look.

After working as an assistant in Kostya's factory for two years, Berel mastered the profession in its entirety, allowing my father to open a sign factory of his own, as he had intended from the start. My father would run the business while Berel, having learned the trade, designed the signs.

My father hired an agent to travel to nearby factories and obtain orders. At one point, when the agent attempted to squeeze out a higher percentage rate from my father for his services, my father decided to look for another agent.

My father decided on a Polish Jew by the name of Tukerman, who worked under the same government office that our business was registered. Tukerman would visit the neighboring villages with his horse and wagon selling tar, which the peasants would use to smear on the wheels of their carriages. As such, his clothes were always covered with grime and he himself reeked of tar, making it unbearable to stand next to him. He was a chatterbox, not quite on the clever side, and he spoke a broken Russian. Nevertheless, my father chose him for the job. Tukerman had a way of latching on to potential buyers unrelentingly, or until they agreed to purchase his wares, and my father believed that he would bring much success to our fledgling business.

When my father proposed the idea to him, he thought he was joking. "Me? I should go around selling your signs? The mere sight of me will cause people to cross the street!"

"Don't worry," my father replied. "All that is needed is for you to wear a new suit and tie, and you will look presentable."

Tukerman still didn't take my father seriously. But my father was true to his word: he purchased a new change of clothes and gave them to his new employee. After putting on the new clothing, Tukerman looked at himself in the mirror and started laughing aloud: "Look at me! I look like an intellectual!"

He set out on his way, and a few weeks later he returned. He entered the house in good spirits and sat himself down on the floor. Tukerman somehow preferred the floor to a chair, and claimed that it was more comfortable for him. I think the real reason was that he lacked a chair in his own home and had grown used to it.

"So did you bring in any orders?" my father asked.

Tukerman laughed and stretched out his hand, as if to say: First things first. Give me what I'm owed!

My father gave him a nice sum of money, and Tukerman opened his satchel and pulled out the contracts he had signed with a number of large companies. Indeed, he had procured us enough work for months to come!

How, in fact, did he manage to convince these companies to purchase our products? "It was simple," he said. "I told them that we employ disabled people—some of our workers are missing a hand or leg, and sometimes even a head as well!" Tukerman gave a laugh.

My father's gamble proved quite successful, and the new agent obtained large orders for us each time he made his rounds. This enabled us to hire various members from the community in our factory.

Among the employees was a woman by the name of Esther, who was nicknamed "Esther the artist." Esther was a lonely woman, who was constantly blaming her parents for forcing her to divorce and remain single. My father took pity on her and hired her to work in our factory. She was simple and sincere but could be a little out of touch.

Officials from the central office once paid our factory a visit, and they saw Esther sitting with her brush, her face stained with various colors. Being that she was officially registered as an artist, the officials asked her jokingly, "And where is Leonardo da Vinci?"

Esther didn't realize that they were referring to the great Renaissance artist, and she assumed that they were asking about one of the workers in the factory. She replied on impulse, "Oh, Leonardo? He just stepped out. He'll be back shortly."

Seeing the success of my father's sign factory, other members of the community copied the idea and opened similar factories, which in turn supplied many families with an ample livelihood.

Unlimited Chesed

My father was a man of true kindness, and truly exceptional generosity.

The terrible wartime economy left us without any money for matzos or other food for Pesach one year. In order to purchase the basic Pesach necessities, we needed around 3,000 rubles, but things were so bad that there wasn't even anyone to borrow from.

My mother was very worried, and each day she asked my father where we would get money for the holiday. One day, my father told her that he had thought of someone who might be able to lend him 3,000 rubles, and the next day after prayers, he would go to him and ask for the money. Hearing this, my mother was reassured and her spirits were lifted.

The next day, after my father returned from the Morning Prayer, my mother asked him, "*Nu*, did you borrow the money?"

My father said that he had. My mother was happy and said, "Thank G-d! Now we will be able to buy what we need for Pesach." But then, suspiciously my father added, "With Hashem's help it will be okay."

Realizing that something was amiss, my mother asked him again, directly, "Do you have the money?"

This time my father tried to avoid answering, but in the end, he had to say the truth: He did borrow the money, but he no longer had it.

Confused, my mother asked, "Was it stolen from you?"

My father replied, "No, it wasn't stolen. I did borrow all 3,000 rubles that we needed, but on my way home I met a Jewish refugee who told me that he also has three children and no money for the holiday and I gave him the money."

My mother couldn't believe her ears. Incredulously, she asked, "Why did you give it all away? You couldn't give him just half of the money? What will we do now?" and she burst into tears.

My father tried to calm her: "Bracha, don't cry. I will find someone else who will lend me the money. Everybody knows me here, and there's no doubt I'll find a way to borrow some more money. But the Jew I met is a stranger. No one knows him here and no one will lend him money."

Looking back, I reflect: My father was not acquainted with that Jew from beforehand. There was no way of knowing if he would ever be repaid; it would probably be more accurate to describe the money he gave him as a gift than as a loan. And yet, he gave him the money he had borrowed for his own Pesach needs without hesitation!

That was my father: there were times when he had more com-
passion for others than he had for himself.

R. Moshe Nissilevitch told me that he remembered the following scenario vividly. My father once prayed at a certain minyan in
Samarkand, at which someone announced that he was collecting
money for an important cause and asked that everyone contribute.
Without thinking twice, my father put his hand into his pocket and
took out all the money he had with him, and without even count-
ing it, gave it all to charity. R. Moshe was astonished by the simple,
unassuming way my father just gave away his money.

I remember that when he would come home with his salary or
other earnings, my mother would virtually have to hide the money
from him, knowing that it would otherwise soon disappear. Before
he left the house, my mother would make sure that his pockets were
empty, for otherwise all the money would be disbursed before returning home.

My father especially enjoyed hosting guests. As soon as he
heard of a Lubavitcher visiting Samarkand, he would jump at the
opportunity to invite him over, and quickly turn to preparing a
festive meal in his honor in the meantime. Once the meal was
ready, he would proceed to ask everyone he saw for the visitor's
whereabouts and instruct them, if they should see him, to notify
him that a meal was waiting for him at the Zaltzman home. Almost every Lubavitcher visiting Samarkand would come by our
home.

My father never complained about his financial difficulties,
and he acted as if he were a wealthy man, promising to give even
more to charity even when he didn't have money at hand. He
would say, "I don't have the amount readily available, but I'm
planning on earning money from this and that, so I can pledge the
money now."

When my mother would hear of his promises, she would say:
"Your future earnings won't be enough even just to pay off our
debts. We must first cover our debts, and only then can we promise
money to others!"

My father would respond in jest: "Let them think that I'm rich! What difference does it make? We have a daughter ready to get married—that sort of reputation can only help!"

My cousin Sarah had lost her father at an early age. Her father, R. Benzion Pil, had joined us in Samarkand in 1945, after his release from a Soviet prison, but died of illness just four years later. When Sarah reached a marriageable age, my father made sure that anything and everything was taken care of, as though she were his own daughter, and he personally arranged a match for her with R. Dovid Mishulovin.

It was difficult to obtain a new *tallis* in those times, but my father wanted to present the young groom with a *tallis* of his own. Without batting an eyelash, he took his own *tallis*—a Turkish-made one of superior quality—and gave it to Dovid. When asked what he would use for himself, my father replied, "I'm not worried about that. I can always borrow!"

My father's goodness and kindness extended to both Jew and gentile. He once went to work and saw a non-Jewish man at the entrance asking for charity. The poor fellow said that he was starving. While the other workers passed by and ignored him, my father bought him a loaf of bread and a bottle of lemonade, and gave him a few rubles as well. The gentiles he worked with couldn't get over it. "See what a Jew is!" they said afterwards in amazement. "That poor man is a Russian like us. Yet we all passed by and ignored him, while the only one who responded to his pleas was Zaltzman the Jew!"

The Girl in the Corridor

It was a bitter winter morning in the year 1945, shortly before the end of the war. The biting cold air was under -10°C, and snow had fallen the day before, sparkling on the ground like towering heaps of crystal. I remember that my father returned home from shul that morning earlier than usual and told my mother that when he entered the hallway of the shul, he saw a girl of about nineteen years of age sitting on the ground, crying and trembling from the cold. Her clothes were torn and dirty, and she was whimpering, "I have nothing… Where will I go tonight? I am starving… Have pity on me!"

Compassionate Jews entering the shul gave her some kopecks before going in to pray. My father gave her five rubles and went inside, but found himself perturbed and unable to focus on the prayers. At that time, corpses were being found every morning in the streets; people perished from the hunger and cold. Who knew what the girl's fate would be?

He returned to the entranceway and asked her where she was from. The girl said that her entire family—her parents, brothers, and sisters—had perished in the Holocaust, and she had been directed to travel to Samarkand.

My father hurried home and told my mother about this girl, adding that it appeared that she was speaking the truth. "We must have mercy and rescue her!" he said.

My mother didn't have to think twice. She got dressed immediately and rushed back to shul with my father, taking along some clean clothes and a warm coat for the girl. My mother took her from the shul to the bathhouse and two hours later she came home with the girl. From that day on, she told her, this would be her home.

The girl spoke a fluent Yiddish with a Polish accent and she slowly learned to speak Russian. She lived with us for half a year as a member of the family. Eventually, she found a job and moved into a rented apartment.

Two years later, she came to my parents and told them that she had been offered a proposal for marriage with a Bukharian boy. He was twenty-six, nice-looking, and was of a fine character, but he had a disability: he had been blind since childhood. Since she considered my parents, who had saved her life, as her own, she wanted their advice.

Her words stunned my parents and they didn't know what to tell her. After inquiring about the young man and seeing that she really liked him, they agreed to the match.

They married and established a traditional Jewish home. He supported himself by asking for donations, as he had done until then, and his wife would lead him down the street. When I would walk near him, he could recognize me by my gait, and his wife would also let him know that I was approaching. I always gave him a nice donation. They were blessed with three healthy children, and when people began leaving Samarkand for Eretz Yisrael, they immigrated there as well.

Sacrifice for a Jewish Education

As hard as providing for one's family was, preserving Jewish life in Soviet Russia was more difficult, and ensuring proper *chinuch*, a Jewish education and upbringing for one's children, was almost impossible. Our dismal financial outlook, of course, didn't make things any easier, especially when that *chinuch* often came at the expense of a secular and professional education.

My father never worried how we would support ourselves if we did not go to university. "The One who gave life will give sustenance," he would say.

When my cousin Yaakov Pil was discharged from military service in 1949, some were of the opinion that he would be suited to teach in a school or work at some other intellectual job. My father, however, was certain that he would be better off opening a store, enabling him to keep Shabbos. "Better a less prestigious occupation in a Jewish atmosphere than a more highly esteemed one amongst non-Jews!" he used to say.

The years leading up to and culminating in the infamous Doctors' Plot of 1953 were very difficult years for Russian Jews. The situation was so dire that when my father bought new earthenware utensils for Pesach, my aunt Rosa criticized him, saying, "These days we have to save money and buy canned goods and preserves so that we will have what to eat on the long trip to Siberia!" That was the prevalent feeling: People were simply waiting for the moment when Stalin would haul us off to Siberia, to "protect" us from the murderous pogroms set to be instigated by the Plot.

I will never forget that frightful scene on Erev Rosh Hashanah. We children were afraid to go to shul, so my father was preparing to go alone. But before he left the house, he turned his head to the heavens and prayed to Hashem in a voice choked with tears:

"Master of the World, what do I ask of you? All I want is for my sons to remain *erlicher Yidn*—devout Jews!"

My father then raised his hands above his head and cried, "Master of the World, if it was decreed that my sons go astray, I ask of You to take me first so that I don't see it!!"

My mother was horrified to hear this and shouted, "How can you talk like that before Rosh Hashana? Our children are *yirei'im u'shleimim*, they are "pious and whole-hearted!" Our children will never compromise on anything. They won't pass a day without donning *tefillin* and will never treat keeping kosher or Shabbos lightly. Other people did not stand strong and their children abandoned our faith, but thank G-d, we are all *yirei'im u'shleimim!*"

My father was not pacified and said, "True, but these are very hard times. Who knows what tomorrow will bring? I'm telling you: If they go off the path, Heaven forbid, I won't be able to live anymore."

Such was the devotion of a true chassid in the Soviet Union of those days.

A New House and a Private Yard

At the end of the 1950s, Chabad chassidim began to move from the Old City and relocate in the New City. We moved as well and bought a house together with my sister and brother-in-law, R. Eliyahu Mishulovin. The house itself was large, and it was surrounded by a huge yard—more than a thousand square meters—containing some eighty fruit trees and bushes.

The house was unusually large for urban Samarkand standards. It had been the former home of a brigadier general in the Russian army who had been given by the government a large plot of land upon which to build a house. A short while after the house was built and the trees were planted, he divorced his wife and married a younger woman. His former wife then moved into a neighboring government house with a window directly overlooking his large yard and would torment him and his young wife without respite. In time, he had no choice but to sell the house, and that is how we came to buy it.

It was a pleasure to sit in the garden, but the windows overlooking our yard bothered us too. On the one hand, this was the first time we had a house with our very own yard; on the other hand, every move we made was observed by our gentile neighbors. The children couldn't go out to the yard, for fear that the neighbors would notice that they did not attend school. We couldn't go outside wearing *tzitzis* or Shabbos clothing because they were watching. We were forced to hide out in our very own house.

If we couldn't do something to get out of their sight, my father said, then all the pleasures of a large garden were worthless. We couldn't be exiled from our own backyard. He finally came to an agreement with the neighbors: In exchange for five meters of land extending across the entire length of the yard, he received their consent to build a high wall surrounding our yard. After that, we were able to host the semi-formal yeshiva that had secretly begun operating in Samarkand and groups of boys would come to learn in our yard on a regular basis.

At the time when R. Mendel Futerfas stayed in our home, after arriving in Samarkand from Chernovitz, my father suspected that one of the gentile neighbors had begun to follow us. My father was extremely on edge, and he would often report to us: "Just as I left the house, he decides to walk his dog. When I went to the market, he was there too, and when he noticed me he bent over as though he was tying his shoelace."

We were sure that my father was exaggerating, and even R. Mendel said that he was just imagining things, but my father insisted. After a while, the neighbor stopped following us, and only then did we realize how closely he had shadowed us during the previous months.

Once, at a *farbrengen* before R. Mendel left Russia, my brother-in-law Eliyahu asked him: "As you are well aware, running a yeshiva and taking care of the *bochurim* studying with us puts us in all sorts of predicaments. Now that you're going, with whom will we consult?"

R. Mendel said, "If you have a question, or if there is a problem, consult with your father-in-law. He is a clever chassid and he understands things well. Do you remember how we all thought that he was imagining things when he claimed that the gentile neighbor was following us? It was only later when we realized how right he was."

CHAPTER 4

The Uncles I Didn't Know

I only knew my uncle R. Benzion Pil during the last years of his life when he lived in Samarkand. I was a young child at that time and many of my memories of him are lost. However, his daughter Sarah was able to recount his life in great detail, even though he had passed on more than sixty years earlier.

R. Benzion Pil was known as a generous man and his story and outsized personality should not be forgotten. During the war, he served time in Soviet prisons, and his family did not know where. He found them again after the war in Samarkand. He died a few years later from illness.

From Poverty to Wealth

When he first met my aunt, my mother's sister Eidel, shortly after their match had been proposed, R. Benzion Pil arrived wearing a new suit, tie, and top hat. In those days, these kinds of garments were reserved for successful business people and my aunt's family was under the impression that he was very wealthy. It was only after the wedding that they discovered that he was under such dire financial straits that he had to borrow a friend's clothes for the meeting.

Fortunately, a short while after the wedding he began to see his own business succeed. He was quite generous and gave away much of his wealth to charity. I heard that R. Mendel Futerfas reminisced about him fondly, saying that he learned how to give *tzedakah* from Benzion Pil. After their wedding, the young couple lived in Kharkov, where there was a small Lubavitcher community that was established during the times of the Tzemach Tzedek (Righteous Sprout), Rabbi Menachem Mendel Schneersohn. Among the members of the community were a number of Cantonists—Jewish boys forced to serve in the czar's army for twenty-five years—who had survived and returned to a Jewish way of life.

Their oldest child was my cousin Yaakov, who eventually moved to the Chabad neighborhood in Lod, Israel, and served as the *gabbai* in the Lubavitcher shul there. Two years after Yaakov's birth, my aunt and uncle were expecting once more. When my aunt went into labor, they called for an ambulance. However, the ambulance driver told them that because of a gentile holiday there were no doctors on call. "Try again tomorrow," he suggested.

My aunt gave birth at home without any medical aid. Tragically, their newborn daughter perished several days later. Additionally, my aunt was stricken with a blood infection, before being rushed to the hospital in critical condition. With the poor sanitary conditions prevalent in hospitals in those days, her condition worsened from day to day. Eventually, they moved her to a separate room where they kept patients deemed to be beyond hope.

While she was there, she had a dream in which her deceased mother appeared with a beautiful casket, saying: "They sent me to take you. Come with me!"

A terrible fear overcame my aunt and she cried out, "Mama, how can you take me away? I have a young boy! I'm not going under any circumstances. Please leave me!"

For a number of minutes she argued with her mother, until her mother finally left.

Her dream continued, and she saw an old Jewish man with a long, white beard carrying a bucket full of water. He entered a marketplace containing a number of booths, and the traders came out asking to drink from his water. The old man refused all of them, saying: "I have no time; I must go to the hospital! There's a sick woman there who needs my water!"

The old man reached the hospital and gave my aunt to drink from his bucket. She could feel her health returning.

When she awoke from the strange dream, she felt much better. From then on, her condition improved daily until she finally left the hospital.

After she made a complete recovery, she asked her brother, R. Avrohom Boruch Pevzner, who then lived in Snovsk, to ask the Rebbe Rayatz for a blessing for another child. After receiving the Rebbe's *brocha*, they bore my cousin Sarah, who would later marry Dovid Mishulovin. Her parents often regretted asking the Rebbe's blessing for a "child" and not "children."

Acts of Kindness

When the famous chassid R. Itche *der Masmid* would arrive in Kharkov to raise money for the Tomchei Temimim yeshiva, my uncle would give him all of the money that was in his pocket. Once, R. Itche asked him, "Why don't you count the money that you give me?"

"Is this my money?" my uncle replied. "Hashem gave me the money and I'm merely passing it on to you."

R. Itche was very impressed with the answer and said, "You have a wife and children whom you need to support. Since, in spite of this, you display such generosity, I'm giving you my blessing that you should have so much money that it will mean nothing to you!"

His blessing did, in fact, come true, and my uncle became very wealthy. He kept very little for himself, using his money instead to perform remarkable acts of kindness, as illustrated in the stories below.

During the 1920s, the Chabad community in Kharkov had expanded, and the central Yeshivas Tomchei Temimim relocated there. It was at this time that my father, along with others in the community, went into photography, as sought-out professions that allowed them to keep Shabbos grew scarce and less lucrative.

On his way home from his shop, my father often passed by the house of his brother-in-law R. Benzion. Once, R. Benzion asked him, "*Nu,* Avremel, how was business today?"

My father sighed and responded that it had not been a successful day. Hearing this, R. Benzion pulled out a wad of cash and pushed it into my father's pocket.

"When you get home, tell your wife it was a successful day."

During more difficult times, when famine struck Kharkov, it was only possible to obtain food with government coupons. Most of the community, and the boys of the yeshiva who did not have these coupons, were literally starving. R. Benzion used his personal connections with officials in the hard-currency *Torgsin* stores, bribing them to obtain cases of fruit. He then went to the yeshiva, placed the cases on the tables, and said, "Eat, eat! You must learn Torah!"

Afterwards, he went to the Meshtchaner Shul and brought food to some community members present, among them R. Mendel Futerfas, R. Zalman Serebryanski, and others. Once, my uncles Benzion Pil and Dovid Pevzner saw a Jew in the street peddling all sorts of candies and chocolates. R. Benzion stopped him and bought sacks full of all kinds of sweets. R. Dovid was surprised by the amount of candy he bought, and blurted out, "Who is all this for? You only have two children!"

"I'll offer them whenever we have guests," he said. "What's important is that this is an opportunity to help another Jew earn a livelihood. He has a family he must provide for!"

There was an old woman who fled with my family to Samarkand from Kharkov. We called her "Bubbe Esther," even though she wasn't related to us.

How did she join our family?

Esther had a son who wanted to marry a certain young woman of whom she didn't approve. They married nonetheless and moved to Poltava. At a certain point, Esther decided to move to Poltava to live with her son, but her daughter-in-law threw her out, crying,

"You didn't want me, now I don't want you!" She gave her mother-in-law enough money for the trip back to Kharkov and the old lady returned, brokenhearted and destitute.

She stood next to the shul holding a small sack. With a tear-streaked face, she would repeat her tragic story to passersby, who would drop a few coins into her sack before going on their way.

One day, R. Benzion encountered the poor, lonely woman. Not content to simply give her money, he invited her to live with his family. With only a single bedroom, a kitchen and a dining room, his home was not especially big. Still, my aunt and uncle provided for her every need as if she were a member of the family.

A Treacherous Trip to the Train Station

During the "Great Purge" Stalin directed against his political rivals during the 1930s, tens of thousands were exiled to Siberia without trial, or simply shot in the GPU dungeons. Under this reign of terror, thousands of citizens became informers for the GPU. Unfortunately, they included a number of Jews, who relayed information about dissidents in the community. The chassidim who fought to preserve Judaism were considered "enemies of the State," and many of them were imprisoned. My uncle R. Avrohom Boruch Pevzner was one of them.

When R. Benzion Shemtov, one of the chassidim of Kharkov, discovered that the secret police were hunting him, he searched desperately for a safe place to stay. No one was willing to undertake the incredible dangers of concealing a fugitive. That is, except for my uncle R. Benzion, who hid him in his home during those frightful times.

It wasn't long before R. Benzion Shemtov realized that hiding anywhere in Kharkov was unsafe and decided to leave the city. Since he was afraid to travel alone, he asked my uncle to find someone who could take him to the train station. My uncle spoke to a number of people, but in spite of the generous amount he offered to pay, no one was willing to endanger himself and his family. Everyone knew what awaited those caught assisting a fugitive.

After several days, R. Benzion Shemtov asked my uncle whether he had found anyone willing to take him to the train station. My uncle was reluctant to tell him the truth.

Understanding the incredible danger that R. Benzion was in, my uncle decided to put his life on the line and travel with him to the train station himself. He dressed R. Benzion in a lady's coat with a large collar and wrapped his face in a woolen lady's scarf to hide his beard. They walked arm in arm, like a woman supporting her elderly mother.

When they reached the train station, my uncle purchased a train ticket for R. Benzion and boarded the coach with him. He remained on the coach until the train started on its way, then quickly jumped off.

Moments later, two men in plainclothes approached him and asked if he saw someone named Benzion Shemtov in the station. My uncle looked at them, a curious look on his face.

"I've never heard of him," he said.

They left him to continue a fruitless search of the rest of the platform.

The Arrest of My Uncle R. Avrohom Boruch Pevzner

My mother's brother, R. Avrohom Boruch Pevzner, the *mashpia* of Minsk, was arrested and released in Stalin's wave of purges. In March 1939, shortly before Pesach, he was arrested again in Kharkov for the crime of spreading Judaism and taken to Kiev where he was interrogated and tortured. Unable to obtain matzah during the holiday, he sustained himself on sugar cubes. He was subsequently sentenced to five years in exile in Kazakhstan.

We recently discovered in a family archive his last letter to his family from his exile in Kazakhstan, written in 1940. Time has left its toll on the letter, but though frayed and illegible in parts, its message reveals an unwavering and devoted chassid to the end.

"If this is my last letter... I inform you, I ask in truth... from Hashem, that He forgive me for all kinds of inadvert, deliberate and rebellious sins, even rabbinic transgressions, whether positive or negative commandments, even minor rabbinic details, because I truly repent for having transgressed them. (And it was never deliberate in order to anger, or in order to cast off the yoke of the kingdom of Heaven, G-d forbid. On the contrary, I have confirmed many times that Hashem is our G-d, Hashem is One, and include myself in His unity). However, since I engaged in thought, speech and deeds that were not from the side of holiness, may Hashem forgive me for all that was negative on my part and send me from Heaven, in his abundant mercy, a complete recovery in all 248 limbs and 365 sinews, along with the other sick people amongst the Jewish people. Please Hashem, I beseech You to heal, in actual deed...

"And if my end has come, I justify the judgment, and request of Him one thing; that my death should be the atonement for all my sins so I will not have to be reincarnated again, G-d forbid. *Hashem is One. Hashem is Alone. Hashem is G-d in the heavens above...there is no other.* This is eternal.

"My sons should recite *Kaddish* as is customary. They should not quarrel with one another, G-d forbid. Hillel and Sholom Dovber should try to learn in the evenings in public if that can be achieved easily.... Yitzchak Shlomo should be careful to pray with a quorum and to say the *Kaddish* for the orphan, *Kaddish Yasom.* That is what I request of all my sons, to listen to the meaning of the words that they are saying.... All my children should conduct themselves in the proper way in which they were raised and certainly with peace and harmony with all, and may Hashem come to their aid materially and spiritually, *Amen*, may it be G-d's will.

"The matter of Jewish burial within a Jewish cemetery is important... but [being deprived of it] does not compare to everything else Hashem has already taken from us in our lives and in our deaths, and to which we have already grown accustomed, so let me suffice with saying it doesn't seem to be a great flaw or impurity....

"I am also confident in the merit of our holy teacher, the crown of our heads, our father and Rebbe [Rashab], of righteous memory, to whom I was devoted heart and soul, in his life and his death, with great love... may it be so. Today the sun warmed the earth, and the frost of the last week has dissipated. This is an opening of the door, and Hashem should help that all things should already be warm and happy, materially and spiritually, in all respects, so may it be. It has already been several days since I began to drink a glass of milk daily, eat butter, and drink plenty of sweet tea. Sugar and sweets I have plenty of...this is the physicality I have to contend with. And who can tell Him what to do, for all eternity."

R. Avrohom Boruch died in Kazakhstan in April 1940. His wife traveled to his place of exile and was with him in his final days. She was able to arrange a Jewish burial for him in the nearby city of Kyzylorda.

R. Benzion Pil's Arrest and Trial

In 1935, the government arrested a group of some ninety businessmen, including my uncles Benzion Pil and Dovid Pevzner. A mass trial was held, and they both received sentences of seven years in prison.

Among the prisoners was a Jew, unknown to my uncles, who had apparently been convicted of some more severe offense and was sentenced to death. When my uncle Benzion Pil heard of his sentence, he decided to use a legal ploy to have the courts reconsider this harsh punishment.

According to the law, someone convicted during a mass trial could appeal his sentence, in which case the entire group's sentences would be reviewed. My uncle hoped this Jew would have better luck during the review.

The appeal worked, but only partially. That Jew received a ten-year sentence instead of the death penalty. My uncle's sentence, on the other hand, was increased to ten years rather than seven. Apparently, the judges were enraged at his audacity to appeal their decision.

The new sentence was disastrous. Soviet law allowed early release for prisoners exhibiting good behavior, but this was limited to sentences of less than ten years. For his heroic act, my uncle would be forced to serve out every last day of his sentence in prison.

My sharp-tongued aunt Rosa berated my uncle. "Why did you ask for another trial?" she asked. "Do you even know that Jew? You could have been out in two and a half years! Now you're going to sit behind bars for ten years while your wife and children have to survive without you!"

"That man has a wife and children as well," answered my uncle. "After ten years, we'll both be able to return to our wives and children. But if he would have died, his wife would become a widow and his children orphans."

My uncle Dovid served his sentence for two and a half years and then returned to Kharkov. When the World War II broke out, he traveled with us to Samarkand. But Benzion Pil remained in prison for ten years to the day.

He was first held in prison in Kharkov, enabling my aunt Eidel to visit him from time to time. During visits, families would be led to the cell blocks, where they would stand on one side of a hall and the prisoner on the other. They literally had to shout to hear each other from such a distance.

Later, all of the prisoners were sent to a place known as the Karelo-Finnish SSR, a Soviet republic founded in 1940. At that time all connection to him was lost. The family had no idea where he had been transported. They sent letters to several police officials trying to locate him, but never received a definitive answer.

By this time, the war had begun, and outside of pure speculation, it was impossible to know the fate of anyone already separated from family and friends. It was the summer of 1941, rumors and reports from the German front seeped in, and the Jews of Kharkov were fleeing frantically towards Central Asia.

Even after letters arrived describing the slaughter of Jews by the Germans, there were still those who refused to believe that the Germans could do such a thing.

My cousin Sholom Dovber Pevzner, R. Avrohom Boruch's son, was eighteen years old at the time. He refused to leave Kharkov, saying that he didn't understand what the great panic was all about. "Do what you want," he said. "I'm staying in the yeshiva."

To our great dismay, we lost contact with him shortly thereafter. Someone later recalled seeing him taken away by the Nazis.

My aunt Rosa Duchman was the one who insisted that traveling anywhere was preferable to remaining in Kharkov. First, she said, "Broch'ke"—referring to my mother—must leave, because she was caring for us young children. Following our family, Rosa and her husband left together with my aunt Eidel Pil and her two children; her husband Benzion remained behind.

Whenever their train entered a station throughout the slow and exhausting journey, the refugees tried to get out of their windowless freight cars and purchase provisions. My cousin Yaakov Pil once went to buy bread at one of the small stations. After some time, with no sign of Yaakov, the family started to worry. The train whistle had sounded for the third time, and there was still no sign of him.

As my cousin Sarah recounts: "We didn't know what to do, but there was no choice. We continued on our journey without Yaakov. As the journey continued, everyone peered into the other trains passing by, hoping to spot him.

"What happened a day later was no less than a miracle. Our train entered a station when we saw another train on a nearby track leaving. To our great joy, there, on that train, was Yaakov! He stood in the doorway, two loaves of bread hanging from his belt, peering into the cars of the other trains in the station, hoping to catch a glimpse of his family.

"We all started to cry out to him. He turned in our direction and saw his family, and without thinking twice, he leapt from the moving train. He fell to the ground and, miraculously, survived with only a few minor bruises.

"Once we had all calmed down, Yaakov told us that after he had found some bread, he returned to the station, saw a train waiting on the platform, and jumped aboard. It was too late by the time he realized his mistake, but he decided to stay on the train in the hopes of finding his family at one of the stations ahead."

Survival in Samarkand

During the desperate war years in Samarkand, my uncle Boruch Duchman's work as a *shochet* proved invaluable. In general, his *shechita* was held in high regard, and even though there were a number of other Lubavitcher kosher slaughterers, esteemed chassidim like R. Nissan Nemanov, R. Hillel Azimov, R. Mendel Futerfas, and R. Shmuel Dovid ate only from my uncle's knife. When I lived with my uncle during my father's imprisonment, butchers would come in the middle of the night and pound on the walls of the house, waking him to come and *shecht*.

Once, as he was walking through the Uzbek Quarter before dawn, on his way back from the slaughterhouse, he realized that there was a gentile following him. Unable to run on account of his poor health, he continued on his way. The streets were extremely dark. Most people would carry lanterns when walking outdoors at night to light their way.

Soon enough, the gentile caught up with him, struck him on his back and escaped. Uncle Boruch returned home terrified and shaken. My aunt Rosa asked him what had happened and he told her everything. She looked at his back and found a deep slash in his winter coat. The cut extended through his jacket and shirt as well, stopping short at the *tallis katan* he wore underneath.

At that time, many people were drafted into the army. My cousin Yaakov was drafted as well and served through the duration of the war. When they summoned my uncle Boruch for the draft, he claimed that he was much older than the age stated on his passport. He changed his birthday years ago, he said, to convince his wife to marry him. He did, in fact, look quite old. His beard was white, he was quite heavy and moved about slowly.

The draft officer believed his story and agreed not to take him, writing "excuse accepted" on his draft card. He continued to receive draft notices, and each time he would bring his draft card with the draft officer's decision and they would exempt him.

Uncle Boruch's *shechita* became something of a family business. My aunt Eidel Pil would remove the veins as required by Jewish law, and her daughter Sarah, a young girl at the time, would make deliveries. Private business was illegal in those days, and a kosher business more so, but a young girl like my cousin aroused much less suspicion than an adult. After my aunt Rosa had packaged an order, she would place it in a bag and conceal it with various dried fruits.

My cousin Sarah related that she once brought a package to R. Benzion Shemtov. After opening the package, Mrs. Shemtov said to her, "Tell your aunt not to send so many bones next time."

R. Benzion, overhearing heard her comment, rushed into the room. "Listen," he said sternly. "Even if she brings you *only* bones, or even stones, say 'Thank you.' The girl doesn't know where her father is! How can you say such things to her?"

He turned to Sarah and said, "Sarah'le, your father is alive and he'll return to you soon."

Reunited At Last

After his release in 1945, my uncle Benzion Pil had no idea where his family was and where to begin searching for them, and he feared the worst. He was aware that the Germans had occupied Kharkov, and knew all too well the fate of the local Jews. He did all he could to chase away these thoughts, and he trusted in Hashem that the merit of his charitable deeds would lead his family to a place free from war.

At one stage, he heard from a woman who knew his family that many Jews had fled southeast to Samarkand. Telephone lines barely existed then, and the postal service had not functioned since the war, so he set out on the arduous trip to Samarkand, in the hope of meeting his family there. How great was his joy to discover, after a few weeks' journey, that his family had survived and were all healthy and well!

Although finally reunited with his family, his good fortune did not last long. Soon after, he became grievously sick, and after a four-year battle with illness, he passed away in 1949, just one month before his son Yaakov was discharged from the army.

Yaakov Pil's Homecoming

With the end of the war, the Russian army discharged the older reservists from duty, but held on to the younger conscripts. Yaakov Pil had been sent, in the meantime, to a military camp in the Far East, near Japan.

Throughout his service, Yaakov had been injured several times, but he also experienced many miracles. During one battle against the Germans, while sheltering in a bunker, one of his comrades had to go outside to relieve himself. Afraid to go out on his own, and knowing Yaakov's good heart, this non-Jewish soldier asked that he accompany him, and Yaakov agreed. Just as the two left the bunker, the Germans launched a massive bombardment of the area. When the explosions subsided and the two soldiers returned to the bunker, they were shocked to find that a bomb had directly penetrated the bunker and killed everyone inside.

Yaakov was discharged towards the end of 1949, and by unbelievable Divine Providence, arrived in Samarkand eleven months to the day of his father's passing—the very last day he could recite *Kaddish* in his father's memory. His appearance threw the family into a terrible dilemma: As his father's only son, they had to tell him the terrible news and allow him to say the last *Kaddish*. However, they simply couldn't bring themselves to share the bitter news with him so quickly.

When Yaakov asked of his father's whereabouts, his family told him he had fallen ill, and was in critical condition at the hospital. They would take him to see his father right after he ate something. As he was served lunch, one of the family members placed a note beneath his plate, bearing the news that his father had died eleven months earlier, and that he should quickly go to shul in time to say the last *Kaddish*.

After reading the note, Yaakov rushed to the Bukharian shul on nearby Dinovskaya Street and merited to recite his first and last *Kaddish* of his father's year of mourning.

Years later, on a trip Sarah's husband, R. Dovid Mishulovin, once made to Crown Heights, he was approached by a certain woman, who offered her unreserved assistance. With tears in her eyes, she explained that she would forever feel indebted to Sarah's father, R. Benzion Pil.

"When I lived in Kharkov, I was once ill and needed to be hospitalized. R. Benzion came to visit me in the hospital, bringing along a package of food for me. After he left, I discovered twenty-five rubles—a sizeable sum in those days—hidden beneath my pillow."

R. Benzion's kindness didn't stop at those twenty-five rubles either, as the woman continued. "At that time, we lacked Soviet citizenship, but R. Benzion would use his government connections, and bribed the right officials to obtain working papers for people in the community. It's only because of him that we were able to live securely, as legal citizens."

CHAPTER 5

The Postwar Years
under Stalin

My bar mitzvah was held in our house. We lived on the second floor of apartment 6, Chudjumskaya Street, Toopik 1 (*toopik* means a dead-end street, and each such street branching off a main street was assigned a number). The year was 1952, a terrible year for the Jews of the Soviet Union; with the fear and uncertainty in the air, no one could think about organizing a full-scale bar mitzvah celebration.

In the evening, a few loyal, trustworthy Jews gathered in my home: Uncle Boruch Duchman, Dovid and Eliyahu Mishulovin, Moshe Nissilevitch, and Berke Chein, who was hiding in our home at the time. Together with my father and brother Berel, we were a total of eight people. Quietly, we sang the tune preceding the Chassidic discourse traditionally delivered by the bar mitzvah boy, and other melodies.

There was a disagreement as to the question of a gift. All the prayer books in those days were well used and torn, and there were none available in the *Arizal* rite normally used in Chabad circles. Only one Jew by the name of Osher Shlaif had such a *siddur*, of the *Torah Ohr* edition, and in extremely good condition. In exchange for the *siddur*, however, he wanted three hundred rubles, an enormous amount of money. My aunt Rosa claimed that it was more important to buy me a winter coat, but I insisted on the *siddur*. I eventually prevailed, and they bought me the *Torah Ohr*. I was thrilled, but I remember one relative of ours flipping through its pages before she remarked, "For this book three hundred rubles? I would have expected a lot more pictures."

Shocking Arrests in Samarkand

Unlike the purges in the years prior to World War II, which were directed at the general population, a wave of arrests between the years 1948 and 1953 targeted Jews specifically, religious and irreligious.

In Samarkand, many Jews were arrested for the sole crime of being associated with Chabad chassidim. That was enough to earn one the title of counter-revolutionary.

R. Simcha Gorodetzky (as will be discussed later) had sent a number of yeshiva-aged youths from Samarkand to learn in Tomchei Temimim years earlier, after the yeshiva had moved to the area on the Rebbe Rayatz's instructions. These graduates had a great effect on their community upon their return, spreading Torah and Judaism in Samarkand and its environs. Many of these chassidim were arrested during this time.

One of those arrested was Rabbi Avrohom Chaim Ladayev who, during the war, built a ritual bath in the cellar of his home. "Avrohom Chaim's *mikvah*," as it was known, was used by many Lubavitch refugees then sheltering in the city. After the war, R. Avrohom Chaim grew fearful of the persecutions targeting the Jews and drained the water from the *mikvah*. He stuffed the empty pit with blankets and rags and covered it.

Apparently, someone informed the secret police about the *mikvah* and their agents were dispatched to arrest him at home, where they found him sitting calmly at his table. With the arrests being accompanied by a massive media campaign, the police had to find a way to present him to the public as a guilty, dangerous criminal. They dragged him down to the cellar—where they had been told that the *mikvah* was located—emptied the pit of its contents, threw him inside, covered him with the blankets and photographed him. His file now carried the picture of a traitorous Jew evading the law.

I will never forget the horrifying time that agents of the KGB, or MGB as they were called then, marched through the streets of Samarkand to arrest R. Zevulun Leviev, grandfather of the renowned philanthropist Lev Leviev. When a household member spotted the police nearing the house, R. Zevulun ran to his hiding place. As someone associated with Chabad chassidim, he knew that the only real question was *when* he would be arrested, and had planned for this eventuality long in advance. Most of the houses in Samarkand were built with double walls, with enough room for a person to hide in the space between. As the KGB approached, R. Zevulun slipped into the walls of his house.

It seems that whoever had informed the KGB supplied them with the information about the hiding place as well, for when the policemen didn't find him, they began to poke the walls with their bayonets. Eventually, they approached his hiding place and stabbed him in the head. It was nothing short of a miracle that he wasn't killed instantly by the bayonet. He shouted out in pain and his hiding place was discovered.

I recall the way he was dragged out of his home and taken to prison. At the time, we all lived in the Jewish quarter of the Old City as in an enclosed ghetto; everyone knew each other. Whenever the KGB came to arrest someone, they would arrive with an entourage of men to search the individual's home for incriminating evidence. The entire procedure would take about two hours, during which time the news spread like wildfire throughout the Jewish quarter, bringing hundreds of Jews—men, women, and children—pouring into the streets. When the secret police discovered their target in his home and jostled him forcefully into the black KGB truck, everyone would shed bitter tears, for they knew what his end would be.

Such arrests became a daily event, but even by the standards to which we had grown accustomed in those days, R. Zevulun's was a shocking sight. That vivid scene still stands before my eyes today. I saw spurts of crimson blood gush from his temple as two KGB beasts dragged him and dumped him into their black truck. Policemen armed with rifles and grim expressions stood guard on either side of him. We watched the scene torn, brokenhearted, but with our hands tied, helpless as we were to rescue him from his plight.

In those bleak days, they also arrested Rabbi Mulla Chizkiyahu, the only Chassidic rabbi of the Bukharian Jews, the *shochet* Mulla Yosef, and others.

Another Jew they arrested was a very simple fellow called Rebbi (a common name among Bukharian Jews at that time), who could barely read and write. Why accuse him of instigating activity against the government?

"We don't care whether or not you know how to learn," snarled the interrogators. "We know that you say the Psalms after prayers, in accordance with one of the enactments of Rabbi Schneersohn. That's enough to incriminate you for associating with a counter-revolutionary organization."

It was at this time that my uncle R. Boruch Duchman was warned of his imminent arrest by a number of local Jews. He fled immediately and hid with relatives in another neighborhood of the city until Stalin died, about two years later.

The relatives of the Bukharian Jews who were arrested did not even dream that they would ever see their loved ones again. No one knew what happened to them, but all assumed they had either been shot to death or would soon die of forced labor in Siberia. There was no hope on the horizon.

A year before the beginning of the wave of arrests, R. Moshe Yachovov, a Bukharian Chabad chassid and friend of R. Mendel Futerfas, passed away. When the arrests began, my mother said: "R. Moshe is a lucky man. He died in his bed, was given a Jewish burial, his children accompanied him to his resting place, and they can visit his gravesite. As for the dozens of Jews who were arrested, who knows if they will merit a Jewish burial, or if their relatives will ever be able to visit their graves?"

Ultimately, as will be related, the situation improved somewhat after Stalin's death, and most of the arrestees returned to their homes. My mother then repeated the well-known saying: "A person can return from anywhere; except from *there.*"

The Fictitious Doctors' Plot

On January 13, 1953, the official Communist newspaper *Pravda* ran a report from TASS, the authorized news agency of the Soviet Union. "Vicious Spies and Murderers under the Mask of Academic Physicians" went the headline, and the article read as follows:

A terrorist group of doctors, uncovered some time ago by organs of state security, had the murderous goal of shortening the lives of leaders of the Soviet Union—the Politburo—by means of medical sabotage.

An investigation has established that participants in the terrorist group, by exploiting their position as doctors and abusing the trust of their patients, deliberately and viciously undermined their patients' health and even killed them, through incorrect diagnoses and false treatments. Cloaking themselves with the noble and merciful calling of physicians and as men of science, by taking the path of these monstrous crimes these fiends and killers have desecrated the holy banner of medicine and defiled the honor of scientists....

The majority of the participants of this terrorist group...were bought by American intelligence. They were recruited by a branch-office of American intelligence—the international Jewish bourgeois-nationalist organization called the "Joint" [the Joint Distribution Committee]. *The filthy face of this Zionist spy organization, which covers its vicious actions under the mask of charity, is now completely revealed....*

Unmasking the gang of poison-doctors struck a blow against the international Jewish Zionist organization.... Now all can see what sort of philanthropists and "friends of peace" hid beneath the honorable sign-board of the "Joint."

The investigation will conclude shortly.

The names of nine individuals who had been arrested were listed, all of them top doctors in Russia at the time. Six were Jewish. Thus began the infamous blood libel later termed "The Doctors' Plot."

The newspapers and radio reported this along with "commentary" of their own, which was in fact little more than anti-Jewish incitement. Commentators and various writers called upon the public to be wary of the "enemy of the people" and asked all citizens to be on the alert for "terrorists in the guise of doctors."

In all sorts of public venues—schools, universities, factories, army camps, and foremost, in all medical institutions, "explanatory meetings" were held. The speakers, members of the party and secret police, defamed the "terrorist doctors" and called upon the public to be wary of any additional fraudulent doctors.

The anti-Semitic rhetoric intensified. A swell of reports about robberies, corruption, and fraud began to appear in the major newspapers on a daily basis. The common denominator in all of these crimes was the suspects' obvious Jewish names. At first, the papers didn't refer to Jews explicitly, and instead preferred to speak in a variety of euphemisms—rootless cosmopolitans, the bourgeois, or Zionist agents. Within a short time, however, they stripped their kid gloves and began writing explicitly: We mean the Jews, reactionary Jews working for Zionistic and capitalistic purposes, and so on.

The Russian nation, deeply influenced by this massive propaganda campaign, accepted the party line. Gentile patients were afraid to be treated by Jewish doctors. Numerous Jews were fired from their positions, especially in institutions of science, education, and medicine.

The incitement grew and so did our terror. We awaited the show trial in helpless dread. If the doctors were found guilty as charged—and there was no doubt that they would—the Jews of Russia would be in grave danger. The ensuing pogroms would be even more lethal, and more ferocious, than those the Jews had suffered under the czars.

The few non-Jews who understood it was all pretense didn't dare speak out against the national effort. At that time, a non-Jew by the name of Kriyakov, who worked with my father, said to him: "So

Zaltzman! What do you say about the new Beilis trial?" (The Beilis trial was, of course, the infamous 1913 Kiev blood libel directed against the Jew Mendel Beilis.) This time, an entire nation was being put on the dock.

After Stalin's death, the Doctors' Plot was revealed as a component in a complex scheme. The plan had been devised by Stalin and calculated to the minutest of details. The doctors were to be incriminated, the public would be enraged, and at the last moment Father Stalin would come to the protection of the Jews. His "protection" would entail a mass exile of the Jews to Siberia.

Rumor had it that Stalin had a timetable to execute this expulsion plan: The doctors would be tried on March 5, then executed a week later, on March 12. Immediately after that, the expulsion would begin to be implemented. Although this information was mainly circulated orally, most Russian Jews did not doubt it to be true, or that Stalin's sudden death spared them from this fate.

Two to three weeks before the designated expulsion date, dozens of trains were reportedly readied at stations in all of the large cities of the Soviet Union, waiting to take droves of panicked Jews to Siberia. In covert areas in frozen, faraway Eastern Siberia, camps were already set up, with 40,000 barracks built to contain the million or so Jews who were expected to survive until then.

As the date for the trial of the doctors approached, we suffered from incessant insults and degradation. We were humiliated and persecuted wherever we went, on the street, at work, and by our neighbors. The antipathy reached such intensity that Jews refrained from leaving their homes. When Jews were assaulted on the street and the police were called, they would tell the attackers, "Don't strike them now; in a little while we'll be able to beat them publicly, with full government support."

My brother-in-law Aryeh Leib Demichovsky lived in the city of Minsk. He looked noticeably Jewish and when he once stepped on a bus, the non-Jewish passengers began to taunt him. No one cared to intervene on his behalf. When he tried to defend himself, an army officer grabbed him by the neck and threw him off the bus.

Under these unnerving circumstances, every passing day seemed to take a year. Our hearts beat in constant fear as we waited with bated breath. Our fate hung precariously in the balance.

In February 1953, a 15-kilogram bomb was planted at the Soviet embassy at 46 Rothschild Street in Tel Aviv. The building was severely damaged. The Soviet Union reacted in fury and cut off all diplomatic ties with Israel. The Russian papers publicized the bombing vociferously, mounting additional fuel on the fire of malicious hatred.

No Rejoicing, But a Sigh of Relief

On March 4, 1953, the Soviet radio broadcaster took to the air. In a saddened voice, he announced that the mighty Stalin had fallen seriously ill and lost consciousness. This official announcement of Stalin's illness was unusual for the Soviet Union, as the government always refrained from announcing any illness in their top echelons. We suspected that Stalin had died, and that the milder public announcement was to prepare the citizens of the country for the truth without causing any chaos. But this was no more than a suspicion, and his death was not yet confirmed.

All through the day, we sat fixed to the radio, listening raptly to every piece of news. We hoped against hope to finally hear the news we had been awaiting for the past thirty years.

Finally, the official announcement was made that Stalin, wicked enemy of the Jews, had died. The top government radio broadcaster, Yuri Levitan, himself a Jew, dramatically announced that a special news release would be broadcast shortly in all the radio stations throughout the Soviet Union. We understood this to be the long-awaited news, and sat listening with bated breath. Levitan then continued solemnly: "On the fifth of March, at 9:50 p.m. Moscow Time, the heart of the First Secretary of the Communist Party of the Soviet Union, Chairman of the Supreme Soviet Council, the Generalissimo Iosif Vissarionovich Stalin, stopped beating."

We immediately all rushed to the newsstands to purchase the latest paper. Indeed, on the front page was a photo of Stalin lying dead in a coffin. How precious this picture was to us! And how we wished to have seen this image sooner!

Stalin's body was temporarily laid in state in the Pillar Hall of the Soviet Union adjacent to the Kremlin, the most prominent hall in Moscow. A formal farewell ceremony was attended by the leaders of other countries, both Communist and Democratic, who had come to pay their final respects to Comrade Stalin.

Stalin was not laid to rest in the distinguished Novo Dyevitchye Kladbishtche Cemetery near Moscow, nor was he cremated, with his ashes deposited in the Kremlin Wall, as was customary for other Soviet government officials. Rather, his body was placed in the mausoleum where Lenin had been interred, so that anyone and everyone could have the "merit" of seeing his grave. Indeed, we considered it a great merit to see him lying in a coffin!

What caused Stalin's sudden death? Like everything in those days, the details of his death were murky; cloaked in shadowy enigma then, they remain disputed until today. Some said he had suffered a stroke and held on for three days before dying. Some said he died in the midst of a psychotic episode, which occurred with some frequency in his later years. Some claimed that he had planned to have the members of his government shot before they decided to preempt him.

The *London Chronicle* reported another fascinating account of Stalin's death from someone said to be very close to Stalin, who had defected to England immediately upon his death. That night, the Leader had called Voroshilov, a senior figure in the governing committee who would later hold the official position of "Premier of the Soviet Union," and gave him a note ordering that every Jew in the Soviet Union be exiled to Birobidzhan, where they would be murdered. Stalin's goal was to complete what Hitler had initiated.

Voroshilov took the note from Stalin and read it. This new craze of Stalin's, sure to further harm Russia's foreign policy, infuriated him. In the spur of the moment, he ripped up the note and threw it back in Stalin's face. This act of impudence, of a degree that Stalin had never before experienced, so shocked and angered him that he had a heart attack on the spot and died.

Others said that Stalin had been poisoned by the head of the KGB, Lavrentiy Beria. One of Beria's motives was said to be the fear he shared with several senior officials that an expulsion of the Jews would lead to a third world war, the result of which they were sure would be US victory and Russian decline.

A Series of Unusual Actions

In the meantime, we were clueless of the events transpiring at 770 Eastern Parkway, in distant New York. We couldn't have imagined how the Rebbe experienced and lived with our daily sacrifices for Torah and Judaism, but after we were freed from Russia we came to realize that, in the words of the Purim *Megillah*, "Mordechai knew everything that had happened." And like the righteous Mordechai in his day, the Rebbe worked to obliterate the evil decree facing Russian Jewry through otherworldly, heavenly channels.

Years later, in New York, I heard about a series of intriguing happenings that took place at the Rebbe's *farbrengens* during those stormy winter days of 1953.

At a Shabbos *farbrengen* towards the end of 1952, the Rebbe suggested that the chassidim present sing a somewhat unusual song. It was during one of the Chassidic melodies customarily sung between the Rebbe's talks that he suddenly asked, "Does someone here know how to sing *Ani Maamin*?"

Ani Maamin was a soulful anthem dedicated to the ancient Jewish belief in the *Moshiach*. It had never before been sung at the Rebbe's court, but one person present did know it. He began to sing, and was quickly joined by the rest of the participants. As soon as the melody began, the Rebbe's expression changed and became very serious. He motioned with his hand for the room to sing more forcefully and he too joined in. The song certainly had considerable power: According to one well-known story, a group of Jews had defiantly sung it while being marched to their deaths during the Holocaust. But why sing it now? What could have prompted this impassioned expression of hope, and of anguished yearning?

In all probability, no one at the *farbrengen* could appreciate this sudden instruction to sing *Ani Maamin*. Of course, millions of Jews on the other side of the world were indeed facing a crisis of truly terrible proportions, but no one present had any way of knowing the severity of what was transpiring behind the scenes in Russia.

During the *farbrengen* of Shabbos Shemos, the Rebbe referred explicitly to Stalin and to Soviet Jewry. He spoke of the astonishing sacrifices being made to keep the Torah and *mitzvos* in the face of awful economic hardship in Russia. In hindsight, it is clear that the Rebbe's repeated references to the indomitable Jewish spirit were an attempt, by divine means, to ensure that the Jewish people would withstand this latest threat.

At the Purim *farbrengen* of that year, a large crowd had gathered to spend the conclusion of the festival with the Rebbe at 770 Eastern Parkway, in distant New York. Tens of attendees had left Russia just several years prior, some after having sat in jail for long periods of time, beaten and crushed by the force of Stalin's iron arm. Though far away, they could not help but reflect upon their brothers still locked in captivity, trapped in the terrible danger that lay behind the Iron Curtain.

The *farbrengen* went on all night and towards morning the Rebbe told this story:

"During the Russian revolutionary period, the Rebbe Rashab told the chassidim to participate in the elections that were to establish a Provisional Government. There was one chassid who went to vote but was so completely removed from matters of this world that he knew nothing of what was occurring in the country. He went to vote solely on the Rebbe's say so. Naturally, he did so after immersing in a *mikvah* and fastening his *gartel*, as one does while fulfilling the Rebbe's instructions. He followed the throngs of people making their way to vote, and after observing them for a short while, learned the proper voting procedure.

"After he had cast his vote, he noticed a noisy group of people gathered near the voting station. The crowd began to shout 'Hurrah!' repeatedly, so, still unaware why or for whom they were chanting, he stood there and joined the crowd. 'Hurrah!' sounded very much like the two Hebrew words hoo and ra, meaning 'He is evil,' so, along with the crowd, he too began to proclaim: 'Hoo-ra! Hoo-ra! Hoo-ra!'"

As he related this, the Rebbe mimicked the chassid. With a big smile on his face, he cupped his hands together and proclaimed "Hoo-ra!" three times.

When the Rebbe finished recounting the story, he turned to his right and repeated the story and once again put his hands together and said "Hoo-ra!" three times. Then he turned to his left and repeated it again, doing as the chassid did.

The crowd of chassidim at the farbrengen were completely taken aback. As astonished as they were by the peculiar scene playing before their eyes, they understood that they were witnessing something beyond their capacity to fathom. No one could explain the Rebbe's actions, but it was clear that something heavenly had just transpired.

Reactions to Stalin's Sudden Death

Rather than greeting Stalin's death with the joy that met the death of Haman, of Purim infamy, people were at first stunned. So unprepared for the shock of it all, most citizens were simply unsure how to respond. The entire population of the Soviet Union had been raised from their youngest years singing praise of the "Father." They had heard radio programs or read newspaper articles every day that lauded Stalin and his personal concern for every citizen throughout the empire. Now, it was hard for them to imagine how Russia, and indeed the entire world, could go on without him.

People believed that Stalin, as Father of the Nations, preserved peace in the world. I remember a children's song that described the residents of the empire asleep in their beds at night, while light continued to shine from just one window—where Stalin sat awake, concerned with the peace of all people.

The delusion had reached such an extent that, despite the massive incitement campaign against the Jews Stalin had perpetrated, there were Jews who cried upon hearing of his demise. A woman who worked with my father tearfully complained: "*Oy*, R. Avrohom, we had someone who cared about us so much and now G-d has taken him away too!"

But after the initial shock, the Jews of Russia breathed a sigh of relief. There couldn't have been a better ending to the Doctors' Plot.

It was in the middle of the holiday of Pesach, just a month after Stalin's death, that we first heard that the doctors had been released. In those days, not everyone owned a radio, but the landlady of the building we lived in at the time did, and as I walked out of the house one day, I was startled to hear the radio reporting that false witnesses had incriminated the doctors. One woman who had reportedly conceived the plot had been sentenced to death, and others would be imprisoned or exiled.

I was the first person in the community to hear the good news. I ran to my uncle R. Boruch Duchman, and then to the Mishulovins, where R. Berke Chein was then hiding, and conveyed the wonderful news.

My uncle R. Boruch would always try to lift the spirits of the people around him, and would repeatedly declare that whatever occurred was for the benefit of the Jewish people. He had stood strong throughout the Doctors' Plot, and insisted that this, too, would turn out for the best. When I told him about the doctors' release, he said that the day would come when Stalin would be denounced and his body thrown out of Lenin's mausoleum.

Back then, this sounded like a wild dream but it was only a few years later that Khrushchev decided to reveal the true face of Stalin. He declared Stalin to be a malicious man, responsible for countless atrocities, and the former leader's remains were removed from public display to be interred alongside the other Russian notables by the Kremlin wall. Forty years later, with the collapse of Communism, all the remaining statues of Stalin were removed from public areas. I remember thinking at the time: My uncle's "prophecy" has been fulfilled.

Following Stalin's death, the situation in Russia changed significantly. Almost all political prisoners were freed, including many chassidim who had been exiled to labor camps in Siberia. This included those members of the Chabad community who had been arrested in 1946 and '47 for attempting to escape Russia.

Thus ended a terrible era in the lives of Jews in the Soviet Union.

Stalin's Atrocities Are Revealed

Three years after Stalin's death and Khrushchev's rise to power, Khrushchev delivered a top-secret address in front of the members of the Twentieth Party Congress. In the course of the four-hour speech, he criticized actions taken by Stalin's regime, particularly the purges of the military and the upper Party echelons and the development of Stalin's personality cult, all the while invoking Lenin's true vision and reaffirming the ideals of Communism.

To preserve the secrecy of the talk, all foreign Communist representatives were told to leave the room, and only the fourteen hundred Soviet representatives remained to hear the speech. The shock that pervaded the assembly was indescribable. Some members fainted, while the others could scarcely believe what they were hearing. No discussion followed the speech, and the representatives returned home stunned beyond words, many falling into depression as a result. Two members committed suicide soon after.

Portions of Khrushchev's speech were published in a small red booklet and copies were sent to all of the Communist centers throughout Russia. Every city received one such booklet and they would read it at secret meetings in the presence of sworn Communists.

My cousin Yakov Pil had received many awards for his service in the Soviet army during World War II. As such, he was involuntarily made a member of the Communist party and was completely trusted. Whenever secret booklets such as these would arrive at the Communist center in Samarkand, he would bring the booklet home for a night. Following Khrushchev's secret speech, Yaakov took home the booklet for a night as well and that is how we found out about the historic event.

The ways of Hashem are wondrous indeed. Just five years before, Stalin led the Nineteenth Party Congress and his portrait was plastered across the front page of all the major Russian newspapers. By the Twentieth Congress, he had been thoroughly denounced and his crimes revealed.

CHAPTER 6

Our Distinguished Guest: R. Berke Chein

My memories of R. Berke Chein begin with my childhood in Samarkand. He first came to Samarkand together with the other Lubavitcher chassidim who had fled to central Russia during World War II. When the Lubavitcher refugees formed a community and opened yeshivas and secret schools, R. Berke became a teacher and many parents wanted their children to be his students. One day my father came home and happily announced that he had been able to arrange a spot for me in R. Berke's class.

I was six years old at the time and I was very apprehensive about this piece of news. R. Berke, I had heard, punished his students with a *kontchik*—a leather strap fastened to a rod—as was customary for schoolteachers of old. One student, Mottel Kalmenson, had told me that he was a good teacher and never hit anyone, but I was still worried. Mottel, I thought to myself, is R. Berke's nephew, so he might receive special treatment.

When I joined R. Berke's class, I discovered that although a *kontchik* did hang on the wall, R. Berke never used it. Mottel Kalmenson was right: R. Berke was a good teacher. And, over the years, I learned that he was much more than that.

An Attempt to Leave Russia

When the Soviet government agreed to allow Polish refugees to return home after the war, R. Berke, along with many other Lubavitchers, tried his luck at faking Polish citizenship. He traveled from Samarkand to Lvov, where community activists—led by R. Leibel Mochkin and R. Mendel Futerfas—arranged the forged documents for him. This was, it hardly needs to be said, very dangerous work, and those who were caught paid with long years of imprisonment and forced labor in Siberia. Many would only be released after Stalin's death, when their punishment was annulled.

Since obtaining a Polish passport was such hazardous work, the activists gave priority to families with children still in need of a Jewish education. After much effort, R. Berke was able to obtain Polish papers for himself, his wife, and their two young sons, as well as for his in-laws, R. Shneur Zalman and Menuchah Kalmenson and their own sons.

This was during the summer of 1946. At the appointed time, he showed up with his family at the Lvov train station, not knowing that the secret police were following them. They waited with pounding hearts for the moment they could board the train to safety: After just half an hour of travel, they would finally reach freedom across the border.

Suddenly, a police car pulled up beside them. When R. Berke saw the car, he sensed that *they* had come for him. A moment letter, a man dressed in civilian clothing emerged and in the typical KGB fashion, "politely" asked R. Berke to accompany him. R. Berke managed to say a few words to his family and asked them to recite Chapter 20 of Psalms on his behalf. His wife cried out to the policeman, "Where are you taking him?" The policeman eyed her coolly and replied, "He will return in a while."

The train was supposed to come at any moment, and in those few minutes, the Cheins had to make perhaps the most fateful decision of their lives: Who was going to continue with the plan to leave Russia and who would stay behind with R. Berke?

R. Berke's wife Feigel had already made up her mind and firmly
declared: "I'm not traveling anywhere." If her daughter was staying,
Mrs. Kalmenson announced, then so was she. Ultimately, only the
Kalmenson sons boarded the train. The train clattered noisily away
and the dejected Chein family returned to the city.

A few months later, another train was arranged to transport
purported Polish citizens out of Russia. Mere hours before the
train's departure, some community fixers discovered an opportunity to include an additional two boys in the group. Mrs. Sarah
Katzenelenbogen, known as "Mume Sarah," arrived at the Chein-
Kalmenson residence and suggested that the two Chein boys, Meir
Simcha and Mordechai, seize the chance to escape.

Feigel was not home, so this time, it was up to the boys' grandmother to make the crucial decision. She took the boys to the train
station and sent them off; their mother only found out what had
happened with them when she came home a few hours later and
asked where her two sons were. Another two months later, and another
train was approved for departure, and the family decided that their
grandfather R. Zalman Kalmenson should join the boys, so they would
not remain as orphans of the living. And so it was that Feigel remained
in Russia alone with her mother, without her husband or children.

Living As a Fugitive

R. Berke was taken to the cellars of the KGB and after a long, painful interrogation he was sentenced to death. Eventually, they reduced his sentence to eighteen years imprisonment, and then finally
to ten years.

Throughout this terrifying time, Feigel worked behind the
scenes to smuggle her husband out of jail. She did not rest day or
night, and by an extraordinary miracle, after two years she managed
to bribe a few of the right people and have R. Berke released. The
Cheins lived for a short while in Lvov, where R. Berke's two brothers
resided, during which time their daughter Freida was born.

Not long afterwards, the authorities decided to once again pursue anyone connected to the great escape from Russia of 1946-47 who hadn't been arrested yet, or like R. Berke, had been arrested and released early.

As was their way, the secret police descended upon several homes the same night, so that no one would be able to warn anyone else. They arrested several activists still in Lvov, one of whom was R. Berke's brother, Dovid Leib. R. Dovid Leib's wife managed to run to R. Berke and warn him. Minutes later, agents showed up at R. Berke's house. Miraculously, he had managed to flee the house with only his *tallis* and *tefillin*, just before they showed up.

From that point on, a dangerous and exhausting chapter in R. Berke's life began, as he was forced to wander from one hiding place to another, his freedom hanging by a hair. Too afraid to even notify his family of his whereabouts, it also marked the start of a long period of separation from his wife lasting until 1958.

At first he concealed himself with a family in Lvov and did not even step outdoors. When he felt the noose tightening in Lvov, he traveled to his aunt Bas-Sheva, the wife of R. Yehuda Kulasher (Butrashvili), who lived in Malachovka, a suburb of Moscow.

It didn't take long for the police to visit his aunt's house and ask whether they had any guests. R. Berke was in the middle of his prayers, completely unaware that anything else was happening. The police however noticed his figure from behind, wrapped in *tallis* and *tefillin* and facing the wall, and asked who he was. R. Yehuda asked them not to disturb him since he was praying, and incredibly, they left.

Naturally, after such a close encounter, R. Berke was afraid to continue staying with his aunt, so he left. But even though his fervent praying had very nearly gotten him caught, R. Berke refused to be daunted by the police. He remained particular about even the smallest details of Chassidic practice all throughout his wanderings, even when it was immensely dangerous to do so.

For some time, R. Berke went from one Lubavitcher family in the suburbs of Moscow to another, until it became clear that he had to leave. Instead, he decided to return to distant Samarkand, hoping that in a place far from Lvov and the center of Russia, he would be left alone.

The trip from Moscow to Samarkand, a train ride of a few days, was dangerous. Passengers were checked several times during the long journey by conductors, as well as by policemen, who would enter the train at various stops to verify that no one was transporting illegal merchandise. Each passenger was required to present his passport and other documents. Needless to say, were anyone to check R. Berke's papers and discover he was a wanted man, he would have been in serious trouble. But staying in Moscow was no longer an option, so despite the danger, R. Berke felt he must travel to Samarkand.

The Hidden "Afikoman"

Miraculously, R. Berke made it to Samarkand without incident, and once there found refuge in the home of the Mishulovin family, old friends of his.

I was a little boy when, while visiting my friend Michoel Mishulovin, I saw a stranger in the other room talking to his elder brother, Eliyahu. Although R. Eliyahu was only nineteen, he was considered an intelligent young man and R. Berke was comfortable conversing with him. When they saw me, they closed the door, and I realized that he was a Jew in hiding, whose presence was to be kept secret. As such, I didn't tell anyone what I had seen. Afterwards I found out that it was R. Berke Chein.

Nobody in Samarkand knew that R. Berke was in the city. In order to guarantee that none of the family members would spill the beans by mentioning "R. Berke" by mistake, he decided to call himself "Chaim." It wasn't a lie, since his full name was Chaim Dovber.

In general, R. Berke was very particular about telling the truth. He said that the Rebbe Rayatz was once asked what to do during a KGB interrogation; it's forbidden to lie, but of course you couldn't tell the truth either. The Rebbe Rayatz answered that lying wasn't permitted, but the truth still had to be concealed.

So when we spoke about R. Berke, we would call him R. Chaim. My aunt Rosa Duchman, a well-known wit, nicknamed him "the Afikoman." Like the highly sought-after piece of matzah on the Pesach Seder night, he was thoroughly hidden.

R. Berke stayed with the Mishulovins for a few months until he began to fear that he had been noticed, and it was decided that the time had come for another hiding place. After much deliberation and a careful investigation of the possible hiding places among residents of the city, staying with us emerged as the next best option. Eliyahu Mishulovin spoke with my older brother Berel about relocating R. Berke to our house and my brother discussed it with our parents. They gave their consent and R. Berke moved into our home.

My Righteous Mother

I was about ten years old at the time. My parents told me that we would be having a guest, a Jew who had no other place to live. They warned me that nobody was allowed to know that he was in our house.

Our home consisted of two rooms and a small corridor. The first room was a dining room, living room, kitchen, and a bedroom for my parents, sister, and myself. The second room, which was not heated in the winter nor cooled in the summer, was for R. Berke. My brother Berel slept in that room too. In the winter we would try to set up a kerosene heater to warm the room, but in the summer the room was sticky with thick humidity.

The bedroom was connected to a little porch facing the yard, but during the day, R. Berke didn't dare to go out on the porch lest one of the neighbors catch sight of him. He was holed up in the heat of his room all day, but absorbed in prayer and his personal divine service. Late in the evening, he would go out on the porch to breathe some fresh air.

I remember that during the long summer days, my mother would tell R. Berke to go rest a bit. He would point to the cemetery that could be seen from the window of our home and say, "Over there, we will rest a lot. Now there's no time for that."

Some Bukharian families lived in our courtyard, but our apartment was above ground level and separate from the rest. This was a big advantage when it came to hiding R. Berke, but it created an uncomfortable problem. In those days we had no bathroom and used an outhouse some forty or fifty meters away from the house. It was a small structure that housed a hole in the ground partially covered by some wooden boards.

R. Berke certainly couldn't go out to the yard every time he needed to relieve himself; before the day was out, all of our neighbors would know of the presence of a foreign man in our home. Lacking an alternative, he used a chamber pot, which had to be emptied a number of times daily. We were only young boys, hardly attentive to these small details, so the burden fell upon our righteous mother.

She did everything with sensitivity, not only to keep things secret from the neighbors, but also so that R. Berke wouldn't notice and feel uncomfortable. She would wait until R. Berke was immersed in prayer, at which time he wouldn't see or hear anything going on around him, and then hurriedly cleaned up. She did this not only for the first day, or week, or even the first year of his stay, but for the entire five to six years that R. Berke was an intermittent guest in our home.

There were no washing machines in those days and my mother would wash all of our clothes, and R. Berke's, by hand. She would place the clothes in a pot of hot water and soap, rub them with soap on an iron washing board, and then rinse them clean. It was hard work indeed. R. Berke tried to do the job himself a number of times, but my mother wouldn't hear of it. "How can I allow him to tear himself away from his service of Hashem, from his praying and learning?" she would say. "For me it is the greatest privilege!" R. Berke pleaded with her to hire a gentile woman to do it, but we couldn't bring a stranger into the house as long as he was hiding there. Instead, my mother tried to also do the laundry when R. Berke was still praying to avoid making him feel uncomfortable.

Over the years that R. Berke stayed with us, he became sick several times. Naturally, my parents couldn't take him to the doctor or call one in. How we managed each time I don't remember, and looking back, I can't understand how we did. I do recall one time though, when he was so ill, dangerously so even, that we had no choice but to call in a doctor. My parents explained simply that we had a guest who had become sick.

My parents, as the Mishulovin family had before, knew the price they would pay if discovered hiding a fugitive from the Soviet police. But did they have another choice? They couldn't throw a person into the clutches of the KGB. Once I heard the adults discussing a possible story to tell in case he was caught, G-d forbid. They would claim not to know R. Berke: this poor fellow had simply showed up at their door without a place to live, and as compassionate people they had pity and took him in. Of course, the KGB wouldn't buy the story; still, knowing that they at least had a cover story in place helped to calm them somewhat.

One day, sometime into R. Berke's stay with us, some government official came by our house to check the residents' logbook. He entered our home and noticed that the door to the second room was closed; as usual, R. Berke was in his room praying, and as the inspector opened the door, there he was. My parents said that he was praying and could not be disturbed, but apparently the official suspected that something wasn't right and began to ask questions about this man. He had to be bribed so he wouldn't talk.

After that incident, R. Berke relocated to his other hideout—the Mishulovin home, and moved back and forth several times over the years. The inspector, however, continued to return to our house every month and demand money to keep his mouth closed.

A Chassid in Every Detail of Life

R. Berke's stay greatly enriched Chassidic life in Samarkand and contributed immeasurably to our Chassidic education. As young boys, we observed R. Berke's behavior and learned how a chassid should act, not only while praying and learning but also during the mundane moments of day-to-day life. R. Berke was a living example of the saying: A chassid walks as a chassid, eats as a chassid, and sleeps as a chassid. In every detail of his life, his Chassidic character, piety, and discipline were apparent.

R. Berke once told us that in his youth his behavior had been completely different, and that he had been absorbed by far less lofty concerns. As a young man, he had been obsessed with earning money: His very first words, he told us, were "Mama" and "money," and as a child, he loved money so much that he used to kiss the stuff. By fourteen, he already had extensive business dealings and quickly became very successful. He would trade merchandise for such large sums that he had to wrap the money around his entire body in order to hide it as he traveled from city to city.

But when he was a little older, he began to wonder about his future. He wondered whether he would always be immersed in the world of business, and so exposed to the cheating and lies that seemed so unavoidable. So moved was he that he decided to change his life and become a preschool teacher. He also worked on his personal character and in time he transformed himself from being a penny-pinching hoarder to a generous donor to charity.

When we heard this, we realized that this is what being a chassid is about. R. Berke's story was an example of true mastery of self, and a demonstration of the mind's power over the heart. This, we understood, is how we are to overcome our lesser instincts, how to break the *yetzer ha-rah* (the Evil Inclination). The book of *Tanya* (a work of Chassidic philosophy by R. Shneur Zalman of Liadi, the founder of Chabad), holds up as an ideal for the everyman: the figure of the *Beinoni*, the "Intermediate Man," who through extraordinary discipline and faith manages to rise above his nature and emulate in deed the perfectly righteous. To us, R. Berke was the embodiment of this heroic figure. He fought his lower inclination all of his days, and succeeded in ruling over it.

Immersion in the Morning

R. Berke's day began by immersing in water. There was no *mikvah* in his first years in Samarkand, and despite the danger, he would instead use a small river at the city's edge. Early each morning, while the townspeople were still asleep and the streets were empty, R. Berke would leave the house. As an additional precaution, he would don dirty rags as though he was homeless, tuck his beard into his coat, and walk to the river. He did this every day throughout the summer, but when he became sickly as winter neared, we thought he would stop. We were wrong, and even during the frigid winter months, he carried on.

During those years before a ritual bath was set up, we boys would also immerse in the river or in a lake, and slightly later on in the morning, we would pass through town on the way there. Ordinarily we made the trip by tram, and walked on Shabbos, but when during the summer the town center became a hangout for some of the crasser, more vulgar locals, we felt it was inappropriate to do so. We thought to skip our Shabbos morning dip and suffice with the previous days' immersion, maintaining that it wasn't proper for us to see the sights of the town center on the holy day of Shabbos before prayer.

When R. Berke heard of this idea, he rejected it. There was nothing in the world that could substitute for the holy act of immersing before prayer. A young Chassidic man had to develop the self-restraint to look only within his immediate four cubits, but in no way were we to forego immersing in the *mikvah* on Shabbos before prayers.

Even in later years, when R. Abba Pliskin's *mikvah* reopened, R. Berke preferred to immerse in the river in the summertime. He was afraid that his daily visits to the illegal *mikvah* would arouse suspicion and might eventually betray its location. He also preferred not to bother R. Feivish Genkin who, along with his wife Chasha, had become responsible for operating the *mikvah*. Only during the winter, when the river was extremely cold, did he immerse there.

The Secret Sukkah

After immersing in the *mikvah* in the morning, R. Berke would proceed with his daily routine: He recited, word by word, the entire book of Psalms, ate a little something, and then sat and learned Chassidus until ten o'clock. The morning prayers took him two hours, until noon. Then he would put on his second set of *tefillin*, as per the view of Rabbeinu Tam. For R. Berke, just putting on *tefillin* was quite an undertaking, as he tried to ensure that his observance of the *mitzvah* would be of the highest possible standard.

If he noticed that someone else's *tefillin* were of superior quality or in better shape than his own, he felt that making do with his would be inadequate. Instead, he regularly asked to borrow our *tefillin,* and once he was no longer forced to hide, would walk to the homes of certain Lubavitchers to do so. There would be one person whose head *tefillin* he found to be of a higher standard, and the hand *tefillin* of another, so R. Berke would borrow from both of them. He also had a custom of reading the *Shema* from parchment before he began his prayers. In general, when R. Berke heard of some way to enhance his religious observance—a *hiddur*—he tended to adopt it immediately.

He would finally finish praying at 1:00 p.m. and then sat down to eat lunch. After such prayers, even eating became a mindful exercise. Careful not to eat ravenously or gluttonously, he would take a slice of bread, cut it into little pieces, and put one piece at a time into his mouth, chewing it slowly. That's how he ate everything he was served. According to R. Berke, it's best to eat slowly even for reasons of good health, so as to aid proper digestion; people were just indulging themselves when they ate quickly.

During the long summer days, he would rest at two o'clock for an hour. Whenever he went to sleep, he was particular not to cover his feet, a practice mentioned in the Alter Rebbe's *Shulchan Aruch*. At three o'clock he sat down for his regular regimen of Torah study on a range of topics. During the long summer days, he would have sufficient time in the afternoon to recite *Tehillim*, the entire book of Psalms, again. Then it was time for *Mincha* (the Afternoon Prayer), some more study, *Maariv* (the Evening Prayer), followed by another study session that included the Code of Jewish Law and Chassidus.

R. Berke would also say *Tehillim* before praying on Shabbos and afterwards he would review the week's Torah reading with *Targum*, the Aramaic translation of the Torah text. He then recited *Tehillim* again before the afternoon and evening prayers, each of which took him over half an hour.

R. Berke longed to pray with a minyan and we tried to the best of our ability to make this happen. Since he couldn't leave the house, we'd arrange, whenever possible, for the Shabbos minyan to be in our home.

Since no one yet knew of R. Berke's presence in Samarkand, his participation in the Shabbos services presented us with various challenges. The Zaltzman and Mishulovin families, who did know the secret, comprised less than ten men, so additional men had to be invited to participate, thereby placing R. Berke in jeopardy. Whenever we held a minyan in our house, we were faced with the dilemma of whom to invite, and only reached a decision after first consulting with R. Berke.

Obviously, R. Berke could not actually pray in the same room as us. He would hide in his room in utter silence and follow the service from there, quietly answering *Amen* and *Boruch Hu u'voruch shemo*, and reciting *Kedusha* and *Modim* along with us. His joy in participating in a minyan was indescribable.

Sometimes we only had nine men and needed R. Berke to make the ten. We couldn't announce his presence by simply proceeding with the minyan, but were loath to forego it altogether. Instead, we would count a child holding a *Chumash* as our tenth man, and claim that we were relying on this somewhat obscure halachic solution for the minyan.

For the High Holidays and Sukkos, R. Berke would always go to the Mishulovin home. Eating in the sukkah at our house was dangerous since it was located in a shared yard, while the Mishulovins' yard was private. R. Feivish Genkin constructed a sukkah for them with a double wall that created a secret compartment containing a sukkah of its own. If someone would visit, they wouldn't dream that behind that sukkah was another smaller one, in which R. Berke was spending the holiday, praying and learning.

The Mishulovins were also able to host a larger minyan to accommodate the bigger High Holiday crowds. Additionally, it was safe to blow the shofar there, whereas our neighbors would have likely heard those kinds of sounds coming from our house. So, we preferred that R. Berke move in from the High Holidays and onwards.

I will never forget how, when he was finally able to openly join the minyan, R. Berke poured out his soul in heartfelt prayer on Rosh Hashana and Yom Kippur. I lack the words to describe the broken heart of this chassid, for years estranged from his rebbe and family, stuck in hiding, and uncertain of when his sorrows would finally come to a close.

He prayed at length on those days, and with copious tears; even a heart made of stone would melt listening to him. The silent *Shmoneh Esrei* prayer of the morning service alone took approximately an hour and a half; his recitation of the psalm prior to the shofar blowing took about forty minutes, as tears coursed from his eyes so heavily that he could barely say the words. The rest of the congregants would wait for him to conclude before proceeding. Observing R. Berke's prayer, we boys tried to emulate him and pray at length: we were ashamed to complete *Shmoneh Esrei* in less than half an hour.

We would often watch R. Berke as he prayed. We noticed how, in his intense focus on the words of the prayers, he would sometimes grind his teeth. He might do it on a regular weekday, but more so on the High Holidays. We saw his total immersion in prayer, and the tears that regularly poured down his cheeks, especially during *Shmoneh Esrei*. When I eventually left Russia, it was hard for me to grow accustomed to the fast-paced prayers common elsewhere.

At a later point, when R. Berke was finally able to appear in public, Lubavitcher men and boys in Samarkand would enjoy his hearty *farbrengens*. I remember how on one Shabbos Mevorchim—the last Shabbos of the month—they sat down together after the prayers. They made *kiddush*, said *l'chaim* and waited for R. Berke, who was still in the middle of reviewing the Torah reading, and whom they were too shy to interrupt.

I was seventeen at the time and was the *chutzpanyak*, the outspoken one of the group. I entered R. Berke's room and said, "These young men are busy throughout the week and now they're sitting here to *farbreng* for Shabbos Mevorchim. You haven't finish reviewing the weekly portion, so now we have to sit and do nothing? Soon everyone will leave and go home!"

Had I said that to someone else, I would have surely been tossed out of the room, but R. Berke, with his refined, gentle character, indicated with a movement of his head and a wordless, "Uh huh," that I was right and that he would try to finish up quickly. Still, he didn't want to stop in the middle because he was accustomed to reciting the entire portion without interruption, and couldn't do otherwise.

Every year, on his birthday, he committed to enhancing his religious observance in some way, a custom he said the great R. Hillel of Paritch used to do. He related that once on his birthday R. Hillel resolved to begin sweeping the floor of his house from the door inwards, as opposed to the common fashion of sweeping directly out of the house, out of respect for the *mezuzah* fixed to the door.

During *farbrengens*, which often turned to discussion of various famed chassidim, R. Berke would speak of R. Itche *der Masmid*, one of the most revered chassidim of the day. He said that R. Itche would always speak of R. Hillel of Paritch and R. Isaac of Homil, and then proceeded to explain that when a chassid speaks often about another chassid, it's a sign that he is close to his level. I thought to myself, if R. Berke often speaks of R. Itche *der Masmid,* they must be similar as well.

Seven Years of Separation

From R. Berke's flight from his home in the dead of night, throughout his subsequent wanderings throughout the Soviet Union, and while he sought refuge with the Mishulovin and Zaltzman families in Samarkand, his wife Feigel remained in Lvov as an *aguna*—a woman whose husband is missing—mothering their newborn daughter Freida. Feigel had no idea what had happened to her husband or where he was. Had he been caught and tried? If not, then what? Where was he hiding? R. Berke assumed that the secret police examined any mail his wife received, so he dared not send her anything, lest they both fall into the clutches of the KGB.

Once R. Berke felt comfortable in our home, my mother began coaxing him to update his wife about his situation. "At least," urged my mother, "let her know that you are alive, and not in jail, but with Jewish families." R. Berke disagreed, insisting that the KGB would see the letter and then likely discover that he was in Samarkand.

My mother pleaded with him to have mercy on his wife—by then she had been living for years without any information about her husband—but R. Berke insisted that his wife did not want to know where he was. The KGB were probably interrogating her every so often, so as to extract information from her about his whereabouts. "She would prefer not to know, and not have anything to tell anyone," he stated firmly.

However, as time passed, my mother came up with an idea. Her brother, R. Dovid Pevzner, lived in Lvov and R. Berke's wife would visit his home often. My mother thought of writing a letter to her brother asking about R. Berke's daughter Freida, who had been born three months before his escape. She assumed that her brother would understand why she was asking: Why else would she ask about a child she had never seen? This way, his wife would realize that he was in Samarkand, among chassidim.

However, R. Berke did not agree to this either. He was afraid that the KGB would figure it out and then all would be lost. That's how great our fear was under Stalin's rule.

A story I heard from R. Moshe Nissilevitch many years later illustrates R. Berke's tragic predicament during those days.

One night, R. Berke went to see R. Moshe, who was heavily involved in all of R. Berke's affairs. In a most serious tone he said, "I want to consult with you about a crucial matter that must remain private." R. Moshe promised to keep it a secret and R. Berke began to share his deep anguish: "I cannot describe the pain I feel for the suffering of my wife, Feigel, and all that she has endured these past few years," he told R. Moshe. "Even now, she doesn't even know what happened to me. There is still no end in sight to my troubles, and I don't know when I will be able to reunite with my family. Perhaps the Torah forbids me from leaving her in such a situation, perhaps I should divorce her..."

There was a dreadful silence. R. Berke and R. Moshe stood there with tears mirrored in their eyes. R. Moshe's head was bent over in deep agony. He couldn't bear to hear the things R. Berke was saying and he didn't have a word to utter in reply. R. Moshe told me how he felt his insides twisting and churning within him, and that had the earth suddenly opened its mouth, he no doubt would have disappeared into it.

R. Berke continued to speak, half to himself. "I hope she will find a good man and get married. With time, I hope she will forget me and lead a normal life." He then turned again to R. Moshe and asked him directly, "According to the Torah, do I have permission to cause her so much suffering, day in and day out?"

Choked by tears, R. Moshe could not respond. He finally managed to croak, "I cannot advise you... What can I say? We will think about it together and we will decide what to do."

The next day, R. Berke went to R. Moshe again and said, "I didn't sleep all night and I tried to think about what I should do. I finally decided that according to Torah I am forbidden from divorcing her. Where is my trust in Hashem? In a moment, He can change the situation so that we can reunite!" R. Moshe was overjoyed to hear this from R. Berke and warmly encouraged his decision.

An Attempt to Forge Identity Papers

R. Berke continued to hide in our house and in the Mishulovin home, immersed in his spiritual world and busying himself all day with prayer, Torah, and the service of G-d. No resolution could be seen on the horizon.

Throughout this time, there were meetings between our families about what to do for R. Berke; his present situation could not continue. The families came to the conclusion that the only thing that could be done was to change his identity papers so that he would become a "new" man. There were three men at that meeting, including R. Moshe Nissilevitch and R. Eliyahu Mishulovin, and on the spot they decided to form a Jewish court of law in order to issue a divine mandate guaranteeing the success of this initiative.

At first they thought to change his name from "Chein" to "Shein," a common name that would entail a change of just one letter, but then decided that it was too similar. They had to give him an entirely new identity and erase the name "Chein."

It wasn't sufficient to alter R. Berke's identity papers. In the Soviet Union every person had a ledger that stated all of the places he had worked in the past and the reasons for leaving each job, allowing the KGB to amass information on every person, from places of work both present and past. He would have to obtain and appropriate an existing employment record from someone who had died. In time, they located a ledger that belonged to a deceased Jew by the name of Goldberg, and decided to adopt the name. In order to act on all these ideas, however, they needed someone with connections in the Interior Ministry. Thus the next stage in their scheme was hatched, one that at the time seemed completely irrational.

A twenty-five-year-old woman by the name of Zina worked for R. Tzvi Hirsh Lerner. She had arrived in wartime Samarkand after her entire family had perished in the Holocaust, in the city of Vilna. While there, she made connections with some of the clerks in the Interior Ministry—ties that might help R. Berke.

Aside from the danger inherent in forging papers and preparing new documents, placing the fate of R. Berke into the hands of this simple, anonymous woman added a frightening new dimension to the plan. Nevertheless, with no other option, they decided to tell R. Tzvi Hirsh about R. Berke and his plight, and to ask him for his opinion.

R. Tzvi Hirsh, a fine and loyal Jew himself, was let in on the secret. They told him that there was a great Chassidic Jew on the run from the authorities. For years, he had been forced to part from his family and hide in Samarkand. Now the only thing that could save him was a new set of papers from the Interior Ministry. Having heard that his employee Zina knew some clerks there, they wanted him to convince her to help out.

Although he knew the danger that this entailed, R. Tzvi Hirsh agreed to get involved. He told Zina about an unfortunate Jew who needed new documents and promised her a nice sum of money for her help. To his great surprise, Zina said she would help, but wanted to do so solely for the sake of helping another Jew, without receiving a penny for her efforts. When R. Tzvi Hirsh conveyed her answer, we were all surprised. In Russia of those days, it was very rare for someone to do this sort of thing without ample reward.

Within a short time all the information was prepared and given to Zina. We prayed that everything would go smoothly.

According to the plan, the entire process would be over within two months. Zina got to work as everyone else anxiously awaited the results. The days passed by torturously, as if in slow motion. And then one day the bad news came: The police had caught a group involved in an identity document forgery operation.

We were all terrified, especially R. Berke. R. Tzvi tried to contact Zina to find out if she knew what had happened, but he could not locate her, and we began to fear for her too. Unfortunately, we soon found out that she, along with some other Jews from the Bukharian community, had been arrested counterfeiting. You can imagine our shock. Our first reaction was that we had to send off R. Berke. Although Zina did not know where R. Berke was, during her interrogation she was likely to confess that she had been asked to deal with the matter and they would be able to track down both R. Tzvi Hirsh and R. Berke.

However, after some consideration, we decided to try to contact Zina and find out whether she had been discovered with R. Berke's documents. Legally, it was permissible to visit inmates in prison, so R. Tzvi went to see her. His visit appeared natural since she was his employee and he certainly wanted to know what had happened and how she was faring.

Zina realized how frightened we all were and she asked R. Tzvi to convey a calming message to R. Berke. She said, "Please tell him that he can remain in the city in peace and quiet as he has until now, because nobody will be able to get anything out of me. Even if they cut me to pieces, I won't reveal a thing."

It was encouraging to hear this, but of course we couldn't rely on her—who knew if she really would withstand the interrogators' torture? We were unsure how to proceed.

In the meantime, we received more information about the arrest of the forgery ring and in bits and pieces were able to understand what had happened. A few people with connections in the Interior Ministry had been using them to forge documents in exchange for good money; Zina had in turn persuaded them to help her forge documents for R. Berke. In order to obtain the new identity, a form had to be filled out with all of the applicant's personal information. She retrieved the form from the Interior Ministry and filled it out.

It was precisely at this time that the police discovered the scheme and set off a wave of arrests, in the course of which they caught some of the forgers red-handed. Zina was arrested when the police officers found the form in her pocket with R Berke's false information. Realizing that the form was intended for someone who wanted false papers, the police tried to extract this important information out of Zina.

However, she was a noble and pious woman and she kept her promise by refusing to surrender a thing. Despite the torture inflicted on her, she repeated her claim that she did not know the person they were after. She said that she had been walking down the street when a stranger had approached her and claimed that he did not know how to fill out a legal form and asked her for help. She helped him but had mistakenly put his form in her pocket before walking away. She had no further information about whom it was for.

A public trial was announced, to be held in the local courthouse. I was thirteen years old at the time, and it was decided that my brother Berel and I would attend the trial in order to learn whether Zina would actually be sitting in the defendant's chair, and if she was, what she was accused of. Critically, we had to know whether the name "Goldberg" would be mentioned, or whether she would be accused of something else entirely.

Since it was a public trial, our presence was not unusual. I sat down in the front and listened in fear to the court proceedings. I recognized Zina sitting on the defendants' bench—since we lived in the same neighborhood—alongside another three Jews from the Bukharian community. I listened to every word, and despite not understanding all that was said, I was certain that among the confiscated documents was one with the name Goldberg, and that Zina had been implicated with these documents.

At the end of the trial, the judge read the sentence: The two Bukharian Jews who admitted to their guilt were sentenced to seven years in jail. A third got three years. Zina, who had denied everything, was sentenced to six years in jail. When we told R. Berke, he was beside himself. "For my entire life I will be indebted to this young Jewish woman who sacrificed herself for my sake and stood up to the police interrogators," he said.

Zina was sent to complete her sentence with a forced labor stint in Siberia, but because of her good behavior she was released after three years. R. Berke wanted to meet her in order to pay her and thank her personally for saving him from falling into the hands of the Soviet authorities, but she refused. She said she did not want a Jew to feel uncomfortable because of her and she did not want to be paid. She had acted exclusively for the sake of Heaven. A short while later, we heard that she had left Samarkand and returned to her birthplace, Vilna. "*Oy!* Who can measure the power of a Jewish spirit?" said R. Berke.

That terrifying time had us consumed by despair. Although still a young boy, I wondered why G-d had done this. No one knew how to proceed, and a short while later the situation became bleaker with the notorious Doctors' Plot and the resulting eruption of anti-Semitism. The papers were full of loathsome propaganda against the Jews and the atmosphere in the Jewish communities was at an all-time low.

You can imagine how R. Berke and all of us felt. We knew that we were hiding a traitor who wanted to cross the border illegally. The government was seeking to besmirch the Jews, and revelations like this were immediately blown to disproportion and used to paint us as counter-revolutionaries.

My mother would comfort R. Berke and say, "Don't be distressed. The time will come when Feigel will come here and you will both travel to Eretz Yisrael and join your sons."

But it also seemed so outlandish, and so removed from reality. R. Berke said sorrowfully, "*Oy*, I am here in a situation worse than that of a dog. A dog can roam freely in the streets, while I have to hide indoors all day. As long as I have no identity papers I'm trapped without a hope. I don't know what tomorrow will bring—will I remain here, will I be in a Jewish home, or will they arrest me? If they arrest me, they will send me to Siberia. Then what? Feigel will remain an *aguna*, a woman unable to remarry forever."

At that time, my mother's optimism seemed like salt on an open, raw wound.

It was only after Stalin's death on March 5, 1953—four days after Purim—and the release of the doctors in the middle of Pesach, that things started looking up. The situation eased, to the extent that R. Berke finally acceded to my mother's pleading and agreed to let her write a letter to her brother in Lvov, with regards for Freida'le, R. Berke's daughter. As my mother anticipated, R. Berke's wife understood the hint and quickly sent a letter in response. You can imagine how excited R. Berke was to see his wife's handwriting. He read line after line as his shoulders heaved with broken cries.

A Secret Meeting in the Dead of Night

As time passed, life became progressively easier. Nikita Khrushchev, the new Premier of the Soviet Union, decided to grant pardon to hundreds of thousands of political prisoners, including those who tried to cross the border illegally. We thought that perhaps R. Berke would benefit from this; if the prisoners had been released, maybe his file had been expunged. If so, it was time to use his old papers with his real name.

But it was still hard to shake off that long tenured feeling of terror and R. Berke was afraid to use his real name after so many years of hiding. He consulted with Eli Mishulovin and Moshe Nissilevitch, and R. Moshe came up with a radical idea to find out whether anyone in the KGB offices was still looking for him.

In those years, there were Jews who were called to the KGB offices from time to time to be grilled for information about the Jewish community. I cannot describe the fear we felt knowing that the sting could very well come from within, from one of our own. As R. Chaim Zalman Kozliner once put it, the situation we lived in was such that if someone was just suspected of collaborating with the KGB, he was "forgotten" as far as the Lubavitch community was concerned. No excuses would help. It made no difference that the KGB often used these Jews against their will, and it was very hard to remove oneself from their clutches.

By chance, R. Moshe Nissilevitch was friendly with one of these alleged co-operators. The story behind their companionship was as follows: In 1946, when many Lubavitchers succeeded in sneaking out of the country to Poland via Lemberg (Lvov), R. Moshe also

tried his luck—but was too late. He miraculously avoided imprisonment, but the KGB was looking for him, so he changed the name on
his official documents to Sholom Friedman.

When he arrived in Samarkand, he told everyone that his name
was Moshe Friedman. Although his papers bore the name "Sholom,"
many people already knew him as Moshe and he couldn't change that.
If he were caught and questioned about it, he could claim to have two
names, Sholom and Moshe, and that he used one name on his papers
and the other in everyday life. Most of the community, including me,
did not know that his family name was actually Nissilevitch. Only a
few people who knew him from before the war knew it.

One man, of whom we were all wary, knew R. Moshe well and
was aware of his past, including his failed border crossing attempt.
He also knew of the name change from Moshe Nissilevitch to Sholom Friedman. In fact, it was this man who had forged the documents. He had been caught and imprisoned along with the activists
involved in the escape and, like the others, was released after Stalin
died. When this fellow then arrived in Samarkand, R. Moshe saw
him and became deeply afraid of being informed on.

However, R. Moshe was never called in by the KGB. Over the
next few years, his impression was that the man was not the informant he was suspected of being; despite having fallen into the KGB's
net, he had remained G-d-fearing and hid from them whatever he
was able. Once he reached this conclusion, R. Moshe decided to
meet with him, all the while keeping his eyes wide open for any
hints of deception.

The two would converse for hours, and the man would tell R.
Moshe of the searing guilt he felt over his visits to the KGB office.
Every Wednesday, the day he had to go to the office, was a terrible
day for him, he said. "You cannot imagine what I go through during
the interrogations. The interrogator attacks me like a wolf. He bangs
his fist on the table and terrifies me with threats of what they'll do
to me if I don't talk.

"When I say that I have nothing to tell them, he orders me to go
to a certain house and see whether there is a minyan there on Shab-

bos, and he warns me, 'You know, we have other people who work with us; they will tell us the truth. If you try to lie to us, you will suffer forever.'"

This is what he would tell R. Moshe, and R. Moshe believed and empathized with him.

None of us in Samarkand knew of the connection between the two, because R. Moshe kept it to himself. Now, with R. Berke's circle of confidants considering the resumed use of his original documents, R. Moshe thought of consulting with this fellow to find out whether the KGB was still interested in R. Berke and his whereabouts. Naturally, before doing this, he had to get R. Berke's approval.

When R. Moshe asked R. Berke about the plan, R. Berke nearly fainted. "Are you serious?" asked R. Berke. "You've lost your mind!" But R. Moshe had excellent powers of persuasion and he managed to convince R. Berke that this was the right move.

R. Moshe lost no time. He left immediately to speak with his contact, and after making the appropriate small talk—as only R. Moshe knew how—he began to slowly and carefully inquire whether the KGB was interested in R. Berke. The man told R. Moshe that they had never asked about R. Berke. Had the police been on the lookout for him, he added, he was sure they would have asked him to gather information.

After receiving this piece of news, R. Berke was very happy but still a little nervous. R. Moshe decided that R. Berke should meet with the man himself so he could hear it from him directly. Arranging a meeting like this was complicated and dangerous, for it would reveal R. Berke's hiding place, which at the time was the Mishulovin home. They certainly would not agree to have this man come to their house to meet R. Berke. It would endanger not only him but the Mishulovin family as well.

R. Moshe simply decided not to tell anyone else of the meeting and to call it for the dead of night, once everyone was asleep. The Mishulovin's house had a private yard, and R. Berke hid in a small shed in the yard. At a certain time of night, R. Berke would open the gate for them, and then they would enter his room and speak by candlelight.

When R. Moshe's man heard that R. Berke was in the city and wanted to meet in order to hear the information from him directly, he became very excited. He knew R. Berke very well and they had not seen each other since their arrests in 1946. The man knew of the dire noose still clutching at R. Berke, and had no need to be told of his sons and his wife, and how they hadn't seen or heard of him in years. He knew it all.

Late at night, R. Moshe brought the man to the gate of the Mishulovin home. The gate was unlocked, and the two entered R. Berke's hiding place. With the electric light turned off, the room was lit only by the weak glow of a candle. It is impossible to describe their emotional reunion. They reminisced for a long time, fell upon one another and cried.

After R. Berke heard directly from him that his name had never been mentioned in the KGB interrogations, he was convinced of the veracity of his words. The man advised him to use his old documents and after the meeting, R. Berke decided to do so. He registered as a resident of the city, and after years of hiding, he was now legal.

"Regards" from R. Berke

After becoming a legal resident, R. Berke relaxed somewhat and finally agreed to write a letter to his wife, in his own handwriting, to inform her that he was living among Lubavitchers and doing well. Still afraid the authorities back in Lvov were looking for him, he refrained from writing his location. He also refused to send the letter through the post, for fear the KGB would read it. He insisted on finding someone who could deliver it personally.

My brother Berel lived in nearby Stalinabad (now known as Dushanbe) after he married, and just then—it was sometime in 1955—he was sent by his work to attend a conference in Moscow. On his way there, he passed through Samarkand. Eli Mishulovin considered it vital that one of us give R. Berke's wife the letter and his personal regards, and so he arranged with my brother to meet at the train station in Samarkand.

When they met, Eli gave Berel two missions: first, that he travel to Riga and raise money to assist R. Berke in settling down in Samarkand, and then to Lvov, to give R. Berke's wife the letter and regards. Eli handed over the letter in an open envelope, along with R. Berke's permission to read it, if he felt the need to.

Berel did not dare to read the letter, but one line that could be seen through the envelope sent shivers up his spine. In Russian, R. Berke had written, "You surely remember that when we met and decided to marry, we said that wherever we live and wherever we will be, we would never forget one another."

Still today, as I write these lines, I am amazed by the sacrifices people expected to make in those years. A young couple met and decided to marry and what did they talk about? Not about buying a house, or about furniture, but to ask one another to keep their commitment alive whenever and wherever they would end up.

Berel first went to Riga where he met Chabad chassidim such as R. Yisrael Pevzner, R. Mulle Pruss, R. Notke Barkan, and others who warmly welcomed him and gave him generous donations. From there he continued on to Lvov.

He did not want to go directly to Feigel's house for fear that it was under surveillance, so the meeting took place in my uncle Dovid Pevzner's house. Feigel met him there with her daughter Freida. When she heard the reason for their meeting, her joy was immense. Taking the letter, she wept tears of joy as soon as she saw her husband's handwriting, and then read it through with tears streaming down her cheeks.

Despite her strong desire for more information about her husband, she did not ask my brother who he was or where he came from. She knew that you don't ask these questions in Russia. All she asked was, "Did you personally see my husband?"

When Berel said that he had seen R. Berke, she couldn't believe her ears. She asked him the question again and again, with several variations, to make sure that Berel had indeed seen her husband.

My brother told her that not only had he seen R. Berke, but that he had even shared a room with him for two years. He said that R. Berke asked him to send his regards and to tell her that he was healthy and living among Lubavitchers and that he was strong in his belief that they would unite again soon.

Feigel's joy was boundless. My brother felt that his trip to Lvov was well worth it.

Fully reinstating his original identity was an achingly slow process, and it was another year before R. Berke even dared to tell his wife where he was. Finally, once all of his papers were in order, he rented an apartment and asked her to come to Samarkand. A group of us went to the train station to meet Feigel and her daughter and bring them to R. Berke's new home. I cannot possibly describe how excited R. Berke was to meet his wife and ten-year-old daughter, who had barely been three months old when he last saw her and their long separation began.

The entire Lubavitch community in Samarkand welcomed R. Berke's wife with great honor. We knew how much this woman had endured over the years she had been alone. In addition, she was a distinguished woman, highly refined, and of tremendous piety.

After arriving in Samarkand, Feigel related that a year earlier, in 1957, she convinced her mother to submit a request to join her husband and grandsons who had left Russia earlier. Her request had been accepted and she was already in Eretz Yisrael.

Leaving for Eretz Yisrael

After his reunification with his wife, R. Berke began to think about the possibility of arranging an invitation from a relative in Israel, so that they could in turn request an exit visa. In those years, fear still hung heavily in the air and hardly anyone dared to submit such a request. The few who did gather the courage to do so knew that it would be a year before they had an answer, which would most likely be negative; that was always the answer.

Sending an emigration application to OVIR, the visa department of the Interior Ministry, was out of the question for R. Berke, who had been arrested for the very crime of trying to leave the country. However, he thought that his wife should request to reunite with her parents in Israel. Perhaps he would also be granted permission to leave after that.

R. Berke sent a letter to his father-in-law, asking—not overtly of course, but by hinting—that they seek the Rebbe's advice. His father-in-law passed the question on to his grandson, R. Berke's son Mordechai, who was at the time studying in the Tomchei Temimim in New York. He was to present the question to the Rebbe: Should his mother ask for permission to emigrate? The Rebbe's clear answer surprised them all: "Your father should submit a request for the entire family to leave and G-d will help them."

Mordechai was taken aback. Nobody had even considered this possibility. R. Berke was still technically an outlaw in the Soviet Union; how could he run the risk of applying? He expressed his reservations to the Rebbe, who smiled warmly and dismissed his fears with a wave of his hand, saying, "They won't catch on."

Indeed, R. Berke received an invitation from his father-in-law in his name and received permission to emigrate only half a year after submitting his request. Another half a year later, before Rosh Hashana of 1960, they received their travel passports. R. Berke didn't want to spend one extra minute in the Soviet Union. They packed their bags and left for Moscow in the middle of Sukkos, and then headed for Israel via Vienna just a couple days later. Our joy for the Chein family was boundless.

Joy and Tears Together

After R. Berke left for Moscow, R. Moshe Nissilevitch was struck by an idea for obtaining Jewish books and copies of the Rebbe's talks. To carry out his plan, I would have to travel to Moscow immediately and deliver a message to R. Berke before he left for Israel, one that could not be transmitted through anyone else.

In those days, we hardly ever received any of the Rebbe's teachings. The books and pamphlets that tourists occasionally brought and left in shul were immediately snatched by the KGB and taken to the "Ministry of Culture." There was only one other way to obtain Chassidic discourses, talks, and other books: The few people who received permission to emigrate first had to go to the Israeli embassy in Moscow in order to arrange their paperwork. Upon entering the embassy, they would be greeted by a small sign that read, "The walls have ears," and an embassy official would motion to them to keep quiet. The official would take them to a bookcase and signal that they could take whatever books they wanted to leave with relatives still closeted in Russia. This is how we occasionally got a hold of Jewish texts, which were subsequently distributed throughout the Soviet Union. It didn't happen very often.

Now, R. Moshe came up with an original idea, as he often did. Samarkand was an ancient city, popular with tourists for its various sights and attractions. Jewish tourists visiting the city would naturally make a stop at the shul, and here R. Moshe spied an opportunity. Although we were afraid to pray at the shul, we could go there occasionally and take books that tourists had left behind—if we had a pre-arranged hiding place.

R. Moshe was enthusiastic about his plan and convinced me to fly to Moscow to ask R. Berke to bring the idea to the Rebbe in New York. That way, when someone reliable next traveled to Samarkand, he could be informed of the hiding place. We could rely on R. Berke to inform only the right people. So I flew to Moscow and told R. Berke the idea.

It did seem like a great plan, but unfortunately, it was also too complicated, and in the end nothing came of it. Moreover, there was no need for it. By the 1960s, Russia had begun to establish warmer political relations with the West, and many tourists began arriving from across the globe, bringing with them prayer books, *Tanyas*, and various other Chassidic works, which reached us safely.

During R. Berke's short time in Moscow, he stayed with his father, R. Peretz, who lived in the Perava suburb. I remember seeing a strange sight that Sukkos in Moscow, one that I had never seen before. Over the sukkah was a roof that could be removed during meals, and upon it lay a pile of snow. With the moderate climate in Samarkand such that it never snowed that time of year, this snowy sukkah made for an odd sight.

While in Moscow, I met R. Michel Vishedsky of Chernovitz. He had also come to Moscow to give something to R. Berke. In those years, it was exceedingly rare for a Lubavitcher, and someone whom you could trust, to leave the Soviet Union for the West.

When I flew back to Samarkand, I felt broken and crushed. I was thrilled at the thought of R. Berke spending the last day of the festival—Shmini Atzeres—in Kfar Chabad, Israel, but I could also feel the spiritual vacuum that had been created in Samarkand with R. Berke's departure. I thought to myself: Here I am, landing in Samarkand, while R. Berke is landing in the Land of Israel!

On Shmini Atzeres, we sat and *farbrenged* for the first time in years without the presence of R. Berke. As the Zohar puts it, "Joy was fixed in this side of my heart; crying fixed in the other." Of course, we were happy that R. Berke's suffering had finally come to an end, far from this land of torment, as he reunited with his sons after fourteen years apart. Yet, we were now left bereft of a chassid like R. Berke, and a sense of sadness still tugged at our hearts. With whom would we *farbreng*, beneath whose radiant light would we warm ourselves? Where would we hear sweet Chassidic prayers as pleasant as R. Berke's?

I'll never forget that Shmini Atzeres *farbrengen*. I sat alongside my friends R. Mordechai Goldschmidt, R. Michoel Mishulovin, and R. Yaakov Lerner. We said *l'chaim*, sang, cried, and then we said *l'chaim*, sang, and cried some more. So we carried on, well into the night, until we drifted off to sleep with our heads on the table.

CHAPTER 7

Secret Worship Services

During the war years, the government's occupation with the conflict and the resulting dreary economic situation left them with neither the time nor the manpower to maintain vigilance over religious activity. Nearly all the local shuls were crowded with worshippers, while schools and yeshivas were opened with relative ease. However, Samarkand's teeming religious life and aura of liberty vanished entirely with the conclusion of the war.

As mentioned previously, the Polish and Russian governments signed an agreement in 1946 allowing Polish citizens to leave the Soviet Union and return to their homes. Many Russian Lubavitchers leapt at this golden opportunity by feigning to be Polish refugees and trying to escape through the border city of Lvov (Lemberg). Within a short time, Samarkand was emptied of the thousands of Jews who had once filled its streets. At the same time, the government cracked down on those who remained, tracking and persecuting them for their religious observance.

The Chabad community remaining in Samarkand mostly comprised families who were afraid to take the risk of crossing the border. Among them was our family, the Mishulovin, Goldschmidt, Schiff and Lerner families, my uncle R. Boruch Duchman, R. Eliyahu Paritcher (Levin), and a number of others. There were also some Lubavitcher families who had tried crossing the border but were unsuccessful and forced to return to Samarkand broken-hearted.

Included in the latter category were the brothers Dovid and Eliyahu Mishulovin, both in their late teens at the time, who had decided to depart on their own in the hopes of joining a family with permission to cross the border. They were unsuccessful and returned home. Despondent as they were about their failure to escape, they were relieved to have evaded the clutches of the KGB and avoid arrest.

We were little children at the time, yet to this day I recall how R. Dovid Mishulovin and his younger brother, R. Eliyahu, returned from Lvov, their eyes ablaze with terror. The fear was so palpable that when Eliyahu would go out in the street he would hold one of the Communist newspapers, *Pravda* or *Izvestia*, in the crook of his arm. In public he spoke only in Russian and refrained from speaking in Yiddish to Jews who were not religious. He did everything possible to avoid suspicion for associating with anything Jewish and, specifically, with chassidim.

In those onerous times, it was impossible to maintain a school or yeshiva; even maintaining a steady minyan of ten men for prayers was not feasible: We were too frightened to enter the shul in Samarkand. Only the elderly men prayed there.

Ironically, the regular prayer services in the official synagogue made arranging a secret minyan for the youth more of a challenge. Soviet law officially granted freedom of speech and religion after the age of eighteen. A child under eighteen, however, was considered a minor, and while children couldn't be punished under the law, it was forbidden to engage minors in religious activities. The offending parents would be accused of promoting religious propaganda and, as a consequence, their children would be taken to government orphanages.

The shuls were officially under the purview of the government's cultural department, and each one had a ring of informants recruited by the KGB. Everybody knew about the informants, and they scarcely tried to conceal their activities themselves. At times these traitors proudly flaunted their position, boasting that the government only allowed the existence of their shuls because of them. The sincere and venerable Chabad chassidim did not attend these shuls, only joining in the secret services and *farbrengens* in private homes.

Since going to shul was forbidden for us children, our parents and the older boys wanted to organize a secret service that we could attend. The setback, however, was that since we were young children and not yet bar mitzvah, we were unable to form a minyan on our own. Our fathers were required to join us if we were to have ten men, but if they were not present at the shul, it would be clear evidence that they had formed a secret minyan elsewhere.

Then again, they longed for us to experience a proper *davening*, to listen to a *Borchu*, or to the Leader's Repetition, and to answer *Amen* at the appropriate points in the prayers. I remember that when I was ten years old, my father would wake me up for the sunrise minyan at the shul, reasoning that the informants were still asleep and would only arrive later. In that early hour of the morning, the only people who came were the simple day laborers who simply wanted to pray with a minyan. But that was during the war years. When the persecution heightened, my father wouldn't dare take the risk of bringing me to the main shul. For the most part, we didn't have much of a choice and I stayed home alone, without a minyan.

A Minyan Without a Torah Scroll

With the approach of the High Holidays in the month of Tishrei, the adults knew they had to devise a plan to form a minyan, despite the menacing danger. Aside from the importance of having a proper prayer service for us children to experience, the boys over bar mitzvah age, like my brother Berel, Dovid Mishulovin, his brother Eliyahu, and Moshe Nissilevitch, needed a minyan. Jewish law recognized them as adults, but as long as they were under eighteen, they were still banned from synagogue attendance. It would also enable R. Berke Chein, who was hiding in our house and the Mishulovin house at the time, to pray with a minyan. Other adults would also have to participate, since there weren't quite enough youth on their own.

With great difficulty and effort, they organized a secret minyan for the holidays. At times we had to start very early and finish before services began at the main shul; other times we began only once they had ended. At all times, the goal was to maintain a low profile, to protect both the minyan and its participants.

Our greatest challenge was obtaining a Torah scroll. We did not possess one of our own, and had no way to get hold of one. Asking the *gabbai* of the shul would no doubt be our undoing, as the authorities would thereby instantly discover our activities. Taking one without authorization was also risky; sooner or later the "burglary" would be discovered and the ensuing commotion would quickly lead the government to our activities. Often enough, we had to suffice with reading the weekly Torah portion from a printed *Chumash*, if only to preserve the structure of the service and not forego the Torah reading altogether. That was the best we could do. Even R. Berke Chein, who under regular circumstances was painstakingly meticulous in his religious observance, was forced to settle with this arrangement.

On very rare occasions, when one of the trustworthy shul-goers fell ill, we had our chance. The *gabbaim* were told that this fellow was too unwell to walk and had requested that we organize a minyan in his home. Naturally, we took care to keep this information from leaking to any of the known informants at the shul.

You can imagine our dread the day we heard that one of the informants had uncovered our secret and reacted by saying, "That's an old trick of theirs. This is just an excuse for the purpose of borrowing a Torah scroll and arranging a minyan for the youngsters!" From then on, we had to be more cautious about any future such schemes.

The *Shiva* That Lapsed into Twelve Months

R. Eliyahu Schusterman, an older and distinguished member of the shul, passed away on the 18th of Elul, late in the summer of 1951. It was understood, even by the informants, that a minyan would be organized in his home for the first seven days of mourning, as is customary. We children avoided participating in this minyan, seeing that the regular members of the shul were there, informants included. But, after several days, they grew weary of partaking in this particular minyan and soon returned to attending official services. This granted us children the ability to warily sneak in and join the specially arranged minyan.

When the seven days were over, some people suggested that the minyan nevertheless continue to operate. He had been a prominent individual, so the proposal seemed befitting, and everyone agreed. The Torah scroll remained in his house for three more weeks, until the end of *Shloshim,* the traditional second stage of mourning. The real reason for the suggestion, of course, was to facilitate a minyan for the young boys during the High Holidays, which just happened to fall during that time.

A month elapsed, and the people attending the minyan, all of whom were Lubavitchers, noted that no one had batted an eyelash in their direction. Even the informants no longer made an appearance. They therefore resolved to continue to pray there every Shabbos. Conducting daily prayers there would have been dangerously noticeable, and they did not want to jeopardize the existence of the minyan altogether. Amazingly, the *gabbaim* forgot about the Torah scroll that remained in R. Eliyahu Schusterman's house. We were finally able to have a minyan on Shabbos and holidays, complete with a Torah reading!

A year passed and the *gabbaim* still hadn't mentioned anything. We wanted to find a place for the Torah that was safer and more concealed than the semi-official minyan in R. Eliyahu's house, so we opted to transfer it to one of our homes and keep it there for whenever it was needed.

Several months went on in this fashion, until the Doctors' Plot commenced, and harassment against the Jewish population intensified daily. The situation was so harsh that we were frightened to keep the Torah scroll in our homes. Despite the miraculous manner we had obtained the Torah, we seriously considered returning it to the main shul in order to alleviate our fear it would be found, a discovery that was sure to mark our fateful end.

I must mention the great merit of Gittel, the wife of R. Michoel Goldschmidt, who insisted that under no circumstances should the Torah be returned to the shul and the secret Torah readings come to an end. She took the Torah and hid it in her house.

A Torah Disguised as a Dead Child

The heightened persecution of Jews accompanying the Doctor's Plot finally subsided after Stalin's death, and once again we felt emboldened enough to arrange a secret minyan from time to time. But with the Torah scroll came a new set of complications. Generally, we were hesitant to hold gatherings of any sort in the same place for too long, but transporting the scroll from house to house presented a real problem. It was a large, weighty Torah, and every time we shifted its location, we were afraid that people would notice and report us to the authorities. In addition, Halacha only permits transporting a Torah from one place to another if it is to be read from at least three times. Therefore, we would hold Shabbos services in a single house for two weeks in a row, despite the enhanced danger from prying neighbors.

To simplify transferring the Torah, we shortened its wooden rollers so that they wouldn't protrude as much, and would sometimes wrap it in a blanket to give it the appearance of a child. Once, we arranged to hold a minyan in the home of R. Refael Chudaidatov, a prominent Bukharian Jew who participated in our Chassidic services. He went to the Torah scroll's location, draped it in a blanket, and took a taxi home. When he got out of the car, a gentile

neighbor on the street noticed the bundle he was carrying and instinctively assumed it was a child. However, after noticing the
wooden rollers jutting out slightly from the blanket, she became
suspicious and determined that it was a dead child, its severed legs
dangling from the coverlet.

It was a short while prior to Pesach and the woman had been
told that Jews use the blood of Christian children in their matzos
for the holiday. Something clicked in her superstition-addled mind
and she immediately called the police to arrest the Jew who had
undoubtedly just slain a gentile child in cold blood.

R. Refael was completely oblivious to all of the action occurring
just outside his window. He entered his house and gingerly placed
the Torah in the cabinet. A few minutes later, a group of men dressed
in plainclothes arrived at the house, along with the woman who had
reported sighting a Jew clutching "the body of a dead Christian
baby." In the courtyard they encountered R. Refael's son Moshiach,
and they asked him where the old man who had just entered the
courtyard had gone. Moshiach, who understood they had come to
arrest his father, rushed home to warn his father to flee.

The two undercover policemen, along with the woman, entered
the house immediately behind Moshiach. Refael was standing in
the entranceway and the woman identified him at once, crying:
"That's the man!"

They began to search the house. Paralyzing fear and apprehension
clutched the hearts of R. Refael and his family. He asked the uninvited
guests what they were hunting for, but the men did not reply and
continued to wreak havoc as they rummaged about the home.

Suddenly, the woman noticed a familiar package in the cupboard,
and pointed it out to the policemen. The men approached the cupboard, cautiously unraveled the blanket, and discovered a Torah scroll!

All at once the tension dissipated. When asked what the scroll
was for, R. Refael explained that since it was the day of his father's
passing, there was a Jewish custom to read from the Torah. He was
an elderly man, so the policemen resolved not to bother with him
and turned to go.

When Moshiach noted their hesitation, he began to yell: "Why did you make this fuss? Why did you scare my father so much? I'm going to call the mayor, whom I know quite well, and they will dismiss you from your jobs!"

The policemen began to defend their actions, saying that they had done nothing wrong intentionally and had only come because the woman had called. They asked the family's pardon and left immediately.

The High Holidays in Samarkand

The High Holidays in Samarkand were an experience unto themselves. From the beginning of the preceding month of Elul, a change could be discerned in the town's atmosphere. The people of the community grew introspective, as each individual tried to improve on his or her own religious observance, and focus less on material pursuits. One could sense that the Days of Awe were approaching.

The two days of Rosh Hashana were solemn and awe-inspiring. Our minyan took place in a private home and was made up of some fifteen to twenty men, each sitting in his place, totally immersed in prayer. We were very careful not to utter anything unrelated to the holiday, and even when we needed to communicate, we preferred to motion with our hands so as not to get caught up in idle talk. Every free moment was devoted to reciting Psalms.

At one point, we found out about the Lubavitch custom to arrange, by roster, for *Tehillim* to be continuously recited for all forty-eight hours of the holiday. Although we hadn't enough people between us to arrange a full minyan for each shift, we divided up the hours and each of us took a shift. The shifts would begin ten minutes early and end ten minutes late, so as to ensure a seamless transfer, without any breaks. In that manner, *Tehillim* was recited constantly, with the exception of the times of the actual prayer services.

As I write this, the memories draw me back to those wonderful days, as I find myself back in shul for the High Holidays. I struggle to describe the feelings that engulfed us in the small room that held our minyan.

R. Berke Chein stands in one corner, covered with his *tallis,* and saying Psalms in a soft and tearful voice. R. Moshe Nissilevitch stands in another corner, words gently drifting from his mouth. Dovid and Eliyahu Mishulovin sit with their prayer shawls over their heads, reciting Psalms with tremendous concentration.

As the minyan starts, everyone begins to *daven* with intense focus, each person as their ability and energy permits. Each person looks inside his prayer book and utters every word clearly, trying his best to think over the meaning of the Hebrew words.

My father had managed to get a hold of a traditional Chabad *Tehillas Hashem* prayer book from an individual in Moscow. His desire to acquire it was so great that he paid seventy rubles to buy it from him—the equivalent of an entire month's salary. Having obtained the *Tehillas Hashem,* we could more accurately recite the prayers according to our custom.

When the leader reached the *Shmoneh Esrei,* the silent portion of the prayers normally recited together with the minyan, some congregants would still be making their way through the various earlier stages of the prayers. Although we always made sure we had enough people together before beginning *Shmoneh Esrei* and enough people ready to answer to the Leader's Repetition, we never tried to hurry anyone. We simply didn't dare interfere with someone else's prayer.

The silent prayer always had a unique aura; whispered voices rose and fell, with the sound of quiet sobbing in the background. One cried, another sighed, and yet a third shed tears silently onto the pages of his prayer book.

After the Leader's Repetition on Rosh Hashana, we would try to wait for those still praying on their own so that they too could be with the minyan when the time came for the blowing of the shofar; while waiting, the others recite Psalms. With Reb Berke leading the proceedings, the shofar-blowing ceremony, including its prefatory prayers, lasted an hour. Before it was over, his tears intermingled with drops of sweat, had soaked his prayer book and the table where he stood.

After prayers of this intensity, even the way we walked down the street on the way back home was changed. We walked with a focused mindfulness, our heads bowed, looking only within our immediate vicinity. We hurriedly ate the festive meal so as to provide sufficient time for the Afternoon Prayer, and the river-side *tashlich* ceremony—to cast off sins as bread crumbs into the flowing water. If I do not err, R. Berke would not eat during the two days of Rosh Hashana, partaking only of the two nighttime meals.

I particularly remember Yom Kippur in Samarkand. R. Moshe Nissilevitch would come to the house where the minyan was held with his prayer book and *Tehillim* and remain there until after the fast. From the time he entered the house, he would stand opposite the wall covered with his *tallis,* murmuring words of *Tehillim* or praying quietly. R. Moshe always made an effort to stand the entire day. He said it was his father's custom, and it was one that he kept his entire life. That was his Yom Kippur; completely engrossed in his prayers, oblivious of the goings-on around him; always praying at his own pace, even if the minyan was ahead of him. His quiet, hoarse voice could barely be heard, and every so often a tear would make its way down his cheek. His *Shmoneh Esrei* was quite lengthy, as he tried to enunciate each word properly. He would often repeat words of the prayers, apparently to ensure that he had pronounced each one just so. Certainly he was careful not to utter any unnecessary words outside of the prayers.

After leaving Russia, it was difficult to grow accustomed to the type of conduct we observed elsewhere. During my first Rosh Hashana in Israel, I still cried as I prayed; but to be honest, those tears were less from the atmosphere of Rosh Hashana itself than from my longing for Rosh Hashana in Samarkand.

One *Esrog* for All of Samarkand

On Sukkos, we were easily able to build sukkahs in our yards. It was accepted practice for all Bukharian Jews and the authorities wouldn't prevent it. Arranging the services on the Days of Awe was just as difficult as on a regular Shabbos, but at least we could spend Sukkos *farbrenging* in the fresh autumn breeze, nestled within the cozy sanctuary of our sukkah.

I have fond memories of reading in the sukkah the fragments of the Rebbe Rayatz's *Likutei Dibburim* that we had managed to assemble in Samarkand. We would peruse its pages thirstily, mesmerized by the descriptions of chassidim of previous generations. So long as there were no disturbances from unfamiliar knocks on the courtyard door, we would sit in our glorious haven and revel in the splendor of the Rebbe's talks and teachings.

Sukkos presented us with but one major problem: obtaining an *esrog*. Of the Four Species customarily assembled and used for the festival—the willow, myrtle, palm-frond, and citron—finding the citron, or *esrog,* in that part of the world was always the greatest challenge. Some years were better, requiring less effort, and some years proved more difficult.

As in the stories of the Jewish *shtetls* of yesteryear, at times we had to suffice with just one *esrog* for the entire community, usually obtained at the last minute, with great difficulty and at enormous cost.

I recall the days preceding Sukkos of the year 1949, during the frenzied years under Stalin's rule. Sukkos was fast approaching and we lacked even a single *esrog*. R. Avrohom Borochov, a wealthy man and a close acquaintance of the chassidim in Samarkand, traveled to Moscow and purchased a single *esrog* for 10,000 rubles, a tremendous fortune at that time, paying for it entirely with his own money.

On the other hand, the palm leaves and myrtle sprigs were easy to come by, thanks to the devotion of young men such as Yitzchok (Itche) Mishulovin, Aharon Makovetsky, Berke Schiff, and others, who would travel to Georgia where these plants grew and return to

Samarkand with a stash of them. Willows weren't a problem either; they grew in abundance by the rivers near Samarkand.

One can only imagine our great joy when one year we heard that the Rebbe had, for the first time, allotted an *esrog* for Samarkand. With only one *esrog* to hold during the prayers, and such a prized one at that, the Sukkos morning services naturally took a very long time.

Extra-long Sukkos prayers aside, possessing only one *esrog* presented us with a dilemma. We knew that there were hundreds of Jews residing in towns around Samarkand who hadn't the privilege of owning an *esrog*, or even access to one. We therefore took turns every one of the Intermediate Days of Sukkos traveling with the *esrog*, from town to town, to enable these Jews to perform the *mitzvah* of gathering the Four Species, despite the danger this entailed. I remember that when we arrived at these towns, a long line of the local Jews would have already formed at a pre-determined spot, awaiting the *esrog*'s arrival.

The righteous women of Samarkand wanted to perform the *mitzvah* as well and the scrupulous among them refrained from eating before reciting the blessing on the Four Species. Naturally, they desired to fulfill the *mitzvah* in the morning, as soon as the men concluded prayers, but we felt that it was of great importance to set out to the outlying towns as early as we could. The men's reasoning was that women were not obligated to take the Four Species, though it is customary for them to perform the *mitzvah* as well. This was a hot topic that surfaced every year and the arguments it caused could get quite lively.

Farbrengen with a Member of the Communist Party

Immediately following the Sukkos festival comes Simchas Torah, a day dedicated to the joyous, often raucous, celebration of the Torah. In Chabad circles, however, the celebration begins a day earlier, on the eighth day of Sukkos, or Shmini Atzeres. Our Shmini Atzeres tradition in Samarkand was to *farbreng* with R. Yosef Schiff, the son-in-law of the elder chassid R. Yerachmiel Chadash, a student of the original Tomchei Temimim yeshiva in Lubavitch.

The *farbrengen* would begin once we had concluded the afternoon prayers. When the sky darkened, signaling the end of Sukkos and ushering in Simchas Torah, we would remain in the sukkah, and continue *farbrenging*. To avoid the halachic concern of *bal tosif* —sitting in the sukkah longer than required—we would put bedboards over the canopy of the sukkah, rendering it halachically invalid, and carry on.

R. Yosef Schiff had studied in Tomchei Temimim in Nevel until he was drafted to serve during the war. After being wounded in battle, the authorities suggested he join the Communist Party and generously filled out the paperwork for him, as was customary in those days. Of course, he was forced to accept their "suggestion"; refusing to join would have been dangerous. That is how R. Yosef became a member of the Communist Party, or as they used to say, referencing the red membership papers, "an owner of the red card."

Divine Providence had placed him in a position to assist many Jews. As a Party member, he had special standing in many offices, and was appointed chairman of a government agency under which numerous factories operated. Many Shabbos observant Jews received employment in factories under his management.

Of course, holding a *farbrengen* in his house was a serious hazard. Organizing an illegal gathering was crime for an ordinary citizen, but it was an incomparably more severe crime for a Party member to do the same. Even worse, it wasn't just any gathering, but a Chassidic one.

However, R. Yosef was a bold man who found great pleasure in acting upon his convictions, perhaps especially when it was difficult or dangerous for him to do so. Often, when one of his workers had *yahrzeit* or when it was a special day on the Jewish calendar, he would close his office door and arrange a minyan for the afternoon prayers. He would tell his secretary and workers that he was in an important meeting and wasn't to be disturbed under any circumstances. If someone knocked on the door to enter, he would raise his voice and shout: "I told you already, don't bother me! I am meeting with my employees!"

The fact that R. Yosef was a member of the Party placed extensive restrictions upon him. He was unable to publicly display his Jewishness and certainly was not able to attend shul. On account of this, he would often hold a minyan in his house, especially during the High Holidays. He said that if he was discovered, he would claim that he had arranged the service for his elderly father-in-law, R. Yerachmiel Chadash, who had trouble walking to shul.

In the midst of the Rosh Hashana prayers in his home one year, while the leader was chanting the liturgical poems, a messenger arrived from R. Yosef's office, requesting that he come immediately to meet some senior officials from the municipality. Naturally, we were very frightened. Prayer shawls were instantly flung off, and in a panic, we tried searching for a place to hide. The only one who was not anxious was R. Yosef. He calmed the crowd, and then strode outside to greet the unexpected guest and send him off. In an even and authoritative voice, he explained that he could not leave since he was in the middle of a meeting with his neighbors for the purpose of enlisting them for the annual cotton-picking. In those years, cotton was considered "white gold," and its harvest was of national importance.

Hakafos at Shul

We would *farbreng* in a private home until very late on these final nights of the holiday, but we had to be careful that we were not noticed. For years, we would have to take off our shoes following the *farbrengen,* for the traditional Simchas Torah *hakafos* dancing. We danced in our socks for hours and sang in hushed tones so the neighbors would not overhear us.

In the years after Stalin's death, when we felt freer, we had the idea to convene for dancing at the main shul in the Old City. Long

after the official prayers, once the rest of the community had finished with their festive meal at home, and after our own *farbrengen*
had wound up, we made our way to the shul. It was nearly midnight
and the city streets were deserted.

A few of us hurried ahead of the group and climbed over the
fence that surrounded the yard of the shul, to unlatch the front gate
for everyone else. When the entire group had assembled, we entered through the front gate and headed straight into the sanctuary,
where we began to dance with song and unadulterated joy. Those
were the days before electric timers, so the lights were all still on,
the sanctuary brightly illuminated. Finally, we were able to revel in
an authentic *hakafos*, grasping Torah scrolls in our arms, with unre-
strained singing and dancing. Our hearts soared with the rhythm of
the Chassidic tunes and our joy knew no bounds.

On the next Simchas Torah, as we strolled towards the shul, our
thoughts turned to the members of our community who had already
completed the official *hakafos*. After their hurried dancing session,
they had returned home, and after the conclusion of their meal, were
already fast asleep in their beds. But it was Simchas Torah! We resolved
to gather some of the older men to include them in our *hakafos*, and
set out in groups of twos and threes. This was after R. Berke had been
reinstated as a legal citizen and he led the way.

When we arrived at a home, we knocked at the door. Once the
man of the house had been rudely awoken, he would demand:
"What is it you want? We are sleeping!"

R. Berke, who was the oldest of our little rabble, would say:
"Please open up."

The poor fellow wouldn't dare to refuse R. Berke, and once we
entered the house, the "show" began. R. Berke, who had already had
some vodka, would approach the stunned householder and chastise
him, saying: "Sleeping now, on Shmini Atzeres night? It seems you
are gravely sick—let me feel your heartbeat."

After pretending to examine him, R. Berke would say: "*Aha*,
you have a serious illness indeed. It's not a physical illness, but a
spiritual illness. Don't be upset, I have good medication for you:

Learn a chapter of *Tanya* every morning before your prayers. But, in the meantime, we have to do something to immediately remedy the situation..."

R. Berke would call over one of the men in our group, bottle of vodka in hand, and then turn back to the homeowner: "I am an excellent doctor for illnesses such as these. Just open your mouth and my assistant here will pour in some medicine, straight from the bottle. Don't be afraid. It has a bit of a sting, but trust me, I have lots of experience with this. After you take the medication, you will immediately get up and join the dancing with us, and you will be as good as new, completely healed!"

R. Berke would perform the act so superbly that we would be clutching our sides in laughter. It was utterly impossible to go back to sleep after R. Berke's treatment. They all drank the *l'chaim* that we, the esteemed doctor's faithful assistants, made sure went down their throats. Naturally, after drinking a little, they joined the dancing, just as R. Berke had predicted. And, even if they didn't come to join the dancing at shul, enjoying a good night's sleep was definitely no longer an option.

CHAPTER 8

The Legendary Chassid: R. Simcha Gorodetzky

I n Samarkand, R. Simcha Gorodetzky was a figure of legendary proportions, the very symbol of a chassid and a man of sacrifice. I first saw R. Simcha in 1955, after his release from a lengthy and brutal imprisonment. During my childhood, R. Simcha had been exiled to Siberia, serving time in the freezing Arctic climate for his "crimes" of spreading Torah and Judaism.

Although I did not see him for most of my childhood years, R. Simcha was a central figure in my life from the stories I heard about him from my mother and from the elder chassidim. But beyond my own impressions, R. Simcha was truly a seminal figure in Chabad Samarkand and for the broader regional Jewish community.

Chabad in Bukhara

The original Jews of Samarkand were Sephardic Bukharian Jews, named after the city of Bukhara, Uzbekistan, the former capital of Central Asia. According to the locals, they are descended from Persian Jews who arrived in the region at the start of the second millennium CE. Indeed, they've had a spoken language similar to that of Persian Jews for generations. Even further back into the past, tradition has their origins with the Ten Tribes banished from the Land of

Israel by the Assyrians. The fact that the Jews of ancient Persia and Medea, the purported ancestors of the Bukharians, are believed to have absorbed some of the Jews from the Assyrian exile lends support to this tradition.

The earliest Chabad presence in the Bukharian region was in the year 1890, when R. Shlomo Leib Eliezerov, a chassid of the Rebbe Rashab and the Rabbi of Hebron, Israel, arrived there. The purpose of his trip was to collect money for the Jewish community in Hebron. While there, he worked on repairing the *mikvahs* as well as organizing the provision of kosher meat in Samarkand, Tashkent, and the surrounding cities and towns. The local Jews requested that he accept a temporary rabbinical position in Samarkand, which he did, and for the next thirty years he would return periodically to strengthen Jewish life in the area. When the Communist government came to power, he was forced to flee and return to the Land of Israel.

The brilliant Halachist and chassid R. Avraham Chaim Noeh contributed to the revival of Bukharian Jewry as well. In the year 1911, while still a young man of twenty-one, he left the Land of Israel with the mission of bolstering Jewish life in Bukharia. His efforts were primarily focused on Samarkand, where he served as its rabbi. During his stay in Samarkand, he wrote a treatise in Bukharian entitled *Chanoch LaNaar,* detailing the laws of *tefillin* for boys of bar mitzvah age. He would wear the customary Bukharian garb—including a turban and kaftan—and was known by the local Jews as "Avraham Chaim Mendelov Noeh," the "Mendelov" being a typical Bukharian reference to his father, R. Mendel Noeh.

Then, in 1925, the Rebbe Rayatz sent a young chassid to Samarkand by the name of R. Simcha Gorodetzky.

R. Simcha was born in 1903. In his youth, R. Simcha learned in the underground Tomchei Temimim yeshivas in Rostov and Cherson. One day while learning, he suddenly fell ill. He had a throbbing headache and felt weak and limp. The student supervisor, R. Chatche Feigin, took him to the doctor, and after his examination, R. Simcha was told that he needed to rest. Rather than remain in the yeshiva, the doctor said he should go home to recuperate.

R. Simcha refused to adhere to the doctor's orders and declared he would not leave yeshiva until they asked the Rebbe. R. Chatche conceded and they traveled together to the Rebbe Rayatz. While R. Simcha remained in the corridor outside, R. Chatche entered the Rebbe's room to report on R. Simcha's condition and the doctor's orders. The Rebbe then requested that R. Simcha enter the room.

When R. Simcha entered the Rebbe's study, the Rebbe told him: "I heard from Chatche what the doctor said about your health and his orders that you should return home. In truth, you aren't in any condition to learn full-time in yeshiva. At the same time, you should remain in Tomchei Temimim and I will give you another path. If you listen to me, I promise you that you will recover and live many healthy years.

"I will send you," said the Rebbe, "to visit outlying Lubavitcher settlements. You should inquire into their welfare and see where a *shochet* is needed, or a *mohel*, and so on, and report back to me."

This was during the most difficult period that followed the Bolshevik Revolution. Starvation and fear were the lot of all the people of Russia, and the Lubavitchers in these far away settlements suffered in particular. They were terribly impoverished, and moreover, they felt distant and removed from their Rebbe. Now the Rebbe was soliciting R. Simcha to become his special emissary, to travel to these places and bolster the spirit of chassidim there and then report back to him.

As a loyal chassid, R. Simcha did not hesitate for a moment and instantly accepted the Rebbe's mission. He later recounted that the moment he boarded the first train, he began to feel better. As the train wound its way through the countryside, he felt his headache dissipating and his body gaining strengthen.

R. Simcha fulfilled his mission faithfully. He journeyed from one settlement to the next and delivered regards from the Rebbe to the chassidim and asked about their welfare. In turn, the chassidim, elated to receive regards from the Rebbe, implored him to convey their requests to the Rebbe. They poured out their bitter hearts and cried to him about their troubles and difficulties.

As R. Simcha listened to the trying plight of the chassidim, he remembered with a chill that at the end of his journey he would have to repeat it all to the Rebbe. When he returned to the Rebbe, he went in for *yechidus*—a private audience—and began to give his account. He told of the troubles of the individuals he encountered in his travels, but he was reluctant to tell the full story because he did not want to cause the Rebbe sorrow. Unable to find words, he began to stammer. The Rebbe noticed and said: "*Nu, nu,* continue, continue… as my emissary you must tell me everything."

R. Simcha then told the Rebbe of one man's request, and the difficult situation of yet another chassid, and finally the man who apologized for failing in his duty to raise Passover funds for the destitute because he had just lost his son to illness. Hearing this, the Rebbe suddenly burst into tears. R. Simcha, who could not bear to witness the Rebbe's sorrow, could not continue his report, and instead stood silently, wringing his hands. The Rebbe understood his silence and said: "If it is hard for you to say it all, put it in writing and hand it to me instead."

R. Simcha Is Arrested

One of R. Simcha's many arrests for his communal work occurred prior to his departure to Samarkand. As per usual, the government had assembled an incriminating file on him containing dozens of falsified reports. As the judge recited paragraph after paragraph from the file during his trial, he read out, "Rabbi Gorodetzky organized propaganda against the Soviet government and during a search of his apartment we discovered live ammunition in his possession."

R. Simcha interrupted him: "What ammunition are you talking about?"

The judge withdrew a *Tanya* from his drawer, hurled it angrily onto the table, and roared: "That's your ammunition!" (They were correct of course; the *Tanya* *is* our ammunition).

The two years that he spent confined in a prison cellar did not break his spirit, nor did it affect his devotion to the Rebbe Rayatz. As soon as he was released from jail, he continued to work in the service of the Rebbe.

Love for Simple Jews

R. Simcha continued to carry out other missions that the Rebbe assigned to him until he married, and then continued to do so immediately after his wedding. When he was absent from home for an extended period of time, his new wife would stay with her parents in Kremenchug.

There were no telephones then, and movement was complicated by the Revolution and the anarchy that followed it. Letters did not arrive on time in those years and the fear hanging heavily in the air nearly broke the ties between people. It is therefore no wonder that when R. Simcha's wife gave birth to a daughter, he did not know of it until he went to the Rebbe in Rostov, where he rejoiced upon hearing the good news.

On that visit, in 1926, when he went in for his audience, the Rebbe said to him: "After marriage it is difficult for you to travel from place to place. Now I will send you to one location where you will remain—to Samarkand, to the Jews of Bukharia, where you will become their spiritual leader."

This new mission meant traveling to a foreign land, far from the Rebbe and any other Chassidic community and living amongst and working with a group of Jews almost entirely unfamiliar to him, both by nature and custom. With an unquestioning sense of duty, R. Simcha accepted. He only asked that, in light of the birth of his first child, he wanted to first travel to Kremenchug. After seeing his wife and baby, he would continue ahead on to Samarkand.

But the Rebbe, perhaps concerned that the family in Kremenchug would object to him being sent so far away, urged him to go straight to Samarkand. "Your wife will follow you there," he said.

For a chassid who had lived all of his years in a Chassidic community in the heart of Russia, Samarkand would have felt like the end of the world. But R. Simcha set off directly to Samarkand. Upon his arrival there, he rented an apartment in the Old City, where most of the Bukharian Jews lived. After a short while his wife and infant daughter joined him.

R. Simcha was very impressed by the warmth and devotion of the people in the local community towards the Rebbe—the *Admor*, as they called him—which resulted from the guidance of the chassidim who had been previously sent there by Lubavitch rebbes, namely, R. Shlomo Yehudah Leib Eliezerov and R. Chaim Noeh.

In the shul in the Old City, he encountered a very simple Jew who would recite *Tehillim*, the book of Psalms, with great enthusiasm. The Jew's pure, wholehearted faith tugged at his heart. His name was Reuven Akilov and he was well known in the community as something of a simple, uneducated person, but R. Simcha reveled in his wholehearted sincerity and once asked him: "Do you know the meaning of the words you're uttering?" Reuven responded that he did not. R. Simcha asked him about the first line of *Tehillim,* "Happy is the man who has not walked in the counsel of the wicked." R. Simcha asked Reuven, "Do you know what the words *Ashrei ha'ish* mean?" He did not. "What about the next words, *asher lo holach?*" R. Simcha persisted. Reuven did not know. R. Simcha pressed on. "What about the words, *b'atzas reshaim?*" At this point, Reuven's eyes lit up with recognition, and in an angry voice he exclaimed: "A *rasha* is a very wicked person and he should be beaten!"

R. Simcha enjoyed going to the shul and observing this man say *Tehillim*. He recalled that prior to one of his trips the Rebbe Rayatz had told him: "If you happen to encounter a simple Jew who believes in G-d with simple faith and you love him, you will know that you have an affinity for communal work and you are fit for *shlichus*, to be sent on such missions." He was certain that the Rebbe had been alluding to Jews like Reuven.

In time, I also came to know Reuven, and remember how he would pray with the Chabad minyan and mingle amongst the community. Whenever there was a class in *Likkutei Torah*, he would sit in and listen, even though they were delivered in Yiddish, a language he didn't understand. When he was asked about this, he explained himself by way of the following scenario: A person was sitting nearby a gang of thieves who were playing with a deck of cards. Suddenly, the police arrived and arrested them all, including the innocent individual. "But I have nothing to do with them! I don't even know how to play cards!" he protested. But the police were unconvinced. "You're coming with us to the station; we'll sort things out over there," they said. "I want to be here with the chassidim now," Reuven concluded. "In the World to Come, we can sort what exactly I understood from the class."

A Letter from the Rebbe Rayatz

R. Simcha worked diligently to bolster the level of Torah and Judaism in Samarkand. He organized schools, the Tiferes Bachurim yeshiva, and even sent ten gifted young Bukharian men from Samarkand to the secret Tomchei Temimim yeshiva in Poltava. These students later returned to serve as local beacons of light, illuminating their respective communities with the flame of Torah and Chassidus. Alongside this, R. Simcha also supervised the town's kosher slaughter and *mikvahs*. In short, he shouldered the responsibility for all of the Jewish needs of the city. It wouldn't be far-fetched to say that he effected a genuine spiritual revolution in the heart of Samarkand.

Many years after R. Simcha's passing, I came across a letter that the Rebbe Rayatz wrote about him and I realized that everything I had heard about him was merely a fraction of his deserved praise. The letter, written in January, 1929, was addressed to the renowned scholar and adherent of the Gerrer Chassidic sect R. Menachem Zemba, as part of the Rebbe's attempts to raise funds for Jewish schools. It reads as follows:

"Who is the one who put his life in substantial danger by traveling to Bukharia; who, with the help of Hashem, founded schools in

Samarkand, and for three months brought together some 800 young children studying under the tutelage of 45 teachers; who generated such enthusiasm on the parents' part that they committed to contribute to their children's tuition, and to establish a special community committee to pay for the rest; and who founded Tiferes Bachurim, where young businessmen, factory managers and laborers—eventually around 150 students—gathered to learn Torah?

"R. Simcha worked tirelessly for an entire year. His work was performed entirely in secret, until, when it became known who had been directing all of this activity, the NKVD came to arrest him. Because someone had come from Tashkent requesting that R. Simcha travel back with him to found schools there, as he had in Samarkand, he left that night and was saved.

"For three months the Yevsektzia worked to destroy what R. Simcha planted with the blood of his heart, with the sweat of his brow, with trembling and awful fear. Twenty teachers were deported to prison where they were tortured terribly and put on trial. About eight teachers fled and escaped, and the rest remained until, after much effort and expense, the detainees were released from their confinement, thank G-d.

"R. Simcha stayed for four months in those outlying cities and labored with blood and heart setting up schools, and, thank G-d, he was successful. Until today, about eight months since he was forced to leave that region altogether—his image had been circulated amongst the regional GPU offices, along with orders that left his fate in no doubt, should he be caught—the sound of Torah can, thank G-d, still be heard ringing in Samarkand from the 400 students still there, may they live and increase. Dozens upon dozens of students in other towns are also learning, although unfortunately there is no money to support them, may Hashem have mercy.

"R. Simcha did not let up from his work, Heaven forbid. He traveled to the ends of the Caucasus region, where our brethren the Mountain Jews dwell, may G-d be with them. He then journeyed to the city of Derbent, where he found some thirty young students learning under the guidance of a teacher; now, through his tremendous work efforts and with Hashem's help, 360 students learn there today. After four months of continued labor, the secret committee that he established there informs us that they are able to increase the number of those learning to 500. However, in order to pursue this, they need outside assistance; not much aid, merely 150 rubles a month. How painful it is that their meager request cannot be met. The conditions of the place require great care and R. Simcha is in much danger, so he plans to travel on to Kuba, a large city full of G-d-fearing Jews and those who know Torah."

This letter attests to R. Simcha's tireless activities and accomplishments from the first years of his arrival in Samarkand. I have often wondered what it was that motivated R. Simcha. What pushed him to put himself and his family aside in order to pursue his mission, even as the secret police hounded after his every step, looking into every institution he established and every religious activity he was behind?

I can only imagine that one thing and one thing only stood as his motivation—he was compelled to fulfill what the Rebbe wanted. For the sake of this goal he was prepared to endure fire and water. He was a chassid, a devoted follower, a *shliach* who carried the awesome responsibility of representing the Rebbe himself; a *mekushar* who was spiritually bound together with the Rebbe.

Ten Years in Siberia

A spiritual revolution of that magnitude that R. Simcha effected would obviously not go unnoticed by the Communist authorities. The secret police, who viciously combated anyone championing religion, constantly sought to catch him red-handed in his religious activities. Threats and persecution were R. Simcha's lot from the day he arrived in Samarkand, and he lived through many frightening experiences and several arrests.

R. Simcha was arrested in the early 1940s, once again for the crime of spreading Judaism, but this time with some other fictitious accusations as well. A group of Bukharian Jews had fled across the border via Iran and escaped to Israel. The investigators accused R. Simcha of organizing the escape and demanded that he admit to it. He was held in custody for two years without a trial.

In an act of depraved cunning, the interrogators told R. Simcha that his wife had also been arrested and was sitting in a nearby cell. He heard a voice that sounded very much like hers whispering to him from beyond the wall: "Simcha, tell them everything; it will be easier for me."

When the interrogators saw that R. Simcha was unconvinced, they moved him to another interrogation, and then another cell. Along the way, R. Simcha noticed a small piece of paper that seemed to have just fallen on the floor, and picked it up. It was note addressed to him, he saw, and seemed to be written in his wife's handwriting: "Simcha, what are you thinking? The children are likely to remain complete orphans, bereft of father and mother. Tell them everything."

The note was signed "Rashke." Everyone called his wife "Raya" and only her parents and closest relatives called her Rashke. Somehow, the NKVD knew even this minutest of details, and had managed to forge her signature.

After a lengthy period of exhausting interrogations, he was sentenced to death in 1944; shortly after, the sentence was commuted by a general order by Stalin to twenty-five years of hard labor in Siberia, where he was sent along with R. Chizkiyahu Kayikov, one of the students he had sent off to Tomchei Temimim who had since been serving as the rabbi of the Bukharian Jews in Samarkand. Both were released from Siberia after Stalin's sudden death. "After ten years of exile, thank G-d, they freed me," he wrote in his diary.

I remember that in the early 1950s, my brother-in-law R. Eli Mishulovin told me that his friend Mottel Simcha's—as R. Simcha's son Mordechai was known—showed him a letter that his father had written to him from exile. In his absence, R. Simcha tried to provide some guidance for his only son, and instructed him how he should conduct himself. Among other things, he wrote that he should take responsibility for the family's livelihood and that he should assist in marrying off his sister. R. Simcha did not want them to wait until he returned from exile. The letter concludes with words of inspiration: "All the concealments are like passing clouds," R. Simcha wrote, "but Torah and *mitzvos* are eternal."

My mother had told me that R. Simcha's wife Raya had been unable to come to terms with his imprisonment. She was so devoted to him that if Simcha was not home, she said, why should she live? The doctors warned her to make peace with her lot because otherwise it could adversely affect her health, but Raya could not do otherwise. She left her children with her sister and began scrambling from place to place, trying to do everything she could to assist her husband, but it was all for naught. When she finally recognized that she could do no more to change his sentence, she returned home in despair. All attempts at consolation were to no avail, and in the end, the doctors' prognosis was realized; she had a stroke, which left half of her body paralyzed.

When R. Simcha was finally released and returned home, he was devastated to see his wife's condition.

Visiting R. Simcha in Tashkent

After his return from the prison camp, R. Simcha and his wife Raya resided in their son Mordechai's home in Tashkent. In the course of my travels for communal and business purposes, I occasionally visited Tashkent and I tried to visit R. Simcha while I was there.

The first time I met him, it felt like I was suddenly standing before a man who had emerged straight from legend. As I greeted him, all those stories began to race through my mind and I found myself too shy to even look at his face. On his part, he cut a surprisingly unassuming figure, but to me he was a giant of a man. He was the very embodiment of *mesiras nefesh*, of self-sacrifice, yet he acted with such simplicity and humility.

After talking to R. Simcha, I went inside to say hello to his wife, whom I knew from the time she had lived in Samarkand. As I mentioned, she was partially paralyzed and R. Simcha took care of her. She was unable to talk clearly and communicated mainly through hand motions.

She was happy to see me and recognized who I was. Although a stranger may not have been able to understand her, since I had heard her speak before, I could still understand what she was saying.

She pointed to herself and said: "Simcha returned home and look at what condition he found me in."

I couldn't control myself and tears welled up in my eyes. Here was a woman who had turned over heaven and earth to try to secure her husband's release, and look at what happened to her! I couldn't bear to stay any longer and quickly left the room in tears.

I thought to myself: Fountains of ink and forests of quills will not suffice to describe the dedication of these true heroes.

Generally when I went to their house, his son and daughter-in-law were at work and only R. Simcha and his wife were home. He would go out of his way to ensure that my stay was a pleasant one. But instead of first asking whether I was hungry, as soon as I arrived he would tell me to wash in order to eat and then serve me a meal himself. The truth is that since I couldn't buy food from the stores and had to suffice with what little I had brought from home, I was always hungry for a fresh homemade meal on these trips.

He always addressed me, using the respectful Yiddish plural, which made me feel very uncomfortable. I was just a twenty-year-old *bochur*, while R. Simcha had passed the fifty year mark—most of those years spent in self-sacrifice, with the brutal interrogations and the long imprisonment he had lived through—and after all that, he spoke to me so full of respect. But that was R. Simcha. He was refined and modest, always the first to greet someone and respectful of everyone.

On one visit, when I came out of the guest room, where R. Simcha would always receive me, to wash my hands for the meal, I noticed someone enter a side room and take food out of his bag. With his ragged cap and threadbare clothing, he seemed to me to be some poor vagrant down on his luck. It looked as though he was asking R.

Simcha about me, so I quickly went into the dining room so that the man couldn't see me.

When R. Simcha entered the dining room, he asked me: "Who are you hiding from?"

I asked him: "Who is that poor man?"

R. Simcha said, "That is Asher Sossonkin."

I had never heard that name before and I remained in my place, still wary of the guest.

R. Simcha realized that I didn't know the man by his last name, so he used his more familiar nickname, borrowed from his home town: "It's R. Asher *Batomer*…"

Aha! Now that I knew who it was, my fears evaporated.

A few minutes later, R. Asher came into the dining room, and I saw this special chassid for the first time in my life. I meekly went over to him and greeted him. R. Asher asked me: "Are you the son of Avremel Zaltzman?" When I acknowledged that I was, he asked me how my father was faring, and about the Samarkand community in general.

I recalled stories that I had heard about him from the older boys, about his fervent prayer and his outstanding love of his fellow Jew. He had also helped my father start a business of selling bread. Later I heard that R. Asher was so kindhearted and generous that when he would go to the *mikvah* and notice a Jew who did not have clean clothes, he would leave his own clothes for that person and take the other man's old garments. Perhaps that was what I saw during my visit with R. Simcha.

In 1964, R. Simcha was allowed to leave for Israel. Regrettably, his wife Raya died in Tashkent. His work with the Bukharian Jews, starting in 1926, had begun well before the arrival of large numbers of Ashkenazi Jews fleeing the Nazis in 1941.

Although some of the local Bukharian Jews sent by R. Simcha Gorodetzky to Tomchei Temimim had returned as full-fledged chassidim, who would regularly learn *Tanya* and *Likutei Torah* themselves, for the most part they lived on their own and were not actively involved in the Ashkenazi Lubavitch community. This separation was primarily due to differences in language and culture, but it was exacerbated by the wariness that had become second nature among Russian Jews in the terrible years under Stalin's regime. As youngsters, we had little to do with them; this would change over time. But there were several Bukharian Jews that I do remember from my youth whose relationship to our Chabad community was strong and memorable, most notably the remarkable R. Refael Chudaidatov.

CHAPTER 9

Our Bukharian Champion: R. Refael Chudaidatov

O ne of the most colorful and beloved individuals in Samarkand was a Bukharian Jew by the name of R. Refael Chudaidatov. My memories of him begin from my early childhood years. R. Refael lived in the Bagishomol quarter on the outskirts of the New City not far from the train station at the city limits. At that time, we lived in the Old City, about eight kilometers away.

R. Refael, who always sought to spend time with Chabad chassidim, would cover the distance on his bicycle. I remember watching him pedal on his bicycle through the narrow alleyways of the Old City with his long silver beard blowing in the wind. The sight of an older person on a bike was peculiar at first, but that was his mode of transportation; in general, he was almost as active in his older years as in his youth.

R. Refael's roots in the Bukharian community and his deep desire to be involved with the Chabad community left him somewhere in the middle. Wary of possible informers and even cautious of those within their own community, the chassidim did not run to embrace him, and to a certain extent they disregarded him; meanwhile, the Bukharian community treated him as though he had defected to the Ashkenazic camp.

Nabbed by the Police

R. Refael was born in 1898. In accordance with the Bukharian tradition of marrying young, his wife Rochel was only thirteen when they married; he was nineteen. I knew his wife well; she was a pious, clever woman of fine character. Shortly after the marriage, R. Refael began working as a merchant. At that time the Communists were still only taking tentative steps in Russia and hadn't advanced into the Muslim countries of Central Asia. But after a protracted battle with the Muslim Basmatchi resistance movement—*basmatch* being a Turkic word for "bandit"—they invaded Samarkand and began implementing their new rules, and of course persecuting and robbing the wealthy citizens.

R. Refael had obtained a certain document from the government certifying that he was an international businessman, along with a permit to move freely abroad. This way, he was able to continue doing business, including his dealings in Bukharia which was still a separate, independent country; the Communists incorporated it into the new Soviet republic of Uzbekistan in 1924. One time, before one of his trips to Bukharia, one of the *chachamim*—the "wise men," or leaders of the community—Chacham Yosef, confided to him that he was in possession of a significant trove of gold, silver, and pearls. His grandfather had bequeathed it to his father and after adding to it his father bequeathed it to him; he had also added to it over the years. Since the Communists had taken over Samarkand, Chacham Yosef was afraid they would try to get their hands on his wealth and he wanted to send it to his relatives in independent Bukharia. With his special permits and status as an international businessman, R. Refael wasn't checked so thoroughly at the borders, so Chacham Yosef wanted him to transport his treasure to Bukharia.

By nature a good-hearted person with tremendous trust in Hashem, he did not think twice and immediately agreed to do it. When Chacham Yosef asked him whether he realized the extent of the danger, R. Refael replied, "Our sages say that someone sent to do a *mitzvah* is not harmed." Knowing R. Refael, I can be certain that he actually considered doing the mission a privilege.

When R. Refael was about to leave, his acquaintances asked him to take along an orphan boy to his relatives in Bukharia so that they could send him to the Land of Israel. R. Refael readily agreed to help with this too and took the boy and the treasure chest with him to the train station.

Before boarding the train, he managed to get in another *mitzvah*. A Jew, whom he did not recognize, placed a small valise into his hand and begged of him, "You are a businessman, and they won't search you. Do me a favor and take this suitcase from me for a few minutes. Take it with you onto the train and I'll take it back once we are aboard." R. Refael agreed and went to board the train, laden with good deeds.

Before he entered his compartment, two policemen suddenly approached him and told him that he was under arrest and ordered him to follow them. R. Refael was very frightened, but did not lose his cool. He firmly told the policemen that he was an international merchant with business dealings in Bukharia and he could not miss the train. The policemen were unimpressed and began to drag him toward the police station.

In the meantime, one of the policemen disappeared, and only one policeman remained, still with a firm grip on R. Refael as he tugged him toward the police station. On the way, the boy accompanying R. Refael asked him, in Bukharian, what the policemen wanted from them. When the Russian officer heard the boy speaking to R. Refael in a foreign dialect, he began shouting, "What's he saying?" and he slapped the boy so hard that blood began to flow from his nose.

The policeman, afraid that he would be accused of assaulting a child for no reason, quickly went to fetch some water to wash the child's face. At precisely that moment, a wagon passed by with two Jews R. Refael recognized who were on their way to Bukharia. He quickly threw Chacham Yosef's treasure into the wagon and asked them to pass on the box to the Chacham in Bukharia. The treasure, which eventually reached its destination, was saved from the police, and so was he.

Miraculously, the policeman did not notice the box that had been thrown into the wagon and after returning with water and washing the boy's face, he continued with the two of them to the police station. At the station, R. Refael began to make a commotion and cried, "What do you want from me? I am a certified business-man with business to conduct in Bukharia and because of you I missed the train!"

With the country's abysmal economic state in those days, the government was intent on confiscating as much money and valu-ables as from their citizens as they could. The police, then, were unfazed by R. Refael's protestations and insisted on examining his suitcase. R. Refael said that the suitcase was not his and that a stranger had given it to him, claiming that he needed to use the bathroom and would return momentarily.

"We already know," they said as they wrested the suitcase from him. As it turned out, the policemen had been following that man all along. With the suitcase in their hands, they calmed down and released both R. Refael and the boy.

Jailed as a Traitor

To further expropriate their people's wealth, the Communist au-thorities regularly demanded that citizens "sell" them their gold and precious stones in exchange for worthless rubles. They had all sorts of methods to coerce people to sell them their valuable metals.

One day, the authorities called for R. Refael and said, "Since we know you to be a certified merchant with freedom of movement and other privileges, we trust you fully. And, because we consider you to be one of ours, it's now your job to convince other Jews to cooperate with us and sell us their valuables. In our estimation, you can obtain at least half a ton of gold for us from them."

When they finished their speech, they brought in a relative of his whom they had incarcerated in an attempt to extricate his valu-ables and told R. Refael to go off with him to a side room in order to convince him to accede to their demands. When the two were alone in the room, the relative said that he was considering giving them a fifth of his property so that perhaps they would leave him alone. He begged R. Refael to advise him how to proceed.

R. Refael, who knew that their desire for wealth knew no bounds, told him not to give a single ounce of gold. If he capitulated, R. Refael reasoned, they would torture him until he gave them everything he owned.

The two men were unaware that on the other side of the thin wall sat an investigator who was listening intently to every word that was said. After they finished their conversation, the interrogators called in R. Refael and began to yell at him, "We thought you were loyal to us! It turns out that you are a traitor and you are working against the interests of the country!"

R. Refael desperately tried to wiggle out and claim that they hadn't understood his words and he had meant just the opposite. They didn't buy his excuses and locked him up.

During his stay in prison, his wife came to visit him often, bringing along packages of food. On one of her visits he managed to tell her, "Go to Tashkent and tell Afanasyev I've been arrested."

Over the years, R. Refael had formed good ties with various politically influential people. One of them was a Russian gentile by the name of Afanasyev, who had previously been a high-ranking official in Samarkand until he was transferred to an even more senior position in Tashkent.

R. Refael's wife managed to locate the government office where Afanasyev worked and went there with her brother-in-law Tzion, R. Refael's brother. They decided to wait for the man outside of the building at the end of the workday.

Before long he came out, and the two of them told him of R. Refael's arrest. He listened intently and said that they should return to his office the following morning. The next day, he handed them a letter to pass on to one of the ruling officials in Samarkand. He warned them to take care of the letter since, if the contents were disclosed, both he and they would be shot.

They returned to Samarkand and transmitted the letter to the designated party and within a few days R. Refael was released.

After he came home, he told his family that one night that week he had seen an old man in his dream who told him, "Your wife is pregnant. When she gives birth to a girl, name her Yeshuah."

Several months later, his wife gave birth to a baby girl and they called her Yeshuah. Yeshuah is the mother of the chassid R. Moshe Chaim Cohen, who later became one of the outstanding students in our yeshiva in Samarkand and currently resides in Crown Heights.

R. Refael the Agronomist

Before R. Refael moved to the Bagishomol district, he lived in the Jewish ghetto of the Old City. Seeking to ingratiate themselves with the Communist authorities, many Jews in that area would inform on one another, Heaven help us. The situation was so bad that a secret relayed under the most private conditions would be known to the government the next day.

R. Refael, who couldn't stand this ugly behavior, abandoned his house in the ghetto and moved to the New City, to the distant Bagishomol quarter that at the time was nearly outside of the city altogether.

In those days, the government in Samarkand turned a blind eye, to a certain extent, to members of the clergy, such as the rabbis, the community *shochet,* or the *mohel.* Generally, they sufficed with marking these individuals as citizens "stripped of all rights" and banned from holding government jobs. Still, they were encouraged to work, in order to bring revenue to the government.

R. Refael took advantage of this opportunity and founded a Soviet-style agricultural settlement. Located about twenty kilometers from the city, the settlement contained vineyards for wine manufacture and a factory for drying fruit. As an extension of this settlement, he obtained a large plot of land in the Bagishomol area, where he planted additional vineyards and built another fruit-drying factory, along with large storage houses for the fruit. In these places, he hired Jewish employees and paid them ample salaries.

Apparently, his great success aroused the envy of the government and they dispatched inspectors to find problems to complain about. Since the fruit would ripen at the end of summer, it once happened that the fruit arrived at the factory during the High Holidays, at a time when R. Refael and his Jewish employees did not work. Some informers used this opportunity to whisper to the authorities that the fruit was outside of the factories and might rot.

The inspector sent by the government arrived at the factory on Simchas Torah and saw R. Refael and all of his employees celebrating and not working. R. Refael welcomed the inspector, served him some vodka until he was drunk, and then sent him home.

R. Refael, who knew that he would soon be accused of activities that were against the economic interests of a Communist society, decided to beat them at their own game. At that time, there was a serious shortage of truck tires that was crippling a number of local industries. As soon as the High Holidays were over, R. Refael traveled to Tashkent and used his connections to buy a large quantity of tires. A short time after he returned to Samarkand with the tires, he was summoned for an interrogation at the head office overseeing his factory.

As expected, they accused him of celebrating a Jewish holiday with his workers instead of working on behalf of the Soviet economy. R. Refael shouted angrily, "You are not ashamed to accuse me of lack of concern for the economy? You all know about the tire shortage that nobody was doing anything about—I was the only one who cared enough to make a special trip to Tashkent and bring hundreds of tires here, and now this is how you treat me?"

Luckily, they accepted this and instead turned on R. Refael's accuser.

The settlement and the fruit factory were a source of livelihood for dozens of Jews. They did not have to work on Shabbos and holidays and they earned up to ten times the going salary. R. Refael was a very talented businessman. He purchased extremely cheap fruits from Asia and, once dried, sold them throughout Siberia for a good price and a tidy profit. This enabled him to pay his workers

fifty rubles a day when a typical employee earned five to seven rubles a day. With the remaining money he invested in various farming tools.

When the Joint Distribution Committee found out about the
Jewish enterprise they decided to get involved. To help, they bought
tractors and other heavy tools for working the ground.

Several years went by until the Communists heard that R. Refael's thriving settlement ran like a capitalist operation. The employees were earning too much money, and it had the support of the
Joint—a bourgeoisie Jewish organization connected with Ameri-
cans and imperialists. The results were swift and painful. The government announced the closing of the settlement and destroyed the
entire operation.

During World War II, R. Refael used warehouses to shelter
hundreds of the Polish Jewish refugees that had flooded the city and
even supplied them with food. Along with Dzura Niazov and other
Bukharian Jews, he went from house to house asking, chastising,
and begging people to pledge towards a food fund for their starving
brothers and sisters. Rather than wait for the refugees to come to
them for help, they would meet them at the train station and immediately arrange lodging for them in Bukharian Jewish homes.

They say that R. Refael would take from the food his wife prepared for the family and feed it to the refugees. When she complained and asked, "What should I give our children to eat?" He
replied, "Our children have parents who take care of them, but these
Jews have nobody."

A Painful Disappointment

Tragically, our tremendous fear of informers was occasionally the
cause of some very painful incidents. In the early years, when we
hosted *bochurim* learning in our home, we tried to hold any communal gatherings in remote locations so that unwanted guests
would stay away. The windows were always covered on the inside

with blankets so that no one could see into the house or hear anything from within.

We once held such a gathering. a *farbrengen* in honor of 19th of
Kislev (a holiday marking the liberation of Rabbi Schneur Zalman
of Liadi, the first rebbe of Chabad) in the Old City, at the home of R.
Dovid Mishulovin. Since R. Dovid's house was located quite a distance from our own, we felt assured that no one would discover us.
It was a dark and cold night and a downpour of rain pelted against
the window panes. At a little before midnight, we suddenly heard a
loud knock at the gate of the courtyard. We instantly fell silent and
strained our ears, waiting for the knocking to stop so we could continue the *farbrengen*. The knocking persisted, then intensified. We
decided that all of the younger attendees should hide behind a
closet and R. Dovid's wife, Sarah, would go out and see who was
knocking so late at night.

The others remained in the room and peeked from a tiny crack
in the window. We saw Sarah arguing with someone. After two long
minutes she returned and reported that it was R. Refael Chudaidatov, who had come from Bagishomol to attend the *farbrengen*. Our
hearts melted. He wasn't a young man, and he had to travel by bus,
then walk for twenty minutes in the pouring rain from the bus stop
on the cold and dark streets until he reached the Mishulovins'. After
all that effort, he was turned away.

It wasn't easy for us to return to the table and continue with the
farbrengen. The *bochurim* came out of their hiding place, but in our
hearts we despaired of this terrible exile that was causing us to fear
each other.

To R. Refael's credit, it should be noted, although he suspected–
and sometimes saw clearly—that we were hiding things from him,
he never got angry or offended. He understood us and knew that we
were frightened of everyone.

Saved by a Prayer

R. Refael's son, Shemtov, worked in the agricultural sector of Samarkand rearing sheep. When some gentiles once fabricated a story about him, claiming that he wasn't meeting the government's expectations, he was duly arrested and interrogated. R. Refael had good connections with senior officials in town who were capable of helping to secure his son's release from jail, but at the time, he was in a resort in the Crimea together with his wife.

Due to the seriousness of the situation, the family informed him of Shemtov's arrest via telegram. Since they were afraid to write the details of what had happened, they merely wrote that Shemtov was "sick"—a code word for getting arrested—and that they were waiting anxiously for him to return.

After sending the telegram, they awaited R. Refael's arrival, but days passed and he did not show up. In the interim, Shemtov was suddenly released.

The next day, R. Refael arrived in Samarkand in elevated spirits. "What's new?" he asked. "Did they release Shemtov yet?"

The family told him about Shemtov's release. But why had he delayed in coming and why was he in good spirits before knowing that his son was released?

With his usual smile, he told them, "After I got the telegram, I thought, how will I help when I get to Samarkand? I might be successful and I might not. I opted to travel directly to Rostov to the Rebbe Rashab, where I prostrated myself on his grave and told the Rebbe what had happened."

Then, speaking in the third person, as he often did, he continued: "Refael stood and cried, 'My son was arrested. Help us, Rebbe!' I davened and cried and I begged the Rebbe to intervene on High. Refael was sure that his prayer was accepted and Hashem would help. I returned with a peaceful heart, confident that the Rebbe would do everything to release my son from jail."

A Cup of Water that Saved the Day

R. Refael was the kind of person that if he heard that help was needed with any Jewish-related matter, he would immediately offer his assistance.

In Samarkand there was one *mikvah*—the ritual bath essential for the perpetuation of religious Jewish life—in official operation. It was called "R. Abba Pliskin's Mikvah," after the chassid R. Abba Pliskin, who took care of it during World War II. As a rule, official Soviet law did not forbid religious practice outright, so most of the attacks against religion had to be made under pretense. So it was at the time of the notorious Doctors' Plot, when the government took advantage of the atmosphere of incitement against the Jews to close such institutions, including our *mikvah* in Samarkand.

At first, people went to other cities in the vicinity that still had a functional kosher *mikvah*. In time, G-d-fearing families constructed their own secret *mikvahs*, but these had a big disadvantage: Afraid that word would get out, these families were unable to tell anyone outside of their immediate circle about them.

I came across one such secret bathhouse when I stayed at the home of a member of the Chabad community in Tashkent. On Shabbos morning my host said, "Let's go to the *mikvah*."

I asked, "Where, here?"

He brought me into the kitchen and said, "Can you guess where it is?"

I didn't know what to tell him. How could I guess? I saw an ordinary kitchen and that was all.

Then he raised the linoleum to reveal a row of wooden boards. I immediately understood that underneath the boards was a *mikvah*.

In the 1960s, once our fear had subsided in the wake of Stalin's death, the young men in Samarkand decided that the time had come to publicly reopen one of the local ritual baths so that it would be available for the benefit of all. In order to open the *mikvah*, the government had to approve, but we were all afraid to get involved. R. Refael agreed to make the request.

There were a few advantages in R. Refael doing this. Firstly, he was a longtime resident of the city and spoke the local language; secondly, he was an older man, and most of the government's religious battles were directed against religious education of the young. Finally, he had tremendous trust in Hashem—*bitachon*—and was not the least bit daunted by the government. "Why are you so worried? You need more *bitachon*," he would often say.

The government officials who listened to R. Refael's request immediately began to look for reasons to deny it. Their main opposition was that health laws demanded extremely high hygiene standards for public venues. The water would have to be changed after each person immersed in it, and since this wasn't very practical, the *mikvah* could not be opened. R. Refael maintained that the *mikvah* was up to the sanitary requirements and if they wanted to be sure they should send someone to check it.

After much effort, the government announced that they would be sending an inspection committee to determine whether the bath was up to the health regulations and could be opened to the public. Needless to say, R. Refael was there when they arrived. The inspectors, who came with the goal of not allowing anything to open, immediately said that the water was dirty and people could not immerse in it. When R. Refael heard this, he protested and claimed that the water was perfectly clean and they were just making things up. For emphasis, he took a cupful of water from the *mikvah*, said a blessing out loud, and drank it.

R. Refael's willingness to unhesitatingly drink the water left the committee members speechless. In the end, they allowed the *mikvah* to open.

Permission from Moscow to Build a *Mikvah*

Towards the end of the 1960s, the government began to provide visas to leave the country and the Soviet terror finally abated. R. Refael wanted to take advantage of this change and build a new *mikvah.* Until then, R. Abba's reopened *mikvah,* while tolerated by the authorities, remained somewhat semi-official; employees of the government were still too nervous to use it. By building alongside the government-approved shul in the Old City, R. Refael thought he could have the government recognize the *mikvah* as an approved ritual bath for the city.

Since all religious matters were officially under the authority of each city's cultural department, R. Refael met with the department head in Samarkand and asked for permission. Although, as I mentioned, there was no legal problem in building a *mikvah,* the official was afraid to give R. Refael a permit. He advised him to travel to Moscow, to the main office for cultural and religious affairs in the Soviet Union and ask there. "If in Moscow they give you permission, then you have a green light to build and nobody here will dare to countermand instructions issued in Moscow. And between me and you, why would the department head in Moscow care about what is going on in distant Samarkand? Surely he will give you permission."

R. Refael accepted his advice and traveled to Moscow. He stayed with his brother, Tzion Chudaidatov, who ran the large Hotel Uzbekistan, where Uzbek government officials usually stayed when in Moscow, as did other influential people. Thus the hotel afforded Tzion good contacts with the government in Moscow.

Through his connections, Tzion arranged a meeting for his brother with one of the bureaucrats in the main office for cultural and religious affairs. R. Refael told the official that he had come from Uzbekistan because Jewish law requires ritual immersion in water. To this end, he wanted to build a *mikvah* in the yard of the Samarkand shul. The bureaucrat, who did not care what went on in a Muslim state so far from Moscow, printed a permit for R. Refael on his department's official stationery.

R. Refael wanted to be sure that he wouldn't be bothered once he started construction, so he decided to obtain an additional permit from the relevant local department. To do so, he gathered a minyan of Jews, among them R. Yaakov Buroshanski, and asked them to accompany him. They would confirm that the Jewish law dictates that men immerse before prayer—the implication being that the *mikvah* was primarily for the old men who already frequented the shul.

Despite their fear of the government, they agreed to go with R. Refael after he convinced them that he was leading the group and they were only there to confirm the dictates of Jewish law. When the group appeared in the municipal office, the department head told them that once they had received a permit from Moscow there was nothing to be nervous about.

R. Refael did not delay and immediately sent his son Moshiach to obtain bricks and other building materials. He hired workers and they began the construction.

The KGB Gets Involved

The informants who regularly prayed at the shul, whose job it was to report on anything unusual, soon told the KGB about the ongoing construction. R. Refael received a summons from the KGB offices, where the head of Jewish affairs, the accursed Tatar Aktchurin greeted him with eyes that glowed from anger. He forbade R. Refael from continuing to build and even threatened him with negative repercussions.

Unafraid, R. Refael said, "I have a permit from the Moscow office for culture and religion and the head of the local department gave me permission to build as well. You haven't the authority to stop me."

R. Refael knew that the two entities—the department for culture and religion and the Jewish department of the KGB—were at odds with one another. The officials in the department for culture and religion considered themselves officially responsible for all religious matters in the city, while the KGB considered themselves in charge of all aspects of life in the country with the authority to override official laws.

Aktchurin decided to stir up the local populace against R. Refael and published a nasty and slanderous article in the local paper under the heading, "The Charlatan Refuses to Desist." The article included a litany of R. Refael's supposed sins and crimes, from religious activities to his ties with Zionists, and so on; all completely fabricated, but standard fare, and an easy way to turn the accused into a political criminal.

In light of these developments, R. Refael decided to travel to Moscow and consult with his brother Tzion. His brother was well acquainted with a Jew by the name of Lifschitz, who was the right-hand man of the head of the Communist Party of Uzbekistan, Sharaf Rashidov.

Rashidov lived a life of indulgence, leaving the actual work of running the government to Lifschitz, the de facto leader. Tzion called Lifschitz and after briefly explaining to him about the *mikvah*, Lifschitz promised to help R. Refael. He called the heads of the local Party committee and censured them, "What do you want from this Jew? Leave him alone!"

In the meantime, the besmirching of R. Refael had adversely affected his son Bechor's financial future. He was studying neurology in Moscow at the time and had just been sent to serve as the head of the department of neurology in Samarkand's central hospital. When he showed up with the written appointment he had received in Moscow, the hospital administration told him that with his father branded as an opponent of the government, they could not accept him.

Bechor tried to appease them: His father belonged to the old generation, he said, and how could they hold him back because of his father's views? After all of his attempts failed, he tried reaching out to Lifschitz. When they met, Bechor began to apologize for his father's actions. But this time, Lifschitz didn't like his apologetic tone and responded sharply, "You're acting contrite for your father's actions? You ought to give him a medal for his contribution to the economy of the Soviet Union! In the first years following the Revolution, he started a number of Soviet *kolkhozes*—we owe him a debt of gratitude!"

In the end, the KGB prevailed and Bechor was forced to leave Samarkand.

An Exit Visa in Place of an Apology

Apparently, something had started to move in the meantime. The rebuke dispensed from the highest Party echelons had frightened the local bureau head. He met with R. Refael and wanted to conclude the matter peacefully. R. Refael said, "I am ready for peace but first you have to publish a retraction in the paper, saying that all the accusations against me were lies." The man refused. "You want the Communists to apologize and declare that they were mistaken and you were right? That will never happen!"

R. Refael realized that things had ended in a stalemate. Once the KGB had publicly opposed the *mikvah*, they could not allow it to be built, even at the expense of conflict with other government officials. Instead, he figured he might benefit from the situation in another way. He said, "If you are unwilling to apologize, at least grant an exit visa for me and my family. How can I live here after you've blackened my name?"

The Party head, eager to conclude the matter as soon as possible, agreed to this request and promised to expedite his request for a visa.

Love for His Fellow Jews

R. Refael loved his fellow Jew to a degree that I have not seen in anyone else. He related to everyone in the community like a member of his family: When told of a *mazel tov* for someone he knew in Samarkand, Tashkent, or somewhere else, he was genuinely happy. A pleased smile would spread across his face, tears of joy glistened in his eyes, and he would bless Hashem for that Jew's special occasion. When he heard less wonderful news about a family that he knew, he cried. At a funeral, he would go right over to the coffin, beg for forgiveness, and recite chapters of *Tehillim* in tears, as if the deceased was a close relative of his.

His fine custom of asking for something to eat or drink whenever he went to someone's house was well known. By making the appropriate blessing before eating, he explained, he left a blessing in the house. He would do this everywhere, even when visiting a shul. The Chabad community in Nachalas Har Chabad remembers this special custom as well, since he kept it up even after immigrating to Israel and settling there.

Although R. Refael had been close to R. Simcha Gorodetzky during his years in Samarkand and maintained a warm connection to the Lubavitch community, he was not a born and bred Lubavitcher chassid. Nor had he ever learned in Tomchei Temimim. Nonetheless, his Chassidic spirit and devotion to the Rebbe were remarkable—and never was this clearer than when he moved to Israel. He had always dreamed of moving to the Holy Land and living the remainder of his years in Jerusalem. He had relatives there, and when his daughter began attending university there after they arrived, his wife wanted to live there as well. The Bukharian community of Jerusalem waited impatiently for R. Refael's arrival. But when he heard that the Rebbe wanted new immigrants to settle in Nachalas Har Chabad, R. Refael did not hesitate. With astonishing simplicity, he changed all of his plans and life ambitions to move there. He did not settle where he thought it was suitable and comfortable, but unquestioningly carried out the Rebbe's wishes.

R. Refael received an incredible reception when he arrived in Israel in 1971. Representatives from a host of different communities, political parties, and movements, including the Agudath Israel party, came to visit him. They invited him to speak at their conventions or work for them, explaining how important and holy their work was, and they promised pay and prestige. Not all that familiar on the differences between parties, R. Refael admitted to them, in all honesty, that he believed everything they said, but he would soon be traveling to New York. Once there, he would ask the Rebbe for his opinion and do whatever the Rebbe advised.

An Incident at the Mount of Olives

R. Refael was a Jew with simple faith in miracles. He knew that his grandfather had purchased several adjacent plots for the family on the Mount of Olives in the 1920s, long before the establishment of the State, and was buried there. Once in Israel, relatives explained to him that after Mount of Olives had fallen into the hands of Jordanians in 1948, they desecrated the gravesites there and made it impossible to identify many of the graves, even after Israel regained control. After the Six-Day War, the relatives looked for the family's plot but failed to find it. They bought a plot in a different cemetery and suggested that R. Refael buy plots next to theirs.

R. Refael decided to check things out for himself. Although over fifty years had passed since his grandfather had been buried, he was not deterred. This is what he reported afterwards:

"I arrived at the Mount of Olives and walked among the graves. I looked for some sort of clue, but found nothing. After several hours I was tired and I felt despondent. I continued walking among the graves with tears falling from my eyes. Suddenly I saw an old man. I did not know where he came from. He asked me, 'What happened? Why are you crying?'

"I told him that I was looking for my family's plot. To my great surprise he told me, 'Don't cry. I know where it is.' He took me by the hand and led me to the right section. Needless to say, I fell upon the graves in tears, but then I remembered the man who had brought me there and wanted to thank him. When I looked for him he was nowhere to be seen. He had disappeared!"

After examining the area, he saw that there were two plots available nearby. His wife Rochel had always spoken of her desire to be buried beside her husband, but R. Refael had never committed to the idea, since in Samarkand it was customary to bury men and women separately. However, after he found his grandfather's plot and had seen the two empty spaces, he realized that it was a sign that his wife was right.

CHAPTER 10

Making Matzah

It is a well-known principle in kosher law that a small amount of forbidden food can become *batel b'shishim*, of no significance. That is to say, if one part of non-kosher food gets lost in sixty parts of kosher, it is considered legally nullified and the entire admixture may be eaten. But, with regards to food prohibited on Pesach—*chametz*—there is no such allowance. If even a trace of the stuff becomes absorbed into food on Pesach, all of the food is forbidden.

Flour can of course become *chametz* once it has been in contact with any moisture for a mere eighteen minutes, at which point we suspect that it has begun to ferment and leaven. For these reasons, G-d-fearing Jews are especially meticulous on Pesach, and even outlandish-seeming precautions against eating *chametz* have their place and legal justification.

Those who are particular in their observance of Jewish law, chassidim especially, are careful to bake matzah for the festival of Pesach specifically from wheat that has been guarded against any contact with water from the moment it has been harvested. This matzah is referred to as *shmurah* matzah—literally, protected or guarded matzah. Back then in Russia, with the wheat fields owned by the government, an intricate and secretive operation was necessary to obtain even a small quantity of flour for our purposes.

During the war, with the city bursting with refugees, and while famine and deprivation plagued the land, it was unfeasible to even consider having *shmurah* matzah. We were simply thankful to have the opportunity to bake regular matzos together with the local Bukharian Jews with the few halachic stringencies we were able to incorporate into the preparation and baking processes. With the flight of refugees at the conclusion of the war, those of us who remained in Samarkand were suddenly forced to manage all Jewish matters on our own, in addition to the physical and monetary difficulties we already faced.

Eventually, a band of older Chassidic *bochurim*, including myself, decided to take on the task of matzah production. We purchased wheat in the local market, exerting maximal effort to acquire the cleanest unwashed kernels, seeing as it was common among the Uzbeki merchants to wash the wheat before bringing it to market. We would then painstakingly inspect the kernels for worms and other refuse. There was no electricity at home, so we worked by the light of a kerosene lamp, calling to mind the Talmudic depiction of women checking kernels by the light of the lamps used for the Sukkos festival.

After inspecting the wheat, we would bring it to a mill powered by a waterfall, in the outskirts of the city. Like all property in Russia, the mill was government owned, so it was illegal for individuals to grind their own wheat there, and certainly not for religious purposes. After a hefty bribe, the owner of the mill, an Uzbeki by the name of Osman Aka, agreed to give us possession of the mill for two days.

Cleaning the large millstones was hard work. The base and runner stone, as the two millstones are called, weighed about 500 kilograms each. With great exertion, we detached them and began scraping them with small sticks and a special brush. Osman, afraid that we would destroy the stones, would stand to the side, pleading with us to stop scraping so hard. We spent a large portion of the time we had possession of the mill scrubbing and scouring the thousands of crevices in the millstones. The remaining time—about two hours —was spent grinding the wheat.

The day that we kashered the mill was a momentous event. A large number of community members, including yeshiva boys and even the small children, would trek up to the mill and help in the process.

R. Feivish Genkin was a simple Jew from Samarkand and a manufacturer of ovens by trade. Despite his simplicity, R. Feivish was unusually punctilious when it came to performing a *mitzvah*. The extent of his scrupulousness was such that even R. Berke Chein, who was highly discerning in his observance of kosher law, agreed to eat in the Genkin home. R. Feivish owned a gasoline-operated blowtorch that he would bring to the mill. After we concluded scraping out all the nooks and crannies, he would pass his torch over the cracking and scorch any remaining particles of wheat. Only then was the mill ready to be used to grind the wheat for our matzah.

It was only in the 1950s that we were able to obtain some wheat that had been watched from harvest. There was a righteous and G-d-fearing woman in Georgia who grew wheat in a small field near her house, specifically for making *shmurah* matzah. We made contact with her and every year, after the harvest, she would send us seven to eight kilograms of wheat. She received similar orders from Lubavitch communities in several cities in Russia. She would parcel the wheat in paper sacks, ensure they were well wrapped, and send them via airmail. We usually received the package after Sukkos.

We purchased a large hand-powered coffee grinder with iron millstones and used it to grind the wheat. The wheat had to pass through the grinder many times in order to produce fine flour, and between uses, we would tighten the metal disks to draw them closer together. Ultimately, from the eight kilograms of wheat that the Georgian woman sent us, we generated six kilograms, give or take, of sifted flour.

Since grinding wheat by hand demanded tremendous physical exertion, we spread the work over several weeks. Every Thursday night a group of *bochurim* convened at the home of a member of the community and while one would grind the wheat, the others would study something of the Rebbe's teachings and *farbreng* together.

Those evenings had a special aura that could have only been generated by the painstaking care we took in executing this *mitzvah*.

After a quarter of an hour, the *bochur* grinding the wheat would grow weary and another would take his place. It was a very slow and measured process; each week we would grind just over a kilogram of wheat. That is how we spent long winter nights until we had completed grinding all eight kilograms.

By the end of the process, we would have five kilograms of matzos, prepared to the most scrupulous standards. It was enough to supply each of us with the minimum amount required for the Seder nights, but generally it was not enough for the rest of the holiday meals. This made it difficult to observe all of the halachic provisions associated with the traditional festive meal. *Kiddush,* for example, must be recited in conjunction with a meal, which normally means eating matzah right afterwards. Instead, after making *kiddush,* we would drink another glass of wine to stand in for the matzah.

One year, having reached the middle of Pesach with only two matzos remaining, I went to my friend Michoel Mishulovin and asked him whether he had any extra so I could have two matzos for the Shabbos meals during the intermediate days of the holiday. It turned out that he had just one matzah left. When I heard that, I told him to take one of my matzos instead.

A Motorcycle Motor and a Coffee Grinder

The tedious, sluggish output of the coffee grinder troubled me for some time and I struggled to find a creative solution to this predicament.

In those days, almost everyone had a motorcycle. It was the most convenient means of inner-city transportation. One day, I thought of connecting a motorcycle motor to the coffee grinder, which would drastically reduce the labor needed to operate the mill. I replaced the handle of the grinder with a wheel and then connected the wheel to the motor. This enabled the disks of the grinder to churn very quickly.

I put this mechanism together at the Mishulovin home, since they had volunteered a room for the cause and were one of the trustworthy families in Samarkand. Moreover, the racket made by a motorised grinder would likely arouse the unwelcome curiosity of neighbors. The Mishulovins' house, however, was at the end of a street, with its walls facing a cemetery. We didn't need to worry about quiet neighbors like those.

I was thrilled that my innovation proved successful and the mill ground the wheat quickly and efficiently. The setback was that the motor began to heat up dramatically and needed water poured over it to cool off. Of course, we were afraid to do so, since the water would come in contact with the wheat and render the entire batch of flour unfit for use. Instead, we would periodically turn off the motor and wait for it to cool off by itself. Despite the difficulties, within a short amount of time we were able to grind nearly all the wheat and we were ecstatic.

Unfortunately, our joy was short-lived. The device was efficient, but the axle turning the mill was rotating too rapidly and towards the end of the process, it suddenly blew out. As the engineer of the contraption, I felt terribly guilty. We were relieved that at least we had already ground most of the wheat, but we needed to devise a new and better plan for the following year.

Watching the Harvest

In the meantime, we came up with a new idea: As in Georgia, summers in Samarkand invariably had no rain at all. If we could only obtain a large amount of locally produced wheat, we could easily protect it from water after the harvest and have enough wheat for all of our needs.

We asked R. Refael Chudaidatov to shoulder this new undertaking. He knew the language of the local farmers and was familiar with the Uzbek mentality. He also knew all the Samarkand collective farms, or *kolkhozes*, and would be quick to befriend their owners. My brother

Berel had a late model motorcycle and he offered to drive R. Refael, if he wasn't afraid to ride with him. R. Refael smiled at my brother and said, "Afraid? I have driven such a bike before you were even born! Let's go." They concocted a story to explain to the farmers why they needed the wheat and they left in search of a *kolkhoz*.

The closest *kolkhoz* where wheat was grown was thirty kilometers from Samarkand. When they arrived there, the Muslim Uzbeks were in the midst of eating their midday lunch of pita bread and green tea with chunks of sugar. As soon as they noticed R. Refael, with his flowing white beard, they stood up and honored him by inclining their heads and shaking his hand.

On top of having to convince the farmers to supply them with the wheat, and explaining why they needed such a large amount of wheat, R. Refael and Berel had another challenge. Eating matzah at the Seder constitutes the fulfillment of a biblical commandment, and as such, a Jew is required to be directly involved with all of the stages of its preparation, with the express intent of doing so for the purpose of the *mitzvah*. For R. Refael and Berel, this meant they needed to personally sit on the tractor during the harvest, while formally declaring that the harvest was "for the sake of the *mitzvah* of matzah." To this end, R. Refael concocted an entire story so they would not suspect this to be something related to religion: "I am soon marrying off my grandson. There is an ancient custom among Jews that at a grandson's wedding, all guests are served *lepyoshki* (flat bread) baked from wheat cut by the groom's grandfather himself." R. Refael then added with a wink, "Of course, we will pay you well for it." The bribe was necessary since the law did not allow a *kolkhoz* to sell any wheat to private citizens, as it was considered embezzlement of state property.

The chairman of the *kolkhoz* was amenable to this special request and told them that when the wheat would ripen in another two weeks, they could come and harvest it themselves. After agreeing on financial compensation, they returned to Samarkand.

Two weeks later, as the two prepared to leave, we started to plan a way to move the large quantity of wheat to Samarkand. Traveling by train with sacks of wheat was not an option because police officers would check the passengers and their packages. If they inspected the sacks, it would seem to them that we were transporting stolen wheat to sell, which is a criminal offense. In the end, we rented a truck that belonged to someone we knew. We cleaned the floor of the truck thoroughly, bought ten new bags, and R. Refael and Berel set off. Arriving at the *kolkhoz,* they were greeted by a sea of ripe wheat swaying in the wind, ready for harvest. As agreed upon, they climbed onto the tractor, proclaimed *"lesheim matzos mitzvah,"* and began the harvest. The tractor did all the work and at enormous speed: it cut the wheat, removed the husks, and shot out pure kernels of wheat. Within a half hour, the new sacks were filled with two hundred kilograms of wheat. Berel said that it was the first time they saw the work of a combine harvester. It was amazing to see wheat flowing in such large quantities directly from the field into the sacks.

This arrangement continued throughout the ensuing years until our departure from Russia. Each year, a few of us would travel to the *kolkhoz* to harvest the wheat.

On one occasion, Yitzchak Mishulovin went along with R. Refael for the cutting of the wheat. On the return journey, R. Refael sat near the driver and Yitzchak sat atop the sacks in the back of the truck in order to guard the wheat. From his perch above the sacks, Yitzchak suddenly felt a few cool drops of water land on him. Lifting his eyes, he saw that the skies were clear, so he yelled at R. Refael to halt so they could check where the water was coming from.

The driver refused to stop as he was afraid the police would discover the undocumented merchandise, but Yitzchak pounded on the roof until he came to a halt. It turned out that near the driver's seat there was a basin of water used for cooling the motor should the need arise. The water was in a large rubber bowl and the jerky ride made it spray up from the bowl. Having no choice, Yitzchak stood for the rest of the journey as he tightly clutched the sides of the rubber bowl to prevent any water from splashing on the wheat.

Genuine Millstones

Now that we had such a large amount of certified water-free wheat, it clearly would have been absurd to grind it all with a coffee grinder. The only alternative was to return to the municipal flour mill, clean it well, and grind our large stock of wheat there. Truth be told, knowing how difficult it was to clean the heavy millstones, it did not seem right to me that after carefully watching the wheat from the time of harvest, we should be forced to compromise and use those millstones for grinding: However hard we worked to clean all the crevices on the stones, it was impossible to reach every miniscule crack and remove all the old flour.

Additionally, since the mill was powered by water, there was the distinct possibility of moisture combining with our wheat, which was of course very problematic. On one occasion, we even discovered that actual dough had formed around the base stone. We plastered the base stone with several layers of paper, but it couldn't compare to millstones that were reserved for Pesach use.

Due to all these factors, I was determined to construct a genuine mill so that we would be able to grind all the wheat on our own. Overall, it would be less expensive, and moreover, halachically, it would be superior.

I proceeded to the mill to scrutinize the grinding process and learn how the machinery functioned. Then I headed to the factory where millstones were manufactured and introduced myself as a chemistry student who needed small millstones for grinding various compounds. Thank G-d, they didn't ask any questions, and agreed to sell me a new set of millstones. Made from natural stone, each one was around sixty centimeters across and weighed some eighty kilograms, heavy enough to grind a large quantity of wheat. Artificial millstones were also available, but we had determined that the natural ones would better suit our purposes.

They prepared the stones with the necessary grooves including, as requested, a special hole in the corner of the runner stone. We would insert a wooden pole into the hole in order to rotate the stones manually. I then went to an old Jew who was a carpenter by trade and asked him to construct a sturdy table for me, following a sketch I had drawn. When the table was completed, I brought it to a shed in our courtyard, positioned the stones on the table just as I had seen at the mill, and we began to grind.

Rotating the grindstone was hard work for one person. It was tricky too, since by turning the handle, he would block the wheat from the feeder above the mill from falling into the hole in the center of the top stone. To make things easier, I tied some rope to the handle so we could work in pairs, each person pulling the stone a half-rotation. Within a short amount of time, we managed to grind about twenty kilograms of wheat relatively easily and in the best possible way: entirely by hand, with new millstones.

Despite our success, I wasn't satisfied. For starters, the grain being dispensed from the bucket of wheat over the mill still didn't have an unobstructed path: When the rope was pulled across the mill, some of the wheat would spill on the rope and fall to the sides. Furthermore, after all the tugging at the mill, with a person pulling in either direction, the table had nearly collapsed. Most importantly, my goal had been to grind enough wheat for our community to have enough *shmurah* matzah for the entire Pesach holiday. This was still far beyond our abilities.

I decided that the following year I would again try to attach a motor to the mill, but this time with a bona fide motor. When I told my friends about the plan, they didn't think it would be successful and claimed that assembling such a machine would be too costly. I told them I'd be arranging it all myself and wasn't asking anyone to chip in towards the cost; only if it proved successful would we divide the expenses amongst us.

To be honest, building a genuine motorized mill was not a simple operation at all, for both technical and practical reasons. Technically, it was necessary to obtain an engine that could operate on a household electrical outlet, with enough power to move the heavy grindstone. According to my estimation, the engine needed to generate 1.5 horsepower. Typically, however, such an engine rotated at

1,800 times per minute, which would be much too fast for our purposes and cause the stone to fly in all directions. Although I had never studied physics or mechanics, I realized that I would need to create an entire system of gears to reduce the number of rotations.

After figuring out which wheels and hinges were needed to build the system, I had to overcome the practical obstacle: How does one obtain an engine, wheels, and hinges in Soviet Russia?

It sounds simple—just go to the store and buy a motor!—but in Russia of those years, traveling to a factory that manufactured motors and providing a reasonable explanation for the purchase was the only way.

I knew of an enormous workshop by the train station that repaired train compartments, and where I assumed a motor could be obtained. Once again, I presented myself as a chemistry student, and after providing a bribe (of course), they offered to sell me a small 1.5 horsepower motor. The workshop also had a lathe, so I could order the necessary axles, wheels, and gears as well. After showing them a sketch that I had drawn beforehand, they prepared all the components according to my specifications. Together with a number of shafts and wheels I had purchased at the same factory, I began to assemble the contraption in the shed in my parents' courtyard.

After long weeks of concerted effort and toil, the long-awaited moment finally arrived. I switched on the motor and the home-made apparatus began to work! The wheat entered between the stones and flour poured into the sack. Mazel tov!

Within one hour we were able to grind fifteen kilograms of flour, and in just a day and a half we finished grinding all of the wheat for the entire Samarkand Lubavitch community. I can hardly describe to you the feeling of elation that coursed through our veins. We instantaneously burst out in song and danced around our very own mill.

Baking the Matzos

After grinding all of the wheat, we went to bake the matzos. In earlier years, a few families would gather together in the *padriad*—the
Bukharian communal matzah bakery—and bake all of the matzos
they needed in just a few hours. But now that we had enough to
feed the entire Chabad community, we needed some more time.
Instead of working in constant fear that someone would raise
alarm about the religious commotion going on in the bakery, we
looked for someone willing to rent his house to us for a few days so
we could freely bake our matzos with all of the extra precautions
customary in Chabad.

There were years that we baked in the home of R. Yitzchak
Chai Ladayev, a former student in the underground Tomchei
Temimim in wartime Samarkand. Other years, the "bakery" was
situated at the home of Binyamin the Fisherman, so called despite
the fact that he never caught fish, neither from the sea nor the
river; he simply purchased fish from the fishermen and sold them
in the market.

Binyamin the Fisherman owned a large yard that held an oven
for baking matzos. The Bukharian ovens were constructed like
the ovens of Talmudic times. Unlike today's matzah ovens, where
the fire burns on the side and the matzos are placed on the floor of
the oven, in the Bukharian ovens, the fire was on the bottom and
the matzah dough had to be pressed against the roof and walls of
the oven.

One had to be something of an expert to make the matzos properly stick to the walls without falling into the burning coals below.
Our first attempts at this were pretty hopeless, so before we had
mastered the art, we asked the Bukharian women to fill in for us
amateurs. As time elapsed, we learned the ropes and our yeshiva
boys replaced them.

In the earlier years, Dovid Mishulovin and Berel did most of the
work. Later on, when we grew older, Michoel Mishulovin, Yaakov
Lerner, Mordechai Goldschmidt, and I joined them. As the years

The author standing near the Mishulovin home,
where R. Bentcha's cheder was located

Former students of R. Bentcha Maroz at a Chamah meeting in Samarkand.
From left to right, seated: Berke Schiff, Yoske Shagalovitch, Michoel
Mishulovin. *Standing:* Mordechai Goldschmidt, Zalman Friedman, Moshe
Nissilevitch, Berel Zaltzman, Aryeh Leib Schiff, and the author

The Rebbe Rashab

R. Avrohom Zaltzman with
his daughter, Sarah

The author's
parents,
Avrohom
and Bracha
Zaltzman

R. Avrohom Zaltzman working as a photographer

The author with his sister,
Sarah (Mishulovin)

The author's brother, Berel Zaltzman

Yaakov Pil as a soldier
in the Soviet Army

The author (*right*) with his cousin
Yaakov Pil

The author (*above*) with his friend
Michoel Mishulovin

From left to right: Eliyahu Mishulovin, Berel Zaltzman, and the author

The young men who brought Mrs. Chein from the train station. *From left to right:* Mordechai Goldschmidt, Aryeh Leib Schiff, Moshe Nissilevitch, Berke Schiff, and Yaakov Lerner. Mrs. Feigel Chein is seated (*lower right*).

Rabbi Avrohom Chaim Noeh

Rabbi Shlomo Leib Eliezerov

R. Moshiach Chudaidatov

R. Refael Chudaidatov

R. Berke Chein

R. Simcha Gorodetzky

Mordechai Goldschmidt
(riding the donkey) and
Yaakov Lerner, enjoying
the outdoor excursion
while kashering the
mill for the making of
Passover matzah

The founders of Chamah: *Left to right*: Berel Zaltzman, Moshe Nissilevitch, Leibke Schiff, and Berke Schiff (note the *Tanya* on the table wrapped in a copy of *Pravda*)

Left to right: Leibke Schiff, Berel Zaltzman, Moshe Nissilevitch, and Berke Schiff

R. Moshe Nissilevitch

The young men of Chamah: *From left to right:* Eliyahu Volovik,
Yaakov Lerner, the author, Pinchas Krugliak, and Benzion Chein

Jewish boys who studied Torah in the underground classes

Students of the underground yeshiva in Samarkand: *From left to right:*
Avrohom Zerach Notik, Tanchum Boroshansky, Yosef Yitzchak Zaltzman,
Benzion Goldschmidt, Benzion Robinson, Shmuel Notik

Berel Zaltzman in a workshop in Stalinabad

R. Mendel Futerfas

The author's wife, Shoshana, at the time of their marriage

R. Efraim Fishel Demichovsky with his first grandchild, Chana Zaltzman, the daughter of Hillel and Shoshana

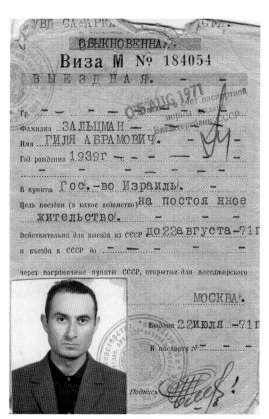

The exit visa for
which the author
waited fifteen years

The author says,
"Goodbye Mother Russia"

R. Moshe Nissilevitch sharing the joy of Purim with Israeli soldiers

The author (*left*) with R. Moshe Nissilevitch

Chamah activists in Israel with Bukharian children in front of the cabin in which Yeshivas HaBukharim of Kfar Chabad was initiated. Standing (*from left to right*): Berke Schiff, R. Avraham Chaim Ledayev, R. Zevulun Leviev, the author, R. Moshe Nissilevitch, Lipa Klein, and Yehoshua Raskin

The author at Chamah's stand at the Moscow International Book Fair in 1989

Revisiting Samarkand: The author and his brother, Berel, in Registan Square,
Samarkand's main tourist attraction, in the heart of the Old City

The author receiving *lekach* (honey cake) from the Rebbe for a sweet year

passed, others got involved in the matzah baking as well: Yitzchak Mishulovin, Yosef Volovik, Moshe Lerner, and Benzion Gold-schmidt.

The difficulty with employing local workers was that they were not accustomed to our stringencies and extra precautions. For example, in the process of attaching the matzos to the oven walls, they would place a vessel of water near the oven, and prior to sticking the matzos they would dip their hand in the water and smear it on the matzah! The water gave the matzah dough a stickier consistency, thereby keeping it glued to the walls, but this was one of the first things we eliminated. The water was used throughout the day and it was almost certain that remnants from the first matzah batch remained in the water and had likely leavened.

Since we baked the matzos without smearing them with water first, we had to force the matzos onto the walls of the oven to make them stick. The extra force weakened the oven to the extent that by the end of our baking, it was close to falling apart. This enhanced the halachic standard of our matzos in a way we hadn't anticipated: Every year we used a new oven.

To stick the matzos to the walls of the oven, we used a small round cushion. The matzah went on one side, and on the other side was a pocket-like depression. We would stick our hand into the pocket and press the matzah dough onto the wall. The drawback with using the same cushion repeatedly was that any dough residue on the cushion would become leavened after eighteen minutes. At first we cleaned and scraped the cushions between each matzah with a specially designated brush, but that didn't satisfy us. The speed at which we needed to work made us unsure they were being sufficiently cleaned. Moreover, we were afraid that the hot glove hastened the leavening of the matzos.

It finally dawned on Berel that there was a simple solution. By attaching a piece of paper between the cushion and the matzah, they wouldn't come in contact with each other. There would be no need to clean anything, as we could simply replace the paper with each new matzah.

Placing paper into the oven seemed dangerous, so the idea was rejected at first, but after several attempts we managed to thrust the cushion with the paper in and out of the oven quickly enough for the fire to not singe the paper. We prepared a large ream of paper and two or three cushions. One of the boys would stand near the oven fastening paper to the cushions with safety pins, and replace the paper after each use.

Every year we bought new plywood covers for the tables. We would also cover the table with paper and changed the paper every fifteen minutes so that no dough over eighteen minutes old would remain in the bakery.

To perforate the rolled-out matzah dough, the local matzah bakers would use a wooden rolling pin into which small nails had been inserted. Of course, it was very hard to clean this rolling pin. We first scrubbed it with a metal brush, but when we tried to kosher the nails by passing a flame over them, we almost burned the rolling pin itself.

We decided to replace the wooden rolling pin with an iron one that we would be able to kosher. Over time, we prepared a rolling pin to which a number of wheels were attached. This enabled us to quicken the piercing process and keep the matzah exposed for even less time.

R. Eliyahu Mishulovin, a Chassidic young man of deep inner character, served as the supervisor. He was especially particular regarding the cleaning of the rolling pins. Under his watch, we would use pieces of glass to scrape off virtually the entire outer layer of the pins. He also carefully checked the mixing bowls. It happened more than once that after everyone had checked the utensils and declared them clean, he would find a tiny scrap of dough which we had all somehow overlooked.

It would break my heart to see R. Eliyahu crying with regret when he found something improper or noticed a detail no one had paid attention to. In Hebrew, the extra measure or special care one takes in the performance of a *mitzvah* is referred to as a *hiddur*, literally the adornment, or beautification of the commandment. Oh, how these *hiddurim* touched him to the very core of his soul! Each year he would make a list of issues that needed to be corrected the following year. But the next year he would cry again, saying that we had not yet achieved the proper *hiddur*. At the same time, however, it was heartwarming to know that we had such Chassidic young men amongst us.

It truly was the most ideal matzah production we could have hoped for. From the time we began grinding the wheat ourselves until I departed from Russia in 1971, we were able to grind all of the *shmurah* wheat every year with our special millstones and bake the matzos in new ovens.

In the late 1950s, we began receiving packages of *shmurah* matzos from Kfar Chabad in Israel. When we first received them in the original packaging with the seal of approval from the Chabad rabbis, it was hard for us to believe that they could bake such large quantities while ensuring that they were baked within eighteen minutes.

When R. Simcha Gorodetzky departed from Russia, we asked him to take a look and report back to us whether these matzos were prepared according the standards we were accustomed to. A short while later, he informed us that he had visited the matzah bakery in Kfar Chabad and they were careful with all the precautions that we were particular about. "However," he continued, "you should continue eating the matzos you bake yourself. There is no greater *hiddur* than that."

CHAPTER 11

The Founding of Chamah

Much of our communal work in Samarkand over the years was done under the auspices of an organization named "Chamah." Though Chamah originated with the activities of just a few young men in Samarkand, including myself, as the years went by, it flourished to become a successful and accomplished international organization to this day. The founder of the organization was R. Moshe Nissilevitch, a young man at the time with a quiet, reserved nature that belied a fiery passion that burned strongly within. R. Moshe was a person who was involved in community work—*askanus*, in Hebrew—with all of his heart and soul, a man who was a true inspiration to all those who crossed his path.

R. Moshe became bar mitzvah before the outbreak of World War II, after the yeshivas and shuls had already been closed down by the Communists. Without many alternatives, his father brought him to the underground Tomchei Temimim yeshiva in Kutaisi, Georgia. "I see that only the Chabad chassidim and their spirit of self-sacrifice can stand up against this evil regime," he said, pleading that they accept his only son.

Those were difficult times and the Kutaisi region had been hit hard by famine. The directors of the yeshiva explained that there was literally no food for the boys. At times, they were starving for bread.

"Whatever is the lot of the other boys will be the lot of my son as well," R. Moshe's father said, and he left his son at the yeshiva.

In the coming years, R. Moshe studied diligently, placing special focus on the study of Chassidus. He benefited from being in the presence of many great Chabad chassidim, such as R. Betzalel "Tzalke" (Chersoner) Wilschansky, R. Nissan *der geller* (the blond) Nemenov, and R. Shmuel (Kutaiser) Notik—all men of extraordinary devotion and sacrifice. When the yeshiva relocated to Samarkand during the war, R. Moshe came as well.

In 1946, R. Moshe tried to join the chassidim fleeing Russia with forged papers, but the government, having caught wind of their scheme, was on the hunt for those who hadn't yet left. Forced to relocate as far from the border as possible, R. Moshe returned to Samarkand with a changed identity—so as to avoid future repercussions for the "crime" of trying to leave. He now introduced himself as Moshe Friedman, but was more commonly known by the nickname his blond hair earned him: "Moishke *der geller*—the blond."

An Outrageous Goal

Not long after the Stalin era, sometime around 1954, R. Moshe spoke to my brother Berel and the Schiff brothers, Leibke and Berke, about founding a local Jewish organization. Its objectives were to be the preservation and promotion of Judaism, and providing economic assistance for Jews in Samarkand. In those years, these goals were completely outrageous, but R. Moshe gave that first meeting a sense of thrill and intrigue and managed to get some of the others excited too.

The young men were invited to the lobby of a hotel. Moshe had brought with him a *Tanya,* the basic text of Chabad Chassidism, hidden inside that day's edition of *Pravda.* There, they laid their hands upon the *Tanya* and gave their word to act with complete and utter devotion to an organization whose activities would be in accordance with the Rebbe's guidance and directives. Of course, this proclamation was more symbolic than practical, for in those years we had no tangible means of communication with the Rebbe in New York. We were scared to even mention the words "rebbe" or "chassid."

A year or two after the first meeting, when I was sixteen, R. Moshe approached me and said, "I see you have a talent for *askanus*. I suggest that you join us in our holy work."

I had always nurtured a burning desire to be involved in this sort of activism and readily accepted his invitation. He told me to come up with some original ideas for future activities, saying that we would meet in a few days and I would share my ideas. I did as he suggested and soon became a close friend of R. Moshe's.

At first, the organization was called Chevras Ahavas Yisrael, the "Fellowship for the Love of a Fellow Jew," or by the acronym "Chai," which means life. But soon after, while studying the *Shelah*, a classic proto-Chassidic work, R. Moshe came across a discussion of the tremendous virtue of inspiring increased religious observance in others. To reflect this priority, he renamed the organization Chaburas Mezakei Ha'Rabim—the "Society for the Promotion of Public Merit"—or simply, "Chamah." I came up with my own meaning for the acronym: Chabad M'Bris Ha'Moatzos—Chabad of the Soviet Union.

The organization was not structured as one might expect today, with a board of directors, several divisions, and so forth. We were, after all, just a handful of members, each of us serving as both director and activist. Nonetheless, we were successful along a number of fronts, both in the material work and the educational work of spreading the light of Torah and the teachings of Chassidus. Needless to say, we acted in total secrecy, keeping the organization hidden from even our closest relatives.

We raised money clandestinely, ensuring that donors would have no idea of the final destination of their particular donation. With this money, we purchased food and distributed it to hundreds of Jewish families before the holidays. In the winter months, when by law one could only obtain a small amount of coal, and only with government coupons, we managed to illegally obtain large quantities of coal to donate to Jews in need.

R. Binyamin Malachovsky and R. Moshiach Chudaidatov, the son of R. Refael, were the ones who took charge of this project. They knew an evangelical Christian who was married to a Jewish woman and saw it as a privilege to help the Jews, the Chosen People. He worked at a railroad station packaging coal from arriving transports and distributing it in the city in accordance with predetermined quotas. When a transport of coal was about to arrive, he would send us a message. R. Binyamin and R. Moshiach would then drive over with a truck under the cover of night and load it with large amounts of coal. In this fashion, they managed to smuggle hundreds of tons of coal for the Jews of Samarkand.

"How Is Aunt Nechama?"

From the time the organization was founded, we searched for ways to inform R. Menachem Mendel Schneerson, the seventh Lubavitcher Rebbe, about our work, but this proved to be difficult. Reporting our activities in writing was too dangerous, and for a while we were unsuccessful in sending out any information. Instead, we decided to wait for the opportunity to do so when someone would be leaving the country; through him, we could convey a full report to the Rebbe in New York.

When my uncle R. Boruch Duchman left Russia in 1958, we gave him detailed reports about our work, but we never received a response.

In 1960, R. Berke Chein received permission to leave Russia. As soon as R. Moshe Nissilevitch heard, he went to meet with R. Berke. He quietly told him the story of the founding of Chamah and about our activities and asked him to give a detailed report to the Rebbe.

The next day—a day before he left—R. Berke approached R. Moshe with great excitement.

"After our conversation last night," he related, "I studied the Torah reading of that day, the third section of *Vezot Habracha*. There, Moshe [Moses] blesses the tribe of Yosef [Joseph] that their land be blessed with 'the sweetness of sun's produce.' In explaining this blessing, the commentator Rashi writes that Yosef's land produced sweet fruit because it was well exposed to the sun. But instead of using the Hebrew word used in the verse for 'sun'—*shemesh*—Rashi uses the word *chamah*: This is a clear allusion to your organization, Chamah!"

R. Berke was so enthused by this sign of divine approval that he asked R. Moshe to accept him as a member of the organization before leaving Russia.

After R. Berke left, we hoped to receive some indication from the Rebbe that he had heard about our work, perhaps by way of the secret letters that we occasionally received from abroad. These letters were written under various fictitious names by Nissan Mindel, a member of the Rebbe's secretariat, as though addressed to relatives and inquiring about their welfare in Russia, but between the lines some secret message would be conveyed. All of them were signed *Zeide* (Grandfather)—the code name for the Rebbe.

To our sorrow, the political situation in Russia at that time was still precarious and people were extremely fearful, especially when it came to communicating with the West. As such, we did not receive any response from the Rebbe. Despite the hardships, our work expanded throughout this time and we also drew many young Bukharian Jews closer to our community, as will be related later.

Before Rosh Hashana of 1966, when Naftali Estulin, one of the first students in the Samarkand underground yeshiva, left Russia, R. Moshe once again gave him a detailed report about all of Chamah's activities and asked him to pass it on to the Rebbe. We asked him to reply with a letter written in Russian. Letters written in Hebrew were censored by a Jewish translator and there was reason for concern that such an individual would understand any hidden messages contained within.

About a month later, we finally received the long-anticipated letter. In the letter, Naftali wrote that "*Zeide* wants to know how 'Aunt Nechama' is doing and if she has enough helpers." "Nechama" was of course a common Jewish woman's name, but it was obvious whom, or rather what, it referred to. This line was short but full of meaning. The very fact that the Rebbe had heard of our work and inquired about it encouraged us tremendously.

Our activities at Chamah had expanded by then, and R. Moshe wrote to the Rebbe that "Aunt Nechama" believes she needs additional people to help her. A while later, the Rebbe responded by saying that Aunt Nechama should look for helpers from within her own social circle.

At that time we received another letter from Naftali Estulin. Naftali managed to slip into the letter references to statements the Rebbe had made at recent *farbrengens* along the lines of the Talmudic adage, "If the ox falls down, sharpen your slaughtering knife." R. Moshe interpreted this as a reference to the Soviet Union, alluding that it would soon fall apart. This caused a great upsurge of activity amongst our members, especially by R. Moshe. There was an aura of anticipation felt in the air, a feeling that we had to prepare for the coming of *Moshiach* (Messiah). In fact, R. Moshe was unwilling to paint the walls of his house as he expected all of us to be traveling to the Land of Israel shortly.

The Rebbe's answers encouraged us to expand our activities. Although the KGB still spied on regular citizens to uncover illegal activity, they didn't actually carry out many arrests at that time and we took advantage of our relative liberty by expanding our communal work.

To fulfill the Rebbe's directive to increase the numbers of Chamah operatives from amongst our own, we looked for youngsters who had the ability to keep a secret, even from their parents. We taught the most trustworthy boys, and they, in turn, transmitted their knowledge to additional boys. We were thus successful in teaching the Hebrew alphabet, Torah, and Talmud to hundreds of Jewish children.

We saw from experience that the boys who joined in our communal work would progress on all fronts. Their association with our group set them apart from their irreligious environment and infused them with a passion for spreading Torah and Judaism.

Over the course of the years, we occasionally encountered various hardships. One such time, during the 1960s, we wrote to the Rebbe and described the situation to him. The response we received encouraged us immensely. I personally was tremendously affected by the reply, to the extent that I made a number of copies which I sent to fellow chassidim in Tashkent and other cities.

The following is a free translation of the Rebbe's response: "One must constantly remember that it is the nature of [G-d, who is] Good, to perform acts of goodness. When one thinks positively, things will improve all the more; and when one is constantly happy, any concerns will dissipate. When one merits to assist another Jew materially, and all the more so spiritually, one is fortunate of that which there is no greater fortune. Everything has its end, and when the end arrives one sees that there is nothing to worry about."

The KGB *Farbrengen* Inquiry

As much as we tried to maintain secrecy in all of our work, especially in regards to the *farbrengens* we arranged, there were times we were lax. One such occasion, and a most memorable one indeed, was in the late 1960s, when a *farbrengen* commemorating the birthday of the Rebbe Rayatz took place on a Shabbos.

We conducted the preceding prayers and the *farbrengen* in one of the homes in the Bagishomol neighborhood: there was a huge yard in the Bagishomol neighborhood that was home to R. Refael and R. Moshiach Chudaidatov, R. Moshe Nissilevitch, R. Berel Yaffe, R. Binyamin Malachovsky, and others. At this particular *farbrengen*, we went a bit overboard and didn't keep things at our usual standard of secrecy. We allowed many more people than usual to participate, and even several of whom we were suspicious. The political climate was a bit calmer at that time, so we continued to *farbreng*, forgetting for the time the potential danger involved, and placing our trust in Hashem.

A short while later, one of the most reliable members of our group was summoned by the KGB. One can just imagine the fear that gripped him. He didn't tell anyone about the summons and just decided to pretend as if nothing had happened. When the appointed day arrived, he simply did not show up. When he received a second summons, he decided to visit relatives in Moscow for the summer. But upon his return, he received yet another summons; the authorities had not forgotten about him. He realized that he could no longer hide, and lacking an alternative, on the set day, he headed out for the lions' den.

As luck would have it, he fell into the hands of the notorious interrogator Aktchurin. Aktchurin was a Muslim Tatar appointed by the KGB as the local supervisor of Jewish affairs. He had earned quite an evil name for himself amongst the Bukharian Jews.

At the beginning of the interrogation, Aktchurin and his underlings first made it clear that they knew as much about our member as he knew about himself. They yelled at him and mentioned well-concealed facts, which until that moment, he was sure that nobody knew about but himself.

After that introduction, which was intended solely to intimidate him, Aktchurin asked him a direct question: "Do you know Moishke the Blondie, the head of the Jewish mafia?" Moishke the Blondie, of course, was none other than R. Moshe Nissilevitch.

"We know that he organizes underground Jewish schools," he continued. "Legally it is permitted, but everything has to be registered in the government offices."

Our friend saw through the smooth talk. He knew where they were heading with that. They pretended that the crime wasn't serious and that it was all just a matter of registration. That way, he would feel comfortable telling them what he knew with the assurance that the information wouldn't harm anyone.

Instead, he decided to deny having any connection with R. Moshe. "I don't know a man with such a nickname. And I don't know about these activities that you mentioned!"

Aktchurin then continued, "We know what you organized in the Bagishomol neighborhood. You organized a..." At this point he took a paper from his drawer and read from it, letter by letter: "F-A-R-B-R-E-N-G-E-N!"

After he left the KGB office unharmed, our friend immediately hurried to R. Moshe and told him in detail all that had happened.

It appears that they knew plenty about our work, and if they so desired, could have easily brought our activities to an end. It was only because the political situation was indeed more relaxed at the time that they did not arrest us. We understood that their main objective was to frighten us.

Nonetheless, we requested from our colleague to disengage from further communal activities, in the event that he would be summoned once again for interrogation.

1,500 Children Studying in Secret

Perhaps Chamah's biggest project in Samarkand was its network of classes geared for the local Bukharian children who until then had little if any knowledge of Judaism. We established underground schools in which children learned how to read and pray in Hebrew and basic concepts of Judaism.

These classes began with some of the grandchildren of the Bukharians whom R. Simcha Gorodetzky had brought into the Chabad fold as young men, many years earlier. Slowly but surely, more students joined, and in time, they came to number well into the hundreds.

Being that we didn't have sufficient manpower to teach the ever-increasing number of students ourselves, we selected the brightest boys of the group, boys who were mature and able to keep a secret, and taught them ourselves. They, in turn, relayed the knowledge they had acquired to the younger students.

R. Yosef Ladayev was in charge of arranging the classes and pairing them with appropriate teachers. He lived in the Old City, and knew the Bukharian boys and *bochurim*, which made him suitable for the task.

Since the majority of these children learned in public schools, the underground learning took place either in the early morning hours or in the evening. At 6:00 a.m., the teacher would arrive at a given house and teach the children the Hebrew alphabet and selections from *Chumash*. Sometimes the learning would take place in the home of one of the children without his parents' knowledge. As the oblivious parents slept in their bedroom, their son would open the door for his teacher and friends and they would learn in the next room.

Whenever I recall how these righteous young children, these little *tzaddikim*, would arise early in the morning to study Torah, I am overcome with amazement. Although young children typically try to avoid learning; although their parents weren't forcing them to study, or were perhaps unaware of the studies altogether; these boys, only nine, ten, and eleven years of age—on their own initiative—arose at the crack of dawn and studied Torah energetically. What a wondrous phenomenon it was!

I will never forget our excitement upon hearing the following episode, related to us by R. Yosef Ladayev:

Early one morning, one of the young boys unwittingly woke up earlier than usual. Unaware of the time, he walked over to his friend's house where the learning was to take place. To his surprise, the gate of the yard was locked. He knocked quietly on the gate until his friend opened the door. It was only then that he realized that he had arrived two hours early. But the boy did not return home. Instead, he entered the room they used for learning and slept with his head on the table, waiting for his friends to arrive.

A number of boys progressed quickly in their studies and desired to learn more and more. These exceptional students eventually joined our underground yeshiva, where they studied according to the Tomchei Temimim schedule.

Parents Threaten to Inform

In those years, nobody dreamed that there would come a day when they would be able to leave Russia; most parents envisioned a future for their children in the Soviet Union. They wanted them to excel in their studies so they would be accepted to a university—the ultimate achievement as far as Jewish parents were concerned. For this reason, many parents did not look favorably upon the fact that their children were being distracted from their studies, or worse, stopped attending school altogether to study in an underground yeshiva. Their children wouldn't earn a degree by studying in a yeshiva, they would not learn a profession, and might never find financial stability.

Although we were careful to keep our activities secret, many parents were aware that R. Moshe Nissilevitch was at the head of the underground classes. Once, a woman burst into R. Moshe's home and said to his wife, "I must urgently speak with your husband."

After a few moments, R. Moshe entered the room. The woman bellowed at him, "If you entice my son to learn Torah with you, I will inform on all of you to the authorities!"

Soon after, R. Moshe received similar threats from another woman. Fearful that all of our underground activities would be jeopardized, R. Moshe had no choice but to ask the two boys not to come to learn anymore.

In the end, one of the boys returned to the underground classes. R. Moshiach Chudaidatov noticed that the boy was not attending the classes, and not having heard of his parents' threats, he spoke with him about the importance of learning Torah and convinced him to return. This time, though, his participation in the classes was kept secret, so that even his parents didn't know.

A few years later, these two boys left Russia. Today they are parents to Chassidic families and their children are learned, devout Jews, several of them Chabad rabbis.

A Noble Child

Keeping a secret was a non-negotiable condition for anyone who wanted to be accepted for study. In those years, all it took was for one boy to start chattering and the entire underground network would be in grave danger.

After we'd teach the older boys, they would assist us in recruiting additional students. First, we told them to speak to their Jewish friends in public school and gauge how serious they were and how good they were at keeping a secret. These boys would then be included into our group. Thus, each student formed a class of his own and transmitted what we had taught them to other students.

Once, a few older students recommended a certain boy, not yet bar mitzvah, who sensed that his friends were learning Torah and wanted to join. They were afraid to tell him about the group because even though he understood that it was secretive, his name alone reeked of trouble.

His grandfather was a gentile policeman and infamous in Samarkand for his cruelty. During World War II, he caught Jews, accused them of various crimes, and threatened to give them over to the police. The Jews, refugees mostly, had no choice but to bribe him so that he would leave them alone.

His son, the boy's father, though not in the police force was known to be even crueler than his father. He had married several times, to both Jewish and non-Jewish women, and treated them all terribly. This boy was the son of a Jewish mother, a refined woman who suffered immeasurably from her husband until they divorced.

Initially we refused to allow him to get involved. We trembled at the mention of the boy's name and what might happen to us if we were to accept him. However, our students told us time and again that he was a good boy and could keep a secret, and we finally agreed to include him. He really was a good boy and was successful in his learning. I myself taught him *Chumash* and some basic Talmud. After a few years, he immigrated to Israel where he married and established a fine, large Chassidic family. He is currently a rabbi and mentor in a Bukharian community and his children are chassidim and G-d-fearing Jews.

In the 1980s, on a trip to the Land of Israel, I discovered this for myself. One Shabbos afternoon, I passed by a large shul in a Bukharian neighborhood. I glanced through the window and saw a rabbi giving a speech, the crowd listening avidly.

When I asked for his name, I was amazed at what I heard. He was the boy from Samarkand whom we had almost refused to accept into our classes!

KGB-Endorsed *Siddurim*

As our educational activities expanded, there was an urgent need for prayer books for the hundreds of children who learned in what was quickly becoming a network of classes spread across several towns. Aside for purposes of prayer, we needed these *siddurim* to teach the alphabet and for general reading practice. There were already volumes of the *Chumash,* Mishna, and Talmud in the shuls, but prayer books were used more often and wore out quickly.

We found out that Rabbi Yehuda Leib Levin, the chief rabbi of Russia, had printed Sephardic rite prayer books for the main synagogue in Moscow. These *siddurim* were printed by the order of the government, with the sole intent of publicizing to the world that Russia was a free and democratic country. It was obvious to all that only a small number of the prayer books, if any, would reach other shuls, with the majority of them remaining in storage back in Moscow.

At that time, R. Mordechai Goldschmidt was planning to visit his in-laws in Moscow and was thus assigned the job of purchasing these books. The *siddurim* were held in storage by the shul *gabbai,* but in order to buy them, Mordechai had to first convince him that he wasn't a KGB agent. He also had to be cautious that this *gabbai* would not in turn tattle on him, seeing as anyone who held an official position in a shul was a government appointee. We hoped that in exchange for a nice sum, he would agree to the deal.

Mordechai gained the *gabbai's* trust and he agreed to sell the prayer books to him. But how was he to remove so many *siddurim* without drawing unwanted attention? Mordechai went to shul for a number of days, and each time he took a few dozen books, until he removed a total of 850 books. We paid fifteen rubles for each book, which was a considerable sum at the time.

Over a short period of time, we were able to send all of the prayer books to Samarkand, and from there we distributed them to the cities and towns where the learning took place.

This "*siddur* operation" gave new wind to our activities. Although many of us were reluctant to pray from prayer books printed by the KGB, for the hundreds of children who needed them, it was a wonderful solution. And if such a *siddur* was discovered in someone's home, it wasn't a terrible crime, since it was "kosher": the prayer books had been printed in Moscow, not in Israel or America.

Black and White Shoes

When we expanded our activities and began engaging and teaching the local Bukharian children, we would often bring them to participate in our *farbrengens*. However, there were some elder chassidim who protested bringing them into the fold in this way.

"Back in Lubavitch," they said, "the yeshiva students knew that when new boys arrived they were to be befriended. But to actively seek and attract new people to our community? Such a thing was unheard of!

"What's more," they continued, "this is a dangerous project that could have you arrested. At such a time, when we were all in danger of spiritual annihilation, we must first look out for our own community, and only afterwards be concerned about the Bukharian Jews."

We, however, thought and acted otherwise. Nonetheless, an opportunity arose to ask the Rebbe when my sister and her family left for Eretz Yisrael in 1969. We spoke with my brother-in-law R. Eliyahu Mishulovin and asked him to pose the question to the Rebbe. We agreed that he would write back to us in code. The sign would be: Does *Zeide*—the Rebbe's regular alias—like only "white shoes," or does he like "dark shoes" as well?

A short while after they arrived in Israel, we got an answer: *Zeide* didn't understand what difference the color made. He liked them all equally and they were all important in his eyes!

Extending Programs Beyond Samarkand

After a number of years of working in Samarkand, and in light of the Rebbe's instructions encouraging us to broaden our activities, we now focused on the idea of arranging learning programs in the cities and towns around Samarkand. Thousands of Jews lived in these towns, and their children attending public schools lacked even a minimal knowledge of Judaism.

This task was given to R. Refael Chudaidatov. As a local, he was familiar with the surrounding areas and knew many of the local families personally. We arranged for him to travel to the communities he was acquainted with and arrange classes for the children.

R. Refael, always an energetic Jew, accepted the task with joy. He traveled to the nearby towns and spoke with the local Jews, who were happy for the opportunity to have their children learn Torah. R. Refael hired knowledgeable men from the Bukharian community to teach the children, the classes taking place either before or after their daily studies in public school.

If someone were to ask one of these teachers where the money came from to fund the work, and who was paying them, we made sure that Chamah would not be implicated. Instead, we had a story prepared: We would say that a man had died, and in his will he had requested that R. Refael arrange classes for children and pay the teachers with his money. We knew that the Muslims of Uzbekistan considered a will sacred and nobody would dare try to stop him.

Thank G-d, the project saw more success than we had expected and within a short period of time a few hundred children were learning in these Torah classes. According to my calculations, throughout the years—until 1971, the year I left Russia—more than 1,500 students learned in our programs in Samarkand and the surrounding villages. When I think about this today, it's hard for me to believe the success we had with so many children, under Communist rule no less. For while the government did not arrest people at this time, the threat of arrest continued to instill fear into all our hearts.

Financial Support for Teachers' Salaries

Where did the money really come from? Among the members of Chamah were a number of businessmen, myself included, and we were able to set aside significant sums for the teachers' salaries. The practice among the Chassidic young men in Samarkand was to donate 20 percent of their profits to charity, as per the Alter Rebbe's directive in his *Tanya*. In the months that we earned more than usual, we were happy to set aside even more than that figure.

Another source of funding came from the aid packages that we received from the American Jewish organizations, Ezras Achim and the Joint Distribution Committee. These packages were sent to individual families and contained various home goods—clothing, like shirts and blouses, some other fabric items, as well as Parker pens—items that could easily yield a nice sum on the black market. The packages from Ezras Achim were larger and more valuable than those from the Joint, and when sold on the black market, could go for nearly one thousand rubles—enough money to support a family for almost a year!

Many of the people who received these packages needed them simply to be able to put food in their mouths, but sometimes they were sent to people who weren't so desperate for the additional provisions. They would sell the packages on the black market and give the money to charity.

One time, shortly after my marriage, I received a package from my father-in-law in Minsk. Upon opening the package, we found numerous expensive items, and I understood that the package had originated from abroad. Having heard that such packages were pur-

chased with money set aside for *tzedakah* and as such I did not want
to benefit from it. Thank G-d, I earned a sufficient livelihood to be
able to support others and had no need for charity myself.

However, there were a number of items in the package that my
wife liked very much. I donated the rest of the package to Chamah,
as well as the black market value of the items my wife kept.

When my father-in-law heard about this, he was not pleased.
"Who gave you permission to sell my package? I received the package and sent it to my daughter!"

It turned out my father-in-law, R. Efraim Fishel Demichovsky,
received the package from his former teacher, Rabbi Shlomo Yosef
Zevin, who had become a prominent rabbinic figure in Israel. The
package was sent from Jerusalem as a wedding gift for his daughter.
This is why he wanted us to use the contents of the package and was
disappointed to hear that we had sold it.

Occasionally, I would also receive packages from Ezras Achim.
I didn't want to be tempted to use its contents, so I would bring the
unopened package to Chamah's "headquarters" so that it could be
sold to benefit the organization. We didn't think twice about giving
from our own money for the benefit of communal work.

R. Moshe Nissilevitch, like many other Lubavitchers, was a
manual laborer whose salary wasn't enough to support his family.
He was among those who truly needed the food packages. There
was a long period of time when R. Moshe did not receive any food
packages and his financial state was dreadful.

One day he received a package from Ezras Achim that was
worth a lot of money on the black market. This was before the summer, about which time the members of Chamah held a meeting to
discuss using the upcoming summer vacation from public school to
expand our work. Such an expansion meant an increase in our bud-
get and the need to procure extra funds to finance our operations.

Aside from R. Moshe Nissilevitch, the participants at the meeting were businessmen: R. Dovber (Berke) Schiff, R. Mordechai
Goldschmidt, my brother Berel, and myself. We were all aware that
the summer would offer a unique opportunity for teaching children

and each of us contributed large amounts until we had amassed the sufficient funds to double our work.

Being aware of R. Moshe's dire financial situation, we were astonished when he brought the package to the meeting. "This is my participation in the summer expenses," he said.

We protested. "You don't have food for your children!" we said.

"I should soon be receiving a package from the Joint," R. Moshe defended himself. "I will be able to use that to support my family."

We refused to accept his explanation. "Who knows if the package will ever come?" we protested. "And even if it does, the package from the Joint is not worth as much as this one. Use this package for yourself, and if you receive a package from the Joint, you can donate it."

R. Moshe remained unswayed by our objections and donated the package to Chamah. I think he didn't even tell his wife about it, although I am certain she would have agreed herself.

An Open Miracle in the Air

With the classes having expanded to well outside of Samarkand, we decided it was important to make rounds of the surrounding towns from time to time to ensure that all was going well. The supervisor was R. Refael Chudaidatov; he had organized the classes, knew when they were held, and who the teachers were. Each time, a different member of Chamah joined him.

This was no simple matter. The classes were all kept under total secrecy, and when the teacher and students would see an unfamiliar person walk in with R. Refael, they would grow suspicious. However, after R. Refael would reassure them that this was "his" man, they would greet him warmly.

Once, I went with him to Charkhin, a town not far from Samarkand. We arrived at around four o'clock in the afternoon and I was pleased to see twenty-five children learning Torah energetically. They had no desks or chairs and instead sat in the manner of the Uzbeks, leaning against the wall, or seated on a carpet spread on the floor.

On one Wednesday in the Hebrew month of Av, R. Moshe asked R. Berke Schiff to accompany R. Refael on a visit to a number of towns a few hours' drive from Samarkand. R. Berke was reluctant at first, as his brother-in-law was getting married the following week and the traditional pre-wedding call-up to the Torah and *kiddush* were to be held in his home on Shabbos. But R. Moshe persuaded him to go. "You should be back by tomorrow night," he said. "There is no reason to worry."

R. Berke Schiff went with R. Refael to a number of cities, among them Margilan, Andijan, and others and they were happy to see that the classes were taking place as expected. On Thursday, R. Berke wanted to return to Samarkand, but R. Refael insisted that they visit the city of Fergana as well, and from there they would fly back to Samarkand.

After visiting the classes in Fergana, R. Berke and R. Refael hurried to the airport. R. Berke approached a clerk to purchase tickets to Samarkand. To his dismay, all the flights to Samarkand had already departed. The next flight would only leave on Friday morning.

R. Berke returned to R. Refael, disappointed. Noticing his frustration, R. Refael suggested that he purchase tickets on a flight to Tashkent. "From Tashkent it will be easy to find a flight to Samarkand that will leave late tonight or early tomorrow morning," he said.

R. Berke consented and immediately purchased two tickets to Tashkent. They boarded the plane and before long they were on their way.

Some time into the flight, to their surprise, the pilot announced that due to bad weather, the plane could not land in Tashkent. Instead of turning around, they would take a detour all the way to— Samarkand! From there, after a short stopover, the plane would continue on to Tashkent. The two men were amazed. This was some miracle!

When the plane landed in Samarkand, they grabbed their hand luggage and began heading for the door of the plane. Noticing them, the flight attendant called out: "Hey, where are you going? We are soon continuing to Tashkent. Go back to your places!"

They explained that their real destination was Samarkand and they had only taken this flight out of necessity. Some of the passengers, overhearing their conversation, commented: "Now we know why we couldn't land in Tashkent!"

The ramp was lowered especially for them, and the two disembarked and made their way home.

CHAPTER 12

The Underground Yeshiva

By the winter of 1959, a small group of young men had gathered in Samarkand, hoping to be able to study Jewish texts. They arrived individually and stayed with different families, but there was no formal structure for learning. My friends at Chamah and I realized we had an opportunity to arrange a schedule of learning based on the model of Tomchei Temimim—the central yeshiva of the Chabad movement founded in Lubavitch. We had already established a network of classes to teach younger boys, under bar mitzvah age, how to read and pray in Hebrew. Those classes, though underground, were going strong.

Despite the risks associated with any independent educational institution, especially a Tomchei Temimim connected with the Chabad movement, a new generation in Samarkand were not deterred from hosting the yeshiva students in their homes. Nevertheless, the creation of a new underground "yeshiva" took place almost inadvertently.

There had not been a yeshiva in Samarkand, clandestine or otherwise, since the end of World War II. When the Lubavitch chassidim of Russia fled to Central Asia during the war, the underground Tomchei Temimim yeshiva followed them into exile. Ironically, it was during the war years that the yeshiva flourished. The Communist police, preoccupied with the war against the Nazis, did not put much effort into the internal war against those "enemies of the state" still faithful to religion. Chassidim took advantage of this lull and founded prayer groups, yeshivas, and schools in Samarkand and Tashkent. These operations were officially secret and "underground," but in reality they operated almost overtly.

With the end of World War II, persecution began once again. In the first two years after the war, when most of the Lubavitcher chassidim were able to escape the Soviet Union, the yeshiva moved with these refugees to a large DP camp in Poking, Germany, and then to Brunoy, France.

The Lubavitchers who remained in the Soviet Union were unable to contend with the Soviet secret police and there weren't many children of yeshiva age left. The few who remained were older teens too afraid to even think about learning in a yeshiva. Still, there were some isolated boys who learned on their own, or as a pair, according to the system of Tomchei Temimim. As such, the learning of Tomchei Temimim never completely ceased to exist in Russia.

We were one of the few Lubavitcher families to remain in Samarkand. After my older brother Berel became bar mitzvah, my father sent him to Tashkent, where he learned together with R. Lipa Klein under the guidance of R. Zalman Buberer (Pevzner). Additional Lubavitcher children in Samarkand included Michoel Mishulovin, Mottel Goldschmidt, and several more whose names I don't recall. We learned in our *cheder* with R. Bentcha Maroz until the age of ten.

In the beginning of the 1950s, a spurt of anti-Semitism erupted and became rampant throughout the Soviet Union. Stalin ran a propaganda campaign against the Jews in general and religious ones in particular, climaxing with the notorious Doctors' Plot.

At this ominous time, one rumor followed the next: Stalin was planning mass pogroms against the Jews in which hundreds of thousands of Jews would be massacred, and those who survived the pogroms would be "rescued" by Stalin and separated from the provoked Russians by being exiled to Siberia. One can understand that under such circumstances, one's head was preoccupied with only

the most basic objectives: How can we escape? How would we survive? As such, almost all learning in the homes of Lubavitcher families in Samarkand collapsed. Even then, a few families—mine included—took the risk of bringing a teacher to their homes to teach
their children for an hour several times a week.

After the miraculous and sudden death of Stalin on March 5,
1953, the situation eased a bit, though no one dared yet to organize
regular classes. Only a few yeshiva-age boys succeeded in studying
with R. Eliyahu Paritcher (Levin) in his house. They were Dovid and
Eliyahu Mishulovin, followed by their younger brother, Michoel, and
Mottel Goldschmidt.

Young People Want to Learn Torah

As mentioned earlier, I had started to get involved in communal
work at the age of sixteen through Chamah. By the age of twenty, I
began to make trips throughout Russia on various missions related
to the communal good.

When I returned from one of these trips at the end of the summer of 1959, I noticed an unfamiliar boy mingling with the community. In Russia we knew to be wary of strangers, so I immediately
approached R. Moshe Nissilevitch and asked him about this boy. R.
Moshe told me that the boy's name was Naftali Estulin from Tashkent, and he was the son of the chassid R. Zalman Leib. It was difficult for R. Zalman Leib to hide his son at home and he refused to
send him to public school, so he decided to send his son to Samarkand, in the hopes of finding some sort of program there. At the
very least, he wouldn't be spotted by the neighbors at home in Tashkent and the authorities in Samarkand wouldn't know to look out
for him. At the time, he was around thirteen years old.

For parents, of course, it was not simple at all to send such a
young child to a strange city, not knowing where he will eat or sleep
and who will teach him. But R. Zalman Leib decided to send his
son, no matter what obstacles were involved. Naftali was the first

yeshiva-age student to come to Samarkand from another city. At that time, the boys there still had no regular study curriculum, but the rumor among the wider Chabad community was that in Samarkand there were young boys who study Torah.

Naftali's father waited for an opportune time to send his son to Samarkand. The opportunity soon came in the form of a group of people from Tashkent traveling to a wedding taking place in Samarkand. R. Zalman Leib sent Naftali along with them and hoped that he would be able to remain in Samarkand.

The wedding took place on the 12th of Tammuz, which was also the anniversary of the Rebbe Rayatz's liberation from Soviet imprisonment. Of course, the community took advantage of the opportunity to rejoice and *farbreng* on the special day. At a later point, Naftali told me that at the wedding he noticed one of the bearded men dancing and rejoicing more enthusiastically than the others and he assumed him to be a close relative of the groom or the bride. Upon inquiring, he was astounded to hear that the man wasn't even a distant relative. Naftali wondered, Why then was this fellow dancing so enthusiastically?

Finally, someone explained that he was dancing for another reason entirely—it was Rebbe Rayatz's Liberation Day! The man dancing was none other than the famed chassid R. Berke Chein.

R. Zalman Leib's hopes indeed materialized, and R. Naftali succeeded in adjusting to the Lubavitcher community in Samarkand. After the wedding, Naftali stayed at the home of R. Feivish Genkin in the Old City. R. Feivish had been a soldier during World War I before coming to Samarkand with his wife, Chasha, and eventually joining the community. They were childless, and together they managed the *mikvah*, once it had been reopened. They were known to be able to keep a secret.

Naftali stayed with them for a month without any company, friends, or anyone else to talk to. The couple did not allow him to spend time outdoors and, as R. Naftali recalls, he felt as if he was under house arrest. The only one who came by was R. Berke Chein, who was a frequent visitor of R. Feivish.

Early one morning, after R. Berke had immersed in the Gen-kins' *mikvah* in preparation for prayer, he began enthusiastically reciting the *Shema* from a *mezuzah* parchment with devout con-centration, as was his daily custom. In the meantime, Naftali had woken up and realized that he had forgotten to leave water and a cup beside his bed the night before. According to Jewish law, one is supposed to wash his hands immediately upon waking, ideally be-fore even leaving the bed and walking four cubits. Still, not wanting to bother R. Berke in the middle of his fervent recital of the *Shema*, he went to the sink to wash his hands.

After he finished saying *Shema*, R. Berke said to Naftali, "You walked four cubits without washing? You should have told me and I would have stopped and brought you water!"

Naftali was extremely impressed with Reb Berke's piety and his love of a fellow Jew: "Although he was in the middle of reciting *Shema* and I was just a youngster, he was prepared to interrupt his davening so that I should not walk four cubits without washing!"

One Friday afternoon, R. Berke took Naftali to immerse in the river in preparation for Shabbos, and on their way back, he invited Naftali to his house for Shabbos. Naftali happily accepted, lonely as he was at R. Feivish's house.

Naftali spent an uplifting Shabbos with R. Berke. After Shabbos, when he returned to R. Feivish's house, R. Feivish chastised him and said, "Why did you go to R. Berke for Shabbos? He doesn't have enough food for his own family!"

After he had spent some time in the house of R. Feivish, Eli Mishulovin came to visit Naftali. He spoke with Naftali several times to assess his level of learning and, crucially, whether he was able to keep a secret.

In the meantime, some of the community members in Tashkent had noticed Naftali's absence. One of them, R. Gershon Gratzman, "sensed" that Naftali was in Samarkand and believed that he was learning there, so he sent his son Shaika to Samarkand as well.

Another youth from Tashkent by the name of Shmuel Chaim Frankel was in Samarkand at the time as well. His family had lived in Samarkand a few years earlier, and his father R. Yisroel sent him there in 1958 to avoid sending him to public school. Shmuel Chaim stayed in the house of R. Tzvi Hirsch Lerner, a family friend from the time they lived together.

After R. Naftali successfully passed Eli Mishulovin's tests, we began to think about an organized schedule for this small group of boys. Ideally, the schedule would be like that in Tomchei Temimim, with seven hours of Talmud and Jewish law and four hours of Chassidus studied daily.

A "Yeshiva" in Samarkand

Indeed, on the 19th of Kislev, in 1959, a regular learning routine was established. The initial group consisted of four students: Naftali Estulin, Shmuel Chaim Frankel, Shaika Gratzman, and Itche Mishulovin, who had been learning alone until then. The positions of lecturer, Chassidic mentor, and student supervisor were held by one individual: R. Michoel Mishulovin. A short time later, the brothers Eliyahu and Yosef Volovik from Chernovitz joined as well. The next arrival was Shimshon Kahana of Chernovitz, who was soon joined by a few more boys, and eventually two separate classes were formed.

The learning first took place at the home of my brother Berel on 6 Tchlekskaya Street, in a small one-room cottage in the yard, where several of the boys also slept. The cottage lacked heating, and its only table served a dual purpose: By day it was used as a table and at night as a bed. Shmuel Chaim Frankel recently reminded me that I arranged for heating by means of some mechanism with a fan that blew hot air. The boys dubbed it "Hilke's patent." (I myself do not recall this detail!)

These underground studies were kept secret in the strictest confidence. For example, Shmuel Chaim was originally staying with Tzvi Hirsch Lerner, a family friend. But later, Shmuel Chaim disappeared. Tzvi Hirsch did not know where Shmuel Chaim had disappeared to; he only knew that Shmuel Chaim would not return to them anymore. Unbeknownst to him, Shmuel Chaim was now staying with one of the host families for the underground yeshiva.

As long as the boys were with their respective hosts, they were literally like prisoners under house arrest; only late in the evening would they go out for a breath of fresh air.

One day, says Shmuel Chaim, we were told that a knowledgeable Torah scholar from Tashkent, R. Mordechai Kozliner, would come to test us. "Many years later," Shmuel Chaim recalls, "I realized that this knowledge was to our advantage, because we all prepared seriously and reviewed for the test, as we were nervous that we would not know the material."

Although the learning followed the schedule of Tomchei Temimim yeshivas, we never thought of calling this learning program by the holy name of "Yeshivas Tomchei Temimim." After all, it consisted of just a few boys learning here and there in private homes, and although it certainly had a Chassidic atmosphere, it wasn't exactly the yeshiva atmosphere that comes with a few dozen students learning together.

On the other hand, a feeling developed deep within me that although it wasn't a yeshiva in a large, prestigious building, the unique holiness of Tomchei Temimim was present nonetheless. During the *hakafos* dancing on Simchas Torah, I remember endeavoring to lead the seventh and final of the *hakafos,* whose accompanying prayer was the origin of the Tomchei Temimim name, and is associated with the yeshiva. I would recite the words *"Tomeich temimim hoshi'ah na"*—"He Who supports the sincere, please deliver us!"— with great fervor and enthusiasm, praying silently to Hashem: Please protect these students, who study as in Tomchei Temimim, that they be able to continue learning without any disruption, G-d forbid!

The first to use the name "yeshiva" to describe the boys' studies was the legendary chassid R. Mendel Futerfas. After he moved to Samarkand, he would ask whenever I visited him, "What's happening in the yeshiva?"

At first, I didn't understand his intention. Was he being ironic and making fun of the learning we had arranged? But R. Mendel was entirely serious. "What do you think a yeshiva is?" he said. "A place where hundreds of students sit and learn? No! If even a small number of boys learn the Talmud, Halacha, and Chassidus according to the schedule of Tomchei Temimim, it is a yeshiva!

"Tell me," continued R. Mendel. "do the boys study Chassidus four hours a day, in the morning and the evening?" When I replied in the affirmative, R. Mendel ended the discussion. "Nu," he said. "If so, this is Tomchei Temimim!"

"Even If There Is a Yeshiva, No One Will Tell You!"

Shortly after the learning commenced, boys began to arrive in Samarkand from other areas. One of them was Moshe Leib Rutner, from the town Munkatch in the Carpathians.

Moshe Leib Rutner's father, a pious, G-d-fearing Jew by the name of R. Yaakov Chaim who had raised his children to be observant Jews, was looking for a place where they could study and be raised according to the Torah.

Since the Carpathian region was only conquered by the Communists in 1946, the Carpathian Jews were not as accustomed to secrecy as were the Lubavitchers, who had been hounded by the government for years, and many of whom had been imprisoned. As such, when R. Yaakov Chaim heard that there was a yeshiva in Samarkand, he was sure that he would find it as soon as he arrived. If not, he figured that he could ask in the local shul and would be directed to the right place.

When he arrived in Samarkand, he quickly realized that there was no one to speak to, so he went to the shul in the Old City which, on account of its constant surveillance by the authorities, was frequented only by the Bukharian Jews and a few older Lubavitchers. Inside the shul, he met R. Feivish Genkin.

When R. Feivish heard that this Jew was looking for a yeshiva for his son, it sounded somewhat suspicious to him; anyone looking for a yeshiva should have known that the shul was the last place to talk about such things! Besides, R. Feivish himself knew nothing about the yeshiva, as its existence was a total secret. After a lengthy conversation, R. Feivish realized that he was an honest and reliable person and a devout Jew. He then told him that he had also heard a rumor about a yeshiva but any effort to discover its location would no doubt be in vain. Even if a yeshiva actually existed, he would surely not be told about it. R. Yaakov Chaim realized he wouldn't get anywhere, so he returned to the Carpathians, brokenhearted.

Heaven must have seen his genuine desire that his children study Torah, and Divine Providence orchestrated events in the most extraordinary way: One summer a few years later, my brother Berel went to the Carpathians for a family vacation, as the climate there was mild even during the hot summer months. He heard that there were G-d-fearing Jews living in Munkatch, and as fate would have it, he came to stay with the Rutner family.

When he saw how the house was run in accordance with Halacha and how the father longed for his children to learn in a yeshiva, he suggested that he send one of his sons to be our guest in Samarkand. Perhaps, he said, it would help him to slowly integrate into the Jewish community there. At that point, Berel still made no mention of any learning.

Indeed, young Moshe Leib Rutner showed up in Samarkand sometime later, and before long, he joined the learning in the yeshiva. An exceedingly humble, quiet young man, he threw himself into his studies completely, with a burning desire and total devotion, and we saw that his new-found yeshiva learning gave him new life. Still, his speech and manner of conduct was so unassuming we didn't even realize the extent of the hidden qualities the young boy possessed.

In years to come, after arriving in America, Moshe Leib continued his studies in the Skver yeshiva in Monsey and developed a strong relationship with the Ribnitzer Rebbe, Rabbi Chaim Zanvil Abramowitz, with whom he had become acquainted with in Ribnitz. Following his marriage, it became apparent that he also possessed extraordinary business acumen. With the Ribnitzer Rebbe's blessing, his business prospered, and he began to distribute charity generously. Among his projects, he established an educational institution named "Darchei Noam Ribnitz" in Williamsburg, for children from nine to thirteen years old to get together in the evening hours to learn Mishnah and Mussar, and hear stories to strengthen their faith.

When I later met up with Reb Moshe Leib, he reminisced about those years of self-sacrifice studying in the underground yeshiva in Samarkand, when each knock on the door made one's heart skip a beat. Now he has speaking engagements in various places, he told me, and every time he talks about his experiences in our underground yeshiva, it brings his listeners to tears.

Envelopes from Moscow

Another outstanding student in the yeshiva was Moshe Miller, who came to Samarkand from Apsha, also in the Carpathians. His parents got word of the yeshiva in Samarkand and resolved to send their only son to study in the yeshiva of a city they had never heard of. His mother cried and worriedly asked: "Where will he sleep, where will he eat?" Moshe, a young teen at the time, tried calming her and said: "On the contrary, you should be happy that I am going to learn Torah!"

Moshe succeeded in his studies and also learned the skill of *shechita*. Now, we are proud to say that this student, having managed to learn *shechita* while studying in our underground yeshiva, was later appointed as a *shochet* in Bnei Brak, Israel, and served in this position until retirement.

The parents of some of the boys who learned in the yeshiva did not even know the most basic information about where their children were. Certain parents not only didn't know where the yeshiva was located, but didn't even know that their sons were in Samarkand!

In one such case, the parents were sure that their son was working in Moscow. That had been their son's original plan as well, before being convinced to come learn in the yeshiva. So that his parents remained oblivious of his true place of study, the boy would give us his letters and we would send them to our friend Moshe Katzenelenbogen in Moscow, who would forward them to the boy's parents. As long as they received his letters in envelopes postmarked from Moscow, his parents had no suspicions that in actuality their son was not working there at all.

Even the parents who lived in nearby Tashkent, who knew that their sons were learning in Samarkand, didn't know any details about the yeshiva and its location. When I would travel to Tashkent for personal or communal reasons, I was obligated to visit the parents and give them regards from their sons, but I would only do so in the most ambiguous manner. I arrived at the parents' house and ensured that only the father would be present during the conversation. I was worried that if the mother would be present, she would ask too many questions, and I would be unable to say anything at all. The father would only inquire if I had personally seen their son and when. They never asked me if they learned, and if yes, where they learned, with whom they learned, or where they ate and slept. They understood that if they asked too many questions, I would simply not deliver them regards the next time I was there.

Thinking back, I realize what self-sacrifice this entailed on the part of the parents. They willingly sent their child to a foreign city, without even knowing where exactly their son was, but as difficult as that was, they were still careful not to ask any "extra" questions.

The *Bochur* and the Most Expensive Car in Russia

The boys who came to learn were sometimes followed by parents and other family members. This was the case with one particular set of brothers; shortly after their arrival in Samarkand, their parents wanted to join them. The eldest son had to work so as to prepare an economic base that would enable his parents and sister to arrive. He signed up to work at one of the factories run by a Lubavitcher in Samarkand, while the younger brother joined the yeshiva.

In the Soviet Union of those years, the government paid the salaries of every worker. In order to save money, every now and then the government forced its employees to receive 10 percent of their salary in lottery tickets. In truth, this scheme of course saved the government many millions, as the total value of profits from lottery sales amounted to millions of rubles, while covering the cost of the few winning tickets cost the state a mere few thousand. The smallest prize was worth twenty rubles, and the first prize was the most expensive Russian car, the Moskvitch.

Of course, everyone preferred to receive cash rather than lottery tickets, which generally accounted for more financial loss than profit. But since people had already received lottery tickets, once the grand drawing took place, each employee would check the paper where the winning numbers were published to see if he might find his name. The newspapers would publish the winning numbers only a week or so after the official drawing, but the winner of the first prize would be announced that very day on several radio stations. Everyone would listen to the radio broadcast, hoping that maybe his luck had finally struck and that he would be the lucky winner. In order to win the coveted prize, both numbers had to match: the number of the specific ticket and the number of the series.

One day, after this older brother heard the number of the first prize winner on the radio, he rushed like everyone else to check his ticket, and his eyes widened in amazement: The number on his ticket perfectly matched the number read on the radio! Regarding the number of the series of tickets, however, something was strange. While his ticket had a three-digit serial number, the radio announcer had read only two digits.

Now, he waited with bated breath for the newspapers to publish the winners to find out whether his series number was right or not. But the paper only came a week after the official draw; in the meantime, he was so stressed that he could not sleep or eat. After a few days, he began to lose weight. He felt like he was losing his mind: One moment it was as though he had become rich overnight, and his next thought was that if the missing serial number turned out to be different from his, then it would all be over. His dreams would end, and he would have to continue to work hard for a living.

He shared his torment only with us, his closest friends. During that week, he went to the newsstands every few hours to see if the newspaper had come out, until the salespeople were sick of his peculiar interest.

The week finally passed, the newspaper arrived, and it turned out that the serial number on his ticket was identical to the lottery draw and that of the first prize—the Moskvitch car!

Winning the lottery ticket of the car was actually worth twice the price of the car itself: In the USSR you could not be rich openly. Rich people and black market business owners were too afraid of being taken to the KGB for an investigation into the source of their income to display their wealth. Thus a wealthy person might be willing to pay twice the price of a Moskvitch for a raffle ticket that entitled him to the best car in the country; he could openly drive the car around, and were anyone to ask how he had money for a car, he could wave his lottery ticket. Now he had to look for just such a rich, discreet person, and after one was found in Tashkent, the brother had found his prosperity.

We were all happy for him. We saw how he worked hard for a living, and we were especially happy that winning the grand prize meant he could move his parents and family to join him in Samarkand, where they would be able to live comfortably.

Endangering Ourselves to Support the Yeshiva

We took various measures to maintain secrecy in Samarkand. Someone might have prayed with us in the secret minyan, even as we withheld other information from them. The studies were the biggest secret.

The secrecy was so great that even our closest family members did not know about the underground yeshiva. Additionally, in order to maintain maximum confidentiality, the location of the studies had to be changed from time to time.

The danger in having boys learning Torah in a private house was that it was illegal on every front. First, the gathering itself was illegal. Second, the fact that the boys came from other cities, did not attend a government educational institution, did not work anywhere, nor have an official address, made their very presence in Samarkand illegal. In Russia of those days, staying in a city for over twenty-four hours without a permit was a criminal act. And obviously, if a yeshiva student was caught red-handed in a home, the host could be accused of organizing secret meetings for Torah and religion as well as hosting illegal residents. This is why we kept it a secret as much as possible.

Many times, the students hiding in the homes of members of the community encountered quite unpleasant situations. For example, they learned at one point in my parents' home at 23 Rosa Luxemburg Street. At that time, my sister, brother-in-law Eliyahu, and their three children lived in the house as well, and because my brother-in-law was sick and had a heart condition, it was very important for the boys to be quiet all day and not disturb his rest. Instead of learning in the living room next to my brother-in-law's bedroom, the boys were forced to learn in my parents' bedroom, which was further away. Therefore, my mother was unable to rest during the daytime because her bedroom was occupied by yeshiva students.

When my brother-in-law's parents would come to visit him, the boys would be careful not to leave my parents' bedroom. Eli's parents realized, however, that something was happening in that room: they heard strange sounds coming from there, and the door was always closed. But they knew not to ask any questions in our homes, especially when no information had been offered beforehand, and never inquired further.

Of course, we were extremely careful that the courtyard gate always be locked. When we once forgot to lock the gate, Eliyahu's parents entered the yard unexpectedly. The boys saw them and rushed toward their usual hiding place in the bedroom, but it was too late. Eli's parents started laughing. "Why are you running?" they said. "Now we understand why that room is always closed and the meaning of the sounds coming from within it!" But the boys were still quite alarmed. Eli turned to his parents and said, "Please, act as if you have not seen anything and do not know anything."

Later, the boys returned to study in my brother Berel's house at 6 Tchlekskaya Street. With its enclosed courtyard and its private, heated hut, one can just imagine the heaven this must have seemed to the boys, in comparison with the previous location.

At that time, when my father or mother would come to visit my brother, he tried very hard to keep them away from the place where the boys learned. No one knew who would be called to the KGB next, so why should anyone have to keep such a secret? No one was sure they could resist the interrogation and torture of the KGB, so people preferred simply not to reveal anything even to their closest relatives. For the same reason, the parents themselves did not want to know too many details.

One time, recalls Shmuel Chaim Frenkel, a young Lubavitcher man in his early twenties was visiting the Zaltzman home at 23 Rosa Luxemburg Street. Sensing that something was going on, in his curiosity, he was eager to find out what it was. He approached my three-year-old niece Rochel'le, the daughter of Eliyahu Mishulovin (now Rebbetzin Rochel Gluckowsky from Rehovot, Israel), and began talking to her as if he knew that people studied in their home.

Everyone was afraid that little Rochel'le would reveal the secret. But to our astonishment, this clever girl swung matters in such a way that she revealed nothing and this twenty-something fellow left our home without finding out a thing. Children were raised knowing how to keep a secret from a young age indeed!

At another point, the yeshiva moved to Dovid Mishulovin's home, on Komunisticheskaya Street. The advantage of his house was that its windows faced the street, and before entering the home one had to knock on the window and would be seen quite easily.

Another benefit was that the house had a basement, the steps to which were located in the foyer leading to the house. In the event that an unwanted guest was about to enter, there was enough time for all the boys to quickly make a getaway and descend to the basement.

It happened once that Yaakov Pil, the brother of R. Dovid's wife, Sarah, came over to visit, and the boys immediately went into hiding in the basement. When Yaakov heard a noise in the basement and asked what it was, he was simply told it was mice. But once there was a more serious situation. A woman, actually a mother of one of the boys who studied there, came to visit Sarah Mishulovin. While all the boys were sitting quietly down in the basement, one of them had to use the bathroom very badly. Still, as long as the woman was upstairs, no one could come out, and he suffered immensely. Since then, they put a pail for the boys to use in case of an emergency.

My Honeymoon

At the time of my marriage, I was in good spirits and a relatively successful businessman. I could have easily gone on a honeymoon with my wife to one of the famous resort towns such as Sochi or Yalta. But what excited me then? That our modest living quarters could serve as an additional place for the boys from our yeshiva to study!

High on my agenda at that time was arranging the various locations where the yeshiva boys could study during the day. My wife and I spent our honeymoon in our "shed," measuring eight by ten yards. This one room served as both our bedroom and dining room. We also had the merit to host four yeshiva students who studied there all day and ate meals cooked by my wife.

After our daughter Chanah was born, we divided the room in two. One side barely fit two beds with a dresser between them, and the other side housed our daughter's crib and a dining table where the boys would study. In this way, my daughter as a baby heard the sweet sounds of Torah study, reminiscent of the great sage of the Mishna, R. Yehoshua ben Chananya, whose mother brought his cradle to the study hall for this very purpose. This is how we spent our first year of marriage, as well as the coming years.

When we considered moving to a new residence, we needed to take into account whether the new location would be able to continue serving as a place of learning for the boys. Indeed, when we moved to 8 Novaya Street, the learning continued in our house. Our new residence had two advantages: first, it was larger than our previous apartment, and second, the extended absences of our new landlord, who was a cobbler. Having learned of a shortage of shoes in Kazakhstan, and that cobblers working there earned a nice profit, he went to work in Alma Ata, the capital of Kazakhstan. During the summer, his wife and children would join him there as well. The landlord's wife allowed me to use their big sun porch while she was away, and the boys were able to learn there in comfort.

By this stage, R. Yosef Volovik had also become a lecturer in the yeshiva, and the students were: Avraham Goldberg, of blessed memory, his cousin Avraham Pressman, now a famous cantor, Dovid Itche Marinovsky, Shmuel Chaim Frenkel, Shaya Gratzman, Naftali Estulin, and one whose name I do not recall. In general, we tried to avoid gathering more than four students in one place, but sometimes we had no choice. Since, as related above, our new home was a good location for study during the summer, seven boys ended up learning at my house. I remember that when R. Yosef Volovik came to us for the first time to give a class, he was surprised to see such a large group of boys in one place.

We later moved again, to 7a Artileriyskaya Street. It was virtually paradise there: The house had three rooms and a completely private courtyard. Additionally, the adjacent inner courtyard had an empty apartment, which we subsequently rented. The boys were thus able to learn without fear of prying neighbors.

Despite all this, the non-Jews outside sensed that their Jewish neighbors were different, and on occasion noticed young Jews entering the courtyard. They tried to disturb us and threw stones at the yard's iron gate.

In order to preserve secrecy, the yeshiva students had to remain inside the house throughout the day. Letting them leave during the daytime hours would only alert the neighbors to the existence of illegal activity. As such, the hostess was required to prepare meals for the boys learning in her home.

The boys, however, found it difficult to remain quietly indoors for so long and would go outside from time to time to dispel some of their tension. Eventually, the neighbors figured out the source of the noise coming from our property and we had no choice but to move the boys to a different home.

During the time the studies took place in our home, my wife was afraid to stay home while I went to work. She was afraid of not knowing what to answer if a neighbor or someone else asked about the noise. When I would leave for work, she would cry and ask to go out with me. She could walk the streets with our daughter Chana'le, then aged three, until I returned from work in the evening. She had her reasons for concern, but I could not agree and asked that she remain at home. "If a neighbor knocks on the door," I said, "it is better for someone to open the door and provide an explanation. If the boys hide with no one opening the door, it will increase the neighbor's suspicions." Realizing that she had no choice but to stay home, my wife cried, "Why didn't you tell me when we first met how my life would be after the wedding!"

The Homeless *Bochurim*

In the first years of the underground yeshiva, there were only three families in on the secret: the Mishulovins, my parents, and the family of my brother Berel. After a number of years had passed, and we saw that the police were not persecuting the Jews as heavily as they had done under Stalin's reign, we relaxed somewhat and expanded to other homes. This enabled us to accept yet more students from other cities and to open additional classes with three to five boys learning in each. Thus we merited to have dozens of precious young men studying in the yeshiva, from all over the USSR: They came from Tashkent, Moscow, Riga, Chernovitz, Gorky, Odessa, Uzghorod, Chust, Apsha, Katta-Kurgan, and other cities.

Still, our ever-present, near-paranoid fear led to more uncomfortable situations. The case of the three students, who had come from out of town to learn and sleep in the home of a certain family, was one of many. One night, after they finished learning, they went out for some fresh air in the yard and began to play a game of soccer. Apparently, they forgot to be careful; it was late, and the sounds of their game could be heard on the street. Their host was returning home just then and, upon hearing the noise on the street, was terrified. He entered the yard and yelled at the boys, "The neighbors know I don't have children your age. Your shouting will cause me problems!" Overcome with anger, he ordered them to take their things and leave.

The boys were out on the street and they didn't know what to do. They decided to go to R. Moshe Nissilevitch. Although he lived about three kilometers away and it was in the middle of the night, they went to his house with the hope that he would let them sleep there. R. Moshe had pity on them and took them in, but they had learned their lesson.

R. Yisrael Pevzner and the Boy from Riga

The Lubavitchers in Russia who somehow caught wind of the Tomchei Temimim in Samarkand considered it a merit to do whatever they could to help us, even though none of them ever asked what was truly going on in Samarkand.

R. Moshe Katzenelenbogen and R. Leib Chatzernov, both from Moscow, constantly kept an eye out for us. When foreign tourists came, they obtained whatever Chabad books they were able and reserved them for us. On one of my visits to Moscow, they produced a

HaYom Yom for me. *HaYom Yom,* an early work of the Lubavitcher Rebbe, is a treasure trove of Chassidic customs, historical tidbits, and profound aphorisms, arranged according to the calendar. When the book arrived, our joy in Samarkand was boundless. We excitedly devoured every line, including the sparing biographies of the rebbes printed in the front of the book, and even read the conditions of membership in the Machne Israel organization directed by the Rebbe, as detailed at its end. The book's every detail was of the greatest interest to us. After photographing each page, we developed the pictures and sent copies to Tashkent.

One special person who endeavored greatly to help us was R. Yisrael Pevzner. He came to Samarkand during the war together with the refugees and remained there afterward. He was an energetic man, a successful entrepreneur, and a generous donor. Outwardly, he looked like a sophisticated businessman, never without a hat and tie, but inside he was full of Chassidic warmth and vigor. On account of his business dealings, however, the government suspected him of illegal activity and pursued him. He was forced to escape from Samarkand and for some time he relocated from city to city until he finally settled in Riga.

R. Yisrael had a well-developed Chassidic "sense of smell," and he somehow found out about our yeshiva and developed an interest in it. He was in constant touch with me concerning the yeshiva, but always acted with greatest discretion and avoided unnecessary questions. When I visited him once in Riga, he told me a story he knew would interest me, that of R. Zalman Levin (also known as R. Zalman Kursker after his hometown of Kursk), a former student of the underground Lubavitcher yeshivas in Russia.

R. Zalman was amongst the wartime refugees in Samarkand, after having escaped from Leningrad along with Rabbis Isaac Karasik, Nachum Volosov, and Yeshaya Gopin. When he learned that the KGB was looking for him, he fled to Tashkent and from there to Moscow. His Shabbos observance made it very difficult for him to earn a livelihood. Once, R. Shmuel Prus, then living in Riga, came to Moscow to visit the home of Rabbi Zalman and his wife, Sarah. He arrived unannounced and saw the poverty in their home; even on Shabbos they literally had nothing to eat.

When R. Shmuel Prus returned home to Riga, he found a job for Reb Zalman in nearby Tukums, a small Latvian town, where the factory director promised to allow him to keep the Shabbos. R. Zalman Levin moved to Tukums with his wife and their two small children—a boy and girl, twins born to them thirteen years into their marriage—and revived Jewish life there. The town synagogue, previously closed after emptying of worshippers, began to host prayers three times daily, as the older locals remembered how to pray from childhood. Kosher meat appeared in the city, since Reb Zalman was certified to slaughter poultry.

The government despised this revival of Jewish life. They quickly moved to ban his activities, arrested him and sentenced him to ten years of hard labor. The synagogue was shut completely, its keys and Torah scrolls consigned to the authorities. Shortly after, they had an article printed in the local newspaper announcing that the synagogue had been closed with the full consent of its management and members. According to the article, the locals were all loyal Soviets uninterested in religion; the recent spurt in the town's religious activity was entirely the fault of this Jew from Moscow, Zalman Levin. Now that he was finally arrested, they were "happily" giving the synagogue over to the government.

With the burden of supporting and educating the children now imposed on the shoulders of their mother, Mrs. Sarah Levin, R. Zalman's family moved back to the city of Riga two years after his arrest. There was a Chassidic community in Riga, with regular *farbrengens* and other communal gatherings, and secret prayers in private homes—all vital contributors to the children's upbringing. Additionally, the prisons where Zalman was incarcerated were in the environs of Riga, so it was easier to bring him food parcels and visit him when special permission was given to do so.

His only son, Moshe Chaim, who by then had already become bar mitzvah, studied with a private teacher who would come to his house for a number of hours a day and study Torah, including the

Prophets and Writings, and the Code of Jewish Law, with him. He had started on the Talmud, but needed a study partner; he benefited greatly from a Chassidic environment.

Since the yeshiva was a secret operation, R. Yisrael Pevzner could not tell the boy's mother, Mrs. Levin, the location of the yeshiva. Rather, he said that he knew of a yeshiva somewhere in Russia and convinced her that when the opportunity arose, she should send her son to learn there. When I arrived, he told her that a man had come who was prepared to take her son to yeshiva, on condition that she wouldn't ask where they were going and where her son would learn and sleep.

She agreed, adding only that she wanted to see the person who would take her son to the yeshiva. The morning before I left the city, R. Yisrael brought me to their home. Sarah Levin asked nothing. Her only request was that I watch over her only son. I was amazed by the heroism of this extraordinary Chassidic woman. Her husband was locked behind bars, yet she was ready to send her son to a distant place, not even knowing where he would be, just so that he could learn Torah.

The next day I left Riga, and a short time later, R. Yisrael sent Moshe Chaim by airplane to Samarkand. I met him at the airport and brought him to the yeshiva.

Today, this young boy has a large Chassidic family and is a prominent Chabad rabbi in a Jewish Russian neighborhood in Brooklyn. I once met with him and we had a friendly discussion, reminiscing over shared memories of the past. He told me that the story of his sending off was actually a bit different than I had thought. His mother would never have allowed him to leave her without knowing his final destination. R. Yisrael told her where we were headed, but didn't tell me that the mother knew our destination. He knew that if I was aware that she knew, I would never have agreed to take him.

During my conversation with R. Moshe Chaim Levin, he shared with me some additional details that, had I known them at the time, would have made me refuse to accept the boy into the yeshiva. In his great desire that the boy be accepted, R. Yisrael had hid these details from me as well.

This is what actually happened:

Shortly after R. Yisrael secretly told Mrs. Sarah Levin about the place of learning in Samarkand, a certain Jew from Uzbekistan arrived in Riga. Mrs. Levin, not imagining how careful we were to maintain the total secrecy of the existence of the underground yeshiva, innocently asked the Jew to take her son to Samarkand to study on his way back.

Knowing how eagerly R. Yisrael was waiting for an opportunity to send her son to Samarkand, she happily informed him that she had found someone who had consented to take the boy.

When R. Yisrael heard this, he became very upset. This fellow was of a suspicious nature and everyone was careful around him. R. Yisrael understood that were the boy to arrive in Samarkand in this way, he would be refused as a new student due to the fear of his companion. In fact, they would deny the very existence of the yeshiva!

He explained the problem to the boy's mother and asked her to tell her guest that her son was not well and could not go with him at the present time. She followed R. Yisrael's instructions and the boy remained in Riga.

A few days later, after her guest had left Riga, Sarah sent her young son alone on a flight to Samarkand, with a transfer in Moscow—a distance of over 2,000 miles—and the rest is history. That was the extent of a mother's desire that her son learn in yeshiva, at a time when her husband was in prison.

On that same visit to Riga, R. Yisrael told me that he had recently been visited by the Rebbe's secretary, Rabbi Nissan Mindel. R. Nissan had a set of *tefillin* that were fashioned out of one piece of leather, which is the halachically preferable method of forming *tefillin*. Being that such *tefillin* were not available in Russia, R. Yisrael asked R. Nissan to exchange them with his own. R. Nissan agreed and left his pair with R. Yisrael. I had the privilege of putting on those *tefillin* and reciting the *Shema* with them.

The Greatest Treasure:
Four Volumes of *Likutei Sichos*

During those years, we were disconnected from any Chabad literature, and only on rare occasions would we merit to receive some Chabad material from tourists who had come to visit Russia. We had no idea of the topics the Rebbe was addressing in his talks, or what he was demanding of the chassidim at any given time. R. Yisrael, who passionately wanted to help us in Samarkand with whatever he was able, told me that R. Nissan Mindel had left with him a two-volume set of *Likutei Dibburim*, a selection of the Rebbe Rayatz's public talks throughout the years. Since not all the Lubavitchers in his area had had a chance to go through them yet, he wasn't willing to give me the books themselves, but suggested that I photograph their pages and develop the pictures in Samarkand.

I was thrilled with this idea and rushed to buy ten rolls of film. R. Yisrael prepared his bedroom for me to photograph the two volumes. Before I entered the bedroom, he asked his wife not to go in so she wouldn't see what I was doing there. She did not ask any questions.

R. Yisrael also told me that tourists who had recently arrived from the United States had brought with them the first four volumes of *Likutei Sichos*. Now a thirty-nine-volume set, *Likutei Sichos* is perhaps the magnum opus of the Lubavitcher Rebbe and a classic work of Torah. According to R. Yisrael, the Chabad Rabbi in Leningrad, known as *der Liepler Rov,* had these volumes in his possession. He suggested that I travel to Leningrad and request that he give them to me. "He will probably be suspicious of you," he told me. "To calm his fears, tell him that Yisrael Pevzner sent you."

I headed straight for Leningrad and made my way to the main shul at 8 Nevsky Prospect Street. Next to the left-hand courtyard, on the second floor, was a small shul where most of the Lubavitchers in Leningrad had prayed before the war. The Rabbi, whose actual name was R. Avrohom Lubanov, lived in a small apartment below the shul. As was to be expected, he was initially suspicious of me and refused to admit that he had the books. However, after I told him that I was a friend of R. Yisrael Pevzner and that he had sent me here, he gave me the set of *Likutei Sichos* without any questions.

It is impossible to describe the joy of the Lubavitchers in Samarkand when I brought home this treasure. We immediately sent two volumes to the chassidim in Tashkent while we learned the other two volumes. After a few weeks we switched with them. It was enough time to review the two volumes from cover to cover. We learned it avidly day and night, devouring every word with great pleasure.

In the meantime, I developed the film with the pictures from *Likutei Dibburim*. It was dangerous to have these pictures, to the point that we did not show them to the boys in the yeshiva. Instead, I would sit together with R. Itche Mishulovin on Thursday nights to copy the Rebbe Rayatz's talks from the book into notebooks. I would compete with R. Itche as to who wrote faster and more nicely. (Truth be told, he won.) It was these copies that we gave to the boys to learn from.

Secrets Even from Close Friends

We once heard a rumor that during a 19th of Kislev *farbrengen* in Leningrad, the chassidim there spoke about the yeshiva in Samarkand, and about the great privilege of raising money in support of a branch of Tomchei Temimim. We were not too excited to hear this; the fact that people knew about our yeshiva in faraway Samarkand frightened us.

That summer, I was due to travel to central Russia for communal matters, and during my travels would be passing through many towns where Lubavitchers lived. At a meeting held before my trip, we decided that if someone asked about the yeshiva during the course of my travels, I would deny its existence. Even if it was someone who was aware, until then, of its existence, I would have to let him know that the yeshiva was no longer active.

This decision caused me tremendous discomfort. During my travels, I went to Moscow to attend the wedding of a friend from Samarkand, Mordechai Goldschmidt. I saw his uncle, R. Yisrael Pevzner, who had come from Riga for the wedding.

R. Yisrael was somewhat aware of the "yeshiva," and had even procured copies of *Likutei Dibburim* and *Likutei Sichos* for us. We spoke amicably about various matters, when he suddenly motioned to me over to a hidden corner. There he gave me an envelope containing 1,000 rubles, an enormous amount of money. It was enough to pay for an entire year's salary! I knew that if I accepted the money, it would clearly indicate that the yeshiva was in existence. Although we were good friends, because we had decided to keep a low profile, I refused to take the money, saying that there was no longer any reason to accept it.

Promising that no one else would know, he pleaded with me to take it until his eyes reddened with tears. I commiserated with him completely. If what I was saying was true, he was pained that the yeshiva was no longer operating; if not, why could he not merit to help? He was an older chassid while I was just a young man. I felt terrible, and so ill at ease that I wished at that moment for the earth to swallow me up alive. After some time, we finally parted with a heavy sigh.

Afterwards, Mordechai Goldschmidt, the groom, told me that R. Yisrael had not given in so easily. He had gone over to Mordechai as well and pleaded that he accept the money, but he also refused to take it.

When I returned to Samarkand, we held a meeting to review my trip. I told them about the uncomfortable situation I had been in with R. Yisrael. My friends understood what I had endured, but they were pleased that I had kept the secret even from him. This was all despite the fact that we did not doubt our friend R. Yisrael for a moment and we needed the money as well. Secrecy was the number one priority.

Those were the precautions we had to take to enable the yeshiva's survival during those difficult times.

Releasing the Students from the Army

The Talmud says: "The law of the land is the law." But this is only so if the rules of the justice system established by the government are not contrary to the Torah's laws.

Governments in the free world are committed to the protection of religious freedom of the individual. A contemporary example of this commitment in the United States military is illustrative. A religious Jew, after becoming a high-ranking officer in the US army, was ordered to remove his skullcap by a superior who felt it did not fit the country's military uniform. The Jewish officer went to court, made a case against the government, won, and was granted permission to wear his *kippah*.

A young man from Israel once sought a blessing from the Rebbe to receive an exemption from the Israeli army draft. The Rebbe replied very sharply: "Who says your blood is redder than the blood of your friends?" The Soviet military, on the other hand, was more problematic for a young Jewish man.

Soviet military conscription meant parting completely with Torah and its commandments. It was a life where you were not allowed to put on *tefillin*, had no time for prayer, no kosher food, no matzah on Passover, and so on. A religious Jew could not keep his Judaism in the army.

The boys who learned in Samarkand were of draft age and we had to ensure that they were released from army duties. R. Binyamin Malachovsky and R. Moshiach Chudaidatov took the leading role in this task.

The process of obtaining an exemption began about a year or more before they had to stand before the draft board. The yeshiva student would go to the local doctor and complain about some pain he had been experiencing. For a year or so, he would return to the doctor several times, complaining about the same "malady" that he supposedly suffered from. We usually chose illnesses that a doctor would have a hard time verifying, such as stomach pains or mental illnesses.

When it was time to stand before the draft board and the young man complained to the military doctor that he suffered from a certain malady, he would be asked to present his medical history. He would show that he had been to the doctor several times in the previous year regarding this complaint.

At the draft office, they did not always rely on the medical history and often ordered potential draftees to undergo tests and X-rays with specific doctors who were trusted by the military. In Samarkand, there were a few Jewish doctors who worked with the army, like Dr. Yosef Levin, Dr. Yitzchok (Izhye) Aharonson, Dr. Abayev and others. R. Binyamin and R. Moshiach were on good terms with them and would send the boys who needed confirmation of their illnesses to be checked by them.

This was a real self-sacrifice on the part of the doctors. They held high-ranking positions, and if caught, they would not only lose their job but could be put in jail. To their credit, the doctors never asked for payment for the services they provided for us. Still, we felt obligated to thank them and R. Binyamin and R. Moshiach would send them various gifts.

It happened quite often that after the doctors in the recruiting center confirmed that a boy had an illness and was unfit to serve in the army, military officials decided to have him examined by another doctor or to have him sent for more tests and X-rays. In such cases, the medical experts who partnered with us on behalf of our boys would turn to the doctor to whom the young man was sent and ask him to do them a favor by issuing a similar opinion to their conclusion. The physicians knew that there would be other occasions in which they would need a favor from the Jewish doctor and they were thus willing to cover for each other.

It was often necessary to go to the draft office and wait for the doctor in the yard outside, in order to remind him that one of our boys was coming that day. One time, during the Shabbos morning prayers, R. Binyamin was told that someone might have informed on them for trying to get Emanuel Ladayev released from the army. The Jewish doctor who worked on his file was very afraid and she was considering reporting what had happened so that the blame would not fall on her shoulders.

R. Binyamin immediately removed his prayer shawl and ran to the doctor's office, located several kilometers away, in order to placate her. She literally cried to him and said, "What do I need this for? I can lose my entire career and be sent to jail!" It took much effort on Binyamin's part to regain her confidence.

Years later, R. Binyamin was speaking to an audience in New York about the self-sacrifice Russian Jewry in those days. After his talk, a young man who had recently left Russia approached him and reminded him of their acquaintance in Russia:

"No doubt you remember that in my youth I wasn't thought of as one of the studious boys in the yeshiva and I spent time with friends who weren't a great influence for me," he said. "My father sent me to Samarkand in the hopes that it would change me for the better.

"When it was my turn to stand before the draft office, I asked for your help in receiving an exemption and was told that a meeting had been held about my case. The participants in the meeting deliberated whether to help me get an exemption or to allow me to go to the army; perhaps the latter would actually make a *mentch* out of me! You maintained that if I were to go to the army, I would completely abandon Judaism. The others accepted what you said and because of your efforts I was exempted. I will never forget your great kindness!"

Support from the Ribnitzer Rebbe

Some of the boys who came to us from the Carpathians traveled through Chernovitz in order to meet the righteous Ribnitzer Rebbe, Rabbi Chaim Zanvil Abramowitz, of blessed memory, and to ask for his opinion regarding their travel to Samarkand. No one knew about a yeshiva for sure, but word got around that learning was taking place somewhere in Samarkand. He told them all to go and gave them his blessing for the trip.

Benzion Rubinson, one of the top students in our yeshiva, actually came from Chernovitz, the city of the Ribnitzer Rebbe. He had arrived in Samarkand at a young age; his father had been sentenced to ten years in prison, leaving him alone with his mother and younger sister, Tamar. R. Mendel Futerfas, who was a relative of theirs and lived in Chernovitz after his own release from imprisonment, arranged for young Benzion to travel to Samarkand.

Every year, Benzion would travel to Chernovitz to spend the summer with his mother and sister. His family, like all of the Chabad chassidim in Chernovitz, was friendly with the Ribnitzer, and Benzion would visit him on his return home. The Ribnitzer never asked him where he was learning, but understood from their conversations that he was studying somewhere, and would give him 1,000 rubles as a donation for the yeshiva. A large sum like that would cover the salary of a teacher in the yeshiva for almost an entire year.

An incident on one of Benzion Rubinson's returns to Samarkand gave us all a serious fright. Upon arriving at the airport, to Benzion's shock, he was apprehended by the police and taken to an interrogation room. He began to panic, trying to determine the reason for his arrest. Had the authorities finally gotten wind of the underground yeshiva?

As the police prepared to search his belongings, Benzion's heart froze: In his suitcase was a pocket-sized *Tanya*, printed in America. G-d forbid that they should find that, he thought. Benzion looked on at the search in dread.

The police turned over his entire suitcase, but miraculously, paid no attention to the little *Tanya*. Then they found his *tefillin*, and asked him what they were. Benzion claimed that he didn't know, only that someone had handed them to him and said he would pick them up from him later. If so, said the commanding officer, leave them here, and if anyone asks for them, make sure to send them to us. They then let him go.

Understandably, after this reception, Benzion was in no rush to continue on to my brother Berel's house and risk leading the police to the learning then being hosted there. Instead, he went over to the home of Rivkah and Chaim Volovik, whom he knew from Chernovitz.

Some time went by, and the *tefillin* remained sitting at the police station; no one dared to go and ask for them. One day, the details of this story made their way to Refael Chudaidatov, who was a bold, defiant man. "How can we just leave the *tefillin* in the hands of those gentiles?" he said. He went over to the police, claimed that the phylacteries were his, and demanded that they be returned to him. After proffering some money to the young clerk, he was handed the *tefillin*.

The Generosity of R. Moshe Goldis

Apart from the Ribnitzer Rebbe, we also received large donations from R. Moshe Goldis, another Jew from the Carpathians. R. Moshe was a successful businessman, as well as an unusually kind man with a heart of gold. When he heard of boys from the Carpathians learning in Samarkand, he decided to visit and inquire about these boys himself. His arrival, however, made us very nervous. We didn't know who he was, and in those years, we kept secrets even from people we knew well. We certainly didn't share information with strangers, but within a short period of time, we recognized what sort of person he was and R. Moshe Nissilevitch befriended him. From then on, until we left Russia, R. Moshe Goldis donated large sums of money to our yeshiva and to our other activities. Thanks to his charitable donations, we were able to arrange learning programs in many locations in the cities and towns near Samarkand.

R. Moshe Goldis was eventually able to leave Russia, arriving in the Land of Israel in the 1970s. The Russians did not allow him to take out any valuables; all of his wealth was relinquished. After we located him in Israel, we helped him raise the funds to buy an apartment in Bnei Brak.

CHAPTER 13

What Was the KGB Looking for in My Workshop?

One of the greatest challenges for a religious Jew in the Soviet Union was making a living without desecrating the Shabbos. In Russia, everybody was obligated to work; the unemployed were considered parasites and their citizenship rights were revoked. All official workplaces were open on Shabbos and anyone registered as an employee was compelled to show up to work on Shabbos. An absence could be put down to religious reasons and lead to being charged with crimes against the state. Since businesses were nationalized and considered state property, if you undermined productivity, you were, in essence, undermining the Russian economy.

Many people tried to find work in small factories and then bribe the manager to look the other way when it came to their weekly absences. The supervisor would usually refuse, afraid that people would find out and report him to the authorities, inevitably causing him to lose his job. The government deliberately created an atmosphere in which employees were encouraged to tattle on their employers in the event that they noticed any illegal goings on.

Only a few individuals managed to find work in small factories without too many other workers around. Then, in rare instances, it was possible to come to an agreement with the manager.

The most common solution in the early years after the Revolution was to work from home. Many religious Jews took advantage of a loophole in the law allowing persons with physical limitations to work at home. The more business-inclined started their own enterprises, freeing them to work without oversight.

Of course, in Communist Russia there was no option of owning a private business. Everything belonged to the government. There was a government office in every city responsible for registering the workers and the industries located in that city. To open a plant, one had to obtain a government permit and strictly follow their official regulations.

Some of the larger factories producing a range of products would open branches in different locations if there wasn't enough room for everyone within the main plant. I was twenty years old, and like many of the Lubavitcher *bochurim* at that time, I had neither a college degree nor a profession with which to support myself. Instead, I went to a government industrial factory that produced household and bathroom products and offered to expand their operations by opening a clothing-labels factory under their auspices. I presumed that they would take an interest in the proposal and agree to my terms.

I presented samples of the cloth labels I intended to produce. The factory managers had no idea how this would work—who would need these labels and who would buy them? I reassured them that production would only begin after I had taken specific orders from clothing companies. Then, to ensure our privacy, I added that most workers in my line of work lived quite a distance from the main factory and I wanted to open a branch in close proximity to their area.

I bribed the managers and they made a simple calculation. It didn't make much of a difference to them if this department was situated far from the main plant, as long as I wasn't asking them to make any investment in it. They approved my request and I opened a factory near the Jewish area in Samarkand. Now I—and anyone I hired—was a registered worker of the government factory.

The Factory Opens

Aside from the bribe, the managers had another motivation for approving my request: In general, they knew that Jewish entrepreneurs could be relied upon to meet the government's "profit plan," prescribing how much each factory was expected to earn annually. I assured them that my division would be able to make an outsize contribution to their overall quota. Over the years, I kept to my word and thus became indispensable to them.

I quickly worked to establish ties with manufacturers throughout the Soviet Union in need of labels for clothing as well as other products and then, after receiving their orders, to produce and ship the labels to them. To reach out to as many clothing factories as possible, I sent agents all over the Soviet Union in search of business. A comprehensive business directory didn't yet exist in Russia, so when they arrived in a city, my representatives would have to locate any manufacturing plants in the relevant industries before arranging to meet with them. Officially, procuring orders was my responsibility, so all of my agents were people I knew I could trust.

One day, a brilliant idea came to my mind. Since nearly every city in the Soviet Union had designated industrial zones, I simply sent out hundreds of letters containing our sample labels, each addressed to the "industrial complex" of a different city in Russia. I had no exact addresses, but in most cities, if there were any large factories, the postal workers knew their location and the letters usually made it to their destinations. Out of the hundreds of factories that received my letters, enough responded to bring us plenty of work and I was able to stop sending out representatives for that purpose. A list of cities in the Soviet Union was all I needed.

Along with the quotas placed on the factories, each worker also had an individual quota. By law, laborers in our field could earn on average between 90 to 100 rubles a month, or with extra hours, up to 120 rubles. If someone began to work enough to justify a larger salary, the officials would instead simply adjust their expectations for the rest of the wage earners in line with his output.

Since our enterprise was able to make large profits, I registered fifteen to twenty people as my employees, while in actuality only four to five people worked there. Officially, the factory's revenue was supposed to go towards paying everyone, but by ensuring that we kept up a reasonable output, I was able to provide an average salary of 120 rubles a month for each of the actual employees, while the others received only a nominal portion of the salary listed in their name.

I was elated to earn a sizable income, from which I could set aside a large portion of the money for the underground yeshiva and other communal activities. The concept of giving our money for communal causes was instinctual to us.

The others, my employees in name only, made their money on the black market or were supported by aid packages from abroad and were thus able to observe Shabbos and the holidays without any trouble. And, as registered workers, the government wouldn't persecute them as parasites. Both sides profited greatly from this arrangement.

Naturally, all of our employees, both those who worked and those who were merely registered as workers, had to be reliable people from the community. If a single person would tattle, it would lead to the arrest of everyone involved and ruin the entire enterprise.

Still, for all of our caution, and although we had located the factory far from the main plant to avoid too much scrutiny from the head office, we were still suspected of closing on Shabbos. From time to time, our supervisors announced that they were coming for inspection on Shabbos. We had no choice. All of us had to be there. On Friday, we would bring various books to the factory and on Shabbos morning we learned Chassidus or reviewed the weekly Torah reading as we waited for the inspectors. Most of the time, they didn't turn up; they just wanted to frighten us. But sometimes they did, and walked around for a few minutes before leaving. They didn't need to see us actively working; they were satisfied just to see us present.

Assessing Our Factory

The government did not rely on these internal inspections—for good reason—so every city was graced with a government "Technical Inspection Bureau." This department was supposed to visit the factories from time to time to check the level of productivity of the workers and to decide whether it was necessary to change any salaries or production quotas. Accompanied by a representative from our main plant, their inspectors would determine how much each worker was capable of producing by scrutinizing the entire operation from top to bottom.

We developed good ties with the head of the Inspection Bureau, Ivan Ivanovitch, after giving him a hefty bribe. When our factory was scheduled for inspection, he would come on his own and ensure that all went well. Nevertheless, assessment day was nerve-wracking.

One day, we were notified by the Inspection Bureau to prepare for an annual evaluation. I told all of the registered workers to be present on this day, assigned a different work station to each employee, and instructed them to refer all of the inspectors' questions to me.

Demonstrating that all fifteen of our registered workers were employed in our plant's production was a tricky task: on a daily basis, only four people completed the very same work. I reserved for myself the most crucial job on the machine producing the labels. I didn't want to risk the chance that someone else would complete our quota too quickly.

My brother Berel had a similar factory, operating under a different government office. Since we had good ties with the Inspection Bureau, we decided that Berel would invite his representative on the same day, so that we could both have our inspections completed simultaneously.

Mysterious Disappearances

The day arrived. At nine in the morning almost all of my workers promptly entered the factory. The chief inspector, Ivan Ivanovitch, was there. Lilia, the gentile representative of our head office, came as well. Only the woman representing the main plant my brother worked for was missing.

Berel asked us to please delay the inspection until the representative of his plant would arrive, and since we had no phone in our factory, he went out to locate a public phone to call her. He wanted her to hurry since everybody was waiting.

My brother was supposed to be five minutes. Ten minutes went by and he still hadn't returned. Mr. Ivanovitch said that while we waited for the other representative to arrive, he would go out and buy cigarettes. More time went by and he didn't return either.

Michoel Mishulovin, who was registered as a worker in my factory, said that until they all returned and the inspection began, he was going to a nearby lake to immerse in preparation for prayer. He left his pocket-sized *Tanya* in my office in case his clothes were stolen and the contraband book discovered.

He left. The minutes ticked by and now Michoel too had disappeared.

There was something very odd about all of this and I began to feel uneasy. But even in my worst nightmare, I did not anticipate what was yet to come.

A half hour went by and the head inspector returned with a pack of cigarettes. I asked him what happened and why he had been gone for so long. He avoided answering me, saying that nothing had happened, but I sensed that something was seriously amiss.

In the meantime, the woman whom Berel had called showed up, but he was still missing. We decided to start the inspection in my factory because it was nearly eleven o'clock. My hands were occupied with producing labels, but my head was elsewhere. I was deeply concerned about Berel and Michoel's whereabouts, frantic even, as I wondered what was taking them so long.

I couldn't dwell on these thoughts because Ivan Ivanovitch was standing over my shoulder with a stopwatch, timing how long it took to produce each label. That way, he could calculate how many labels we could make in a day and how much the monthly salary should be.

After what seemed like forever to me, Michoel came back. Still in the middle of the inspection, I couldn't ask him what had happened.

A Surprise Inspection

By two in the afternoon, the inspection was almost complete when the front door suddenly swung open and in walked Berel, white as a ghost. I couldn't ask him anything either, as he was closely followed by a man, elegantly dressed, who scanned all of the workers with narrowed eyes and a grim expression. His dress and demeanor led me to believe that he was a KGB agent.

As I tried to think of a reason a KGB agent would be in my factory, and wondered how he was connected with my brother's disappearance, another agent walked in, followed by another one, and then another. In less than a minute, the room was under the scrutiny of seven officers of the KGB.

I cannot begin to describe how terrified I was. The first agent who came in, apparently the leader of the group, quietly muttered to himself, "What is this, an underground printing press?"

I quaked inside. If that is what we were suspected of, we were in deep trouble. An underground printing press meant that we were printing anti-government material. In those years, even a simple typewriter had to be registered with the KGB and now we suddenly had an entire underground printing press operation!

In the meantime, Berel had managed to walk past me and he whispered, "I was 'there' and 'they' took my home address." It was unnecessary for him to say what 'there' was and who 'they' were. He said this deliberately so that I would know that his house was under KGB watch. Five bochurim were learning there as a part of our underground yeshiva.

Now I was petrified. I began trembling from a burning heat and an icy cold all at once and felt my body break out in a cold sweat as I struggled to breathe evenly. My thoughts whirled. *Oy vey*, the *bochurim* are sitting right now in Berel's house and the KGB have probably already gone there and caught them learning Talmud at the table. Who knows what they are going through in the KGB interrogation rooms and how well they will be able to keep their mouths shut.

The *bochurim*, Naftali, Shmuel Chaim, Shaya and two others, were high-quality boys who were careful not to say a word about their clandestine Jewish studies to anyone in Samarkand, but KGB agents were experts at getting people to talk. Even a mute would speak for them. What if they did not withstand the torture and revealed that I was connected with the yeshiva? At that time, for various reasons, the coordination of all the classes had come under my responsibility.

The senior agent barked, "Who is the manager here?" My workers pointed to me and the agent motioned for me to approach him. I was in the middle of producing labels and pretended to be oblivious to what was going on. The others also tried to remain calm and maintain a composed look on their faces although all of them were terribly frightened.

The senior official asked me, "Which plant are you under?"

"Zavad Chozbitizdely," I answered.

He asked, "Do you have a rental agreement with the owner of this property?"

I said that I did. Together we left the workshop and went to locate our landlord. The landlord took out our official contract and showed it to the senior agent, who examined the agreement and then returned it.

In the meantime, the agents noticed that amongst all the Jewish workers there was one non-Jewish woman: Lilia, the representative from the main office. A few agents went to speak with her privately in the yard. After a half hour, one agent then removed something from his pocket and showed it to her. She said something to them and then the KGB left our factory without another word.

When Lilia came back in, I asked her what the KGB wanted to know. She said that she had understood from them that they were looking for a particular person. They had shown her a picture and asked whether she knew the man in the picture.

"I didn't know him and I said the truth, that I did not recognize him. Apparently, they had made a mistake."

I did not accept her answer; they had spoken for a while before showing her the picture. We were deeply shaken by the incident, but could not speak freely amongst ourselves since the inspection had not yet been completed. All we could do was comment to one another, "How interesting! I wonder what they wanted."

When the inspection was finally over, I hurried to Berel's house, hoping that the *bochurim* were still there. I was surprised to find that all five of them had left on their own. Apparently, some of our neighbors had seen the agents drag Berel into a car and hurried to my house to tell my father what had happened. My father went to Berel's house and told the boys to leave immediately.

In the evening, I located the *bochurim* and told them that some temporary problems had come up with their continued learning in Samarkand and they should return home instantly. There was fear in their voices as they asked, "What happened?"

I didn't want to scare them, so I just said that for various reasons it was necessary to change the location where they learned and in the interim, they should go home to Tashkent. We would notify them when to return.

Arranging the boys' trip to Tashkent wasn't a simple matter. Tickets weren't always available and since the train station was crawling with police meticulously surveying passersby, meandering around the place with the *bochurim* wasn't advisable. With Hashem's help I was able to purchase tickets immediately and I sent them safely on their way.

The next day, I discovered my first strands of gray hair.

Michoel's Miracle

So what had happened with everyone?

My factory was located behind a yard, set back so that it wasn't easily visible from the street. Beyond the yard was a sand and stone embankment over which the electric train rode. Berel had crossed over those iron tracks when he left to call his office's representative that morning. As soon as he went down the other side, two men in plainclothes approached him, grabbed him, and shoved him into a car parked on the side of the road. He didn't know whether he had fallen into the clutches of thieves or the KGB.

As soon as he was thrown into the back seat of the car, the two men who had grabbed him sat down next to him, one on his right and one on his left, and warned him to remain silent. The man at the wheel began driving quickly. As they rode, the men at his side lifted Berel's hat and discovered his *yarmulke* underneath.

"Why do you wear that?" they asked.

Berel, who was naturally bald, had an excuse ready-made. The piece of fabric on his head, he told them, simply helped to fill the empty space beneath his hat. Then they began quizzing him about where he was coming from and where he was running.

He told them everything "by the book"—that the factory he worked in was undergoing an inspection and explained that he was running to a public phone in order to tell his factory's representative to hurry over.

As the car continued driving along the streets of Samarkand, Berel noticed that they were approaching the KGB headquarters. When the gates opened, he thought it was the end. He was taken to the interrogation room and asked all the same questions again, along with some other inquiries.

During this interrogation, the agents took this information down—including where he lived, which made him very concerned about the fate of the *bochurim* who were learning there. When it was over, seven agents made out for the factory, together with Berel.

Ivan Ivanovitch, who had gone out for five minutes to buy cigarettes, and took half an hour to return, told us afterwards that he had also bumped into the KGB officers swarming the area. When they saw him leave the factory they grabbed him as well and questioned him as to where he was from and where he was going. They detained him for a short while before realizing that he was not connected with us and he was released.

The same fate had befallen Michoel Mishulovin. He said that after he had exited the factory and turned into a small alleyway in the direction of the lake, a man in civilian clothes chased after him, ordered him to halt, and then interrogated him too. Michoel told him that he worked in the area and since he wasn't feeling well, he had decided to go to the lake and refresh himself.

The KGB agent searched him and after failing to find anything suspicious, released him. Michoel realized what a miracle it was that he had left the small *Tanya* in our office. If that book had been in his pocket, the KGB agent would surely have found it and seen that it was printed in New York, which was reason enough to arrest him and accuse him of having ties with the West.

The KGB Asks for Our Files

Although I was in charge of the factory, officially our manager was Aharon Pakanayev, a religious Bukharian Jew. Normally he did not mix into anything that went on in the factory, but I preferred for somebody else to officially represent us to the government and paid him every month to do so. Figuring that he would probably find out what had happened, I told him about the incident and made sure to underplay how terrified we had all been, so he would not be afraid to continue working with us.

We both decided not to say anything to the manager of the main office, a clever non-Jew by the name of Konstantin Nikolayevich Alexandrov, who had worked with religious Jews for many years. We agreed that we would only tell him what had occurred if he found out indirectly.

Not a day went by before I was told that the manager wanted to see me immediately. When I arrived at the main office, he called me into his room, closed the door, and with a pained, fearful look on his face he asked, "Zaltzman, what happened at your plant? Did you make a secret synagogue there? They called me from the KGB! Do you know what the KGB is? Not the OBHS, the KGB!"

The Soviet Union had two national law-enforcement agencies, the OBHS and the KGB. The function of the OBHS was to preserve economic law and order, to battle corruption, theft, embezzlement, and the like. They primarily dealt with crimes against property. The KGB combated espionage, opponents of the state, and political crimes. You could bribe someone in the OBHS, but the KGB was of an entirely different caliber. The call from the KGB offices had frightened Mr. Alexandrov terribly. He was nearly in tears when he spoke to me about it.

At first, I thought that he had found out about the incident that had occurred the day before at the factory, but I gathered from what he was saying that something new had cropped up. He said that he had received a request from the KGB that he send all of the files of the workers at our plant. He tried to stall and said that he wasn't permitted to send personal information based on a phone conversation, and if they wanted the files, they could send one of their people to come and take them.

To his surprise, within half an hour a KGB agent had arrived for our files.

What did they have against us at the KGB office?

Within our small group, we tried to conjure an explanation. At first we speculated that since many of us had submitted a request for a visa in the past—a process overseen by the KGB—they had decided to track us. But on second thought, we discarded this idea. For something like that they would not have arranged such a dramatic raid, or the extra measure of seizing and interrogating everyone who left the factory.

Perhaps, we thought, they had discovered all of our underground work over the years and were trying to collect evidence against us. We went about our work over the next few days with heavy hearts, fearful that something disastrous was brewing at the KGB headquarters. We tried to keep the incident quiet even amongst our friends.

Our encounter with those seven "visitors" to the factory started us off on a new project of sorts. Whenever we saw one of the agents walking with other people in a friendly manner, we knew that the people conversing with them worked for the KGB as well and we tried to memorize their faces. That was how we spied on those who spied on us, but there was one small difference: All we could do to them was be wary, while they could do whatever they wanted to us.

Days, weeks, and then months elapsed and nothing happened. We finally sent word to the *bochurim* to return to Samarkand and it was as if nothing had ever happened.

Mystery Solved

It was only years later that the mystery was partially solved. One day I met the non-Jewish woman, Lilia, whom the KGB had questioned. We were entering a tramway at the same time. By amazing Divine Providence, two of the KGB agents who had raided us that day were also entering the tram. We both recognized them and instinctively moved to the next compartment. This situation reminded us of that inordinately unpleasant day years back.

She asked, "Did you recognize the men who entered the first compartment?"

"Of course," I replied.

"If so," she said, "I will tell you what happened after they raided your factory. A few days later, I was called down to the offices of the KGB. I was afraid to go, so they sent another summons. My husband had worked for the KGB in the past and made a good salary there but at a certain point he felt like the work was too demanding and that it was infringing on his family life. He decided to leave before they considered him a permanent employee, which would make it impossible for him to ever leave.

"When I told my husband what had happened at your factory and about my summons, I asked him to find out what they wanted and what it had to do with me. After inquiring of his KGB pals, he told me that I had nothing to worry about. They wouldn't do anything to me and only wanted to talk.

"I went to the KGB and to my surprise they took out thick files on each of you. They said to me, 'We know they are religious, so we want to ask you: Since you work in their central office, perhaps you know where they go on their vacations?'

"I answered them truthfully. I knew nothing about any trips, and to the best of my knowledge they continued to work even during vacation, receiving double salary according to the law.

"That was all that I said to them, and then they released me."

When I heard this, I finally understood, even if not entirely. As I mentioned earlier, I occasionally traveled on various communal missions. Every time I traveled, I would prepare a formal letter to the director of the central plant requesting vacation, as part of the two weeks' annual leave every worker is entitled to. I told my employees that if anyone came to inspect the plant and asked for me, they should show them my letter and tell them I was on vacation. On my return, I asked whether anyone had shown up and if nobody had, I would destroy the letter as though I had never asked for vacation or taken any time off.

Apparently, the KGB knew something about my trips but did not have precise information. That was why they asked the woman where I went. Luckily, she had no idea about my occasional trips and was positive that I worked instead of taking vacation.

Our conclusion was that the KGB had organized the raid to frighten us. The episode had occurred during Khrushchev's rule, not under Stalin. During that time, they didn't arrest people solely on suspicion, but would still employ these sorts of scare tactics. The fear persisted until we eventually departed from the Soviet Union, and beyond.

The New Employee

In the late 1950s, a man by the name of Yisrael Nachman Zeidman arrived in Samarkand. He had sunken eyes and a frightened expression that seemed to bear testimony to a deep pain and a fear that lay in his heart. He was a quiet, humble, and refined person, and we quickly discerned that he was also a pious man and a great scholar. He respected everyone, young and old, and was the first to extend greetings to anyone who crossed his path.

At the time, we were still young and didn't know the reason for the pained look on his face. It was only later that we found out, discreetly, that before coming to Samarkand he had lived in Ukraine, where he had been arrested and thrown into jail for ten years. When his jail sentence was complete and he finally returned home, he discovered to his horror that his wife had not been faithful to him and he had to divorce her. In an attempt to forget his painful past, he decided to move far away and that is why he came to Samarkand. Within a short time, he married a G-d-fearing woman by the name of Liza, but due to their advanced age, they were not blessed with children. Because of his refined nature, he did not want to live at the community's expense and he worked as a bookbinder, an occupation that allowed him to keep Shabbos.

The first to recognize his special qualities was R. Tzvi Hirsch Lerner, who also came during the war from Ukraine together with his wife and two sons, Yaakov and Moshe. R. Tzvi Hirsch was a good-hearted and kind individual who enjoyed doing a favor for a fellow Jew. He helped R. Yisrael Nachman whenever he could. When R. Tzvi moved to live in the New City, he bought a house with an enclosed yard and arranged a separate apartment there for R. Yisrael Nachman and his wife to stay, free of charge.

In those days, a retiree in the Soviet Union would receive a pension based on a percentage of his salary earned during the last year he worked. Since R. Yisrael Nachman earned a very meager income as a bookbinder, he would not be able to continue to support himself on his pension without help from others. So, when he approached retirement age, R. Tzvi Hirsch took pains to ensure a nice income for him. I had become the manager of a factory by then, so he asked me for my help. He asked me to take Yisrael Nachman into my clothing label factory and to pay him a respectable salary for the year before he retired so he could subsist afterwards on his pension.

It was hard for me to accede to R. Tzvi's request. No manager is thrilled with the idea of hiring someone whose documents state that he spent ten years in prison. The situation was made even more delicate for me since my factory already had many illegal elements: It was closed on Shabbos and holidays, it only employed Jews, some of my employees had submitted requests to immigrate to Israel, and I myself was associated with the local underground yeshiva and other communal affairs.

Every detail on this list was reason enough to avoid another problem, but I couldn't ignore how beneficial this would be for this Torah scholar, R. Yisrael Nachman. I knew that if I didn't do him this favor, he would be stuck with a low income and would be forced to be dependent on others, suffering for the rest of his days. I also couldn't turn down the kindly R. Tzvi Lerner, and I realized the great merit involved, so I agreed to hire R. Yisrael Nachman.

Knowing R. Yisrael Nachman to be more of a bookish person, I tried to make the workload easy for him. Sometimes I would arrive at work a little late, after the other workers had begun working, and as I walked in R. Yisrael Nachman would approach me, flustered, and humbly ask, "What needs to be done today?" He realized the great favor that I had done for him and he wanted to be of assistance in any way he could.

My friend Yaakov Lerner told me that he heard that when R. Yisrael Nachman was younger he would field halachic questions, and had compiled a book of his responses. Apparently, his correspondents would address him using unbelievable honorifics. It all made these scenarios extremely difficult to swallow: Here I was, a twenty-one-year-old youngster, causing discomfort to someone who was not only much older than I, but a pious, revered Torah scholar as well! To prevent this kind of uncomfortable situation, I tried not to enter the factory immediately, but to first walk around outside so that he could see me through the window before I entered. This way he would expect my entry and would not feel ill at ease when I walked in.

I remember that one time we prayed at the Schiff home, and seeing as it was the last Shabbos of the month, we started off by reciting the entire *Tehillim*, as is customary in Chabad. Although R. Yisrael Nachman respected Chabad and its customs, he was afraid to take more time than necessary for the minyan lest the neighbors notice our illegal gathering. He suggested that we pray immediately and say the Psalms afterwards. I was young and excitable, and his suggestion annoyed me. I told him, "Saying *Tehillim* on Shabbos is an enactment of the Rebbe and it cannot be changed. We will first say *Tehillim* and then we will pray!"

R. Yisrael Nachman, the humble person that he was, kept quiet. Years later, when I recall this incident, I cringe for daring to talk so impudently to a person like him.

Factory Turned into a Yeshiva

Throughout all this time, I maintained my involvement with community work, and at one point, we even set up a branch of our underground yeshiva to operate, out of all places, in my factory.

It wasn't too long before then that Nikita Khrushchev, premier of the Soviet Union, began encouraging young people who had completed their schooling to study a trade for two years; only then, those interested should continue their studies in university. Since not everyone is cut out to be an engineer or a doctor, went the thinking, those who wouldn't reach such a position could still benefit the country as manual workers.

After Khrushchev's recommendation was accepted and established as law, I thought of a wonderful idea. Since all of the employees in my factory were "our" Jews, the workplace would be an ideal setting in which to set up a yeshiva for boys, dressed up as a trade school.

At the time, my work was registered under a government office located in a small town called Charkhin around ten kilometers from Samarkand. By law, my factory also needed to be located outside the city. As such, I rented a house not too far from the city and set up my factory there.

When the law went into effect, I registered five *bochurim* as students learning the trade under the tutelage of a previous employee. That was how we ran a proper yeshiva right under the nose of the government. The boys learned under the direction of R. Dovid Okunov, and could come and go freely; outside the city we were far from the KGB's scrutiny and the Uzbek neighbors didn't suspect a thing.

Those days were truly heaven on earth. No one imagined that we had a functioning yeshiva tucked within the factory walls. Teacher and students sat and learned diligently, and if any supervisors appeared, all they would find was a man teaching some boys a useful trade.

The only hindrance was providing the necessary texts for the boys to study from. We were afraid to bring large tomes of Talmud to the factory, the likes of which a non-Jew had never seen, and written in a foreign language, no less. How would we explain away six *Gemaras* lying around the factory? Photocopying only the relevant pages was not an option, as such machines were unavailable in Russia at that time.

Having no choice, we unraveled the bindings of the books and, aside for one complete *Gemara* for the lecturer, only a few pages were brought in at a time. We could hide those few pages when the need arose.

Obtaining Letters of Recommendation from Work

Our manufacturing plant continued operating successfully, and in time I discovered that running my own factory enabled me to help my employees in other ways as well.

Preparing the necessary documentation for an exit visa application and presenting it all to the Office of Visas and Registration (OVIR) was a six-month process, and a complicated one at that. Some of the required papers were difficult to obtain and some simply had to be forged. One of the hardest documents to get hold of was a letter of recommendation from work. The employer had to testify that his employee was a decent, law-abiding individual and recommend that he be allowed to leave Russia since his place of work would not be negatively affected by his departure.

Anyone who asked for this letter directly was likely to get a response between outright refusal and immediate firing. Managers were afraid that if they signed this letter of recommendation, they would pay dearly for it. Indeed, it was well known that many who submitted the paperwork lost their livelihood and had to find work elsewhere. The stain of treason would follow them for life. There were even some professionals and academics who were fired after requesting to emigrate to Israel and had to find menial work as a watchman or a janitor just to get by.

At great risk to myself, and with the help of Heaven, I succeeded in helping quite a number of Jews receive approval for emigration from the manager of our head office—without him even realizing it. This is how it happened:

Those hundreds of letters I mentioned earlier that I would send out advertising our label design and production services were written on the official stationery of the main factory. Of course, our manager had to sign all of them.

When I wanted to give a letter of recommendation to one of the workers, stating that the factory approved of his request to emigrate, I would wait until I had accumulated a pile of hundreds of letters needing the manager's signature. I prepared one or two letters on the official stationery, on which I wrote, in the name of the manager, that he recommended said employee and allowed him to request to emigrate. I put this paper within the pile of papers, after several dozen letters.

When the manager received this pile of papers, he glanced at the first one and signed it, looked at the second one and signed it, and kept this up for several letters, until he got tired and began signing sheet after sheet without examining them. When he got up to the page that I had stuck within the pile, he breezed straight past it, unaware of what he was signing.

After he finished signing all of the documents and returned the pile of letters, I sighed with relief. I immediately put all of the letters into my briefcase and quickly left his office.

I cannot describe to you how tense I was each time I presented him with a pile of letters knowing that within the stack was a letter, or several letters, for OVIR. Had I been caught, I would have been severely censured, and possibly fired along with all of my employees, aside from all the other consequences of being charged with such a serious act of forgery.

To be honest, from time to time I was tempted to stop the whole thing. I thought that, G-d forbid, the manager might receive a call from the KGB, reprimanding him for signing off on so many of his workers leaving the Motherland. Fingers would certainly be pointed at me and I would pay a heavy price. But, in Hashem's kindness, the KGB never inquired into the signatures and no one ever knew. In this way, I was able to arrange these letters for myself and for all of the Lubavitchers registered as my employees.

CHAPTER 14

Shabbos Bereishis
in the Cotton Field

I will never forget the lonely Shabbos I spent, forlorn and dejected, in a remote cotton plantation, far from Samarkand. My mind and heart were focused on the famous Chassidic saying that one's conduct on Shabbos Bereishis, the first *parshah* of the new year, influences his entire year. But there I was, among dozens of gentiles, picking cotton.

After the Revolution of 1917, the Communists replaced traditional farming with collective farms—the *kolkhoz*—and huge government farms—*sovkhozes*. The goal was to cultivate agricultural products for export and bring foreign money into the country. In 1937, the government launched a massive cotton growing campaign. Just as oil earned the nickname "black gold," cotton was deemed "white gold."

The arid conditions of the sunny plains of Uzbekistan and other large swathes of land in Central Asia created excellent conditions for growing cotton. Under their Five Year Plan, the government designated a large area for the crop, dug irrigation canals throughout the area, constructed railroad tracks to transport the cotton, and erected factories to process it.

Nowadays, in most countries, cotton picking is automated from start to finish, but back then, the Soviet Union did not own enough equipment to pluck the cotton from the fields and the machinery that they did have barely operated properly. The picking had to be done manually and it was exhausting and menial labor. It meant spending all day sweltering beneath the scorching sun plucking and separating tufts of cotton and seeds from their tall, unyielding stalks. Since exporting cotton provided the Soviet Union with large quantities of foreign currency, the government deemed cotton picking a national project to which all citizens had to contribute of their time. During the harvest, most high schools and universities in central Soviet Asia were practically closed down as many students were sent off to the *kolkhozes*. Additionally, every factory and workplace was required to send a quota of employees to participate in the massive undertaking. Cities became deserted as thousands of people were sent to the cotton fields, to assure that everything would be picked before the rain season.

The cotton harvest usually began before Rosh Hashana and continued for two months. This placed the religious Jews of those areas in a serious dilemma. A worker sent to pick cotton could be made to stay for a couple of weeks, including Shabbos and Yom Tov, and would only be allowed to go into the city for a day or two to shower, do laundry, and buy some necessities; students sometimes had to work for a month or more. Being absent from cotton picking was risky of course, given its national importance. How could one explain to the authorities why he was neglecting his patriotic duties?

The Muslim Supervisor's Threat

Like every factory, the factory that I managed was obligated to send a delegation of workers. However, all of our workers were Lubavitchers, and there was no way that I would send them to the fields over Shabbos. As an alternative, I hired non-Jews and sent them, on our behalf, to pick cotton. I explained to those in charge that we had a great deal of work to do at the factory and had to keep our regular employees just to meet the quota assigned to us.

The management did not always agree to this arrangement and often insisted that our workers be present to pick cotton in the *kol-*

khoz. I tried sending ten workers for one day, and argued that they would accomplish the same as one worker in ten days, but they weren't convinced.

Each time, I tried to push them off, but once, just after Simchas Torah, they insisted that I send one of our workers for a full week. If I did not, they threatened, they would consider our refusal as an act of defiance against the government and it would result in negative consequences.

Having no choice, I decided to send R. Moshe (Moshke) Valotzky for a few days. He left on Monday for a *kolkhoz* located near a village called Jambol, forty kilometers from Samarkand. He was supposed to return on Friday afternoon. To my surprise, he returned on Wednesday.

"The *kolkhoz* is very far from the city," he explained. "I was afraid that I wouldn't find a vehicle traveling in the direction of Samarkand later on in the week, to be back in time for Shabbos."

The next day, when I arrived at the main office for which I worked, I encountered Comrade Usmanov, a Muslim fellow who served as the factory's Party representative, ensuring that things were being run in accord with the Communist spirit. He began yelling at me in front of everyone. "You should know, Zaltzman," he snapped in a threatening tone, "cotton picking is the duty of every citizen in the Soviet Union. If you persist in not sending representatives from your factory, you will regret it."

As it turned out, Usmanov had visited that *kolkhoz* on Wednesday. When he inquired as to whether someone from our factory was there, he discovered that Moshke had been present only from Monday through Wednesday morning.

I knew that if I didn't calm him down he might carry out his threats against us. I tried to mollify him by saying that I would go personally to pick the cotton myself, but he continued to shout: "When are you going? After Saturday?"

I didn't know what to say. If Usmanov would indeed accuse me of a political crime, he might investigate further and discover that the factory actually closed every Shabbos. All of our underground activities would be placed in jeopardy, including our precious ye-shiva. Realizing that I had no alternative, I relented and said, "Fine, I will go tomorrow, on Friday."

This decision was made in the spur of the moment, but I knew I needed to placate him. He needed to feel that he was in charge if I didn't want him to create any unnecessary fuss.

Obviously, I did not plan for a moment to work on Shabbos. The plan that formulated in my head during those moments was to pretend to work. After all, the main thing was for Usmanov to know that I spent Shabbos with the workers in the cotton plantation.

Morning Prayers Amongst the Cotton

Several times a week, a truck would travel from Samarkand to the *kolkhoz* to deliver food and other necessities for the workers. I prayed that the next truck would leave on Friday so that I'd arrive there before Shabbos. Making my own way there was not feasible, as the *kolkhoz* was difficult to locate. My prayers were heard on High, and the next morning a truck departed. We set out, and once I was sure that we would arrive before Shabbos, I breathed a sigh of relief.

I took three small challah rolls to use for *kiddush* and the meals, and some fish and meat. I didn't bring along my *tefillin* because I was afraid that I would not find a place to hide them, let alone to put them on privately. Instead, I would return on Sunday to don the *tefillin* at home.

As soon as I arrived in the *kolkhoz,* I searched for a place to hide the money I had brought for my return trip. In the end, I left the money in a crack of a tree, and as will be related, I never came back for it. For all I know, it might be lying there until this very day.

In the center of the *kolkhoz* stood a large single-room hut where all the men slept. Each person had his own mattress and whatever meager belongings he had brought with him.

According to the regulations, every worker was to sign in upon arrival, when he received his apron, essentially a long sack tied around the waist into which the cotton fibers were placed once picked. I hurried to the office so I could sign in before Shabbos and receive my apron. However, the supervisors were out in the field with the workers. I approached some of the workers who had come back from the field and urgently asked them who was in charge of the aprons. They didn't understand why I was so anxious. They tried to calm me down and said, "Where are you hurrying to, comrade? You can get the sack later tonight, or even tomorrow morning."

Of course I couldn't explain to them why I was in a rush and I waited impatiently for the supervisors to return. To my good fortune, shortly before sundown all of the workers returned from the fields along with the supervisors and I was able to sign in and receive the apron sack.

Some of the workers, who worked in the main factory that my own workshop was a branch of, recognized me, and knowing me to be a lively sort, exclaimed, "Ho, Zaltzman is here! Things will be entertaining tonight!" They turned to me with excitement and suggested that after supper in town we go to a club and spend the evening dancing and having a good time. I didn't immediately reject the idea, so as not to arouse suspicion for my strange opposition, but I began to think of how I could shake them off without letting on why I refused to go along.

I went with the other workers to the sleeping area where I had been allotted a mattress. I lay down with a bitter taste in my throat. It was Shabbos Bereishis that week—after the joyous conclusion of the Torah on Simchas Torah a few day earlier, the Torah-reading cycle began again that week, and in my mind flashed the Chassidic adage: "The way one starts off on Shabbos Bereishis is the way the rest of the year follows." If this was how my Shabbos Bereishis was being spent, I wondered, in a distant *kolkhoz* filled with coarse, vulgar peasants, what sort of year was in store for me?

The workers, who had rested from their work, tried encouraging me to come along to the restaurant, and then to continue on to the dancing. I told them that I had a bad headache. By then, I was so irritated and distraught that I really did have a throbbing headache.

The workers left for town and as their boisterous chatter faded away, I got up and went outside to pray in the fresh night air. Needless to say, I had not taken a *siddur* with me and had to recite the *Kabbolas Shabbos* prayers from memory. Facing acres and acres of seemingly endless cotton meadows, enveloped by silence and the soft rustle of the wind, I lifted my head toward the heavens and let my mouth sing, welcoming the Shabbos bride into this desolate landscape. I imagined the words flowing softly from my lips, traveling through places untouched by man, and then joining the prayers of my friends back at home before ascending heavenward together. I then recited *kiddush* on two small loaves of challah, ate one, along with some fish and meat, and went to bed. I had a hard time falling asleep, as my mind was preoccupied with ideas about how I'd manage to pray the next morning and how to conceal from everyone that I wasn't working.

In the morning, I woke up along with everyone else and somehow managed to slip away to avoid eating breakfast with the workers. Shortly afterwards, they began to head out for the fields and I quickly donned the apron sack so as not to carry it outside.

We arrived at the field and I looked for a spot that was far from the other workers so they wouldn't notice I wasn't working. I was surprised to find a cool, freshwater stream in a hidden corner of the field and quickly immersed in it. At least I was able to find a *mikvah* for Shabbos! After immersing in the stream, I felt much calmer. I managed to say the morning prayers while walking about in the field and pretending to pick cotton.

In the afternoon, after finishing *davening*, I returned to our living quarters, where I made *kiddush* on the two remaining loaves and ate my "Shabbos meal."

My thoughts journeyed back to my friends in Samarkand and my heart longed to be with them. That particular Shabbos there was a minyan at my parents' house, which was to be followed by a *farbrengen* in honor of Shabbos Bereishis. My brother-in-law Eliyahu would be there, along with others who knew how to conduct a warm Chassidic *farbrengen*. I was sick of this cotton plantation and felt that I had to get out. I couldn't even wait until Sunday morning: doing so would complicate my morning prayers. I began to think of how I could return to Samarkand that night.

The Black Road

Thanks to inquiries I had made earlier, I knew that not far from the *kolkhoz* was the main highway connecting Samarkand and Tashkent, along which trucks would often drive by and take hitchhikers for a fee. The problem was that to get to the highway one had to cross over several fields and vineyards that were guarded by fierce dogs as big as wolves. Anyone trespassing through those fields at night was in danger of being torn to shreds. (A piece of advice I was taught as a child surfaced in my mind: If ever chased by a dog, the best thing to do is to stay still, without budging an inch; running will only tempt it to attack.)

I decided to leave the *kolkhoz* with enough daylight to reach the highway before nightfall. I hiked through the fields and over their ditches and furrows at a quick pace and neared the highway by late afternoon. After praying on the side of the road, then waiting until the sky was black and the stars twinkled brightly, I recited the Evening Prayer and tried to flag down a truck.

This highway was considered dangerous and was known amongst travelers as "the Black Road," since one never knew who might stop by on it. The Black Road was notorious for its stories of drivers having "pity" and stopping for people standing by the road, only to rob them. There were also the reverse cases, in which robbers waited on the road for a victim to pick them up.

I stood there in the inky darkness for a long time, waving my hands and hoping that someone would notice me and stop. After some time, a truck pulled over. When I got in I noticed another passenger sitting next to the driver. In the pitch black cabin I couldn't see the stranger's face. I sat quietly next to the door, hoping that the trip would pass uneventfully.

After a short while, the other passenger asked the driver to turn off the main highway and enter a small village on the road-side. It wasn't far from the highway, so the driver agreed. The com-pletely black, narrow roads made for a frightening ride, but the passenger guided the driver through the village until he reached his destination.

I got down from the truck to let the other passenger out, and after he exited, I climbed back in. While the door was still ajar, the driver asked the man for the money he was owed for the ride. The man withdrew a large knife and in a menacing voice, he snarled, "You want me to pay?"

Sitting between the driver and the brandished knife, a feeling of terror fell upon me. If an argument started, I was likely to be the victim. Fortunately, the driver realized what sort of sinister charac-ter he was dealing with. He quickly drove off as the door banged shut on its own.

After we had both calmed down somewhat, I spoke to the driver and found out that he was going to be passing right near my house. Since I had left the *kolkhoz* before Shabbos was over, I had left my money there and had nothing with which to pay him. When at last he drove near the street where I lived, I asked him to wait a few minutes so I could get some money from my house and pay him. But after his unpleasant experience with the previous passenger, the driver was afraid of waiting and after I got down, he drove off.

It was already three hours after Shabbos, and I hurried home, hoping to catch the remnants of the *farbrengen*. When I entered the house, I was happy to see my friends still sitting at the Shabbos Bereishis *farbrengen*, which had lingered well into the night. They were thrilled to see me. They had thought of me throughout the entire Shabbos and wondered how I was faring, alone in a cotton field among dozens of non-Jews. We continued to *farbreng*, and I related to them all of my experiences of the past day.

Pleasant Moments during the Harvest Season

During those challenging months of the cotton harvest, there were also some enjoyable moments that I fondly recall. Once we had somehow dealt with our annual cotton-picking predicament, we were able to enjoy the Intermediate Days of Sukkos and *farbreng* for hours in the big sukkah that we constructed in our yard or in the Mishulovins'. We did not need to work during those days and had ample time to *farbreng* all day. Even then, our hearts would quicken whenever someone knocked on the door of the yard, but we tried to divert our attention from such interruptions. In general, they were relaxed days and bring back pleasant memories.

Eventually, I was able to reach an agreement in which I would organize a group of my employees to pick cotton on a Sunday, instead of sending one employee for two weeks. One such time, R. Moshe Nissilevitch, R. Michoel Mishulovin, and I went to the *kolkhoz*. We brought along some food from home, as well as a copy of the Rebbe's *HaYom Yom* that I had managed to obtain not long before on a trip to Moscow.

During the lunch hour, we moved away from the other workers and sat to the side, relaxing on a patch of fresh grass near a gurgling stream. The air was pure and fresh. We washed our hands for the meal, ate our fill, and then we proceeded to learn from the *HaYom Yom*. Every entry that we learned was a vast spiritual treasure for us. This was after many years of not receiving any information about the Rebbe, and this small booklet revived us like cool water to a parched throat. It truly felt like Heaven itself.

CHAPTER 15

Mentor and Friend: R. Mendel Futerfas

O f all the great chassidim who fled Russia in 1946, R. Mendel was one of only a few left behind. Of course, he spent many years in prison, but we always held on to the hope that one day we would merit to meet him face-to-face.

Just after the war, as mentioned earlier, a window of opportunity opened for Chabad chassidim. More than one thousand Lubavitcher men, women, and children fled the Soviet Union using purchased or doctored Polish citizenship documents. R. Mendel was one of the leading organizers of this clandestine operation.

R. Mendel decided to get his family out of Russia, while he would stay behind until the last chassid had escaped. This is indeed what happened: His wife and children left Russia and settled in London, while he remained in the lion's den.

Eventually, R. Mendel was arrested by the secret police in Lemberg. Before his imprisonment, he managed to send word to the Chabad community not to worry—he would take responsibility for everything: If any other activists were to be placed under arrest, they should identify him as the ringleader.

The interrogators tried to squeeze any information they could out of R. Mendel. They were aware that he knew every detail of the underground operations, but he never cooperated.

When they discovered that they could not break R. Mendel's spirit with beatings and torture, they tried psychological means to get his cooperation: "You're sentenced to death, you know. But if you were to cooperate, we could save you by giving you a prison sentence instead."

R. Mendel was unmoved. "You know that I believe in G-d. I have no doubt that if G-d wants me to die, even if you were to release me now, I could be run over and killed by a car as I leave here. But if G-d wants me to live, you will never succeed in killing me."

Finally, he was brought to trial and sentenced to death, after which he was led to a room to await his execution. On the way he passed by one of the interrogators, who blurted out, "Well, Futerfas, you're a lucky man!"

R. Mendel didn't understand, but soon learned that a telegram had just arrived from Stalin with instructions to commute unfulfilled death sentences to twenty-five years in prison.

Surviving a Siberian Labor Camp

Upon arriving at the Siberian labor camp, R. Mendel resolved never to work on Shabbos. When the first Shabbos arrived, he remained in the barracks and did not go out to work. Instead of making up excuses, he simply told the warden, "I don't work on Shabbos."

The warden answered, "You will work. Trust me; we have plenty of ways to force you."

"You can do with me as you please—hang me even!" said Reb Mendel calmly. "I don't work on Shabbos." In the end they gave up and R. Mendel did not work on Shabbos.

He succeeded in keeping kosher with no less courage. Obviously, he did not partake in any of the cooked foods distributed sparingly to the prisoners, but instead ate only pieces of bread. The gentile prisoners that observed his conduct told him about a prisoner called Yonah Kogan—it turned out, his friend R. Yonah Cohen—who similarly ate very little and perished.

Reb Mendel understood that under these circumstances, especially in the Siberian cold, he had to arrange hot food for himself every day in order to survive. He resolved that just as wearing *tefillin* is a daily obligation, so too would it be obligatory to eat hot food every day and fulfill the *mitzvah* to "guard yourself carefully."

He obtained a metal container and every day he would take his daily ration of bread and boil it in water. This was his "hot food." If he would find a little vegetable oil, it was truly a meal fit for a king! There were times when all the running water had frozen solid, leaving R. Mendel with the extra task of melting snow and ice. Even when he returned exhausted from his work, he never failed to prepare his food. These "hot meals" helped him to endure the hardships of Siberia.

A Sign of Life from Siberia

Realizing that the Chabad community would be worried for him, not even knowing whether he was alive or dead, R. Mendel sought a way to send out some sort of message.

My brother-in-law R. Aryeh Leib Demichovsky, who as a teenager had served as R. Mendel's courier, told me that once in the early 1950s, a gentile arrived at his father's slaughterhouse in Minsk. Discreetly, he said, "I was just freed from prison in Siberia. A Jew named Mendel Mendelovitch—Mendel the son of Mendel—is there. He's a distinguished person whom we regarded very highly. We cleared a special area for him to pray and none of us disturbed him. When he found out that I was due to be freed, he told me, 'If you see a Jew that looks like me—with a beard and of distinct Jewish appearance—tell him my name, and ask him to spread the word that I'm alive and well, that I hope to be freed soon, and not to worry.'"

Thus, even from behind the walls of a Soviet labor camp in frozen Siberia, R. Mendel succeeded in showing a sign of life to the rest of the community.

In 1953, the tyrant Stalin, may his name be wiped out, suddenly died, and was replaced by Nikita Khrushchev. Khrushchev exposed the atrocities that had taken place under Stalin's regime and liberated nearly all the prisoners detained both during the wave of religious arrests of 1937–38, and in 1947 for attempting to flee the USSR. Among those liberated was R. Mendel. Following his release, R. Mendel settled in the city of Chernovitz, near his close friend R. Moshe Vishedsky and some other acquaintances.

Meeting with R. Mendel

In 1959, after the constant dread of the Stalin era subsided, I prepared to travel deep into Russia to visit several cities, one of them being Chernovitz. Before I left, I spoke at great length with R. Moshe Nissilevitch about R. Mendel's personality. He related whatever he knew about R. Mendel and then cautioned me: "R. Mendel is incredibly sharp, and everything you say should be direct and without any pretense. Otherwise, he will realize immediately and will lose his faith in you."

Before I departed, a nagging insecurity came over me: Would it be wise to disclose to R. Mendel the details of our underground activities, which had already grown substantially? We felt a gripping suspicion of anyone who had been in the lair of the KGB, since we could never truly know what transpired there. Who knows, perhaps the KGB had successfully recruited these former prisoners into its service!

I spoke about my concerns with my father as well as with my brother-in-law R. Eliyahu and they both rejected outright any possibility that R. Mendel could ever collaborate with the KGB. R. Moshe was also firm in his position: "Perish the thought that we should even suspect R. Mendel of such a thing! We have all heard about his strength and composure throughout his interrogation, how he chose to bear guilt for everyone else's underground activities, and much more!" We resolved that he should know everything, with full disclosure, and that he be consulted on a number of pertinent matters.

One of the subjects I wanted to resolve with R. Mendel was the ongoing disagreement between R. Moshe Nissilevitch and R. Berke Chein. During *farbrengens*, R. Berke emphasized that tremendous investment in one's own personal service of G-d was a critical first step before trying to uplift and inspire others. Only after that was accomplished could one's efforts with other people see any success. In contrast, R. Moshe held that if one refrains from communal work until he's satisfied with his own service, he would never find himself truly ready. "Should my neighbor suffer because I am still not ready?" he would exclaim.

When my friends discovered that I would be traveling to see R. Mendel, they asked me to seek his opinion regarding this "dispute."

An Emotional Meeting in Chernovitz

I departed Samarkand, and despite having a number of important missions, my mind was on my impending meeting with R. Mendel. When I arrived in Chernovitz, I immediately set out to see him.

I sought out his address with the utmost caution. The affairs of ex-convicts, especially someone like R. Mendel, were certainly monitored by the government. For that reason, I passed by his home several times before finally feeling assured that there were no suspicious characters around. I knocked on the door. No answer.

One of the neighbors heard my knocks and came to his door. "What do you want?"

"I am looking for Comrade Futerfas."

"Futerfas is not home now. He's probably by his friend, Moshe Vishedsky. He spends hours there every day..."

Fortunately, he was able to tell me R. Moshe Vishedsky's address, which was not far away. I followed the neighbor's directions and soon found R. Moshe's home. As before, I made sure there was no surveillance on the building before knocking on the door. Footsteps approached the other side of the door. A woman's voice asked, "Who's there?"

"*An eigener*," I replied in Yiddish. One of ours.

Silence.

After a moment, the voice called out again: "Who's there?"

"*An eigener*," I repeated. I could make out whispering behind the door. After a few moments, R. Moshe's wife Chashe opened the door. I entered; however, I saw no one. Mrs. Vishedsky asked for my name.

"Zaltzman," I answered loudly, presuming that the others were hiding in another room and could hear my voice. "Is R. Mendel Futerfas here?" A moment later, he emerged. Having last seen him in my childhood, I could not recognize him.

"Are you R. Mendel?"

"Yes. Are you the son of Avrohom Zaltzman?" he asked. I nodded, and we greeted one another with a *sholom aleichem*. I was unable to fight the tears that had gathered in my eyes. R. Mendel was known for being an emotional person and I could see that his eyes, too, were red and brimming with tears.

Hearing our emotional meeting, R. Moshe came out from his hiding place and entered the room and I gave him a *sholom aleichem* as well. There was a tired anguish in his eyes that spoke volumes of the sorrows he had endured. Near his forehead was a deep cavity. I later learned from R. Mendel that he had been terribly wounded while in the labor camps. He had been struck in the head while felling trees and it was a miracle that he survived.

After this brief greeting, R. Moshe left the room, sensing I had come to see R. Mendel.

I sat facing R. Mendel speechless. Here I was, a young man of twenty, sitting with an elder chassid with decades of selfless devotion behind him. R. Mendel sensed this and opened our meeting with an intelligent smile, his face overflowing with affection.

Still, I could sense that he was being very cautious with me. Could I blame him? He didn't know me, and the fact that I was the child of his good friend R. Avremel Zaltzman meant nothing. After all, we all knew of men—faithful chassidim—whose children had not followed in the ways of their parents, Heaven forfend.

However, after a while the ice began to melt. From our conversation, he could tell that I was indeed an *eigener* in the fullest measure, and seeing that there was no reason to harbor further suspicions, he began to ask details about the Lubavitchers of Samarkand and Tashkent, the "great Chabad communities" in those years. He saw that he could get detailed information from me and I withheld nothing, telling him at length all the goings on of our community as well as our underground activities.

In the course of our discussion, I asked R. Mendel his thoughts about the differing approaches of R. Berke Chein and R. Moshe Nissilevitch regarding community activism—if it was necessary to refine oneself before influencing others, or if it was possible to be involved in public life and personal divine service simultaneously. I told him of the heated discussions between R. Berke and R. Moshe during *farbrengens* and how we longed to hear R. Mendel's opinion on the matter.

At first, I suspected that he didn't fully understand my question, especially since he declined to take any side on the subject. Only after I explained the two differing concepts once again did he offer a clear answer.

"Listen," he said. "If the prophet Eliyahu [Elijah] Hanavi himself comes to you and says that there's no need to involve yourself with your fellow Jew, tell him, 'You might be *Eliyahu Hanavi*, but we're still not listening to you,' and continue to assist others."

As we were speaking, R. Moshe Vishedsky entered. Since, not knowing him personally, I didn't know whether or not to trust him, I refrained from speaking about any sensitive subjects.

R. Mendel, sensing my caution in front of R. Moshe, declared: "If you're worried about him, then don't tell me anything either. I eventually tell him everything!"

I was stunned. This was someone who was known to keep a secret?

R. Mendel saw my apprehension. "With us, it's like two bodies with one soul!" He proceeded to tell me at length about the close friendship they had shared since childhood.

The following morning, which happened to be the fast day of the 17th of Tammuz, I returned to R. Moshe Vishedsky's home. During my stay in Chernovitz, R. Mendel never hurried to return home. Apparently, he realized that I wished to spend as much with him as possible and he sat with me for hours in R. Moshe's home, returning home late in the evening. However, he did not allow me to come to his home under any circumstances. He feared that I would arouse suspicion—after all, what business could an ex-convict have with a young man like myself?

There were other chassidim living in Chernovitz at that time: R. Chaim Zalman Kozliner (known as "Chazak"), R. Avraham Shmuel Lebenhartz, and others. Chazak's son, R. Mottel, married and moved to Tashkent, as had R. Moshe's son, R. Michel, who lived together with his sister Dina and her husband, R. Mordechai Gorodetzky. In general, the younger generation would usually move to Tashkent or Samarkand, where the Chabad communities were both larger and younger.

As I left Chernovitz, I was overcome with conflicting emotions. On the one hand, I had finally met a true chassid; I had drawn fistfuls of Chassidic energy and a renewed passion for community work. But on the other, I began to feel a tremendous longing. When will I see R. Mendel again? On the way back to Samarkand, which took more than two weeks, I was engulfed by the memories of my time with R. Mendel, as well as with the new chassid I had been privileged to meet, R. Moshe Vishedsky.

When I arrived in Samarkand, everyone was waiting impatiently to hear the details of my travels, especially R. Mendel's position on the "dispute" between R. Berke and R. Moshe. R. Mendel's clear, sharp answer greatly energized our work.

Even R. Berke took R. Mendel's words deeply to heart. It was amazing to see how he, himself a giant in piety and prayer, who had also achieved incredible self-mastery, expressed such profound reverence towards R. Mendel and accepted his words.

Let the *Avreichem* Decide

After his release from prison, R. Mendel had tried again and again to leave Russia. He applied for an exit visa numerous times and was always rejected. R. Mendel related that one time, as the government official presented him with the formal rejection slip, he began to scream at them: "What do you want from me? How much can you punish a human being? I am a prisoner for seventeen years already: first in Siberia, and now within the four walls of my house!"

"Don't even dream about an exit visa," they answered coldly. "You will never leave Russia."

"We will see what G-d decides," retorted R. Mendel.

Meanwhile, other chassidim had left Chernovitz, either for Tashkent or, for those lucky enough to receive exit visas, for Israel. When Chazak moved to Samarkand, R. Mendel began to consider leaving Chernovitz himself. Among other reasons, he began to believe that the officials there would never grant him an exit visa. Elsewhere, a number of people had already succeeded in receiving visas. like R. Simcha Gorodetzky and the Mochkin brothers in Tashkent and R. Boruch Duchman and R. Berke Chein in Samarkand. Chazak was the first to learn of R. Mendel's thoughts. He had moved to Samarkand and lived close to my home. I used this opportunity to arrange a Talmud class with him. He was an incredible teacher and I gained from him tremendously.

One day, he confided to me that he had received a letter from R. Mendel, who disclosed that he wrote to the Rebbe that he was considering moving to Tashkent or Samarkand. The Rebbe's reply was somehow communicated to him that he should consult the *avreichim*—the younger married men—of Samarkand. Therefore, Chazak concluded, I was to go and consult with our small circle of young chassidim and bring back an answer.

Chazak was not a part of the underground in Samarkand and our policy was to not share information with anyone not directly involved. However, Chazak, the chassid that he was, could sense the existence of some sort of band of young chassidim in Samarkand

and that I was a part of that group. He therefore knew I could be asked to consult with the *avreichim*.

I immediately went to consult my brother-in-law R. Eliyahu Mishulovin, who was considered the "brains" in Samarkand.

He began to analyze the Rebbe's response. On the one hand, it would be a tremendous privilege to have R. Mendel with us in Samarkand, and the Rebbe seemed to be hinting that he approved of such a move. On the other hand, the Rebbe's answer seemed to imply that there was an element of risk that he didn't want to force upon us.

Simply put, at that time there were many groups of *bochurim* in our underground yeshiva. If an ex-convict like R. Mendel, who lived under constant KGB surveillance, would come to Samarkand, additional KGB scrutiny would follow him. It would be obvious that he had some local connections, and the KGB would find out very quickly where he lived, whom he was seeing, and with whom he was associated: nothing was concealed from them. The move could endanger both R. Mendel and the entire underground.

"Go speak to R. Moshe Nissilevitch," my brother-in-law finally said. I immediately set out for the Bagishomol neighborhood, where R. Moshe lived. I told him of the letter that Chazak had received from R. Mendel and about the Rebbe's answer.

"Oh! R. Mendel wants to come to Samarkand!" he said excitedly. However, he too understood full well what kind of dangers would follow R. Mendel to Samarkand. As a rule, the Rebbe exercised special caution when it came to Samarkand. We knew of certain American tourists who, in audience with the Rebbe, disclosed that their itinerary included several cities in Russia. Upon learning that their destinations included Tashkent and Samarkand, the Rebbe asked them to avoid Samarkand. When Rabbi Binyomin Katz visited Russia at around that time, he was explicitly warned by the Rebbe not to visit Samarkand —a trip to Tashkent would have to suffice.

On the other hand, after ten years in Samarkand, R. Berke Chein had received permission to leave Russia and we were without a *mashpia*, a proper Chassidic guide. There was no one to *farbreng* with us or from whom we could draw Chassidic vitality and energy.

R. Moshe examined all the sides of the issue, considering all the possible outcomes. He finally concluded that it would be preferable for R. Mendel to come to Samarkand, in spite of the risks that his arrival would entail.

"We are three, Eliyahu, you, and I," he said at last. "We can serve as a Jewish court of law and rule that Hashem should help us and that everything will be alright."

I immediately relayed to Chazak that the *avreichim* of Samarkand agree wholeheartedly that R. Mendel should come. With great anticipation, we awaited R. Mendel's answer. After a number of weeks, we learned that he had set out for Samarkand.

R. Mendel Arrives in Samarkand

In the days before his arrival, we met to consider how to receive R. Mendel: who would go to meet him and, most importantly, where he would stay. There was no doubt that the KGB was watching him. For this reason, it was important that his home be in the Old City and that he go every day to the shul there. This way, the collaborators at the shul would note his arrival and inform the KGB of it. Otherwise, they would search for him everywhere and cast unwanted suspicion upon us all.

On the other hand, we strongly desired that he live among us, at least initially, so that we could spend time with him. If so, he would need to stay with someone trustworthy, namely, one of us. Being that my family lived in a separate courtyard that opened into an empty clearing, and not a public thoroughfare, it was decided that R. Mendel would stay in our home. We all lived there together: my parents, my sister and brother-in-law, and myself. We would have the honor of *farbrenging* with R. Mendel until he moved to a permanent residence in the Old City. He wouldn't be able to stay with us for long, though. Apart from our concern that the KGB was following him, every Soviet citizen had to register with the local police within twenty-four hours of changing his residence. Since I had seen R. Mendel most recently and we recognized each other, I had the special privilege of meeting him at the airport. I accepted this mission with much excitement.

The airports were infested with KGB agents tracking foreign tourists, so I didn't want R. Mendel, who stood out in his appearance, to remain there even a second longer than necessary. Certainly, we couldn't be seen wandering around together looking for a taxi. Instead, I paid the taxi driver who took me to the airport to wait for us as long as needed. In those years, passengers would descend from the airplane on stairs. From there they would exit the airfield without entering the terminal.

When R. Mendel's flight landed, I was waiting at some distance from the airfield. I spotted him the moment he emerged from the airplane, and I stood facing him, in order that he should recognize me. As he drew near to me, I could see his eyes brimming over with tears.

Once I saw that he had spotted me, I turned away and walked back to the cab, not wanting to approach him. He understood that it wasn't safe for us to walk together and he followed me, carrying all of his bags. Only after we both sat down in the waiting cab and were on our way did we give each other a warm *sholom aleichem*.

The First *Farbrengen*

R. Mendel arrived at our home at 6 p.m. on September 17, 1962. The chassidim and boys who were aware of his arrival gathered in our home. After eating supper, he started his first *farbrengen* in Samarkand. His eyes engraved the faces of each and every one present upon his memory. It was clear that he felt deep *nachas* to be in the presence of throngs of young chassidim after so many years.

We were all somewhat bewildered by R. Mendel's first *farbrengen*. We were accustomed to R. Berke Chein's style, to the way he would always urge us to improve in our commitment to Chassidus through lengthy meditative prayer and by being meticulous with everything we see, hear, and say. Every *farbrengen* with R. Berke was intense and left us introspective, reminded as we were of how much we still had to work on ourselves.

R. Mendel's *farbrengen*, by contrast, was full of Chassidic sayings, tales, and allegories, each with its own lesson. In general, his *farbrengens* were full of joy and enthusiasm. It took a while for us to get used to R. Mendel's style and to learn that all of his witticisms and stories brimmed with Chassidus and *avodas Hashem,* dedication to the service of G-d, with a focus on cultivating within ourselves absolute honesty and an unquestioning sense of duty.

Owing to the Uzbek climate, the weather was still warm and summery, and we all sat out in the courtyard. Eliyahu Mishulovin, who was of poor health, had to retire at about 9 p.m. We were unable to continue the *farbrengen* past then in its present location, since we were near the window of his room and our voices would disturb his sleep. When I mentioned this to R. Mendel, he released a great sigh and said, "Indeed, he is very sick." In that sigh, I could hear his tremendous, heartfelt concern for his fellow Jew.

"Is there perhaps someplace else we can continue without disturbing him?" he asked. "We have a cellar," I answered. The cellar was full of barrels of pickled vegetables that we had stored for the winter. There were no tables or chairs in the cellar, and no electricity. There was just an earthen floor replete with barrels.

Hearing this, R. Mendel stood up and said, "Let's have a look!" We went down together. "Perfect!" he said. "Let's move a few of these barrels, light a candle, and bring down a few chairs. This is an excellent place for a *farbrengen!*"

Before long, we were all sitting in the cellar. A few of us sat on the barrels, some others on the stairs, and a barrel was tipped over to serve as a table. The *farbrengen* went on in this fashion until 3 a.m.

An Uninvited Guest

Since every citizen was obligated to officially register his place of residence, R. Mendel was certain that the police were searching for him since he had left Chernovitz and had not yet notified them of a new address. So concerned about crossing paths with the authorities, or getting us involved by reporting his present location, he began to search for a permanent residence the morning after his arrival. We, of course, wanted him to continue staying in our home and didn't exactly rush to find him his own apartment.

One day, R. Mendel learned that a certain Jew, someone whom he recognized quite well, had arrived in Samarkand. He was an extremely suspicious individual and rumor quickly spread of his ties with the KGB. R. Mendel, certain that this Jew was sent by the KGB to spy on him, was quick to leave our house and to go to the home of a friend who had no relationship with us and our underground activities.

R. Mendel hoped to move his residence to an area of the Old City known as the "Jewish Quarter." All of the Jewish KGB collaborators lived there, while most of the Chabad community lived spread throughout the New City, which had made surveillance difficult for the KGB. R. Mendel wanted to live among the Bukharian Jews in the Old City in order to keep the eyes of the KGB far away from us. Thank G-d, we managed to find a residence for him in the Old City. We were very disappointed, as was R. Mendel, that he had to live so far from us. To make matters worse, since moving to his apartment, this recently arrived individual started to pay him near-daily visits. These visits continued for about half a year, by which time we learned his schedule: he would arrive every day at 11 a.m. and stay until 2 p.m.

"Now I'm at peace," R. Mendel once said. "I know that the 'letters'—meaning the KGB—know where I am and what I do, and I know what precautions to take."

But in spite of the calm he tried to project, these unwanted visits actually made him quite agitated.

Obviously, as long as the "uninvited guest" was around, he did not want any of us to visit and risk disclosing our relationship. We honored his wishes and stayed away. Only on certain occasions, when we knew he was alone, did we dare visit—and even then, we worried that his visitor would learn of our visit.

It happened once that I went to visit R. Mendel, certain that he was alone. When he saw me enter the courtyard, he emerged, extremely uptight and motioned that I leave immediately. I understood that he was with the "guest" and quickly left.

R. Mendel would go daily to the official shul so that he would be spotted by the collaborators swarming the place and seen keeping to himself. R. Mendel's apartment was near that of Binyomin the Fishmonger. Binyomin had also been acquainted with R. Berke Chein and knew of his constant suspicions of the KGB informants whom he avoided for years and years. He once said in his simple way: "This R. Mendel, with all of his precautions, is even worse than Berke Chein!"

Before the High Holidays, the "guest" finally went back to his home and we used the opportunity to *farbreng* again, and then some more, with R. Mendel. During Sukkos, we brought him to the Mishulovin home where he stayed throughout the holiday.

It's no exaggeration to say that we sat and *farbrenged* in the Mishulovin's sukkah day and night. R. Mendel continued to speak, to share, and to confide, hour after hour, until his strength left him and he dropped to sleep on the table or in his chair. When he awoke, he would estimate how long he had slept, in order to know whether or not he needed to wash his hands. If he happened to see a new face, he would start to *farbreng* anew. It would happen every so often that someone would arrive when R. Mendel was sleeping. We didn't allow anyone to enter the sukkah when he slept so as not to wake him. In some cases, they would have to wait hours to have the privilege of sitting with R. Mendel.

In general, we used every opportunity to *farbreng* with R. Mendel. On every Chassidic occasion, as night fell, we would take a cab to his home, take him to an arranged location and *farbreng* with him there all night. In the early hours of the morning, we would bring him back to his home.

After the holidays, the same "guest" returned to Samarkand and resumed his visits to R. Mendel. This continued for another half a year. He would visit R. Mendel for several weeks and then return home for a few days.

The time I spent with R. Mendel was in between visits from his "guest." I was just twenty-three years old at the time while he was fifty-five, but in spite of the age difference we were very close, and he made me feel that we were old friends. He would share his personal thoughts and feelings with me, and would often pour out his heart about the experience of living under such strict surveillance.

I always felt a little strange to have such a distinguished elder chassid expressing himself to me in this way. I figured that his loneliness was so intense that he felt compelled to connect with whomever he could in order to restore his spirit, and that I, having earned his trust, had become a prime candidate for the role.

Among other things, he told me about the visits from his "guest." R. Mendel was always very tense in his presence, knowing that he studied his every action and reported it all to the "letters." The worst was when the "guest" would sit and say nothing for hours.

Once, he told me how the "guest" spoke with great pride about all the *mitzvos* that he had done. R. Mendel answered him very bluntly, "Your *mitzvah* is that you should stop doing *aveiros!*" (The best thing you could do is to stop sinning!)

Another time R. Mendel told him, "The day will come that you will stand before the Rebbe. I'm sure you think that you'll be able to defend yourself and get a stamp of approval for your past, but nothing will help you."

R. Mendel told me once that he was thoroughly familiar with his visitor's past, and knew of all his travels, aside from two years of his life that he could not account for. He had no idea where he was during that time and suspected that the KGB had sent him on some secret mission during those years.

A Personal Friendship

R. Mendel, with his incredible brotherly love, aroused strong affection in all who knew him personally. In those days, although I was very busy running a factory with seventeen employees, I was still committed to the yeshiva *bochurim* and spent much time with them. Yet, I had a strong spiritual thirst that could only be satisfied by *farbrenging* with R. Mendel and I felt compelled to see him at least every other week.

Whenever I would visit him, I felt inspiration that would give me strength for the weeks ahead. R. Mendel sensed this and once when I came to visit him, he smiled broadly and said, "*Aha!* He's back again! It looks like what I give him only lasts a couple weeks!"

All this time together brought about a special friendship between us. Our relationship was not that of a student and a teacher, or even a *mashpia* and a *mekabel*, of mentor and protégé; it was a true friendship. I would share my innermost feelings with him and he took a careful interest in my daily life.

I was always very open with him. He once asked me how much money I earned and how much I gave to charity. I didn't want to lie, so I told him everything. I was happy to know that my answer pleased him.

Once, in the middle of our conversation, R. Mendel asked me all of the details of our activities and I disclosed everything. After speaking about these things for about an hour, he exclaimed, "How could it be that you remember all of these things? Only the *Eibershter,* only G-d, remembers all that is forgotten!"

R. Mendel once suggested a match for me with a particular young woman. I told him that I wasn't interested, but gave no explanation. He demanded to know why I refused to meet her and didn't let the matter rest until I finally told him that I had heard that she had some health issues. He thought for a moment and then became very upset.

"*Oy!* Why are you telling me this?"

"You asked!"

"True," he said, "but now if someone asks me about her, what should I do? Lie?"

When the daughter of R. Efraim Demichovsky was suggested as a possible match for me, I went to R. Mendel to ask his opinion.

"*Ahh…* The daughter of R. Efraim Fishel, Leibke's sister!" He was very happy. "R. Efraim is a nephew of the Rogatchover Gaon and I heard that the girl is attractive too. Your parents want a nice-looking girl for you."

After our first meeting in Minsk, my future brother-in-law arrived with his sister to spend that Tishrei in Samarkand. I met with her several more times and eventually proposed. R. Mendel came to our home to take part in the celebratory *l'chaim* and asked that we arrange the wedding as soon as possible so that he could be present. This, ultimately, was not possible. R. Mendel left Russia in February of that year, while our wedding took place the following May.

Interest in the Yeshiva

Whenever I would arrive, R. Mendel's first question was, "What's new with the yeshiva?"

As I mentioned earlier, I never got used to this question, and never thought of our underground studies as a "yeshiva." It was R. Mendel who taught me that a yeshiva isn't just a building housing regular studies. "What do you think, that it's only a yeshiva if it comprises hundreds of students learning in a big, beautiful building? If *bochurim* are learning according to the schedule of Tomchei Temimim, it's a yeshiva!"

R. Mendel regarded our activities in much the same way as the yeshiva he had founded together with R. Abba Pliskin in Samarkand during the war. "When we first arrived in Samarkand during the war," he told me, "we decided that we needed to hire a teacher for the children. It was literally a time of famine, but since a teacher would need to support his family, we resolved to find a way to give him two loaves of bread every week. And so it was. There were some extremely difficult times when we didn't have what to feed our own families, but the teacher always got his pay.

"So too with you," he concluded. "You need to pay a lecturer enough to support his family. You have to pay some of the students, too. If one particular student doesn't bring enough money into the household, his father may force him to leave the yeshiva to go to work. A second student's mother might rely on what he brings home. In the merit of this money, everyone is able to sit and learn. And so the cycle keeps on going."

R. Mendel had a very high opinion of Samarkand's Chabad community. Once, when I arrived at his home to take him to a *farbrengen*, he surprised me with the question, "*Nu,* are the chassidim there already?" I didn't understand which esteemed personages he was referring to.

"Which chassidim are you expecting?" I asked.

"Berel, Eliyahu, Dovid…" he said, listing all of my peers. "Who are the chassidim today? They are! These are the real chassidim!"

R. Mendel Leaves Russia

In the winter of 1964, the day he had dreamed of for twenty years finally arrived. R. Mendel's application for a visa was approved. When I learned of this, I immediately went to him to congratulate him on the wonderful news. When I saw him, I grabbed his hand and wished him *mazel tov.* Full of emotion, I wanted to give him a Chassidic kiss. He stepped away from me.

"Chassidim should express themselves differently," he said. He explained the type of Chassidic kiss that the Rebbe Rashab gave to his young son and eventual successor, R. Yosef Yitzchok. Once, observing his young son asleep in bed, the Rebbe Rashab was overcome with emotion. Rather than giving his son a kiss, he wrote a Chassidic discourse for him. Years later, when Yosef Yitzchok became bar mitzvah, the Rebbe Rashab gave him the *maamar* and said, "This is a Chassidic kiss."

It's easy to imagine how brokenhearted we were to see R. Mendel leave after his two and a half years with us. Nonetheless, we were overjoyed that he could finally leave Russia.

During our last meeting before his departure, R. Mendel questioned me on all of the details of our activities in Samarkand: how many prayer groups there were and their locations, the number of participants and their ages, the number of children in school, the number of students in the yeshiva, the number of people present at *farbrengens*, and the identities of the activists. He asked me for every detail.

"You yelled at me for "remembering all that is forgotten!" I reminded him.

"It's different now," he responded. "When I see the Rebbe, he'll ask me about all these things. I have to give the Rebbe an exact accounting of everything that's happening here."

He then turned to me and asked, "Hil'ke, do you remember what you said to me when I first arrived in Samarkand?"

I didn't.

"You told me that just by being in Samarkand, one is eventually uplifted spiritually."

I remembered now that R. Mendel hadn't appreciated this comment of mine.

"*Nu, nu,* everyone is uplifted in your Samarkand," R. Mendel continued. "Now I think there's some truth in your words!"

Upon leaving Russia, Reb Mendel Futerfas joined his family in England. In 1973, he moved to Israel to fill the position of *mashpia*, spiritual mentor, at the yeshiva in Kfar Chabad.

CHAPTER 16

Adventures on the Road

My involvement with communal work often saw me traveling the breadth of the Soviet Union. Along with the main purpose of each trip, I would always take the opportunity to meet with the chassidim and other Jews of the cities I passed through. Each trip was a separate story, filled with all sorts of experiences and adventures. Sometimes, just getting there was an event in itself.

A Visit to Lvov

When I traveled to meet with R. Mendel Futerfas in Chernovitz, Ukraine, I decided afterwards to detour to nearby Lvov. My aunt Sarah Pevzner lived there and she had recently lost her husband, my uncle R. Dovid Pevzner, and her only son, Moshe.

The sudden death of my cousin Moshe was painfully tragic. He was a man in his twenties, good looking and healthy. He worked as an electrical engineer in a local government-run plant. A short time after his wedding, he left his house for work in perfect health. Two hours later, he was brought back, dead. He had been working on installing a new electrical machine at a plant together with some Ukrainian anti-Semites working there. They had intentionally switched on the power, electrocuting him instantly.

My aunt was a very strong woman who kept her pain buried deep within her heart. Even under these trying circumstances, with her son dying in his prime and so shortly after the death of her husband, she did not cry. Instead, she sufficed with deep, long-suffering sighs. I felt obligated to visit her and lift her spirits.

Although she barely recognized me—when they moved from Samarkand to Lvov I was only six years old—she was happy to see me, asking about my well-being and hosting me graciously. On the first day of my visit, I went with her to the cemetery and we visited the adjacent graves of her husband and son. I was taken aback to see how, after cleaning the weeds from the graves, she stood there silently and did not shed a tear. She only sighed, shuddering sighs that seemed to hold all the heavy contents of her heart.

During my visit, my aunt suggested that we visit the Botanic Gardens in Starisky Park. I was happy to see that she had retained a joy for life and enjoyed showing me the sights. Starisky Park was a garden with a myriad of colorful and aromatic flowers, shrubs, and trees. The air was crisp with a faint scent of pines, and I breathed the fresh air deeply. Songbirds chirped softly, creating a magical atmosphere. I felt relaxed and refreshed.

Living in Lvov at the time were the brothers R. Shmuel (Mulle) and R. Dovid (Dovidke) Gurewitz, as well as R. Elimelech (Meilach) Lebenhartz. I knew R. Elimelech, but I had never met either Gurewitzes. In those days, we all yearned to meet with the few Lubavitchers still living in other cities of Russia.

On Shabbos morning, I joined with R. Meilach Lebenhartz and we walked together to R. Mulle's. Our meeting was warm and friendly and the three of us then headed together to the *mikvah* before the prayers. On the way, we passed by the house of a certain chassid whose wife had just given birth to a son. We entered the house to wish them well.

From there we continued to the *mikvah* and shul. Our *farbrengen* after the prayers was especially festive and emotional; in those years it was very rare to meet fellow Lubavitchers from other cities and *farbreng* together.

A Terrifying Encounter with the Police

From Lvov, I would continue on to Rostov by way of Kiev. My plan was to utilize my trip as an opportunity to visit the Ohel—the resting place—of the Rebbe Rashab in Rostov. My aunt escorted me to the train station towards evening and together we stood waiting in the passenger area. A cleaning lady washed the floor, as a bored policeman walked before her asking people to step aside so she could do her work.

The policeman approached me, and I felt the handle of my suitcase burn in my hand: The suitcase was full of "anti-Communist propaganda" and I desperately wanted to avoid a confrontation with the law. I quickly stepped aside before he had to ask me to do so. Unfortunately, my preemptive move aroused his suspicion. He stopped beside me and requested to see my passport.

My heart raced. I handed him my documents, and an uncomfortable feeling settled over me. The policeman saw that I had come from faraway Samarkand, a distance of 4,000 kilometers from Lvov, and he asked, "What are you doing here?"

I explained that I had vacation from work and I had come to visit my aunt (which was true). He looked at me suspiciously and said, "Please open your suitcase, comrade."

I trembled. My suitcase held several volumes of the *Tanya*, *Tehillas Hashem* prayer books, and the weekly *Panim el Panim* magazine published by Agudath Israel in New York, which had a long article about the Rebbe's brother-in-law, the Rashag, and the Chabad movement. (The article was of great interest for the Lubavitchers in Russia, as we knew very little of what was going on with the Rebbe.) It was difficult for me to breathe. What would happen if he discovered all of this incriminating material? Although I had arranged my suitcase with towels and clothing on the top, he could still easily find what was beneath them.

Even worse, if he would start asking me about my activities in Samarkand, I would be in real trouble. I began thinking about the boys learning in our house and the danger that might befall them if I was arrested. These terrifying thoughts came one after the next.

In those tense moments, I recalled how R. Moshe Meisels, a chassid of the Alter Rebbe, had once avoided death by following the Chassidic dictum that, "The mind rules the heart." He had been planted as a spy by the Alter Rebbe to subvert the French military campaign against Russia of 1812, which the Alter Rebbe had considered detrimental to Jewish interests. Even when Napoleon himself accused R. Moshe of being a spy, the remarkably disciplined chassid managed to keep his cool. Although I could not achieve such total self-control, I mustered my inner reserves to the best of my ability, and with a relaxed smile I began to open the suitcase. I felt the policeman eyeing me and I continued to smile. After I opened the latch, I started to raise the cover. He continued to watch me and I continued to smile for all I was worth. Then he responded with a smile of his own and said, "Fine, you can close the suitcase. Please move out of the way."

It all took just a few moments, but to me they seemed like an eternity. Before there was any time to think about what had happened, the train arrived. I hurried inside, arranged my belongings, and the train was off. Only afterwards, when I had calmed down a bit, did I think of what could have happened and where I would be had the policeman discovered the material in the suitcase.

Looking for a Place to *Daven*

After I had concluded the Evening Prayer, I began to think about my plans for the trip. The train was due to arrive in Kiev at ten in the morning, leaving me plenty of time until my train to Rostov at six in the evening. Before I left Samarkand, I was told about the widow of a certain G-d-fearing man who, following his death, continued living with her two daughters in Kiev, far from a Jewish environment. One of my goals on this trip was to visit them and encourage them to leave Kiev and move to the Jewish community in Samarkand. I imagined that I would be able to *daven* the morning prayers in their house.

When I arrived in Kiev, I began searching for the widow's address but was unable to find it. After searching for a long time, I began to grow nervous: Where would I pray? I had already said the *Shema* in the morning, but as for reciting the rest of the prayers, and donning both sets of *tefillin*—I wasn't married yet and didn't have a *tallis*—I preferred to wait and *daven* in their house with peace of mind.

I nearly gave up and decided to look for a quiet place outdoors, but then I had an idea. I would look for a Jewish neighborhood and simply ask someone to let me pray in their house. That was no simple matter, but it was definitely preferable to praying in the street.

Having learned from my experience the evening before, rather than take my suitcase with me, I left it in a locker at the train station and took only a bag with my *tefillin* and a bit of food I had brought from home. I walked around the streets of Kiev and noticed a public courtyard with private houses around it. I entered the yard and met a woman who looked Jewish. When I asked her whether I could *daven* in her house, she looked at me in terror and whispered, "*Daven? Daven?* Go to the city park where you will find some old Jews on the benches. From them you can ask to *daven...*"

I did as she suggested and found a small park nearby where old Jewish men and women sat and spoke together in Yiddish. This unusual sight was wonderful to behold. When I went over to them and asked in Yiddish whether I could pray in their houses, they could not believe their eyes—a young man who spoke Yiddish and wanted to *daven*! They were sure that there were no religious youth in Russia anymore and my existence astonished them.

"Who are you? Where are you from?" asked one old man incredulously.

"From Kostanay in Kazakhstan," I answered, as always.

"What is your name?"

"My family name is Breitbein," I said.

"Unbelievable!" exclaimed the man to his wife. "In the Soviet Union there are still young men like him who speak Yiddish and who know how to *daven*."

Showing the Jews whom I encountered on my travels that there were still young people in the Soviet Union who kept Torah and *mitzvos* and spoke Yiddish too was an important mission of mine. The information greatly encouraged these Jews and inspired them.

After they calmed down from the pleasant surprise, one of the old men said, "Go to Kreshtchatik—a main street in Kiev—take the streetcar and get off at the Podol stop. You will find a shul there where you can pray." They assured me that the shul was open all day and wouldn't be closed, despite the late hour.

I followed their instructions and, to my great joy, succeeded in finding the shul. Walking into the yard, I saw an old man sitting and learning Gemara. I greeted him and asked, "Is the shul still open? Can I *daven* there?" He nearly fell off his chair from shock. A young man who spoke Yiddish and wanted to *daven*! He answered in the affirmative and showed me the door to the shul.

I continued to ask, "Is there a *mikvah* here too?" He nodded, surprised by the question, and showed me the *mikvah*. I went to immerse, and a few minutes later noticed that the old man had come in after me, apparently to see what a young man like me was doing in a *mikvah*. When he saw that I was wearing *tzitzis* made of wool, he asked, "Ah! Are you one of the chassidim?"

In Russia of those days, the term "chassid" was generally associated with Chabad chassidim, as there were very few chassidim there from other groups. One of the signs of a Chabad chassid in Russia was his woolen *tzitzis*, which they would wear even during the hot summer months.

In those days, it was very dangerous to associate oneself with Chabad chassidim, so I pretended not to understand his question. "What? *Schidim*? What's *schidim*?"

He asked me again, and I continued to play dumb. When he saw that I did not understand what he was saying—or that I did not want to continue the conversation—he left.

After finishing, I went into the shul and prayed. The old man came in several times, apparently to check whether I was really *dav-*

ening. When I put on my second, Rabbeinu Tam, *tefillin*, I made
sure to do so deliberately and conspicuously, so that he would tell
his friends about the unusual sight and inspire them in turn. He saw
that I was a man of few words and he did not try to ask more questions, such as my name and why I had come to Kiev. In general, in
Russia one got used to not asking too many questions.

When I was finished, the old man invited me to his house to eat
something. I politely declined and told him that I had brought kosher food with me from home. As he marveled at the sight before
him, the old man seemed deeply moved. In Russia of those days, a
religious young man who put on two pairs of *tefillin* and ate kosher
was beyond imagination. He probably thought that Hashem had
sent him an angel from heaven…

At the Ohel of the Rebbe Rashab

That evening, I left for the train station to continue my journey. The
trip to Rostov was long, with many stops. The train departed Kiev
on Wednesday night and was expected to arrive in Rostov on Friday, at 11 a.m.

Before leaving Samarkand, I had heard that the legendary chassid R. Lazer Nannes was planning to travel to Rostov during the
summer. I was thrilled by the rare opportunity to visit the Ohel with
him. Ordinarily, so I heard, the attendant there was suspicious of
visitors and made admission difficult, but R. Lazer was one of the
few select individuals to whom he allowed entry. We therefore arranged to meet in Rostov and go to the Ohel together.

In those days, chassidim didn't consider visiting the resting
places of the other Chabad rebbes in Haditch, Niezhen, and
Lubavitch. We felt safe visiting the Ohel of the Rebbe Rashab in the
large city of Rostov, but these others were all small towns and such
a visit would arouse unwanted attention and suspicion. We also felt
a certain closeness to the Rebbe Rashab who, of all the rebbes buried in Russia, was the closest to our generation. My father, for exam-

ple, had studied in Lubavitch in the time of the Rebbe Rashab and we had heard many firsthand stories about him from numerous chassidim.

R. Lazer's sister-in-law lived in Rostov. He gave me her address and I followed the directions to her house with ease. Her husband was a simple man, but she had seen some great chassidim of the previous generation and had absorbed that "Chassidic flavor."

When she saw a young Yiddish-speaking *bochur* who had come to Rostov to *daven* at the Ohel, she accorded me much respect. She spoke a lot about chassidim with whom she had been acquainted in the past and related the Chassidic stories she remembered. Mostly, she talked about chassidim who learned in Tomchei Temimim.

To her, the highest form of praise for a person was to say, "He was a *tamim*" (meaning wholehearted)—the term for one who studied in Tomchei Temimim. Over the years, however, her Hebrew had gone rusty and instead of saying *tamim* she would say *tamei* (impure). Every time she wanted to describe the greatness of such a graduate of the famous Chabad yeshiva, she would say, with glowing admiration, "He was impure." I had a hard time keeping a straight face.

Soon after, R. Lazer arrived and we spent an uplifting Shabbos together replete with Chassidic melodies and stories. He spoke a lot about the long imprisonment he had endured at the hands of the Soviets and said that one of the things that kept him going was his custom of singing every Chabad song he knew every week after Shabbos.

On Shabbos day, I went with R. Lazer to the shul where the Rebbe Rashab used to *daven*. For security reasons, we did not walk together; R. Lazer walked ahead of me and I followed. We didn't want people to think that we were associated.

Before the Torah reading, the *gabbai* approached me and asked me whether I knew how to say the blessing on the Torah if I were called up. I was taken aback by the question, and after replying in the positive, I said, "Can't you already see that I know how to *daven*?" He replied, "The fact that you are holding a prayer book doesn't necessarily mean that you know how to pray." He then gave me a paper that said *chamishi* on it, meaning that I would be called up for the fifth *aliya*.

As a rule, I did not accept *aliyas* during my travels because the majority of Torah scrolls in Russia had not been checked for many years. Many of them had deteriorated to the point that they were invalid, and any blessing recited over them would have been in vain. However, R. Lazer had told me that this particular scroll was kosher and I accepted.

On Sunday, we immersed in the Don River and proceeded to the Ohel. The Ohel was located in a yard separate from the rest of the cemetery and some Lubavitchers had arranged for the yard to remain locked. The *shamash* let us in, and when we entered the yard, I saw five plots with piles of dirt atop them, as though people were buried there. R. Lazer pointed to one of the five plots, identifying it as the gravesite of the Rebbe Rashab, and explained that the other piles were simply so that other people wouldn't be buried there. We said some prayers quickly, lest we be seen, and hurriedly left.

A Spiritual Rescue

A few years after World War II, around 1948, a young man from Leningrad arrived in Samarkand. His father, a Lubavitcher *shochet*, had died during the siege on the city and the orphaned son had come to Samarkand in order to live in a Jewish community. When his studies met with little success, he began working at a job. Since he wasn't very bright, when it came time for him to be drafted in the army, everyone assumed he would receive an automatic exemption, so no particular efforts were made on his behalf by the community. To everyone's surprise, he was drafted. By the time they realized their mistake, it was too late.

When he finished his service, he returned to his remaining family in Leningrad, and from that point on we lost touch. On one of my trips during the summer of 1959 or 1960, I decided to pass through Leningrad in order to meet with him and see how he was doing.

When I would travel to a distant, unfamiliar city, I always tried taking along a few addresses of Lubavitchers living there, so that if one wasn't home, I could visit another. On my trip to Leningrad I had the address of that man, as well as that of the chassid R. Michel Rappaport.

My aunt Feiga, my father's sister, lived in Leningrad at the time. She was good-hearted, but simple and naïve. As a result, she had been influenced by the Communist propaganda in her youth and became a staunch Communist. So dedicated to the cause was she that she never married, so that family responsibilities would not distract her from her work on behalf of the Party.

My aunt lived in a small house together with her niece Nata. When I arrived at their home, she was happy to see me and we began a pleasant conversation. I wanted to see if she was still a full-fledged Communist or if her blind faith had been eroded after Nikita Khrushchev revealed Stalin's atrocities to the public. I asked her, "Do you still believe in Communism?" to which she replied resolutely, "Of course! Until the grave…"

Realizing that I was looking for a place to stay, my aunt informed me that I would not be able to stay in her home. Firstly, the house was extremely small, containing just one room that served both as kitchen and bedroom for her and her niece. More importantly, were I to stay with her for over twenty-four hours, she would have to register me at the local police station. Her dedication to Soviet law left no room for exceptions.

I decided to try to stay with R. Michel, but I soon discovered that the house was located in a communal apartment. If you've never seen something like it, you would not believe that people in developed countries in the second half of the twentieth century still lived that way. Several families lived together in one apartment, with one bedroom for each family. The bathroom facilities were shared; there was one dining room and one kitchen. Each family had an allotted time slot—a specific time to use the bathroom and to cook in the kitchen.

One can imagine how difficult life was for a religious Jewish family that had to live in an apartment like this with non-Jews. This was especially so with regards to cooking on the communal stove. Before using the stove to cook, a metal plate had to be placed inconspicuously on the non-kosher stovetop. Additionally, one had to be careful that nothing else was cooking nearby so that no non-kosher food or steam would come in contact with the kosher pot.

R. Michel, who was forced to live in such an apartment, rented a summer home outside of the city. Although the summer home was more of a shed than a house, for R. Michel it was a virtual palace. His family lived there by themselves, with no gentile neighbors, and had their own kitchen: What a luxury!

When I came to R. Michel's apartment, he was on his way out to his summer home. He was very happy to see me, not only because I was a fellow Lubavitcher, but because his only son, Itzikel (Yitzchok), had recently celebrated his bar mitzvah and R. Michel wanted to show him that being religious wasn't only for old people. It was possible for a *bochur* in the Soviet Union to be religious as well.

R. Michel was amazed by the Divine Providence behind our encounter, because he had already relocated to the summerhouse and only returned to the city from time to time. That particular day he had come back for just a few hours, and exactly at that time that I arrived.

I told R. Michel of my plans to visit the man who had once spent time in Samarkand, and asked if he knew of him, but he replied that he did not. Leaving my belongings with R. Michel so he could take them to his summer home, I hurried off so that I would make it to the young man's home before nightfall. Actually, while in Leningrad, I came to notice an uncanny scene: Even though the hour was late, and the streets had emptied of people, the sky was still lit like the day. It was then that I remembered hearing of Leningrad's famous "white nights," when it would be close to midnight by the time the summer sun set.

I found the correct address but was told that the man had married—a Jewess, thank G-d—and left the area. I did not have the opportunity to see him, but I met his two sisters and mother who were very happy to meet a young Jew who knew of their family.

From my conversation with them, I learned that their father had brought them up in a Chassidic home, as befitting someone who had learned in Tomchei Temimim in Lubavitch. However, after their father died they remained alone without any Jewish or Chassidic guidance. They also said that they had a younger brother who had been drafted to the army. After speaking for a few hours, I left the house.

Everything is obviously ordained from above. Who knows the true reason behind my journey to Leningrad— to see the man I had planned to meet, or perhaps something far more important? I often encountered this during my travels. I'd be thinking along certain lines, and Divine Providence would lead me in another direction entirely.

After I returned to Samarkand and relayed the stories from my visit to Leningrad, I had an idea: I would try to marry off the girls I had met. I spoke to one of the *bochurim* in Samarkand and suggested that he go there and meet them—maybe one would be suitable for him. They were Jewish girls who had been born to pure, pious parents and they were the daughters of a *tamim*.

He took me up on the idea and went to Leningrad. I was thrilled when I heard that he had met with one of them, they liked one another, and had decided to marry. The wedding took place a few months later in Samarkand.

Later on, the second daughter arrived in Samarkand, eventually marrying another Chassidic young man as well. She was then followed by their younger brother who had finished his army duty. After years of estrangement from Jewish company, the young man barely knew anything about Judaism. I took on the job of bringing him back to Jewish life and hired him as an employee in my factory. With thanks to Hashem, over the years he became more involved until he became a true chassid.

Thanks to Hashem, over the years he and his sisters established Chassidic families with many children and grandchildren.

A Visit to the Great Shul of Leningrad

When I was in Leningrad, I used the opportunity to visit the main shul, where I met a tall man by the name of R. Avrohom Abba. He worked as a *gabbai* in the shul and was also a *sofer*, a scribe. He had in his possession many pairs of *tefillin* that had accumulated from elderly Leningrad locals who had passed on. There was a shortage of *tefillin* in Samarkand due to the growing number of additions to our community, so I bought a few pairs from him. I had been looking for *tefillin* on my trips without success, and the only person from whom I managed to obtain kosher, *mehudar tefillin* was R. Avrohom Abba.

After we became acquainted, he offered to show me the main shul, which was generally only used on holidays. For weekdays, services were in the small shul on the second floor, to the left of the main sanctuary. During and following the war, Lubavitchers had *davened* there, and it had also housed Yeshivas Tiferes Bachurim—a yeshiva established by the Rebbe Rayatz for *bochurim* who had to work part-time to make a living.

R. Avrohom Abba said that the main shul in Leningrad was considered one of the most beautiful in all of Europe. Indeed, when we walked in, I was taken aback by its elegance, and its intricate architecture. I began to walk towards the Ark and suddenly I felt as if someone was walking beside me. I looked carefully behind me and to either side, but no one was there: The shul had exceptional acoustics, such that even something spoken in a regular tone of voice could be heard throughout the building.

On my way out of the shul, I met a Jewish woman of about forty years old in the courtyard. She clearly assumed that a youngster like me did not understand Yiddish, so speaking in Russian, she asked what I, a young man, was doing in the shul. I realized that she knew

Yiddish, and when I answered her in that language, she expressed her amazement at my fluency.

When meeting Jews by chance on the street, I would try to avoid long conversations, for fear of the KGB. But in the short time that we spoke, I would ask who they were, what they did, and if they had been able to raise their children in the ways of the Torah. I will never forget the answer of that woman, after she told me about her only son and I asked whether he had followed in her ways. With tears in her eyes, she quoted the verse from the prophet Isaiah: "Children have I raised and exalted, and they rebelled against me." A shiver ran up my spine as I was witness to the deep, inner pain of a woman whose only child had left the path of Judaism.

Leningrad became a regular stop during my subsequent trips to central Soviet Union. I would make a point of meeting with R. Avrohom Abba and we enjoyed many pleasant conversations. Knowing that I was ready to pay well for a good set of *tefillin*, he would prepare a number of such pairs in advance. Once he had collected a pair, he would improve it until perfection before selling to me. One can imagine the joy of my friends in Samarkand when I returned with beautiful, *mehudar tefillin*. They would compare the new pairs with the ones they had already, and upon seeing that the pairs I had brought were indeed more *mehudar*, would gladly switch their *tefillin* for the new ones.

An Unexpected Meeting with R. Mulle Mochkin

As described earlier, in 1959 I opened a plant on behalf of the government to manufacture cloth labels. Because the labels were very small, we were able to print dozens on a relatively small piece of fabric. I sought out fabric manufacturers where I could obtain large quantities of scrap fabric that these other factories regarded as rubbish; for our plant these scraps were very useful.

One day, I discovered such a plant in the city of Tashkent. After traveling to the plant, I found that there was plenty of suitable scrap, and went to speak to the director, a Muslim Uzbek woman. I prepared a bribe in advance to speed up the transaction, but to my misfortune, another individual followed me into her office. Obviously, I could not offer my bribe in the presence of a stranger, and so lost any interest in speaking to the director at all, lest this stranger interfere with my offer. When I asked about the stranger, the director identified him as her deputy and I understood that I had no choice but to make my offer in his presence.

Using my Russian name, I presented myself as Gilia Zaltzman, the manager of a label production plant. I explained that her fabric scraps would suit my needs and requested that rather than discarding them she should sell them to our plant for a nominal fee so that we could all profit. After hearing me out, she responded that she would consider the offer. I was not too excited by the turn of events. Presumably she would consult with her deputy, but who knew whether he would spoil the entire deal.

Upon leaving the room, I noticed the deputy follow me out. To my astonishment, he caught up with me and asked, "Are you the son of Avrohom Zaltzman?"

I was shocked. "Yes, I am," I answered, "And who are you?"

"I am Shmuel Mochkin," he answered. Sensing that I did not recognize the name, he added, "I am Mulle Peretz's," the name by which he was more commonly known.

I had heard numerous stories of the two sons of Reb Peretz Mochkin, Yosef and Mulle, who had been left behind in the Soviet Union. They failed to escape the country along with their family in 1946 and had spent many years in jail. I had only recently heard that they had both been freed from prison and I was most excited to be meeting him now. We fell upon each other's shoulder with great happiness and shared a long and friendly conversation as if we had known each other for many years.

He then told me, "When I saw you enter, I recognized not only a Jewish face, but also someone that appeared to be a fellow Lubavitcher! I was unsure what you wanted, so I joined you in the director's office so I could hear your request and make sure that it is fulfilled."

From that time on, whenever I was in Tashkent, I would make sure to visit Mulle, and we would enjoy spending time *farbrenging* together.

Jewish Pride in Flight

R. Eliyahu Bisk, son-in-law of the *shochet* R. Yisrael Konson, was born into a Skverer Chassidic family. He had attended university, but remained a true G-d-fearing individual in spite of this. Despite working in a large government factory in Moscow, I heard that he nonetheless remained strictly Shabbos observant, and even served as the Torah Reader for the underground Chabad minyan in Udelnaya, a suburb of Moscow. This was rare indeed. To be an observant Jew in the Soviet Union was difficult enough, but in R. Eliyahu's circumstances, it was nearly impossible. Little wonder it was said about him that he entered the Communist furnace—by both studying in a university and working in a government factory—and emerged unscathed.

It should be understood that in some cases Lubavitcher chassidim considered attending university to be the lesser of two evils, despite all their efforts keeping their children away from government-sponsored institutions: In the Soviet Union, conscription could only be avoided by obtaining a medical or academic exemption. In a big city like Moscow, where it was almost impossible to find a doctor to issue a medical exemption, attending university was essentially the only way to avoid military service.

During my numerous travels to Moscow, I often had occasion to stay at the home of R. Yisrael Konson, which was where I first became familiar with R. Eliyahu.

Once, on a flight departing from Moscow, I noticed R. Eliyahu board before me and take a seat in the front of the plane. He didn't notice me. Now, in those days, everyone was extremely careful to conceal any expression of Judaism, for fear that KGB informants were watching our every move. I was curious then to observe how

Eliyahu would conduct himself when not in the presence of Jewish companions.

If I harbored any doubts about R. Eliyahu, they were quickly dispelled. As he prepared himself for the flight, he removed his kasket cap, revealing a large Chassidic *yarmulke* underneath. He then opened up a *Tikun Korim* (Reader's Aid) and prepared that week's Torah reading for the duration of the flight. It's difficult to describe the thrill I felt from this surreal sight—a chassid amongst dozens of gentiles in Soviet Russia, completely immersed in preparing the weekly *kriah* without a care in the world!

When a stewardess presented him with a meal, I wondered what he might eat. Often these meals contained fruits or nuts that one could eat without any kosher concerns. However, he didn't even look at the meal presented to him, immediately waving it away as he continued to prepare the *kriah*. Later, I noticed him take out some homemade food from his bag to satiate his hunger. I was deeply moved by this open display of his Jewish pride.

CHAPTER 17

Matchmaking in the Shadow of the KGB

L iving a religiously observant life in the Soviet Union was always difficult, but at certain times, such as when the time came to get married, it was even harder. The main problem was the small number of Chassidic families. After the great postwar exodus, very few Lubavitcher families or other religious Jews remained in the Soviet Union. When a young man came of age, you could count the potential candidates for marriage from the entire Soviet Union on the fingers of one hand.

The main problem was finding Chassidic girls. In Chassidic families, the *bochurim* learned secretly and attended *farbrengens* with the elder chassidim, where they absorbed the Chassidic flavor. Without these institutions of Chassidic life, the girls' attitude to Judaism and Chassidus could only be shaped by the atmosphere in their homes. And with the atmosphere in the street and schools antithetical to everything they heard from their parents, the girls found it hard to preserve their Jewish character. So a Chassidic *bochur* looking for a Chassidic girl, or even just a religious girl, had to work very hard until he found someone suitable. In the following pages I will share some stories of Chassidic courtship and matchmaking—my brother Berel's *shidduch* (match), and my own.

My Brother Berel's *Shidduch*

My brother's matchmaker was R. Berke Chein. As noted earlier, R. Berke was on the run for many years before he finally arrived in Samarkand. One of his hiding places had been in Malachovka on the outskirts of Moscow, in the home of his aunt Bas Sheva, the daughter of R. Meir Simcha Chein. She was married to Reb Yehuda Butrashvili—known as R. Yehuda Kulasher, after his hometown of Kulashi in Georgia. It was there that he met Bas Sheva's daughter Chaya Esther.

When R. Berke came to Samarkand and moved into our home, he became impressed by Berel, who was himself a Chassidic *bochur* of good character, as well as being a talented cantor, and a handsome one too. He encouraged Berel to travel to Moscow to meet Chaya Esther.

Berel was involved in a business venture at the time with R. Dovid Mishulovin and R. Bechor Mullokandov, with the intention of opening a factory for producing blankets in Stalinabad (today Dushenba). R. Bechor was a religious Bukharian Jew and he knew how to keep away from suspicious people. He was considered a reliable, trustworthy person, someone with whom one could do business.

R. Bechor brought the necessary money into the partnership; R. Dovid, who had worked for a while in a similar field, brought his knowledge of the relevant machinery; and Berel would travel to Moscow to obtain the equipment needed to construct the machines.

When R. Berke suggested the *shidduch*, R. Bechor and R. Dovid had already traveled to Stalinabad to set up the business and my brother was heading off for Moscow. Of course, this made for an excellent opportunity to meet R. Berke's cousin.

How Rumors Get Around

The Talmud says, "There is no marriage contract without dispute." A friend of my parents had a recollection of the girl's father being overly sensitive in his youth, that he would often cry over nonsense, and concluded that he must be a peculiar sort. They considered the source to be reliable and since when it comes to matchmaking everything is examined under a magnifying glass, my parents decided to drop the *shidduch*. They informed my brother not to bother visiting the home of R. Yehuda Kulasher.

Berel was staying at the home of R. Wolf Nissinevitch who lived in the Moscow suburb of Perlovka, where he met R. Yaakov Notik. R. Yaakov said: "Berel, you aren't in yeshiva now—why don't you get married?"

"Any ideas?" Berel asked.

"Yes," R. Yaakov said. "The daughter of R. Yehuda Kulasher."

When Berel told him about the information his parents had gotten about R. Yehuda, R. Yaakov dismissed it and said: "He is a smart man with a good temperament, a truly pious man, and a genuine chassid. In his youth he was one of the outstanding *bochurim* in the town of Nevel and now he serves as the highly respected rabbi of the Chabad community in Malachovka. How could he be maligned in this way?"

My brother could see that R. Yaakov knew what he was talking about and wondered out loud how a baseless rumor like this had ever got started.

R. Yaakov thought about it and then laughed. The rumor must have developed from when R. Yehuda first arrived at Tomchei Temimim in Nevel as a *bochur,* he said. Coming to the yeshiva, he had not known a word of Yiddish, and since all the classes were in Yiddish, he did not understand anything in his first weeks there. He was a very emotional person and on one occasion, he began to cry bitterly about his trouble adjusting. The other students were surprised by this display of emotion and said: Why is he crying so much? Within a short time he will learn Yiddish and will understand it like any of us.

At any rate, said R. Yaakov, it seems that someone heard this story and decided that R. Yehuda is a peculiar person who cries over nonsense.

After ascertaining that the rumor was baseless, my brother went to R. Yehuda's house to meet his daughter Chaya Esther, or as most people called her, Anya.

An Engagement or a Wedding?

In those days, making an inter-city telephone call was an ordeal, and not just because the KGB tapped every phone conversation. To make the call, you first had to go to the post office and order a time slot. The clerk would then send a telegram to the post office in the desired city, and when it was delivered to the recipient, he or she could book a time at the post office. Another telegram was sent back with the relevant information, and only then could a conversation be held. All this took a number of days to execute.

This is why, even though things can be quite tense when a couple first meet, with the parents wanting to know exactly what's going on, there had been no phone contact with my brother. Out of the blue, a telegram arrived from Berel, which read: "Anya seems most suitable, spiritually and materially. All of the concerns proved baseless. I have decided to make the *t'naim* (engagement ceremony) and await your consent and arrival here. I am wiring money to you."

My parents could not afford a trip to Moscow and R. Yehuda, who very much approved of the *shidduch*, sent money to my parents for the trip.

This was 1954, and in Russia of those days it was understood that when a wedding took place in a distant city, the parents would represent the entire family at the wedding. The cost of transporting all the siblings, aunts, and uncles, was simply not affordable. This was all the more so, of course, when only the engagement had been planned. Thus, the rest of us remained in Samarkand while my parents traveled to Moscow.

The trip by train from Samarkand to Moscow took more than three days and so R. Yehuda sent money for plane tickets. These were no jet planes, however, but old propeller planes; with several stops along the way, this "quick" trip took over twenty-four hours. They left Samarkand on Wednesday at eleven in the morning and arrived in Moscow on Thursday at three in the afternoon.

When my parents met my brother at the airport in Moscow and heard his positive impressions of the girl, my father said to him: "If everything looks good, why should we only make the *t'naim* now and postpone the wedding for a few months? Let's do the engagement and the wedding now!"

Berel thought it would be better to make the wedding in Samarkand where the entire family and his friends could participate. However, citing my uncle R. Boruch Duchman's concerns, my parents said it was not a good time to make a wedding in Samarkand: Two weddings had recently taken place there in our family, and another might arouse a dangerous degree of interest on the part of the authorities.

Berel explained my parents' position to Anya, the *kallah,* and to his surprise, she immediately agreed. Later, she told him that her parents had been urging her to convince him to make the wedding early but she was unsure how to convey their wishes to him.

It was arranged that the *t'naim* celebrations the next day would lead directly into a wedding feast, which is why, when my parents arrived at the Butrashvili home, they saw a huge challah loaf sitting on the table. My mother realized that R. Yehuda and his wife had assumed that the wedding would take place right away and decided to greet the new in-laws in the traditional way, with a large challah. And so, all the guests who arrived for an engagement party found themselves attending a wedding as well.

Going into Business

After the wedding, my brother bought the machinery for his new business back in Stalinabad. With the help of R. Yaakov Krichevsky, he was able to get all the necessary equipment and then immediately left with his new wife for Samarkand.

I missed my brother very much during the weeks he was away and when a telegram arrived that he would be arriving in Samarkand, I immediately inquired into the precise time their plane would be landing. It turned out that it had already landed and I would not have enough time to meet them at the airport. Nevertheless, I rushed to call a taxi and set out towards the airport so as to meet him on the way. Indeed, as I was traveling I spotted a taxi containing Berel and his wife, Anya. I told my driver to stop, and Berel, having noticed me as well, told his driver the same, and we met joyfully in the middle of the road.

After a brief stay in Samarkand, Berel went on to Stalinabad where R. Dovid and R. Bechor were anxiously waiting for him and the equipment. Later on, the *bochurim* Elimelech and Yosef Lebenhartz joined them, so they now had a tiny Chassidic community. With no kosher *mikvah* in Stalinabad and a thirty-six-hour train trip back to Samarkand, they decided to build a ritual bath of their own.

A Jew by the name of Yechiel Samokhvalovitcher—for his city Samokhvalovitch—arrived in Samarkand at this time. He was an expert oven builder and, since they were wary of entrusting an unknown person with the task, the Stalinabad crew convinced him to come and construct a *mikvah* for them there.

The *mikvah* was to be built in the yard of the shul, and if the KGB would come and question Yechiel, they all decided to tell them that his late grandfather had come to him in a dream and told him to go to Stalinabad in order to build a *mikvah* with his life's savings. Fortunately, the KGB did not get involved at all and the job was done by the summer.

Now they had to fill the covered reservoir of the *mikvah* with rainwater. Since, however, they rarely saw rain in the summer, R. Eliyahu Paritcher ruled that they could fill the pit with ice. After bringing a truck full of blocks of ice, they wiped down each block so that they would be totally dry before they filled the reservoir with them.

They assumed the ice would quickly melt in the summer heat, but the reservoir seemed to have been well insulated, because it didn't. Using warm water to melt the ice would invalidate the *mikvah,* so instead they got a gas torch to do the job. The torch had a weak flame, and the ice was quite cold, but oddly, even after a long time, the pit was still not filling up. How disappointed they were when they discovered that the melted water was being absorbed straight into the ground. As it turned out, an expert oven maker isn't always an expert in building *mikvahs* and the cement floor wasn't properly sealed. They had to start all over again and, with Hashem's help, they eventually built a kosher *mikvah.*

Meanwhile, despite putting prodigious effort into the business, it was not as successful as they had anticipated. Without enough demand for their merchandise, they had to close the factory. They understood that their stay in Stalinabad had been arranged from Above, solely so that a *mikvah* would be built there.

Shortly before returning to Samarkand, Berel saw a beautiful blanket for sale in the market. After examining the weave, he learned how it was made and told R. Dovid, who had the necessary technical knowledge to manufacture such a blanket. Together, they offered to sell the idea and plans to R. Bechor outright. R. Bechor agreed, but since he didn't have enough cash on him after their Stalinabad venture, pledged to pay them their share if the new enterprise succeeded. It turned out that the new business was a great success and R. Bechor kept his promise to Dovid and Berel, paying them 5,000 rubles.

A Match for Me

I was in no rush to marry. I longed to leave Russia and always assumed that it would be much easier to leave single than with a family. When I discussed it with R. Mendel Futerfas, he tried to convince me not to wait. He said, "When the time comes and Hashem decides we can leave Russia, we will be able to leave with our families as well!"

As usual, R. Mendel had an analogy on hand. In 1961, the Soviet Union succeeded in sending the first manned rocket into space.

Yuri Gagarin became the first astronaut and the first person to orbit the earth. By the time he landed, he had been transformed into a celebrity and was famous throughout the world. Said R. Mendel, What's so great about Yuri Gagarin? It was the engineers who built the rocket and the spacecraft capable of safely taking a man to outer space who are the real heroes!

Rather, Gagarin's heroism was an act of survival: He had survived in a place that nobody had even been to before. This, said R. Mendel, is also our task, and our challenge. We must lead full Jewish lives—family lives—in a place and time where others have not succeeded.

I had already received some *shidduch* suggestions, one of them being the daughter of R. Efraim Fishel Demichovsky from Minsk. My father remembered him from the time he learned in Lubavitch and also knew that he was the son of the Rogatchover Gaon's sister. In fact, while he was a student in Tomchei Temimim, my father had eaten meals at the home of his grandmother, Feige.

This same grandmother, who served as the main breadwinner of her household while her husband sat and learned Torah, had actually raised R. Efraim for much of his childhood. R. Efraim's mother died a few days after she gave birth to him. Feige took in her infant grandson and raised him in her home. After several years, he went to live with his late mother's brother, R. Yosef Rosin, the famed Rogatchover Gaon, one of the most brilliant Torah commentators of the twentieth century. At sixteen, his uncle sent him to learn in Tomchei Temimim in Lubavitch.

Growing up without a mother affected R. Efraim deeply and he felt the loss all his life. He would often gaze upon his daughter and say, "She might look like my mother." And then, in a wistful tone, "I never got to know her and I don't even have a picture of her."

We also heard that R. Efraim Fishel himself was a *shochet* in Minsk. His oldest son, nicknamed "Leibke Fishel's," was a good friend of my brother-in-law Eliyahu, who knew him as a warmhearted young man with a good head. In short, the Demichovskys sounded like a Chassidic family with a good Chassidic home.

Still, as was always the concern with *shidduchim*, it wasn't unusual to meet a Chassidic, G-d-fearing father whose children were as different from him as east is to west. So despite all that I had heard about R. Efraim Fishel, I wondered about his daughter.

That summer, I had some communal matters to attend to in the center of Russia and decided to use the opportunity to travel to Minsk. My plans went somewhat awry and I got stuck in Vilna until Friday morning. A flight from Vilna to Minsk takes less than an hour, but during the summer the flights were always booked out by vacationers, so getting a ticket wouldn't be easy. If there was room on a flight, I decided, this would be Heaven's way of telling me I should go to Minsk and meet with the girl. When I arrived at the airport, I found out that there was one seat left on a flight to Minsk.

I arrived in Minsk in the afternoon and asked the first taxi driver I saw to take me to the address I had: 29 Dobrolyubovski Proezd. To my dismay, not only did he not know where it was, but none of the nearby drivers did either. There was a Dobrolyubovdikaya Street, but no Proezd. The drivers started looking through their maps and address books and I began to worry where I would spend Shabbos. I knew nobody in Minsk and the only address I had was one nobody could identify.

Finally, one of the drivers said he thought that the street I was after was a smaller lane leading off the larger Dobrolyubovdikaya Street. Having no choice, I went with him and it turned out that he was right. When we entered the lane, I noticed a bearded Jew up ahead. He was walking with two pails for drawing water; not everybody had running water in their homes then. I asked the driver to stop, paid him for the trip, and rushed to catch up with the Jew while calling out, "R. Efraim!"

He turned around and when he saw me with two suitcases, quickly brought me into his house. Only then did he greet me. I realized he was afraid lest he be seen for too long in the street in the company of an uninvited guest. His vigilance was familiar to every Jew who lived in those days in the Soviet Union, but R. Efraim seemed more frightened than I would have expected.

He began interrogating me about where I was from, the purpose of my visit, what I worked in, and what was in my suitcases. It
was like a KGB interrogation and I couldn't understand it. Eventually, I had no choice but to open my suitcases and show him their
contents. There were some volumes of *Tanya* and *Tehillas Hashem*
prayer books, items I always tried to get on my trips to Moscow, as
well as a thick volume of Chassidus that I had managed to recover
on the trip in order to send to the Rebbe. After this search, he
calmed down and told me why he had been so tense.

The previous Rosh Hashana, at night, an unfamiliar Jew had come
to shul and after the services asked where he might be able to go for
the festival meal. The shul-goers all referred him to the *shochet,* who
gladly invited him. But after a few days, a few government agents
came by and wanted to know where the guest was, how "Comrade
Demichovsky" knew him, and other probing questions. It turned out
that the guest had just finished a prison sentence after being implicated
in the Great Escape to Poland from Russia after the war. (It was Aharon
Friedman, the brother-in-law of R. Yitzchok Zilber.) In Russia of
those days, the police kept close tabs on former prisoners, which is
why, when they discovered he was staying with the Demichovsky
family, their suspicion was aroused. What connection was there between Comrade Demichovsky and the released prisoner?

Another incident had taken place shortly before my arrival. A
Lubavitcher friendly with the family also spent a few days in their
home after being released from prison. After he left, policemen
again came and inquired about him and the nature of their relationship. It turned out that in addition to being an ex-convict, he
had dealt in gold and foreign currency, an especially severe crime
in Russia back then. This is why R. Efraim was very nervous about
any guest who landed in his home. As I learned more about R.
Efraim's background, I came to better understand the reasons for
his constant anxiety and caution regarding anything that might incriminate him.

Parenthetically, Berel Silverman, a friend of my future brother-
in-law Aryeh Leib, later told me that a short time after my wedding

he was called down to the KGB and asked whether he knew the son-in-law of Comrade Demichovsky. They wanted to know who this son-in-law was, where he was from, and what he did for a living. Berel Silverman did not know me then and knew nothing about me, so that was the end of that.

R. Efraim and his family had also tried their luck in escaping after the war but had failed. Since, even during the period of the great exodus in 1946–47, the border would frequently close and re-open, they hoped that the day would come when the border would be opened once again. They decided to move to Minsk, which was relatively close to the border city Lvov (Lemberg).

They arrived in Minsk without anything. Even the suitcases containing their clothes and a few personal possessions had been stolen on the way. In the winter they had no shoes and R. Efraim had to wear galoshes tied with string so they wouldn't fall off his feet. Regarding those years he would say, "In one way I was, like our Father Yaakov [Jacob], 'consumed by heat during the day and by frost at night.'"

His oldest son, Aryeh Leib, wanted to help support the family but could not find a job. He was totally illiterate in Russian, having never gone to public school, and without an education he could not get a job anywhere. So, he decided to do some studying, but instead of learning for ten years, he managed to finish high school in two. After another two years in a technical college he graduated as an expert on timber and forestry, which was a sought-after field in the heavily wooded regions of Belarus.

Since everybody had to work in an official capacity, R. Efraim was registered to work in a recycling factory, where he somehow managed to observe Shabbos.

The Soviet Union had a shortage of feathers for stuffing pillows and quilts, a problem that R. Efraim thought of a novel way to capitalize upon. Since he was a *shochet*, having learned the skill as a boy from Rabbi Shlomo Yosef Zevin, R. Efraim told the factory management that he had an idea of how to obtain feathers. He could open a store to clean chickens in the central marketplace, and whoever bought a chicken and wanted it slaughtered would come to him. Afterwards, his wife would clean the chickens and he could give the feathers to the government.

If you've ever tried plucking the feathers of a single chicken by hand, you can imagine how hard it was to pluck feathers all day. But they labored away lovingly, knowing that it brought them a triple profit—the ability to keep Shabbos, to enable hundreds of Jews to eat kosher chicken, and finally, to earn some money.

Although he officially worked for the government factory, the KGB knew that he had a spiritual-religious agenda and wasn't merely slaughtering chickens. Although they approved this special business, he was under constant surveillance. Along with the two times he had been interrogated for hosting guests, it all made him exceedingly wary. This was the reason for his caution when he first saw me.

An Uncomfortable Trolley Ride

I had arrived in Minsk just a few hours before Shabbos. When I entered the house, I saw R. Efraim's wife standing in the kitchen and cooking for Shabbos. She was dressed modestly, as a Chassidic woman, despite the summer heat.

Their daughter, Mussia Shoshana Esther—Shoshana, as she was called—had seen me when I got out of the taxi and ran towards her father. She thought I hadn't noticed her at the time. With the atmosphere turned more congenial after R. Efraim's interrogation, I now saw her standing near her mother, telling her mother that she had recently bought shoes but wanted to exchange them. Since it would be Shabbos soon, she wanted to go right away.

I only intended on staying in Minsk until Sunday, so I suggested that we go together and get to know one another. Our brief outing was a pleasant one, but as we sat on the trolley on the way back home, a young man whom I recognized as a Jew got on at one of the stops. When his glance met hers and they both blushed, I realized they knew one another. As interested as I was in knowing what their relationship was, I didn't dare ask. Still, the discovery raised all sorts of doubts in my mind and made for an awkward ride home.

When we arrived back home, I was even more surprised to see the young man in the house. That was when I realized that he was none other than her brother, Aryeh Leib, or "Leibke Fishel's," as he was known in Tomchei Temimim of Samarkand. He explained that upon seeing his sister with a *bochur*, he realized she was meeting for a *shidduch* and did not want to introduce himself and disturb our meeting.

Our First Shabbos Meal

My first Shabbos meal at my future father-in-law's table had a few uncomfortable moments.

Grapes generally didn't grow in the central regions of Russia as they did in Samarkand, which made kosher wine particularly hard to come by. Like others, R. Demichovsky would buy his own raisins, soak them in water with some sugar, and after enough time the mixture would begin to ferment and turn into wine. Not knowing exactly how much water could be used in this process for the product and still satisfy the halachic definition of wine—without being too diluted—I preferred not to use raisin wine for *kiddush*.

To make matters worse, when the main course was served, I chose not to eat the chicken. Even though I knew R. Efraim to possess a sincere fear of G-d, I still didn't know his technical ability in preparing a knife for *shechita*. I had never eaten meat from outside of Samarkand and didn't want to start now. R. Efraim was a stern person, and could be quite sharp too, but sometimes, a young person's obstinance comes from a holy place, and I decided not to compromise. In fact, I thought, maybe it's better they knew exactly who their prospective son-in-law was!

R. Efraim was unsurprisingly irritated by all this, but at the same time, he saw it as a sign from Heaven that I was meant for his daughter: Years earlier, in Lvov, he had been sitting at a Chassidic *farbrengen* with R. Yonah Cohen. He made *kiddush* on vodka, and after a few *l'chaims*, began speaking proudly of the high kosher standard of his own *shechita*. Reb Yonah interjected, "Efraim, may G-d grant you a son-in-law who is too stringent for even your *shechita!*"

"Since that *farbrengen*," my father-in-law told me, "many chassidim have passed through my home, and they all ate my food without any reservations. You were the first person to refuse to eat my meat, and I understood that R. Yonah's 'curse' was being fulfilled."

My brother-in-law Aryeh Leib also took a pretty dim view of my conduct. He knew how careful his father was with even the minor details of the law, and suddenly, along comes this *bochur* from Samarkand who thought himself such a chassid that he won't even eat in their home! So as to convince me of his father's great *yiras shamayim*, fear of G-d, he told me a story:

One Friday, a woman came to R. Efraim with a chicken she needed slaughtered for Shabbos. After he had performed the *shechita* and sent the woman on her way, he began to have doubts about the halachic quality of his cut. Despite the late hour, he took two trains to travel to the woman's house, and only after checking the chicken and verifying that his original cut had been deep enough, did he travel back home.

Even after our marriage, when I returned with my wife to her parents the next summer, I was unsure what to do: If I still refused to eat in their home, it would be a real scandal. There was no doubt that my father-in-law was a true *y'rei shamayim*, but I had to find out whether he had the same knife-sharpening skills I had seen in my father.

I had studied the art of kosher slaughter in my younger years, following my father's insistence that everyone should be able to *shecht* for himself, or others, should the need ever arise; one never knew how life would turn out. I knew how to prepare a sharp knife, and how to properly inspect one, and I decided to check my father-in-law's knife. The problem was, of course, that I couldn't just ask to see his knife upfront. Besides, if I did, and it wasn't to my liking, would I even have the courage to say so?

Instead, I would find where he kept his knife and check it without him knowing. If I found a smooth blade, I'd start to eat in their home, but if not, I would maintain my refusal and just bear the discomfort.

With a bit of help from Heaven, a woman came by with a chicken for slaughter, and after my father-in-law was finished, I saw that he put the knife on top of a closet. He then went off to shul early, and after the women had gone to light the Shabbos candles, and everyone was occupied, I realized that the time was right. Without anyone noticing, I took the knife, and found a corner of the house to look it over. A heavy weight lifted from my heart when I found that the blade was in fact unbelievably smooth and straight.

Obviously, I never told anyone of this boldfaced chutzpah, but from then on, I ate from my father-in-law's *shechita* without any worries.

From Ninety-Six Synagogues, a Lone Survivor

On that first Shabbos, I saw that the Demichovskys had a guest. Afterwards, my father-in-law told me that he was a simple, quiet Jew who could be trusted to not tell what he knew, quite a compliment for those days. In general, my father-in-law always lamented that he had nobody with whom to share a few words of Torah and Chassidus, and he was even afraid to discuss current events with other people. "I am alone in a spiritual desert," he confided. Over Shabbos, the guest was happy to share some stories of his life and his time in Minsk.

Before the Revolution, my father-in-law told me, there had been ninety-six shuls in Minsk. By 1963 only one was left, a semi-official affair, in a rented apartment. In a candid conversation later on, he told me how hard it was for him to attend this minyan, which mostly comprised a group of Jews lacking the most basic fear of Heaven. On Shabbos he tried to quickly finish his prayers and leave, before they began collecting money from whoever had bought an *aliya*—in order to buy vodka for the *kiddush*. In general, he said, I try to finish the silent *Shmoneh Esrei* before everyone, because when I take a long time, they start grumbling about the "chassid" who insists on praying for so long.

Where Is the *Kallah?*

Meanwhile, throughout my stay in Minsk over Shabbos and until I left on Sunday, I became impressed by Shoshana and her family. Although they lived alone and isolated from other Chassidic families, they were not drawn after the winds blowing in the street and the Chassidic atmosphere was as it should be. On her part, she felt similarly about me. Since she planned on traveling to some relatives in Samarkand for the High Holidays along with her brother Leibke—he was very close with R. Mendel Futerfas and planned on using the opportunity to see him—we resolved to continue meeting there.

When I arrived in Samarkand and told my parents about my visit to Minsk, they were very pleased. R. Mendel, because he had known Leibke since his youth, was similarly enthused by the match. The pair came to Samarkand shortly after, but after a few more meetings I still couldn't decide about the *shidduch.* I thought we could write letters to one another after she had returned to Minsk and maintain a connection that way. However, my father, who was always practical and very decisive, said that it wasn't right to drag things out: If we were interested, we should make a *t'naim,* an engagement ceremony, so as to commit to one another.

That's what we did. We wrote to the Rebbe about our decision to marry and sometime later we received—via Israel—the Rebbe's blessing.

The wedding was set for the next summer, and in the meantime, my *kallah,* my intended, returned home. That winter, R. Mendel received permission to emigrate. "If the wedding would have been set to take place now," he told me, "I would have loved to attend." Of course, he didn't postpone his departure because of me and immediately used the opportunity he had been given to leave Russia.

My father-in-law had a half-brother and two half-sisters through his father, who were not religious. They all lived in Minsk, so before leaving for the wedding in Samarkand, my father-in-law made a goodbye gathering for them. They were all very interested in hearing about his new son-in-law, which university I attended, and what my profession was.

My father-in-law didn't know what to tell them, and when they realized that the groom had not attended university and did not have a degree, they all began to question the match. "You have an only daughter, a talented and beautiful girl, and you're giving her to someone who doesn't even have a profession? How will he support his family?"

My father-in-law responded curtly, "I know he hasn't attended university, but he can do everything!"

His relatives did not bring it up again; amongst themselves they said, "*Nu*, if Efraim agreed to this *shidduch*, no doubt he knows what he's doing." They considered my father-in-law to be a smart man and would often go to him for advice.

Just before the wedding, I caught a cold, so when the *kallah* and her parents announced their arrival, I could not go to meet them. I asked my childhood friend, Yaakov Lerner, to go instead of me. I gave him all the information he needed: the number of the train, their compartment number, and the time the train was due to arrive, around seven o'clock in the morning. I described what each of the family members looked like, the main point being that when he saw a Jew with a beard, that was the man he was looking for.

We all waited anxiously but Yaakov returned home alone two hours later. He said that nobody had gotten off from the train compartment I had given him. He even went inside to look but found nobody with a beard. When he asked the conductor, the man had no idea what he was talking about.

A few hours later, they arrived. They had traveled all night and the train was due to reach Samarkand early in the morning, so they had asked the conductor to wake them up upon arrival. The conductor forgot, and when they woke, it was too late. They had to get off at the next stop and travel back to Samarkand.

A Wedding Without Pictures

We were married in May of 1964. Our wedding was a happy Chassidic wedding that lingered well into the night. My uncle Shimon Zaltzman came from Tashkent and made merry like a true jester, a *badchan*.

In those days, we were cautious not to photograph events such as these, out of fear that the pictures would end up in the hands of the KGB. Eager to know who had attended the wedding, they would no doubt interrogate us about who was there and what was spoken of. It was only in the following days, at a *Sheva Brachos* feast in a more private family setting, that we dared to take a picture.

Back then, people would joke darkly about the Jew who went to the KGB offices to say he was planning to marry off his daughter. Since he didn't want to be called in for an interrogation after the wedding, to be asked who was there and what they had said, he requested that they send one of their men to write a full report. They asked: "Do you perhaps have the guest list with you?" He said yes, he did, and gave them the list.

After perusing it, they said: "Don't worry, we won't call you for an interrogation. More than half of your guests are our men anyway!"

Our First Apartment

After our wedding, I was forced to contend with a new problem. At the time, the entire country was facing a housing crisis, and in larger cities like Moscow and Leningrad things were even worse. Private dwellings were all but impossible to come by, and the only practical option was finding a residence in an apartment building. To buy into a government apartment building, however, one had to be well connected, to know the right people, and be able to grease the palms of the right officials. Obviously, Lubavitchers did not fall into that category, and those who lived in the big cities could only seek housing in the suburbs.

The housing shortage became so bad that it began to raise the age for marriage. When young people knew that there wouldn't be a place to move into after their wedding, they opted not to marry altogether; those who did were forced to come up with creative solutions. Often, parents would split up their own apartment to share it with the young couple. Generally, these apartments only had one room in the first place, so this meant dividing a single room with a screen or sometimes just a sheet. Couples whose parents were able to give a separate room were considered the lucky ones. It's easy to understand how this sort of situation wasn't exactly appealing to young men and women thinking of marriage and instead they preferred to push off marriage further and further, in the hopes that somehow things would be better in the future.

In anticipation of my wedding, I began looking for a small apartment appropriate for a young couple, but even in Samarkand it was no easy task. So it was that I found myself just weeks before my wedding without a place to live and no sign of anything on the horizon.

At a loss, I turned my attention to a storage shed in my parent's backyard and decided to turn it into a home. The shed consisted of a relatively large room, with a hallway of sorts alongside it, but it was being used to house the goat my parents kept for milk. Simply evicting the goat wasn't an option, seeing as the winter rains and cold would have likely killed it. Besides, it was a "Jewish" goat, who had the great merit of providing us all with fully supervised dairy products! One way or another, I prepared a new place for the goat, and we—the newlyweds—took its place.

I couldn't be too picky when it came to furnishing our little abode either. Since I had no money for any new furniture, I tried to make do with what was there. Sitting in our yard was an old bed that had been thrown out years earlier and had since weathered several winters' worth of rain and snow. After a few repairs to ensure it wouldn't completely collapse the moment someone sat down on it, it came into the house, where it joined another folding bed I had found. A relative bought us a clothes closet as a gift, and although we didn't have a proper mirror, we made do with the one attached to the door of the wardrobe. Our luxurious bedroom was ready.

On the other side of the room lay our dining room, which we had also managed to furnish piecemeal. The only items of furniture that were actually new were six chairs that my uncle R. Shimon Zaltzman had given us as a wedding gift. After finding an old table in my parent's house, we now had a beautiful dining room, if you could call it that. Our dining room even boasted a display cabinet I had made by lining two wooden tea boxes from within with silver foil and stacking one on top of the other, in which we kept some porcelain and a few glasses we had received from relatives.

I recall my joy over being able to host boys from our yeshiva in our modest living quarters. For our honeymoon, my wife and I did not travel on vacation; we spent it in our "shed," together with four yeshiva students who studied there all day. Our first home was modest indeed, but our satisfaction knew no bounds.

CHAPTER 18

My Mother's Death and My Father's Immigration to Israel

In the summer of 1968, my mother suffered a heart attack. She was sixty-three years of age. The doctors described it as a severe heart attack and said she would have to be hospitalized for some time. In Samarkand of those days, the hospital had no intensive care unit, or even a reliable supply of oxygen, and none of the rooms were air conditioned. It was very hot, and my mother had to lie there in a stifling room, attached to an IV drip.

We stayed at her bedside throughout her hospital stay. My brother Berel and I, as well as our cousin Yaakov Pil, took turns so that she wouldn't be alone.

"I have no complaints," we would hear her say, "I had the merit to raise a family and bring up children who have remained religious despite all the hardships. I married them off and have seen grandchildren from each of them. True, it would be wonderful to live another ten or fifteen years, but I have no complaints against G-d. Thank Hashem, I have fulfilled my mission in this world." These words were repeated over and over during the three weeks she spent in the hospital.

On Tuesday morning in July, my mother felt that her final moments had arrived. I was there with her at the time and she asked me to call my father immediately. She wanted to say goodbye. Softly she said, "We lived together for forty-three years."

It was hard for me to call my father under these circumstances. I was afraid that he wouldn't be able to bear the emotional burden. Instead I called my brother Berel to explain the situation and he immediately came to the hospital.

Meanwhile, my mother called me and said, "Don't you realize the situation I am in right now?" She asked me to recite *Shema* with her. I began to say *Shema* and then *Boruch Shem,* word for word. *Blessed be the name of the glory of His kingdom forever and ever.* After I said the final word, *"va'ed"* in the Hebrew, she passed away.

Throughout my mother's time in the hospital, my father would prepare some cooked oats for her every morning and bring them to her room. The morning that she died, I stood there waiting with my brother for him to come so that he wouldn't suddenly walk in on his own and see what had happened. We kept going out to the hall to see if he had come.

A short while later, we saw him walking heavily towards her room without the usual bowl of porridge. Before we even had a chance to go over to him, he called out in tears, *"Kinderlach,* children, I know already."

We couldn't understand how he had found out so quickly. She had passed away a mere half hour earlier and our house was not equipped with a telephone. How had the news reached him so soon?

Later, my brother-in-law Eliyahu related that my father had placed the oats on the stove at home in the morning, as he always did, and he had then gone to pray. A short time later, he suddenly returned home and turned off the fire, saying, "The oats aren't needed, and an *onein*—a new mourner—is exempt from prayer." My brother-in-law and his brother Dovid, who were then in the house, berated him for talking that way. "Have you heard something?" they asked him.

"I didn't hear anything," he replied softly, "but I already know everything that happened." And with that, he quickly made his way to the hospital.

My father wanted my mother's funeral to be as soon as possible since, as he explained, the soul is said to suffer terribly as the body waits for the burial. He only asked to ensure that ten men be present at the funeral for a minyan. In Samarkand of those days, all of the preparations for the burial, including the ritual purification of the body, were performed in the home of the deceased. My father remained in the house and sobbed the entire time.

Suddenly, we didn't hear him anymore and an eerie quiet reigned over the house. My brother Berel and I were very apprehensive. What had happened? We began looking for him throughout the house but were unable to find him.

We finally discovered him outside among the fruit trees in the backyard, leaning on one of the trees. We ran over to him and asked cautiously, "What happened? Do you not feel well?"

Our father replied: "*Kinderlach*, I am so broken; I have never felt as broken as this my entire life. I remembered that when our patriarch Yaakov [Jacob] was reunited with his son Yosef [Joseph], his heart was filled with an overwhelming love, and at that point, he decided to direct his intense emotion Above by reciting the *Shema*. I also want to use this moment when my heart is broken. I am saying *Vidui* now—the Confessional Prayer. Please don't disturb me."

We left him by the tree until he was ready.

In accordance with my father's wishes, we held the funeral immediately. The Bukharian custom in Samarkand was to carry the casket to the cemetery by shoulder, without any other means of transportation, as a way of honoring the deceased. Since we resided in the New City and the cemetery was located in the Old City, we carried the casket a distance of over three miles to the cemetery.

My mother was buried next to her sister, our aunt Chaya Eidel Pil. She had died a half year earlier after a prolonged illness and my mother had cared for her the entire time. As per my father's request, we connected the two gravestones with an additional stone bearing the inscription, "Those who were beloved and pleasant in their lifetime are not parted in their death."

At the time of my mother's illness, my sister, Sarah Mishulovin, was living at the home of R. Sholom Ber and Asya Raskin in the suburbs of the city of Gorky in eastern Russia. That year had been a difficult one for her. Her husband, R. Eliyahu, was ill himself, and our yeshiva boys had been studying in their home, which made for an atmosphere of constant stress. On top of all this, her children remained at home instead of attending school, so each knock on the door was cause for even more fear and anxiety. We all decided that she should leave for a vacation and relax, enabling her to—at least temporarily—put her worries out of her mind.

We would communicate by means of letters, and when my mother was hospitalized, Sarah—now on vacation in Gorky—asked why our mother had stopped writing. With each letter we sent her, her worry grew, and shortly before our mother's passing, she sent a telegram stating that if she would not be told why Mother wasn't writing, she would return home immediately. We replied that she could return if she desired.

A few days later, she returned to Samarkand. We couldn't go out to greet her; we were already sitting in mourning at home. As soon as she entered the yard, she ran towards the house, asking, "Where's Mother?" I went out of the house, and when she noticed the first signs of a mourner's beard on my chin, she immediately burst out in tears.

My Father Settles in Israel

At this time, we were all preoccupied with leaving Russia. In the winter of 1969, about half a year after our mother's passing, my father, along with my sister Sarah and her family, received permission to leave Russia. They did so, and settled in Kfar Chabad, Israel, while my brother Berel and I remained in Samarkand with our families waiting for our exit visas. My sister would report to us in letters about her daily life in the Land of Israel.

About a year after they moved to Israel, in April 1970, we were surprised to hear that my father had left my sister's house in Kfar Chabad and moved further south to a town called Kiryat Malachi. We did not understand what had happened with him. After all, he had been so close to my sister and her family for so many years in Samarkand, it was surprising that he would pick up and move away from them so shortly after they had immigrated together. In Israel, he had been living in a well-established Chabad village. What had caused him to leave and live alone in a city we had never even heard of before?

In her next letter, my sister explained: "Don't you know our father?" she wrote. "One fine day he came home from shul and declared, 'I must pack my suitcases because I'm moving to Kiryat Malachi.'" Sarah asked him why he was suddenly leaving. He replied that R. Dovid Raskin, a prominent Chabad activist in the United States, had arrived in *Eretz Yisrael* on a mission from the Rebbe and spoke in shul that day. He relayed that the Rebbe desired to start a new neighborhood in Kiryat Malachi to be named "Nachalas Har Chabad." He was opening an institute for adult Torah study, a kollel, in the neighborhood and wanted Russian immigrants to move there.

My father concluded, "So I decided to move to Kiryat Malachi and I even stopped at the post office to send the Rebbe a telegram with the news."

My sister and brother-in-law asked him how he would manage on his own without a woman to cook and do laundry for him. He said: "Don't worry! I'll manage somehow. The main thing is that the Rebbe should be pleased and that he might have *nachas*."

When we read my sister's letter, we understood the power of genuine devotion, and of having *kabbolas ol,* a sense of duty, to the Rebbe. My father made no conditions; he did not ask questions about how it would work out. He simply packed his bags and left.

The Rebbe did indeed take pleasure in my father's devotion and he blessed him that in its merit he would settle comfortably in his new home and see his sons join him from Russia as well. Indeed, in the summer of 1971, I also received my long-awaited exit visa. Berel had received his three weeks earlier. We were soon reunited in Israel.

My Father Remarries

One day in Nachalas Har Chabad, a fundraiser from Bnei Brak came to my father's house and asked for a donation. Why had he come to a neighborhood of new immigrants with no money to ask for contributions, my father asked the man. "You would be surprised to hear," he replied, "that the immigrants tend to give more than the well-established families of Bnei Brak."

As the two men conversed, the collector noticed that the house wasn't very orderly and understood that there was no woman at home. After he inquired, my father told him about my mother's passing before his emigration from Russia. The man said that he had a wonderful match for him with a virtuous woman from Lod, a city near Tel Aviv. She had come to Israel after the Holocaust and now served as the caretaker of the local *mikvah*.

My father was practical and decisive by nature. He lost no time and went to Lod to meet his match. When he arrived, he saw a religious woman walking down the street and approached her to ask if she knew someone in the area named Eidele, which was the first name he had been given. Surprised to hear her own name, the woman—none other than the very same person he was searching for—asked why he wanted to meet her. Not realizing who she was, my father did not answer right away. It was only after she introduced herself that my father disclosed the reason for his visit.

They conversed for a short while, and after seeing that they were suited to one another, my father proposed. She was shocked at the sudden turn of events. A stranger appears out of nowhere, begins talking to her, and already he asks her if she wants to marry him!

She decided to discuss the matter with her rabbi, who advised her to take her time before deciding. Only after finding out more about my father would she give her reply.

After doing some research into my father and inquiring of people who knew him, she agreed to the proposal. They received the Rebbe's blessing and were married.

For thirteen years, father lived happily together with his second wife, Eidele, who both cared for and greatly respected him. She became involved with communal work in Nachalas Har Chabad and the entire community came to hold her in high esteem. We of course paid her our respect as well, especially so out of honor for our father. After my father passed away in 1984, she moved into a home for the elderly. My siblings and I would visit her whenever we could. Our visits made her very happy and she was proud to introduce us to her friends as her children.

My Father, the Kollel Director

A short time after my father arrived in Nachalas Har Chabad, the Rebbe appointed him as director of the newly-founded kollel, as we learned in a letter he sent to us while we were still in Samarkand. This was the first we had even heard of the concept of a kollel, where newly-married men studied for the year after their marriage and received a stipend; traditionally, only younger men who were bachelors studied in the yeshiva. Explaining what it was, he wrote that this was where he invested his energy now.

We wondered how someone who had been a businessman all his life could suddenly start to run an institution dedicated to Torah study. Once again, we realized what it meant to be a *penimi,* the "inward" person the Rebbe Rayatz had dubbed him so many years earlier. As soon as he heard that this is what the Rebbe wanted, he took to the directive completely and carried it out. He was not distracted by other considerations and had no need for any prior deliberation.

Men who learned in the kollel then told me that their best years of learning were the years when my father served as its director. Rabbi Binyomin Jacobs, later the chief rabbi of Holland, told me as much of the two years he spent there. He was full of nostalgia for those days in the kollel and was still impressed by my father's generosity towards the young men learning there and how he looked out for their welfare.

When the shul they learned in grew cold in the winter, he purchased a heater for them with his own money.

R. Nachman Holtzberg, an erstwhile resident of Nachalas Har Chabad, was extremely close with my father and still speaks of him in admiring, even reverential, terms. He recalled how R. Efraim Wolf, the director of Agudas Chassidei Chabad, the umbrella organization for Chabad in Israel, once entered the kollel and noticed a couple of baby carriages in the corner. Unhappy that the kollel members were bringing their children along with them and thereby getting distracted from their studies, he threatened to deduct the hours they had brought their carriages from their regular stipend. "Are you babysitting here, or learning Torah?" he demanded.

My father began defending the young men: "What do you want from them? They are hardly earning much from learning here as it is and you want to make things even harder?"

But R. Efraim was a man of principle, if rigidly so, and meant what he said. Shortly after, he deducted three hours of pay from several kollel members' stipends. My father couldn't bear to see this happen, and so, at the end of the month, he made up the difference out of his own pocket.

My father gave most of the money he earned in his position to the free loan fund for the members of the kollel that he had founded in my mother's memory. He and his wife Eidele lived off the reparations she received as a Holocaust survivor. If they lacked money for essentials he would supplement their income from his salary, but most of it went to the fund. Often, the money he gave was more of a gift than a loan.

Since he put all his money into his fund, my father wrote to me on a couple of occasions, he didn't know what would happen after he passed away. He wanted to be buried on the Mount of Olives, but a plot there cost $3,000 in those years and he hadn't saved up that much money.

What could I tell him, that he shouldn't worry because of course we would pay for his burial there? I opted not to reply, since I couldn't bring myself to discuss the prospect of his passing.

After some time, he told me that he had asked the Rebbe whether to continue giving all of his money to the fund or to save up for a plot. The Rebbe told him to continue donating and blessed him with long life.

R. Mendel Wechter, a Former Satmar

In 1982, R. Mendel Wechter, a brilliant young member of the Satmar community of New York, was discovered to have been closely involved with the Chabad community, as well as with the study and instruction of Chabad Chassidus. At the time, the Satmar community was deeply opposed to many Chabad teachings and practices, some of the extreme elements of the community dangerously so. Once his affiliations had been exposed, he was forced to leave New York; it was dangerous for him to remain because the Satmars were very upset with him. The Rebbe advised him to settle in Israel. There he found his rightful place in the kollel that my father directed in Nachalas Har Chabad and became its dean. My father took a great liking to him and wrote to the Rebbe that R. Mendel was a true chassid, a fearer of G-d, and a Torah scholar; he had always wanted to have such an individual in the kollel.

I heard that when the father of R. Mendel went to Nachalas Har Chabad to see how his son and his family were faring, his son told him, "If you want to see what a Lubavitcher chassid is, look at R. Avrohom Zaltzman."

On the day he died, my father went to the kollel after lunch, as usual. He then began to ask the members of the kollel for forgiveness if he had been too demanding in enforcing the kollel schedule, or if he had ever spoken harshly to them. R. Mendel, who overheard him asking forgiveness from these young men, was amazed at his humility. It didn't come to his mind that my father would shortly pass on.

When the day's period of learning had concluded, R. Mendel asked my father to review some responsa relating to kosher law and asked that he return them after a few days. To his surprise, my father brought them all back that very night at eight o'clock.

By nine o'clock, after returning home, my father reported not feeling well. A Magen David Adom ambulance came to take him to the Kaplan Hospital, but on the way his condition deteriorated so quickly that they called an intensive care mobile unit. It was there, on the way to the hospital, that he passed away.

We later found a note he had left on the table before leaving the house, upon which was written three words: "Har HaZeisim, Yerushalayim," Mount of Olives, Jerusalem.

We fulfilled his request and he was buried on the Mount of Olives in Jerusalem on January 18, 1984. When we had to decide what to write on his gravestone, we were reminded of something he had told us several times. He disliked seeing headstones with too many honorifics on them, he said, because the deceased has to answer to each one of them. He said that he wanted his gravestone to simply say, "Here lies Avrohom Zaltzman, who had the privilege of learning in Lubavitch." Naturally, we fulfilled his request.

When I later visited my father's grave, I was bothered by the fact that all the other tombstones in the vicinity bore numerous titles of distinction while my father's lacked any such title. Perhaps other visitors would surmise that, save for his studies in Lubavitch, this person was simply bereft of any positive qualities.

I considered adding a line on the bottom of the stone that would read, "The words inscribed here were written at the direction of the deceased." Perhaps then, people would know that there was more to be said of him. I consulted a rabbi who told me, "I can assure you that was not your father's intention!"

CHAPTER 19

Leaving Russia

After Stalin's death and Khrushchev's ascension, there were no more political arrests, but neither were there any significant changes in the attitude towards the Jews. The government continued to scrutinize every move of every Soviet citizen. Every house had to keep a ledger accounting for every member of the household and it was forbidden for a newcomer to stay in the house for more than twenty-four hours without signing himself in the book. This way, the government maintained a close eye, and a tighter grip, on its people.

But in 1956, my uncle R. Boruch Duchman and his wife Rosa received a letter from his brother in Israel, R. Yisrael Noach, offering to send them an invitation to come join him there.

My Aunt Rosa had always been terrified of the Russian authorities. When she saw a policeman, she would cross the street. It was therefore no wonder that, when she saw the letter from Israel, testifying to their foreign ties, she was frightened to even open it.

Invitations from abroad were very rare, and ultimately, despite their deep anxieties, the couple agreed to accept. A few months later, my uncle received an official invitation from his brother and thus became one of the fortunate few able to start the emigration process.

The emigration process was not all that simple. It took half a year until they completed preparing the many complicated documents necessary. By the end of 1956, they submitted the documents to the emigration office, OVIR, a branch of the KGB.

And, surprisingly, despite the tension created by Israel's 1956 Sinai campaign, half a year later, my aunt and uncle were told that their request had been accepted. Back then, this was such a rarity that when a Jew in one end of the country received permission to leave, the news would make it across to the other side. Since we hadn't heard about any other Jews receiving exit visas, it followed that at least in our area, they were likely the only fortunate ones to leave the country that year. The process of obtaining passports took another half a year, which was the norm in those days. Towards the end of 1957, my uncle and aunt finally left for Israel.

A Fictitious Marriage

In 1956, Wladyslaw Gomulka became the premier of Poland and proposed to separate Poland from the Soviet Union. He organized a Communist Party convention in Warsaw and invited representatives from various Communist countries. He did not invite Russia.

Russian Premier Khrushchev decided to attend the convention uninvited. When he and his entourage entered the hall, Gomulka left the dais, approached Khrushchev, and ordered him to leave immediately. Khrushchev warned that kicking him out would cost Gomulka dearly. The two men moved to an inner office where they continued their conversation. It is not known precisely what took place behind the closed doors, but after some discussion, Khrushchev reentered the hall. In exchange for permission to partake in the conference, Khrushchev had conceded to sign a humanitarian agreement with Poland, stating that any Polish citizen who had not left Russia in 1946–47 could present a request to leave now, so long as they could provide a reasonable explanation for not taking the opportunity to leave right after the war.

Chassidim rejoiced over this new opportunity, but very few were able to actually take advantage of it and leave for Poland.

I was a young *bochur* then and I didn't see a future for religious life in Russia. Having long yearned to leave, when I heard about this agreement between Russia and Poland, I decided to take advantage of the opportunity.

There was a Jewish woman by the name of Luba who lived in our neighborhood. She spoke Yiddish with a Polish accent, so I thought she might be a native Pole. I did some research and discovered that indeed she was a former Polish citizen. After I spoke to her, it turned out that she had reasons for not leaving in 1946. Last but not least, Luba also had an only daughter by the name of Genia.

My idea was to have the government register me as married to Genia and then to submit a request for my entire family to leave for Poland. This ruse was not my innovation—many Lubavitchers had arranged similar fictitious marriages with Polish citizens during the previous wave of escapes.

Before presenting her with the idea, I spoke with my parents and brother-in-law R. Eliyahu, and after they consented to my plan, I approached Luba with the proposal, adding that I would pay her if she agreed. She gave her general consent but said that the problem was that her daughter was a member of the Komsomol, the Communist youth group. Genia certainly wouldn't agree to leave Mother Russia. Fearing that her daughter's loyalty to the Party would supersede family loyalties, she wouldn't even discuss it with her. That was life in Russia. There were many instances of children ratting out their parents to the KGB, so effectively had they been brainwashed by the government to total subservience to the Communist ideology.

Having no other choice, I undertook the difficult and dangerous step of speaking to the girl directly. Hashem put the right words into my mouth and somehow I managed to convince her. There was an additional problem, though: She was only sixteen, and by law, you could not marry before the age of eighteen. After much effort, we made some connections in the Ministry of the Interior to bribe the right people and obtained a false identity card for her stating that she was eighteen.

So far, everything was proceeding according to plan. It seemed that the day we had been yearning for would soon arrive and we hoped to soon leave the Soviet Union.

Although we kept the entire plan undercover, the mother was a big talker and she spread the news that Hillel Zaltzman was marrying her daughter and we were all going to Poland. Of course, she didn't tell anyone that it was a phony marriage, but since she and her daughter weren't religious, it was totally obvious. Word spread, and explanation followed: Hillel Zaltzman is marrying into a secular family; surely, it's only in order to leave Russia!

You can imagine how scared my father and our entire family were when the news spread throughout the Jewish section of Samarkand. Luba and Genia proceeded to leave, but before I would be caught, I aborted the deal, and with it my rosy hopes for leaving the Soviet Union.

A Spiritual Experience in Kulashi

My opportunity lost, we remained behind the Iron Curtain. But in 1961, we received an official invitation from my aunt Rosa in Israel. Now, it was our turn to debate whether to submit a request to leave. After all, it was a risky move to make and highly unlikely it would even be approved.

Still, it was extremely difficult for us to come to terms with conditions as they were then. My sister's children had already reached school age and were legally required to be sent to public school where they were at risk of being indoctrinated with Communism and atheism; we were therefore anxious to leave Russia as soon as possible.

At that time, R. Mordechai Gorodetzky, who lived in Tashkent, paid us a visit in Samarkand. Trying to gauge how people in Tashkent viewed the possibility of leaving Russia, my brother-in-law R. Ellyahu Mishulovin asked him casually, "If you received an invitation from Eretz Yisrael, would you submit a request to leave?" Eliyahu was too afraid to ask explicitly and reveal that we had received such an invitation.

R. Mordechai said that he would, adding that he felt that the times had changed. To a certain extent, this encouraged us to begin preparing the documentation.

The process of gathering the documents took half a year, and to our great disappointment, we were turned down. We had the right to contest the decision and so appealed directly to Yuri Andropov, chairman of the KGB, who later became the general secretary of the Communist Party. A few more months went by until we received our answer, which was… negative.

Since the visa we had received from Israel was valid for only one year, we were forced to receive a new invitation from my aunt and start the process all over in order to try again. Once again, the process took a year and, once again, we were turned down.

The years dragged on as we impatiently waited for the day we would be permitted to leave. Although we were continually declined, we lived our lives as though we were about to leave. Why buy furniture—an oven, refrigerator, couch, or any household amenities—when a positive answer might come in another few months? Our hope was always renewed as we thought that maybe *this* time we would be granted permission.

We used to say that when two Lubavitchers met in the Soviet Union, they would ask one another, "How long have you been traveling for?" as if to say, How many years have you been submitting documents? I began the process in 1957 as a *bochur* and only left fourteen years later, with a wife and children!

At one point, we heard a rumor that in Kulashi, Georgia, the Jews got along with the emigration authorities and, in exchange for a bribe, it was possible to obtain a visa. It was decided that I would go and investigate.

If the rumor indeed proved to be true, all eight members of the family would have to move to Kulashi and register as residents of the city. We would then need to receive a new invitation from abroad, and only then would we be able to submit a request to the

Georgian emigration office. Uprooting our family from Samarkand and settling into a new place would be physically difficult, and politically risky. But what wouldn't we try in order to leave Russia?

The Georgian Jews were known to be remarkably brave and courageous. I heard that after the Revolution, when the government closed down many shuls throughout Russia, KGB officers were sent to Kutaisi, Georgia, to permanently seal the local synagogue. The Jews poured out into the streets and protested openly. They surrounded the shul as a human wall and refused to allow the KGB officers to enter. The officers laughed sadistically and sneered, "We'll come back and show you..."

They returned bearing machine guns and other forms of weaponry. The bold Georgian Jews—men, women, and children—marched to the shul and laid their bodies across the ground. They said, "We are not moving from here. You can only enter if you kill us first." In the end, the KGB officers left empty-handed and the shul remained open.

Although Georgia was one of the Soviet republics and Soviet law applied there as it did everywhere else, rumor had it that Georgians were granted slightly more freedom because Stalin hailed from there. When a visitor arrived in Georgia from another Soviet republic, he would be asked jokingly: "Where have you come from? The Soviet Union?"

I went to Kulashi and was astonished to discover a large, vibrant Jewish community that lived as though oblivious to Communist rule. I had heard beforehand that there were two thousand people in the town, most of whom were Jewish and religiously observant, but what I saw surpassed anything I could have imagined.

I arrived there on a Friday and I saw dozens of Jewish women going to the *shochet*, Chacham Yitzchok, to slaughter their chickens for Shabbos. The sight of this older Jew with a long, flowing beard brushing against a long silk frock coat moved me very much. What was dangerous in Samarkand was done openly and fearlessly in Kulashi.

What I saw on Friday afternoon was nothing compared to the moving sight I witnessed on Friday night in the big shul. The place was crowded with old and young, and many children were present. Many of them couldn't even fit in the shul and stood outside!

I had visited many places in Russia but I had never seen young people in shul, and I certainly hadn't seen small children. Hundreds of Jews crowded the hall, *davening* loudly and singing enthusiastically. I couldn't restrain myself and tears of joy flowed from my eyes. When it was time to begin the *Lecha Dodi*, a young boy got up to sing and the crowd followed his lead. Till this day, I haven't forgotten the special melody he used for this liturgical poem. It was worth traveling to Kulashi just to behold this oasis amidst the spiritual desert of Soviet Russia.

The next day, after the meal, Chacham Yaakov addressed the congregation. He spoke for around an hour to an attentive audience. Afterwards, I was told to visit the other shul in the afternoon, where Chacham Refael would speak. He was a young dynamic rabbi in his thirties and a very talented speaker. People flocked to hear him. The shul was packed and Chacham Refael enthusiastically lectured on Torah, Midrash, and Aggada for more than two hours. Although I didn't understand a word—the two-hour lecture was all in Georgian—I was again moved by the scene.

I had a supremely spiritual experience in Kulashi that left a deep impression within my heart, but as for the purpose of my trip, I did not achieve anything. The rumor was false, and despite all their freedom, no one was able to obtain a visa through bribery.

It was time for me to return to Samarkand. With neither trains nor direct flights from Georgia to Samarkand, the only way to travel home was taking a flight to Kutaisi, another one to Moscow, and then to finally fly from there to Samarkand. Finding a seat on a plane during the summer months, however, when everyone was flying on vacation, made things difficult. Indeed, once in Kutaisi, I was unable to obtain a ticket to Moscow.

I had heard that in Georgia it was possible to obtain anything you wanted with appropriate bribery—excluding visas, apparently —and I thus hoped that I'd be able to bribe the right people to get on a flight. I went to the airport and headed straight for the runway, which was still possible in those days, and located the plane going to Moscow.

When I saw the pilot approaching, I went over to him and said, "I must go to Moscow and I couldn't obtain a ticket. I'm ready to pay for it plus more. Can you get me onto the plane?" The pilot regarded me for a moment and then nodded. He said, "Follow me."

We reached the door to the plane and he said to the stewardess, "This is one of my attendants." He gave me a seat next to the cabin, where the stewardesses sat, and we took off. A short while later, the second pilot left the cockpit and I asked the main pilot if I could come in and pay him. We spoke for a bit and I asked him a few questions about flying and navigating a plane. He insisted it wasn't very complicated and offered to let me sit in his seat and play with the controls.

I was too afraid to play with such a toy; at least not while it was aloft and I was aboard it! But the pilot wasn't too concerned.

"Watch, I'll scare the passengers by making the plane pitch downward," he said. Suddenly, he yanked the controls, and the plane dove towards the ground. Standing next to the pilot at the front of the plane, I felt a gentle drop as I watched us hurtle through the vast expanses of clear sky, but from the main cabin we suddenly heard the passengers screaming. "Why are we falling?" they yelled.

The pilot straightened out the plane with a laugh, and thus concluded the Kulashi affair.

Incident at the Train Station

The Klein family of Tashkent, friends of our family, once told us that they had good connections with the superintendent of the local jail, an Uzbek, who told them that when he used to live in Samarkand he was a close friend of the official who issued visas there. He hinted to them that in exchange for a bribe—of course—he would be the go-between.

I immediately traveled to Tashkent, where R. Moshe Klein introduced me to the Uzbek superintendent. We made plans to travel together by train to Samarkand. His friend would come to the station, ostensibly to greet him, and the superintendent would introduce me to him. I agreed to pay the man 1,000 rubles for his services.

We traveled together and throughout the trip, we did not talk to one another, as though we were strangers. We didn't want anyone to suspect a connection between us.

We arrived at the train station in Samarkand at eight in the morning and found his friend waiting for us. The Uzbek introduced me and I gave him the 1,000 rubles. He hadn't yet slipped it into his pocket when suddenly a policeman appeared and stood between us as if to separate us. In the typical KGB fashion, he "asked" us politely, "Please come with me to the police quarters located in the train station."

The Uzbek managed to quickly put away the money; I don't know whether the policeman noticed the money that had exchanged hands or not. In any case, our fear at the moment was indescribable. We tried to remain calm and expressionless and hide the trepidation we felt inside.

At the police station we were told to sit down, before being asked where we had come from and where we were going. When they asked for our passports I thought the Uzbek would tell them that he was the superintendent of the jail in Tashkent and they would leave us alone. But he just handed over his passport and they continued asking questions.

Then they called him into an inner room and I remained alone in the outer room. My heart pounded and I could taste fear on my tongue. After what felt like an eternity, they released us.

Afterwards, the Uzbek told me that they had told him that they were looking for someone who resembled me. Furthermore, it was soon after my father-in-law passed away, and I decided that it was an opportune time to begin growing a beard; my unusual appearance apparently aroused their suspicion.

After this incident, however, the friend of the Uzbek was afraid to have anything to do with me, so once again, this latest plan was shelved.

Cracks in the Iron Curtain

In the middle of the 1960s, the Soviets issued a number of exit visas and many chassidim in Moscow, Tashkent, and Samarkand were given permission to leave. It seemed that perhaps a new, brighter era had dawned, until the Six-Day War broke out. Diplomatic ties between Israel and the Soviet Union were cut and the exit visas stopped.

In the meantime, the miraculous victory of the war had whipped up a whirlwind of spiritual arousal among Russian Jewry. Many Jews who for many years had been members of the Communist Party and whose Judaism had been dormant woke up suddenly with a longing to go to Israel.

Then, two years went by and there was another crack in the re-silient curtain. The OVIR (Office of Visas and Registration) offices once again began issuing visas. At the same time, the Jewish Agency began a campaign to send visas to Jews in Russia. They would locate families in Israel with the same name as a family in Russia and send the Russian family an invitation to reunite.

Suddenly there was a widespread movement of Jews who had received visas asking for permission to emigrate. There were sporadic demonstrations in which Jews called on the authorities to allow them to leave for Israel. The demonstrators were often arrested, but unlike the 1930s and 1950s, when arrests ended with sentences of twenty-five years in Siberia, the arrests of the 1960s lasted mere days and ended with release and a warning. Only very few were actually charged or held for more than a few months.

In Moscow, a group of young Jewish men and women gathered in the thousands on Simchas Torah in the area around the main shul on Archipova Street to demonstrate their Jewishness and their desire to be freed from the Soviet Union. Archipova Street is a very narrow road that scarcely sees any cars passing through, but the police ordered large trucks to drive through the street and force the Jews to leave. The protesters lay down on the road and didn't allow the trucks to pass, forcing the police to drag them off the streets. It was a wild and riotous scene. Many demonstrators were arrested but almost all were released after several days.

We listened to the Kol Tziyon Lagolah (Voice of Zion to the Diaspora) radio broadcast from Israel and heard reports about families who had received visas and had left for Israel. At first, it was a few from one city and a few from another, but then we began to hear reports about dozens leaving in one week, and then dozens in a day. There were times that an entire planeload of emigrants from Russia landed in Israel. These reports breathed new life into us and we began to hope that the day would soon come when we too would receive permission to leave Russia.

In 1968-69, people in Samarkand and Tashkent once again began receiving exit visas. My father, my brother-in-law R. Eliyahu Mishulovin, and my brother-in-law's parents all left the very same month. R. Shimshon Kahana and his mother left after submitting their first request. Then followed R. Dovid Gurewitz's family, the Lepkivkers, and others from Tashkent.

A Trip to Moscow, with the Help of the KGB

We didn't understand how OVIR made its decisions. There were people, seemingly simple people under no suspicion, who were turned down for years. Then there were people who, after they submitted their first request, received immediate permission to leave. The unfortunate ones were sure that the KGB was holding something against them.

We went to the OVIR office in Samarkand and dared to ask for exit visas. "How come in other places they are giving dozens of exit visas and you are refusing us?" we asked. We didn't dare to say, "How come you gave so-and-so and you didn't give to me?" but we asked in a general way. The officials in Samarkand said they did not know of any changes in the emigration laws.

In 1970, an international Communism convention was held in Moscow. This convention took place every five years and was attended by Communist Party leaders from all over the world. We figured that since the Russians would not want the guests to see the Jews demonstrating in Moscow, they would approve requests for exit visas made at this time. Many people planned on demonstrating during the convention in the hopes that the government would want to get rid of them and grant them exit visas.

R. Moshe Katzenelenbogen, who lived in Moscow, called my brother Berel and said that he should come to Moscow, and although he couldn't guarantee anything, there was a good chance that he would receive an exit visa. Berel, together with his neighbor R. Aharon Makovitzky, decided to travel to Moscow. The day after they arrived, my brother called. Spirits were high in Moscow, he said, and I should come there too.

That evening, I walked over to R. Moshe Nissilevitch, told him what my brother had said, and suggested that we travel together to Moscow, for there was a hope that we would be granted permission to leave. R. Moshe stood still and thought for a moment. "*Oy!*" he exclaimed. "*Oy*, how can we leave and abandon all of the underground classes we have arranged and the rest of our communal work?"

In the meantime, his wife overheard our conversation. For the most part, she was the one who had to deal with the upbringing of their children; she was home most of the day, and if someone came to see where the children were, it was she who had to think of an excuse. She would not let an opportunity to leave Russia pass and urged R. Moshe to go along with me to Moscow. R. Moshe listened to his wife and asked me when I planned to go. I said that there was a plane to Moscow that very night. He immediately packed some clothes and we left for the airport.

We arrived at the airport and discovered that due to poor weather conditions, no planes had left Samarkand in the past twenty-four hours. Hordes of people were waiting for a flight, including a large group of pilots who had to get to Moscow but were stuck in Samarkand waiting for an improvement in the weather.

At one of the ticket counters, I noticed a gentile woman by the name of Tamara whom I recognized from my time in public school. I went over to her and asked whether she could use her connections and put us on a flight that night. She said that it wasn't possible that evening, but the next morning the weather would improve and then she could help me.

We decided that R. Moshe would not return home and he slept at my house. We woke up early and rushed to the airport. We wanted to get on the first flight so we could *daven* in Moscow, where it was two hours earlier than in Samarkand. If we left at eight in the morning, after a three-and-a-half hour flight, it would be nine-thirty in Moscow.

I went straight to Tamara, but she said there was no room on the first flight because the thirty delayed pilots had to be in Moscow as soon as possible. However, there might be another flight later that day. I told her we had to get to Moscow urgently. She pointed at someone sitting at the next counter and said, "Go over to him. Maybe he can help you."

I went over to him and told him that I had to get to Moscow. He told me to wait and said he would try to assist me. I was happy about this and immediately gave him a ten-ruble bribe. In those days, when a monthly salary was between 80 and 100 rubles, this was a considerable sum. To my surprise, he refused to accept the money. I tried to convince him but nothing helped. I finally said that when I returned, I would bring him a nice gift from Moscow.

He examined my passport carefully, wrote something in his ledger, and after a few minutes of effort on his part, I received a boarding pass. I wasn't satisfied with that, of course, and asked for another pass for R. Moshe who was sitting a distance away, waiting to see if I'd be successful. He hadn't wanted to come over with me at first, since his long beard made him rather conspicuous.

I pointed at R. Moshe and said that I needed another pass. The clerk looked at him, marked something down again, and asked for his passport. Then, to my surprise, I saw him go over to an old woman and convince her to give up her ticket! He then returned to the counter and wrote R. Moshe's name on her ticket. I ran over to R. Moshe and told him that Hashem had sent us an angel.

I was so overjoyed that I offered the clerk a bribe again, this time, twenty rubles. He continued to refuse. I asked Tamara what the man's name was. At first she didn't want to respond but when I asked again she replied that his name was Vassily Vachidovitz. I asked what his job was and what he was doing at the last counter and she evaded me again. She finally winked and hinted in a way that only someone living in the Soviet Union would understand. He had a special position at the airport, one that made him capable of pulling strings others couldn't pull: He was a KGB agent.

I gasped. I was certain that the KGB knew that Jews were flocking to Moscow in order to demonstrate during the Communist convention. Who knows what would happen to us now! We might be arrested, or worse.

When I told this to R. Moshe, the blood drained from his face. In the meantime, a group of tourists from abroad arrived, and we saw that the man at the last counter immediately left his spot and began following them. It was clear that he was a plainclothes agent whose job was to keep an eye on foreigners at the airport.

When it was announced that it was time to board the plane, we began heading toward the exit, our stomachs knotted with worry. *Boruch Hashem,* we boarded the plane without mishap and breathed a bit easier, relieved that we hadn't been arrested. But we didn't know what awaited us in Moscow. Would they arrest us there? We strengthened our faith in Hashem and hoped for the best.

Three-and-a-half hours later, we landed in Moscow and to our great relief, nobody approached or arrested us. We traveled immediately to Malachovka and were hosted by R. Yehuda Kulasher (Butrashvili), my brother's father-in-law, where my brother Berel and R. Aharon Makovitzky were staying. We *davened* there upon our arrival.

When we met Berel, even before I managed to tell him what had happened to us, he told us that a certain individual in the airport in Samarkand had checked their passports and they suspected that he was a KGB agent. We told them that he was definitely an agent and related what had happened with us. We found it all quite surprising. I am still mystified by it to this day.

In the KGB Office in Moscow

Berel and Aharon, who had been there for a few days already, reported to us on what was taking place in Moscow. All sorts of demonstrations were taking place to draw the attention of the authorities to the emigration issue.

They told us that a day before we had arrived, a recent returnee to Judaism by the name of Tzvi Epstein had decided to perpetrate an act of public disorder. He went to the Red Square near the Kremlin and took out a large sign that read in bold letters "LET ME GO TO ISRAEL." He hoped that he would be arrested and it would make such a commotion that he would be thrown out of the Soviet Union. However, to his misfortune, no one paid any attention to him at all. He stood out in the cold Moscow weather until he was frozen stiff. He then folded his sign dejectedly and returned home.

Berel suggested that we go to the main OVIR office located in the central KGB headquarters at Lubyanka Square and present our request. Berel said he himself had been there the day before and met with two high officials there, one from the Interior Ministry, General Shubov, and the other, General Verein of the KGB.

Protesters were claiming that it was a suitable time to display one's Jewishness, my brother said, so he had told them that he wanted to go to Israel solely on religious grounds. They considered his request seriously and proceeded to verify whether he was indeed religious. They asked him whether he had *tzitzis* and he showed them. They asked whether he had a *yarmulke* and he took off his cap to show his *yarmulke*.

To his disappointment, they said that since he lived in Samarkand, they were not authorized to issue an exit visa to him and he had to present his request to his hometown office. When he tried to insist, they frightened him with the words "Over here nobody insists. If you weren't a father of young children, we would have already arrested you."

Berel's story motivated us to tell them the true reason we wanted to leave and we decided to try our luck. We did not have to make an appointment, as the office had set hours and everyone who came waited their turn in line. We arrived at Lubyanka Square with a shiver, as we beheld the dominating KGB building, recalling the thousands who had been shot in the cellars of this despised building, or sent from there to the northern confines of Siberia. A mere ten years earlier, people were deathly afraid to even pass the building, and now here we were, willingly going in and asking for permission to leave the Soviet Union for the despised Zionist state. A few years earlier, it would have been considered a crime of treason. It almost felt like the "End of Days" had arrived.

This was shortly after the momentous anniversary marking twenty years of the Rebbe's leadership on 10 Shevat 1970, along with completion of the Torah scroll that the Rebbe Rayatz had commissioned decades earlier. We had also recently received a letter from R. Naftali Estulin who wrote that the Rebbe had portentously quoted in a *farbrengen* the Talmudic expression, "When the ox falls, sharpen the knife." We understood that the fortune of Russia was on the decline. These thoughts endowed us with courage, pushing us to enter the lions' den.

We entered the waiting room and saw that the line wasn't too long at all. We sat down on one of the benches and began to discuss what to do. R. Moshe, ever nervous about his conspicuous long, blond beard, asked me to go in first and then relate to him what transpired.

As I entered the room, I immediately recognized the generals sitting there by the precise description my brother had given me. They sat there with their uniforms and their epaulets, with cold apathy in their eyes, instilling fear upon anyone in their presence.

In the secular world, it is considered a sign of respect to remove one's hat, but wanting to show that I am religious and that it's hard for me to live in the Soviet Union, I specifically chose not to. As expected, they asked me why I didn't doff my hat as is customary. For us, I replied, it is not respectful to be bareheaded.

One of them asked, "What do you mean by us?" I said that I was referring to religious Jews. He pressed: "Are you religious?" I said that I was.

One of them asked, "Did you study the Bible?" I said that I had.

"Who taught you the Bible, and what does it say?" I said that my uncle Boruch taught me when I was little. It says there that G-d created the heavens and earth.

"Did you also study Talmud?" I said that I had and then added, "I didn't come here to be tested on my Torah knowledge. In a little while, the time allotted to us will be over and I will have to leave. Please deal with my request."

They asked to see my passport and when they saw the name "Zaltzman," they asked, "Was the Zaltzman who was here yesterday your brother?" I responded that he was and they said, "He was impudent and we wanted to arrest him but we had mercy on his children. As for your request, the decision has to be made where you live. Go to Samarkand and we hope they will give you permission to leave."

I left the room and repeated the strange conversation to R. Moshe. He then went inside and I waited for him in the waiting room.

When he returned, he told me that when they saw his long beard they had been taken aback. "Ho!" they exclaimed. "How long did it take to grow that?" Then they commented, "We don't understand why all of you want to go to that inferno going on in Israel."

R. Moshe answered that we trust in G-d that there will be peace and everything will be okay. Finally, they told R. Moshe the same thing: He had to go to OVIR in Samarkand and they would decide.

Although we left empty-handed, we felt that something had been achieved and that they would transfer the request to the office in Samarkand. We were optimistic that the tide was turning for the good.

When we returned to Samarkand, we immediately went to the local OVIR and said that we had been in the main office in Moscow and they promised us that in Samarkand they would give us exit visas. The officials said there was nothing to discuss. They had not received orders from Moscow about this and the emigration laws hadn't changed so it wasn't likely that we would receive exist visas.

A Surreal Conversation in the Employment Office

A short while later, I received an invitation to a meeting at the Soviet national employment ministry. This was the central department overseeing all of the city's factories and workshops. The head of the department, a Muslim Uzbek, welcomed me with honor and asked me to sit down. He said, "I heard that you want to immigrate to Israel. Why?"

Knowing that the KGB had given him the job to talk to me, I explained that my aunt lived there and added some other silly reasons. Still he tried to dissuade me from considering such a move. Eventually he said, "Imagine what will happen if they draft you into the Israeli army and I am sent to Egypt as a volunteer. Will you shoot at me and kill me?"

What could I say in response to this ludicrous question? "Heaven forbid!" I said. "I know you and I wouldn't shoot you."

That is how our preposterous conversation came to a close. It seemed that he had done his duty and carried out the job given to him by the KGB. When I told my friends about it, they were excited and we realized that something strange was definitely going on.

Good News on Erev Pesach

The day before Pesach, 1971, a government official appeared in the Bagishomol Quarter, in the courtyard where many Lubavitcher families lived, among them the Chudaidatov family, R. Yaakov Boroshansky, R. Moshe Nissilevitch, and R. Binyamin Malachovsky.

The official was looking for R. Moshe, who had already submitted documents to OVIR with the request to leave. He met Mrs. Sonia Boroshansky and asked, "Where does R. Moshe Friedman live?" using the name R. Moshe adopted after his failed attempt to leave Russia in 1946. "I have good news for him. He was granted an exit visa from Russia."

Mrs. Boroshansky blurted out, "We also want to leave!"

Other people who were around and heard the officer's remarks gathered around him and they badgered him that they wanted to immigrate to Israel as well. It was an interesting scene indeed. The official stood there in the middle of the crowd and apologized, "Soon, all of you will be able to go. Believe me, you will all get your visas, but it can't be all at once. It has to be orderly, one by one."

Such an event had never occurred before in Soviet Russia. An OVIR official had come and related to whoever came his way that a certain citizen had been granted an exit visa! Unbelievable!

The news spread fast among the Lubavitch communities in Samarkand and Tashkent and inspired renewed hope. Within a short time, R. Moshe was called to the OVIR office and he received his exit visa. The Nissilevitches quickly gathered their belongings and left.

His brother-in-law R. Binyamin Malachovsky planned on accompanying them until Moscow. Who knew when they would see each other again? He also intended to take back to Samarkand any items they weren't approved to take along with them from Russia, especially the pictures of our yeshiva students that R. Moshe had taken for the Rebbe.

He had another reason for going along as well—to retrieve some of the Jewish books housed by the Israeli embassy.

At that time, the Israeli embassy did not operate in Moscow since Russia had cut off diplomatic ties with Israel at the outbreak of the Six-Day War. However, the Dutch Embassy, which represented Israel and took care of all the required paperwork, also knew about the Jewish books and kept the same system.

R. Binyamin wanted to join the Nissilevitch family on its trip to Moscow in order to bring the *sefarim* back to Samarkand. However, when they arrived at the airport in Samarkand, they saw, to their horror, the infamous head of the Jewish department of the KGB in Samarkand, the Tatar gentile by the name of Aktchurin.

He looked angrily at R. Moshe and his family and gnashed his teeth. He had always struggled to catch R. Moshe red-handed in his activities and had spent years preparing a heavy file against him. Now he had to adjust to the political changes and allow them to leave Russia unharmed.

When they arrived at the ticket counter, Aktchurin came over and began to personally examine their documents, one by one. When R. Binyamin presented his ticket, he asked, "Who are you? Why are you leaving all of the sudden?"

R. Binyamin said that he was the brother of Mrs. Friedman (Nissilevitch) and he wanted to help them in Moscow. Aktchurin ground his teeth and huffed in fury, "They will manage on their own. You don't need to go!" He forced him to remain in Samarkand, even though he had already paid for his ticket.

Finally Leaving!

During the next two years, many additional families received exit visas, and between the years 1970 and 1972, most of the chassidim left the Soviet Union.

In the summer of 1971, I also received my long-awaited exit visa. (Berel received his three weeks before.) Like everyone else, I had no desire to tarry in Samarkand and wanted to travel to Moscow right away to spend a few days there arranging our final papers before the trip. However, my wife was pregnant and she didn't feel well, so I was forced to wait several days while she was in the hospital. As soon as she was discharged, we left Samarkand with all haste.

Arriving in Moscow, we heard that the government was allowing every adult who left Russia to take a Torah scroll with him. The big shul in Moscow, so we heard, had thousands of Torah scrolls from all of the shuls throughout Russia that had been closed by the government. At that time, not believing there would ever come a time when Judaism would flourish in Russia, we felt it imperative to redeem the Torah scrolls. We were sure it was just a matter of time before they were all carted off and turned into leather, G-d forbid.

I went to the main shul and spoke with the *gabbai*. He was suspicious of me as I was of him, but since we were both interested in the deal, we had a mutual understanding. He led me to the second floor to a room that was about ten meters wide and thirty meters long. All over the floor, to the height of a meter and a half, were thousands of Torah parchments removed from their wooden handles. Which scrolls to take? I didn't know how to check them, or how to even reach them. The *gabbai* urged me, "*Nu*, hurry, take off your shoes, go up and pick whatever you want." I learned how to assess the quality of a Torah scroll on the spot and quickly rolled a few scrolls, handling every parchment section to see if the letters were there. The passage of time and exposure to moisture had separated letters from the parchment and many of the *sifrei Torah* were halachically invalid.

I took four with me and remunerated the *gabbai* generously. Since the authorities allowed every adult to take out one scroll, I took two scrolls and rolled them up together as one scroll, and then did the same for my wife. During our inspection prior to our flight out of Russia, they asked me to unroll my scroll so they could be sure I hadn't hidden anything in it, but they did not catch on that it was two Torah scrolls. After all, they were gentiles and unfamiliar with the normal thickness of a Torah.

I cannot describe how thrilled I was when we finally left Russia. My heart beat with profound joy and gratitude that I had lived to see that day.

I remembered what we used to say between ourselves that the word *Mitzrayim*, Egypt, has the same Hebrew numerical value as the initials SSSR (USSR in the Russian language). I felt like I was literally experiencing an Exodus from Egypt of my own.

The Shinau Transit Camp

The Jews who left Russia for Israel at that time traveled via the Shinau transit camp near Vienna. The camp was established by the Jewish Agency, who had located it far from the city as a security measure.

After the plane landed in Vienna, I greatly desired to meet Jews from the West. I was certain that we would be received with a public reception at the airport, but to my disappointment, we met only a grim-faced official who unceremoniously motioned to us to board the bus that would take us to the Shinau transit camp. I later learned that due to security reasons, again, the agency had been instructed to lead us immediately to the bus without any fanfare.

In the Shinau camp itself, we were prevented from associating with unfamiliar people. But safety measures aside, the Jewish Agency had another reason: they didn't want anyone to convince us to change our country of destination.

While in Shinau, I met a number of Lubavitcher families who had recently left Russia as well. Among others, they included the Kozliner, Boroshansky, and Volovik families.

One of the officials asked us where in Eretz Yisrael we wanted to settle, and we said that we wanted to live in Kiryat Malachi.

"Do you know where Kiryat Malachi is situated?" the official inquired. (It turned out it was in the Negev, near Ashkelon.)

"No," I responded. "But I heard that the Lubavitcher Rebbe established a community in that city and wants us to settle there."

The official responded with a sharp remark, expressing his disbelief that we were willing to blindly follow the Rebbe's directives. I realized that he was anti-religious and I didn't bother debating the matter.

The members of the agency provided the immigrants with $70 per person. When I was offered the amount, I declined and said that I had sufficient funds. Before leaving Russia, I had exchanged my rubles for dollars, and being that we were allowed to bring $100 per person, I had $300 for my family. They looked at me as if I was mad. "This is the first time anyone has refused money from us!" they said.

I noticed a man at the camp with a knitted *yarmulke*, writing down the names of the other Jewish immigrants and asking them questions about their parents, grandparents, and family history. Strangely, he seemed to be ignoring all of the Lubavitchers. I went over to him several times and asked him why he didn't mark me and the other Lubavitchers down as well, but he said that it wasn't for us.

I didn't understand his response and continued asking questions until he said, "I am here on a *shlichus,* a mission, because of your Rebbe!"

Later on, I was told that he was from Israel's Ministry of Religious Affairs and had been sent to the camp—as a result of the Rebbe's "Who Is a Jew?" campaign—to apply halachic standards in recognizing Jewish identity, to ensure that only those who were born to a Jewish mother or underwent Orthodox Jewish conversion would be recognized by the Israeli government as Jews.

In the meantime, I had become friendly with a young man named Menachem, an Israeli from the Herut political party who studied medicine in Vienna and spent his vacations working in the Shinau camp. I enjoyed practicing my Hebrew conversing with him and he was impressed with my grasp of the language.

It seemed to me that Menachem was in fact an agent of the Shin Bet, or "Shabak," Israel's internal security agency, assigned to speak with the Russian immigrants. Apparently, Menachem had passed on my name and in the few days that I was there I was visited by various Shabak types who asked me about life in Russia and the Jewish underground.

One day, Menachem informed me that a prestigious man would be coming to speak with me that evening. The person was Isser Harel, who was serving at the time as a Knesset member of the Reshima Mamlachtit party. Menachem secretly told me that he was the man responsible for capturing the Nazi fugitive Adolph Eichmann and the former director of Mossad and Shin Bet. We had a long talk about the Jewish underground in the Soviet Union.

People generally spent a day or two at Shinau arranging their documents and then left for Israel. However, the Jewish Agency had arranged a visit to Israel for a group of two hundred philanthropists from the US and Canada, with a stop at the immigrant camp on the way. Being that many Jews—including many Lubavitchers—were leaving Russia at the time, the agency extended our stay in the camp for over a week in order to impress these wealthy people.

After a few days had passed, many of our group began to complain that they wanted to continue to travel. On my part, I didn't mind waiting a few more days. Thank G-d, I had already broken through the Iron Curtain and was glad simply to have left Russia.

The Jewish Agency constructed a huge tent and held a public welcome for the group of philanthropists. Since I knew Hebrew and was among the younger members of the group, they gave me a special task: I was placed on the dais and honored with reciting the *hamotzi* blessing for bread and cutting the giant challah, as well as saying a few words of greeting in Hebrew.

After the reception, a man from the agency told me that my family would be placed on the same flight to Israel as the philanthropists and asked me to speak with them during the flight. Indeed, I became well acquainted with several of them.

In Eretz Yisrael at Last!

On September 1, 1971, after a flight of several hours, I finally arrived in Eretz Yisrael. Elatedly, I descended from the plane, and unable to restrain myself, bent down and gave the holy ground of Eretz Yisrael a loving kiss. As I made my first steps in the Holy Land, I tried to recall the borders of the land as I had studied them in the Torah: In my mind's eye, I could see the Yarden River on my right, the Great Sea to my left, and over the southern horizon lay the land of Egypt.

At the airport we were greeted by my father, my sister Sarah, and her son, Yosef Yitzchak Mishulovin. I remember my sister instructing my nephew, who had come to the airport on a bicycle, which streets to take on his hour-long ride back to Kfar Chabad.

We made our way to my sister's house in Kfar Chabad and a few days later we moved to our permanent residence in the Nachalas Har Chabad section of Kiryat Malachi, where my father now lived.

The very next day, our daughter Chana'le began attending the Chabad school in the community. I stood there, looking through the window and thinking excitedly: Our dreams have come true at last! Our daughter will never be forced to attend public school in Russia. She will be able to absorb a Chassidic *chinuch* in the pure air of Eretz Yisrael!

Six months later, our son was born, whom we named Efraim Fishel after my father-in-law, R. Efraim Fishel Demichovsky. *Boruch Hashem*, we have received much *nachas* from our children, grandchildren, and great-grandchildren, all of whom are continuing the beautiful heritage of Chabad.

CHAPTER 20

From Dreams in Russia to Reality in Israel

Two weeks after our arrival in Israel, I attended a gathering for newly arrived immigrants in the house of Rabbi Yehosaf Ralbag, the rabbi of Kiryat HaYovel in Jerusalem. Isser Harel, the Knesset member, was there as well, but he acted as though we hadn't met.

Soon after, I was summoned to the Shabak offices in Tel Aviv. I was in a quandary: On one hand, these were Jewish people who had the ability to use the information I had for the benefit of other Jews. But on the other hand, the mere thought of associating myself with what was essentially the Israeli counterpart of the KGB sent shivers up my spine.

It turned out that the Shabak members with whom I met were familiar to a certain degree with our undercover activities, including our covert yeshiva. I related to them whatever I knew, hoping it would enable them to assist other Jews.

As for us, until about 1969, we had known nothing of the wide world beyond the borders of the Soviet Union. The few individuals to receive visas would leave and disappear with the wind, never to be heard from again. If they penned letters, they were extremely brief, out of fear of the censors. They asked, "How are you," and we wrote, "We are fine, thank G-d," and that was all.

We could only guess and imagine what life in the West and in Eretz Yisrael was like. A trickle of information came our way by means of the Israeli Kol Tziyon Lagolah radio station, but the broadcasts were always unclear because the Soviets deliberately interfered with the radio waves to prevent Jews from listening to a Zionist radio program.

Only at the end of the 1960s did we begin to receive more information from letters by family members in Israel. They were written in a cryptic style, but we understood that the immigrants had a hard time adjusting upon arrival in Israel and that even afterwards, life was not all that rosy.

Still and all, we had no qualms about leaving Russia. The physical hardships did not frighten us; an easy, materialistic life was not our goal in relocating to the West. We made a living in Samarkand and did fine. The tribulations we endured in our daily lives were of the spiritual sort, primarily regarding *chinuch*, Shabbos, and so on. It was clear to us that there was no Jewish future for us in this land. So, even if life abroad was very difficult, nothing deterred us from yearning to leave the bitter exile of Soviet Russia.

In 1969, a year after my mother's passing, and still two years before I would leave, my sister Sarah and her husband, R. Eliyahu Mishulovin, received visas, along with my father. R. Eliyahu had heart disease and we thought that my sister could support them. She was a capable and talented woman and we were sure she could honorably provide for herself and her family.

We waited eagerly to hear what really went on in Eretz Yisrael, and before she left we asked her to send us detailed letters about life there. True to her promise, a short time after their departure, we received the first letter. We read about the festive welcome they received at the airport in Lod.

In those years, *aliya* from Russia was very rare and the new immigrants were warmly welcomed. When I heard this, I hoped that emigration from Russia would become so commonplace by the time it was our turn to leave that no one would welcome us at the airport. (*Boruch Hashem,* my wish indeed came true!)

My sister has a talent for vivid writing and her first letter was poignant and emotional. She penned it while sitting on a train, as it snaked its way through the mountains near Jerusalem. "I am traveling by train and my heart flutters rapidly. Where am I going? To Yerushalayim, the Holy City! For thousands of years, Jews dreamed to lay their eyes upon this land, but did not merit to do so. Now, as my heart races, before my mind's eye I can see the phrase, 'Next Year in Yerushalayim.' With what feeling and hope we said these words every year—and now I can confidently declare, 'Next *hour* in Yerushalayim!'"

The rest of her letter described how she arrived at the Kosel, the Western Wall, the remnant of our Beis Hamikdash, the Holy Temple, with tears coursing down her cheeks; and how she caressed its stones and prayed from the depths of her heart for all of us. When we read that she had written part of the letter against the Kosel, we excitedly felt the paper that had touched those holy stones.

In her letters, she tried to depict the enormous disparity between our lives in Russia, haunted by fear every day and the liberty of life in Eretz Yisrael. She wrote how she took a walk after the Shabbos meal in Kfar Chabad without any trepidation, and how she heard sweet songs wafting from the open windows—Jewish songs, Chassidic melodies, and Shabbos hymns.

In another letter, she described how they invited students from the local yeshiva for the Shabbos meal; one was from England, another from Holland, and a third from Brazil. In Russia, we were afraid to meet with anyone from abroad, whereas in Israel, she was able to host *bochurim* from all over the world who learned in the yeshiva in Kfar Chabad.

Each time a letter arrived from my sister, we gathered together eagerly to peruse it. Her words touched us deeply and we greatly enjoyed reading her descriptions of the burgeoning spiritual life in Eretz Yisrael.

That is how it was, until the letter came describing the difficulties the new immigrants had adjusting to their new lives. After a brief period of acclimation, when the time came to start looking for work, her letters took on a sadder tone.

At first, she attempted to use her talent for satire and wrote in jest, using a Russian expression that she had found employment as a "senior assistant to a young janitor." Then she wrote the bitter truth: "I work at the absorption center in Kfar Chabad. What is my 'occupation' there? I… clean… the floor. The water I use is cold and dirty and every bitter tear that falls into the water makes it ever more putrid. The floor has to be clean and I try to clean it well. I had the occasion more than once to scrape the floor at the feet of the tourists staying at the hotel here. I pray that no one who knew me in Russia, and my respectable standing there, should come and see to what rank I have descended here…"

We were shocked. How could such a talented woman like our sister Sarah be a cleaning lady? When they were in Samarkand, my brother-in-law was in business and my sister never even needed to work. Had things reached such a low point? Who would have believed this could happen?

The Illusions Dissipate

We all dreamed of the great life the future held for us after emigration, certain that everyone would find work in the field they enjoyed. However, after reading my sister's letter, we realized that the lives of new immigrants to Israel were not all that easy. All of the fantasies we had conjured about life in Israel shattered into millions of fragments.

R. Moshe Nissilevitch, whose heart and soul were devoted to the needs of the public and to spreading the knowledge of Torah, would constantly mention to me, "Over here we face many difficulties and live in perpetual fear, but when we get there, it will all be good. Tell me, Hilke, do you think the millionaires in Eretz Yisrael won't happily give us just one of their hundreds of millions? We'll have enough money for all our work!"

I always disagreed, countering that Western countries must have a multitude of activists working to promote Judaism. Free of religious persecution, Lubavitchers were surely all busy reaching out to their fellow Jews, and with so many people already involved, we would hardly be needed to contribute to such work abroad. When we eventually arrived in Israel, we discovered to our dismay that we were both mistaken: There was a need for work to be done and there was no money to do it.

I had always been simultaneously involved in the world of business and in communal affairs. I loved the work of spreading the wellsprings of Torah and Chassidus and it had become an inseparable part of my life. Before he left Russia, I told R. Moshe that if he succeeded in continuing with his communal work in Israel, he could count me in.

After all, I presumed that if here in Russia, where our activism entailed literal self-sacrifice and where we lived in constant doubt of what the morrow would bring, I still devoted myself to the cause, then surely I would be able to continue to do so in the West. If I only had a decent wage, I would be happy and willing to be busy all day spreading Torah.

In this too I was somewhat mistaken since, when I arrived in Israel and began working, I found it very hard to get accustomed to a fixed salary. As a businessman, even if I experienced tough times, I had become used to frugal periods being followed by better times. Suddenly, I had to manage on a fixed monthly stipend.

In time, however, things turned around. Our commitment to keeping Shabbos in Russia meant that my sister hadn't been able to attend university and study a profession, but she wasn't going to stick with cleaning floors in Israel.

Before long, she heard about an employment agency in Tel Aviv that used newly developed aptitude tests to recommend a particular field of work to applicants. When she went to get tested, the agency found that she had the potential to be an excellent draftsman, at the time a highly sought after profession in Israel. After completing a drafting course with distinction, she found work with the Jerusalem Municipality planning department. For the most part, she worked on planning smaller thoroughfares and street crossings and redesigning those that had fallen into disrepair.

Years later, she would tell me of her sense of satisfaction whenever she passed through the streets of Jerusalem and recognized one of her street crossings. Perhaps, she would think to herself, a Jewish life had been saved on account of her work.

Monthly Support from the Rebbe

R. Moshe left Russia in July, a few months before me. As was customary in those days, all of his friends and acquaintances came to greet him at the airport. After the initial excitement, R. Moshe asked them how they were doing in Eretz Yisrael. One friend reported proudly that he ran a factory manufacturing blankets, while another dealt in textiles. All of them were eager to show that they had become successful businessmen.

But R. Moshe was not impressed. After his initial shock wore off, he admonished them: "*Oy, oy, oy*. Is this why you came to the Holy Land—to make blankets and rags? *Gevald, gevald...*"

As soon as he could, R. Moshe wrote to the Rebbe about his arrival and about his plans to pursue his communal work together with his friends who were soon coming from Russia. A few weeks passed with no answer forthcoming from the Rebbe.

R. Moshe informed the Ezras Achim charity about his intentions of founding Chamah in Israel. They were aware of our work in Samarkand and had sent us regular packages of valuable goods to help with finances. When they heard that R. Moshe wanted to carry on in Israel, they sent him $1,000 of monthly support, a hefty sum in those days.

One day, R. Binyamin Gorodetzky, the Rebbe's representative in Europe, came to visit. He invited all of the Chabad immigrants to Israel to a special gathering at the Devorah Hotel in Tel Aviv where he was staying. Many of the new arrivals came and R. Moshe was present too.

After he greeted the immigrants, R. Binyamin began to speak about the importance of communal work in Eretz Yisrael. R. Moshe, in his typical unassuming manner, stood quietly in a corner of the hall while closely following the proceedings. Seeing the muted response to his words, R. Binyamin asked directly, "Who wrote to the Rebbe that he wants to continue working in *askanus haklal,* in communal activism?"

The room was silent. R. Moshe was quiet too but he realized that the Rebbe had written to R. Binyamin regarding the letter he had sent.

After the meeting emptied out, R. Moshe went over to R. Binyamin and told him that he was the one who wrote to the Rebbe. "What do you plan on doing?" R. Binyamin asked.

R. Moshe told him his ambitious ideas for spiritual activity among the thousands of immigrants who had come from the Soviet Union and how he was waiting for his friends from Samarkand to come and join him in his sacred work.

R. Binyamin told R. Moshe that he would give him $1,000 towards his work every month. R. Moshe could carry out his plans as he saw fit, and he pledged not to meddle in his work. During the next two months, R. Binyamin sent him a monthly amount of 4,200 *lira,* equivalent to $1,000. Finally, in the third month, R. Moshe received a phone call from R. Efraim Wolf, the director of Chabad affairs in Israel, who said, "The Rebbe sent $1,000 towards your work." At that point it became clear that the Rebbe was personally seeing to it that we were sent the money R. Binyamin had promised each month. This monetary support continued throughout the years, and at one *yechidus* with R. Moshe, the Rebbe referred to this monthly support explicitly, illustrating to us the importance he attached to Chamah's work. It was a great honor and one that hardly any other organization merited to receive.

What are *Mivtzoyim?*

When I finally arrived in Israel from Samarkand with my family, it felt like we had fallen onto another planet. We were utterly confused and disoriented by the rich, teeming life around us. When we were in Jerusalem, we gawked at the fur *shtreimels*, white socks, and other *hareidi* garb. We knew nothing about other sects of Judaism and were clueless as to how to interact with them. It perplexed us to see Jews with shaven beards, but their hair grown into *peyos* and tucked behind their ears. If they had long *peyos,* why was the beard missing?

I envied the look of contentment I saw on the faces of the people on the street, and the ease of spirit it spoke of, like that of a man who feels comfortable in his own home. After decades of anticipation for the day I would finally arrive in Eretz Yisrael, I had envisioned that I would immediately feel at ease in this country. I was disappointed to discover that my constant sense of being out of place seemed to have followed me from Russia. After being dogged by the sentiment for so many years, it was difficult to adjust to a new mindset. However, we burned with an energy and desire to work with our brothers and sisters from Russia, who were by then emigrating by the thousands. After generations of complete estrangement, they lacked even the most minimal knowledge of Judaism, Torah, and *mitzvos.*

Although in Samarkand we were primarily involved in teaching children, we presumed that in Eretz Yisrael, which teemed with yeshivas and religious schools, the immigrant children would receive a proper education and we would not be needed in this field. As new immigrants, we were unaware of the ignorance and the absence of basic Jewish knowledge that was endemic in the local public schools—even in Israel—and how important it was to ensure that the immigrant children received a proper Jewish education.

My own work with Chamah continued almost as soon as I had descended from the ladder of our aircraft, sank to my knees, and kissed the holy soil of Eretz Yisrael.

The very next morning following my arrival, R. Yehoshua Raskin and R. Zalman Stambler came by the Kfar Chabad home of my sister, Sarah Mishulovin, where we were staying. They were among the first people R. Moshe included in Chamah's work in Israel, and they asked me to join them on *Mivtzoyim.*

In Russia, we had never heard the word *Mivtzoyim*, and during the few hours that I had been in Eretz Yisrael, I hadn't had enough time to acquaint myself with the latest Lubavitcher terminology. I asked them, "What is *Mivtzoyim*?"

"We are going to conduct an 'Evening with Chabad' at absorption centers," they explained unhelpfully.

Mivtzoyim, it turned out, referred to the Rebbe's campaigns to encourage Jewish awareness and observance. They then explained that absorption centers were places where new immigrants would commune. Chassidim would arrange evenings of song with a Chassidic flavor at the centers, along with lectures about the importance of Judaism. I was happy to join them. It was my first tentative step toward outreach in Israel.

I'll never forget those "Evenings" that we held back then. Naturally, we spoke to the new immigrants in fluent Russian. We told them that we too had just arrived from the Soviet Union, that we had fulfilled Torah and mitzvos secretly there, and had even organized underground yeshivas.

The immigrants were incredulous. "You were religious in Russia? Yeshivas in Russia? How can it be?"

We explained that it was all done secretly with the support of the Lubavitcher Rebbe and that now too we had come as his emissaries. He was calling on them to take advantage of the opportunity they had in Eretz Yisrael to ignite their Jewish spark laying within.

This message made a significant impression on them and brought them to regard Lubavitch in high esteem. After the lectures, we held a "Question and Answer" session and then we sang Chassidic melodies and danced with them. These were very emotional gatherings.

An Impromptu Performance

About a week after my arrival, R. Menachem Lehrer, director of the Nachalas Har Chabad branch of Tzach, Chabad's outreach arm, called me and asked me to be ready Sunday night at 8:00 pm. I was needed at an "Evening with Chabad" at a military base in Tel Nof. I asked who else would be going along and Menachem replied simply, "Other Lubavitchers."

A military jeep arrived at the appointed time, and R. Menachem told me to join him and enter the jeep. I asked him, "Who else is going? I don't know what to do there."

R. Menachem replied, "Don't worry; plenty of others are waiting for you there."

I didn't realize he was joking. When I arrived at the camp, I was welcomed by an officer who told me to come with him.

"Where are the others Rabbi Lehrer told me would be here?" I asked.

"What do you mean? The *chevreh* are waiting for you!"

I followed him, and I then realized who the *chevreh*," the "boys," were: I was brought into a large hall where I was placed on stage facing hundreds of officers and soldiers. The officer introduced me as a new immigrant who had arrived from the Soviet Union just a week before and they all applauded. I didn't know what I was supposed to do next. I hadn't imagined R. Menachem would arrange that sort of surprise performance for me!

Having no choice, I began to talk in my halting Hebrew. I spoke about the sacrifices we made learning Torah, performing *mitzvos,* and keeping Shabbos, our underground yeshivas, and more. I told them about how the Rebbe had empowered us in faraway Russia. Then I took some questions, and despite how uncomfortable I had felt, it seemed like the soldiers were enjoying it. The entire program lasted an hour and a half, and when it was over, they applauded once again and I was taken back home by jeep.

A few days later, R. Menachem approached me and asked in an excited tone, "What was it that you told those soldiers?"

"Why? Did I do anything wrong?" I asked, concerned.

"On the contrary!" said R. Menachem. "You left a tremendous impression on them!"

A Convention of Scientists

In line with our work in adult education, and with immigrants in particular, shortly after our arrival we organized a convention in Tel Aviv for intellectuals. We brought together immigrant academics and scientists with world-renowned reputations, both religious and irreligious, to demonstrate that Torah and science do not conflict. We assembled hundreds of respected individuals for the convention, including Professor Alvin Radkowsky, a religious scientist involved with America's nuclear submarine program; Professor Alexander Zarchi, a religious Jew and a pioneer in ocean water desalination; Professor Zev Lev, a prestigious chemist from Tel Aviv University; and Professor Berger-Barzilai, who had been Lenin's agent to spread the Communist ideology in the Middle East before he was thrown into prison on his return to Russia. Miraculously freed from imprisonment ten years later, Professor Berger-Barzilai immigrated to Israel, became religious, and occupied a prominent place in the Israeli political class.

It was interesting to see the positive responses we received upon inviting these world-renowned professionals and intellectuals to partake in the gathering. I remember that, when we invited Professor Alexander Zarchi, he responded that we would do better without him. The government despised him, he explained, and he would bring negative attention.

Then he related the following:

"I am engineer by profession. While living in Russia, I was thrown into prison, accused of holding Zionistic views. When I was released, I made it safely to the shores of Israel, where I continued to work as an engineer and became involved in salt water desalination. I was making progress in the field and had discovered a breakthrough in the form of an apparatus I had engineered to desalinate water.

"I approached Ben-Gurion with a sketch of my idea and demonstrated to him how I would implement it. It would be the first system of its kind and it was bound to attract a lot of investment to Israel. To start the project, I asked him for $100,000. He replied that religious Jews can study the Talmud but they can't invent technology. He told me to leave him alone and forget about my plans. That was the extent of his antipathy toward religious Jews.

"Ultimately, I traveled to America and found a company that offered me one million dollars to purchase the patent. I returned to Israel, showed Ben-Gurion the offer, and only then did he agree to help me with the project: He needed validation from America to trust a *hareidi.*"

Still, despite his initial reservations, Professor Zarchi too participated in the event.

After the event, R. Berke Wolf, who was the spokesman for Chabad in Israel, told us: "I paid a visit to see what the Russian Chabadniks have created and I have to admit that this event blew my mind. I have never seen such a terrific and successful organization."

After getting involved with these activities immediately upon our arrival, we ourselves were surprised at our own ability to organize every event down to the last detail.

A Call from the Rebbe

A few weeks after the scientists' convention, we were working in Chamah's office on a new project. The office was no more than a designated room in R. Moshe Nissilevitch's apartment. Suddenly, the phone rang and R. Moshe picked up. After he listened for a moment to the person on the other line, I could see that he was very excited. He motioned for me to take the receiver.

I held the phone against my ear and heard an unfamiliar voice saying, "This is the *mazkirus,* the secretariat." I had no idea what that meant and I asked, "Which *mazkirus?*" The answer was, "The Rebbe's *mazkirus.* Rabbi Chadakov wants to speak to you." It was Rabbi Binyamin Klein on the line.

I remembered having seen Rabbi Chadakov's name and a description of the work he did with the Rebbe when I managed to smuggle a copy of a *HaYom Yom* from Moscow. At the end of the

slim book, below the name of the Rebbe, was the name of the director of Merkos L'Inyonei Chinuch, Rabbi C.M.I. Chadakov.

I became very nervous and I listened to Rabbi Chadakov in a
sort of stunned silence. I had the niggling feeling that the Rebbe was
on the line, and during the conversation I thought I heard a voice
speaking softly to Rabbi Chadakov several times, as though instructing him what to say.

Rabbi Chadakov said, "You have already been working for three
months in Eretz Yisrael. What exactly are you doing?" While I had
only come more recently, R. Moshe had begun working immediately after he had come, a few months prior to my arrival.

I replied, "We hold 'Evenings with Chabad,' organize gatherings, lectures, and *Shabbatons*; we speak with immigrants to encourage them to keep Torah and *mitzvos*, and so on."

Rabbi Chadakov then inquired, "Have you sent any children to
attend religious schools?"

I said, "No."

He asked me, "Have you arranged for one hundred children to
attend school?"

"No."

Rabbi Chadakov continued, "Did you arrange for fifty to go?"

"No."

"Did you arrange for forty?"

"No."

He kept asking and I kept responding, "No." He was down to ten
children. At that point, our Father Avraham's conversation with the
Almighty, in which he attempted to have the city of Sodom spared
from annihilation, flashed through my mind. Perhaps there are fifty
righteous people in the city? forty? thirty?

Finally, he asked whether we had made arrangements for ten
children. My negative reply was greeted by silence. At the other end
of the line I could hear the Rebbe whispering something. "*Nu*," R.
Chadakov said, "then what are you doing?"

Pausing for a moment, I then replied, "Now we know what we
have to do and will begin to work on it."

Education as a Priority

I reported to R. Moshe the details of the conversation and we immediately sat down to construct a plan of action. We enlisted the help of R. Yosef Ladayev, a dynamic individual who had worked with us in Samarkand. He began working with the new immigrants, particularly those from Bukharia. The focus was, as the Rebbe wanted, to have them put their children into religious schools.

We knew that once the immigrants were settled in absorption centers and their children were already attending government schools, it would be difficult to remove them. We decided that the best course of action would be to catch them at the first possible chance, right there at the airport in Lod. As the passengers landed, our little band from Chamah would approach them, find out which absorption center they were being sent to, and arrange to meet with them the next day in order to arrange schooling for their children.

Naturally, the Jewish Agency wasn't too thrilled about this. They even tried to thwart our efforts, but by presenting ourselves as relatives of the newcomers, in most cases we were able to approach them.

Word spread quickly among the new arrivals that members of Chamah could arrange religious schooling for their children, including space in a dormitory, if needed. It reached the point where the telephone number of Chamah's office became known to the émigrés before they even departed from Russia. When our activists were unable to approach the immigrants at the airport, they knew to call the Chamah office in Nachalas Har Chabad. They said, "In Samarkand you took care of our children's religious education. Please come to our absorption center and help us here too." We spoke their language and we wanted to assist them, and the immigrants, who felt alone in their adopted country, were happy to form a connection with us.

In those years, there were hordes of new immigrants flocking to Israel from Russia and Bukharia, and within a short time there wasn't enough space in the Chabad schools for all of the children to be placed.

I remember that we once spoke with one of the principals of a Chabad school, asking him to accept a new group of immigrant children, only to be told that registration was full and that there was no more room. We couldn't understand how, for lack of space, they could reject a Jewish child from learning Torah. We persisted, "In Samarkand, children like these would study in our house, in our sole bedroom, just so they could learn Torah."

The principal said, "If you want, take them into your house now too. Here in our yeshiva, it doesn't work that way. If there is no bed in the dormitory, I can't accept another child."

Eventually I realized that although in Russia we acted in what might be called an undisciplined manner, under normal circumstances, order is essential.

After a while, R. Shmuel Chefer of Kfar Chabad contacted us. He had just come from New York and said that the Rebbe had told him to pass on the message to Chamah that we should try to register Russian children in Chabad schools until there was no room left. Then, we should send the children to other *hareidi* and religious schools.

Since we had so many children who wanted to be accepted to the schools we recommended and we had nowhere to send them, we eventually founded a new yeshiva in Ashdod, with the Rebbe's consent. The yeshiva wasn't very organized; some classes comprised children of various ages, but we were happy that the children were learning in our school and receiving a Jewish education.

R. Zushe Wilmowsky was a friend of Chamah and a constant source of encouragement and support. He once told us surreptitiously, "I know that the Rebbe received some complaints regarding your yeshiva in Ashdod, about how children of different ages learn in the same class, amongst other problems. In response, the Rebbe quoted them the Talmudic adage 'Competition breeds wisdom.' If someone could provide a better alternative for those children, they are welcome to."

At one point, some Lubavitchers suggested that we incorporate our school with the struggling Yeshivas Achei Temimim in Rishon

L'Tziyon. Barely ten children learned there at the time and the merger would revive the institution. After asking the Rebbe and then, based on his instructions, discussing it with the faculty there, we transferred the students from Ashdod to Rishon L'Tziyon. The yeshiva there thus grew by nearly one hundred students.

Since the administration of the yeshiva in Rishon L'Tziyon had no experience in educating Russian and Bukharian children, R. Moshe Nissilevitch and R. Yehoshua Raskin joined the faculty. This way, together with other Chamah activists, they could ensure the children benefited from a high-quality yeshiva tailored to their needs.

For Shabbos, some of us would go to Rishon L'Tziyon in order to *farbreng* with the older *bochurim* staying there and to help them with their spiritual and material acclimation. We worked hard but, with thanks to Hashem, we reaped great results from our efforts.

In the meantime, R. Mendel Futerfas urged us to establish another yeshiva in Kfar Chabad. He organized a meeting in Kfar Chabad attended by R. Simcha Gorodetzky, R. Shmuel Chefer, R. Shlomo Maidanchik, and others. At the end of the meeting, it was decided that the community council would give us a small building if we undertook to renovate it and make it suitable for a yeshiva for Bukharian children. It was agreed that we would run the yeshiva, unfamiliar as they were with the mentality of Bukharian Jews.

We repaired the building and appointed R. Berke Schiff, who worked for Chamah at the time, to run the yeshiva. For two years he received his salary from Chamah, until the yeshiva became financially independent. That was how Yeshivas HaBukharim in Kfar Chabad began.

From then until these lines are being written, some thirty-five years later, we have placed over 30,000 immigrant children into various religious schools around the country. This sacred work continues to this day, and it is thanks to this that multitudes of religious and Chassidic families were established. Many of them can be accredited to the selfless effort of R. Yosef Ladayev, who worked tirelessly to ensure a proper *chinuch* for the émigré children.

The Rebbe Says to Use the Name "Chamah"

R. Moshe Nissilevitch went to the Rebbe for Tishrei, 1971. Those who were in Crown Heights for the High Holidays that Tishrei remember it as a particularly special time. Many recently freed Russian chassidim had come to New York to see the Rebbe. At one of the *farbrengens*, the Rebbe turned to the guests and said that whoever had run a yeshiva "over there," meaning in Russia, should come forward to receive a cup of *mashke* to say *l'chaim*. Some chassidim urged R. Moshe to go forward, but he could be quite reserved and refused to move until someone else went over to receive the *mashke*.

After *Havdalah* on Rosh Hashana, when R. Moshe passed by the Rebbe, the Rebbe asked him why he hadn't come forward when he was called. R. Moshe said that he was shy. The Rebbe said, "Then how do you want to be involved in spreading the wellsprings [of Torah and Chassidus]?"

Before he left for Eretz Yisrael, R. Moshe had a private audience with the Rebbe that ensued for forty-five minutes. The Rebbe asked him, "What are your plans?"

R. Moshe, a man of big ideas, told the Rebbe all of his plans, sure that the Rebbe would agree to them and give him a blessing for their fruition. He said that he intended on hiring ten men with ten cars so they could operate simultaneously across the country.

The Rebbe asked, "When did you leave Russia?"

R. Moshe answered, "Six months ago."

The Rebbe said, "You should know that everything here is connected with money and politics. Where are you going to get the money from to implement your ideas?"

"We'll do fundraising," he replied.

"And what will people say—that a bunch of *shnorrers* have come from Russia?"

"We will contact wealthy men and raise the money we need," he said with some naiveté.

"Start with one and a half people—you and another person working part-time—and one car," the Rebbe advised.

Hearing this sober take on the realities of outreach work and the challenges ahead, R. Moshe was taken aback, and he blurted out, "*Oy... Moshiach* should come already!"

"I also want *Moshiach* to come!" replied the Rebbe, before adding, "But start by getting a desk in the Tzach office in Tel Aviv."

Then R. Moshe asked, "What name shall we use? Should we continue using Chamah, the name we used back in Russia?"

The Rebbe asked whether the KGB knew of the name Chamah and R. Moshe replied that it wasn't possible that they knew it since only a few members of Chamah knew of the name. The Rebbe said, "*Nu*, then continue using the name Chamah. There's no need to operate under the name of Chabad; it's Russian Jews helping fellow Russian Jews."

When R. Moshe returned to Israel, he relayed to us the details of his *yechidus*. R. Yehoshua Raskin then went and purchased an office desk and planted it in Tzach's Tel Aviv branch. Thus we began working as a division of Tzach for Russian immigrants.

We worked in that manner for about a month and a half, until we realized that we couldn't operate efficiently in the Tzach office and we turned to the Rebbe for advice. We received his consent to open our own office and soon thereafter we rented a space in Tel Aviv.

Move Over to Outreach

Although I was already in Israel, having arrived at the beginning of September, I couldn't join R. Moshe on his trip to New York later that month. Of course, I wanted to travel to see the Rebbe as soon as possible, but it took too long to prepare all the necessary papers. It was only a few months later, in time for the 19th of Kislev, that I was finally able to travel to the Rebbe.

When I arrived in New York, it was late, already close to midnight, but I wasn't ready to go to sleep. Instead, I asked my host to take me as soon as he could to 770 Eastern Parkway in Brooklyn—

the Rebbe's shul, the headquarters of Chabad, and the home of
every chassid.

As the famed building came into view, my host pointed out a
glow emanating from a room on its left-hand side. That room was
the Rebbe's study, and despite the late hour, he was still there. The
sight reminded me—with a thousand degrees of distinction—of
that oft-repeated Communist fairytale, about how while all the
citizens of the Soviet Union were fast asleep, one window at the
Kremlin was still lit. There, they would say, sat Stalin—of cursed
memory—worrying about world peace.

Was this not the perfect opposite of that lie? I thought to myself. While the rest of the world is busy with their own affairs, here
sits the Rebbe, who *truly* concerns himself with everyone else's
welfare. How many tears had the Rebbe shed here for us while we
were behind the Iron Curtain? I reminded myself where I had
been but a year earlier, and where I was right now, outside the
Rebbe's room.

When the time came, my cousin's husband, Rabbi Berel Junik,
who was something of a regular in the Rebbe's household, guided
me in my first audience with the Rebbe, my *yechidus*. On a small
note that I would bring in with me to present to the Rebbe, I wrote
a few brief details of my life story. When I entered the *yechidus*,
though, I had a distinct feeling that the Rebbe already knew everything I had been through. The Rebbe asked me what I had done for
a living in Russia, and when I replied that I had produced signs and
labels, he told me to continue with the same line of work in Eretz
Yisrael.

When I returned to Israel, I found work at a sign-making workshop in Tel Aviv, and would contribute to Chamah's activities in the
evenings. R. Moshe was unhappy with this arrangement and
claimed that I ought to be involved with Chamah the entire day.

When I told him that I was only doing as the Rebbe had instructed, R. Moshe countered by quoting the Chassidic adage about
yechidus: "If you go in a fool, you'll come out a fool." Then he added,
"If you would've insisted, with a bit of the right sort of chutzpah,

that you want to go into communal work, the Rebbe would have instructed you as such."

That was how the next two months passed. During the day I produced signs, at night I worked with Chamah, and in my spare time, I argued with R. Moshe.

Eventually, I decided to write to the Rebbe. After first putting down all of R. Moshe's arguments on paper, I then asked directly: Should I continue with the sign making, or move over to outreach work? My letter came back from the Rebbe with the last words underlined. Then, in his handwriting, it read, "May it be with success."

From then on, I threw myself into Chamah's holy work full time, my life's work.

GLOSSARY

The following terms are Hebrew unless noted otherwise. (Spelling reflects Ashkenazic pronunciation.)

Aguna	(lit. "anchored woman"); a woman whose husband has disappeared, leaving her unable to remarry
Aliya	(lit. "going up"); the honor of being called up to Torah to recite the blessings before and after the reading of a Torah portion. Also refers to "going up" or moving to the Land of Israel.
Askanus	Community work
Aveiros	Sins
Avreichim	Older students or young married men
Badchan	Wedding entertainer
Bar mitzvah	(lit. "son of the commandment"); when a boy is called to the Torah at age thirteen, the age of Jewish adulthood
Beis Hamikdash	The Holy Temple
Bittul	(lit. "self-nullification"); a commitment to G-d and divine service that transcends self-concern
Bochur, bochurim (pl)	(lit. "young unmarried men"); used in reference to yeshiva students
Boruch Hashem	Blessed be G-d!

Bris	Circumcision
Brocha	Blessing
Bubbe	(Yiddish) Grandmother
Chabad	The Chassidic movement founded by R. Schneur Zalman of Liadi in the latter part of the eighteenth century; also known as Lubavitch or Chabad-Lubavitch
Chacham, chachamim (pl)	Wise men; title for a sage or leader in Sephardic communities
Chassid, chassidim (pl)	(lit. "pious"); an adherent or follower of a Chassidic rebbe
Chassidus	Chassidism, the movement within Judaism founded by R. Israel Baal Shem Tov (1698–1760); the teachings and philosophy of this movement.
Cheder	Torah school for young children
Chesed	Compassion, lovingkindness
Chinuch	Jewish education or upbringing
Chumash	Pentateuch; the Five Books of Moses
Daven, davening	(Yiddish) To pray or recite the prescribed prayers in the Jewish liturgy
Eibershter	(Yiddish) "The One Above," referring to G-d
Eretz Yisrael	The Land of Israel
Erev Pesach	The day before Passover
Esrog	Citron; used during the holiday of Sukkos as one of the "Four Species"
Farbrengen	(Yiddish) An assemblage addressed by a rebbe, or an informal gathering of chassidim characterized by singing and inspiring talk
Gabbai, gabbaim (pl)	The lay official responsible for the proper functioning of the synagogue and religious services

Gartel	(Yiddish) A sash or belt worn by chassidim during prayer
Gemara	The Babylonian Talmud
Hakafos	(lit. "circles"); dancing with the Torah scrolls— seven times around the reader's platform—on Erev Simchas Torah and Erev Shmini Atzeres
Halacha, halachic	The body of Jewish law, or a single law
Hashem	(lit. "The Name"); G-d
Har HaZeisim	The Mount of Olives, a neighborhood adjacent to the Old City of Jerusalem and the site of a 3,000-year-old Jewish cemetery
Kaddish	(Aramaic, lit. "holy"); prayer recited by a mourner or by the prayer leader
Kallah	Bride
Kiddush	(lit. "sanctification"); the blessing over a cup of wine expressing the sanctity of Shabbos or a festival
Kollel	Institute for advanced, fulltime study of the Talmud and rabbinic law
Kosel	The Western Wall of the Second Temple
L'chaim	(lit. "to life!"); a toast or blessing often exchanged over wine or other strong drink
Lubavitch	Town in Russia which served as the center of Chabad Chassidism from 1813 to 1915 and whose name has become synonymous with the movement
Maariv	Evening prayer service
Mashpi	A Chassidic spiritual mentor
Matzah, matzos (pl)	Unleavened bread eaten on Passover

Mehudar	An enhancement in the performance of a divine commandment; for a ritual object, going beyond the bare minimum required.
Mesiras nefesh	(lit. "giving of the soul"); self-sacrifice
Mezuzah	(lit. "doorpost"); parchment scroll affixed to the doorposts of a Jewish home containing portions of the *Shema*
Mikvah	A ritual bathing pool for immersion as part of the transition to ritual purity
Mincha	Afternoon prayer service
Minyan	The quorum of ten Jewish men necessary for communal prayer
Mivtzoyim	Chabad mitzvah campaigns; outreach
Mishna	The first compilation of Oral Law, ca. 200 CE
Moshiach	(lit. "the anointed one"); the Messiah. One of the thirteen principles of Jewish faith is that G-d will send the Messiah to return the Jews to the land of Israel, rebuild the Holy Temple, and usher in the utopian Messianic Era.
Mohel	A person trained in the practice of ritual circumcision
Nachas	Pride or satisfaction
Ohel	(lit. "tent"); the structure built over the resting place of a rebbe and frequented by chassidim in prayer
Parshah	Weekly Torah portion
Pesach	Passover; the eight-day festival commemorating the Exodus from Egypt
Purim	(lit. "lots"); the holiday celebrating the rescue of Jews from Haman's plot to annihilate them

Rebbe Rayatz	R. Yosef Yitzchak Schneerson (1880–1950), the sixth leader of Chabad-Lubavitch; headed the movement's active resistance against Communist suppression of religion in Russia; transferred the movement to US during the Second World War
Rebbe	A Torah teacher; used primarily to refer to leaders of the Chassidic groups. Today, "the Rebbe" is often a reference to R. Menachem M. Schneerson, the late Lubavitcher Rebbe.
Rebbe Rashab	R. Sholom Dovber (1860–1920), the fifth leader of Chabad-Lubavitch; founder of the Tomchei Temimim yeshiva in Lubavitch in 1897
Rebbetzin	(Yiddish) Wife of a rabbi or rebbe, or a pious woman of great spiritual achievements
Rosh Hashana	(lit. "head of the year"); the Jewish New Year, commencing the ten "Days of Awe"
Sefarim	Holy books, or books of Jewish religious literature regarded as sacred
Shabbos	(lit. "rest"); the Sabbath, a day of rest on the seventh day of the week
Shamash	The custodian of a synagogue
Shechita	Ritual slaughtering
Shema	(lit. "hear"); the daily declaration of faith, recited in the morning and evening prayers and before retiring at night
Sheva Brachos	(lit. "seven blessings"); the seven blessings recited under the wedding canopy; the week of festivities following the wedding during which the blessings are repeated

Shliach	(lit. "one who is sent"); messenger; refers to emissaries of the Lubavitcher Rebbe involved with outreach work
Shmini Atzeres	The eighth day of the Sukkos festival, a holiday celebrated with great joy
Shmoneh Esrei	(lit. "Eighteen Benedictions"); also referred to as the *Amida,* the main section of the daily prayers, recited standing
Shnorrer	Beggar
Shochet	Ritual slaughterer; one who slaughters and inspects cattle and fowl for kosher consumption
Shofar	Ram's horn, sounded on Rosh Hashana and at the close of Yom Kippur
Sholom aleichem	(lit. "Peace upon you"); a common greeting
Shidduch	Matchmaking
Shul	Synagogue
Siddur, siddurim (pl)	Traditional prayer book
Sifrei Torah	Handwritten Torah scrolls
Simchas Torah	(lit. "Rejoicing of the Torah"); festival immediately following *Sukkos,* on which the public reading of the Torah is annually concluded and recommenced
Sukkah	A hut or booth that Jews are commanded to dwell in during the holiday of Sukkos
Sukkos	(lit. "booths"); eight-day holiday celebrated in the autumn
Tallis	Prayer shawl with ritual fringes at four corners, worn during prayer
Tallis katan	Garment worn under a shirt with fringes (*tzitzis*) in four corners

Talmud	Compendium of Jewish law and thought; edited in Babylonia, late fifth century CE
Tanya	Fundamental text of Chabad philosophy; written by R. Schneur Zalman of Liadi in the eighteenth century
Tefillin	(lit. "phylacteries"); small black leather cubes containing parchment scrolls inscribed with the *Shema* and other biblical passages, wrapped with bands on arm and head for weekday morning prayers
Tehillim	The biblical book of Psalms
Tishrei	Hebrew month, corresponding to September–October, in which the High Holidays and Sukkos are celebrated
T'naim	Engagement
Tomchei Temimim	The yeshiva founded in Lubavitch in 1897 by Rebbe Rashab; also refers to its subsequent offshoots
Torah	The Five Books of Moses (the Bible), as well as a term for the overall body of Jewish religious teachings in Jewish law, practice, and tradition
Tzaddik	A wholly righteous person
Tzedakah	(lit. "justice"); charitable donations
Tzemach Tzedek	R. Menachem Mendel of Lubavitch (1789–1866), third leader of Chabad-Lubavitch; son-in-law and successor of R. Dovber of Lubavitch
Tzitzis	Fringed four-cornered garment, or fringes of said garment
Yahrzeit	(Yiddish) The Hebrew date of the anniversary of the death of a parent or close relative observed by lighting a memorial candle and reciting the *Kaddish*

Yarmulke	(Yiddish) Skullcap; the head covering worn to symbolize recognition of G-d above
Yechidus	A private audience with the Rebbe
Yerushalayim	Jerusalem
Yeshiva	Academy of Jewish learning
Yiras shamayim	Fear of G-d
Yom Kippur	Day of Atonement; fast day climaxing the ten "Days of Awe"
Yom Tov	Jewish holiday or festival
Zeide	(Yiddish) Grandfather

ABOUT THE AUTHOR

Hillel Zaltzman was born in Kharkov, Ukraine, in 1939. Fleeing the German invasion in 1941, the Zaltzman family settled in Samarkand, a city in southeastern Uzbekistan, along with many war refugees. There the Chabad community was able to reestablish houses of worship, Jewish schools, and a yeshiva, which operated in secret to avoid persecution by the Soviet authorities. Hillel received his early Jewish education from distinguished rabbis who taught small groups of children at great personal risk. In the postwar years under Stalin, with more frequent arrests, the Zaltzmans hid a fugitive rabbi in their home for six years.

At age sixteen, Hillel joined a newly-formed clandestine group called Chamah, whose goals were the preservation and promotion of Judaism and to provide economic assistance to the Jews of Samarkand. They founded a network of underground classes for children and a fund to help needy Jews obtain coal and food packages. Through their efforts, an underground yeshiva also emerged in Samarkand, housed in private homes. At age twenty, the author traveled extensively through the Soviet Union in connection with his community work, while taking the opportunity to visit and bolster the morale of isolated Chassidic and religious Jews. In 1971, after a fifteen-year wait, he finally received his exit visa and he and his family left for Israel.

In Israel, Rabbi Zaltzman and his friends saw a continuing need for Chamah—to help Russian immigrants adjust to their new home. They created programs to introduce new immigrants to Jewish culture and started schools for Russian and Bukharian children. Zaltz-man moved to New York in 1973, where he established a New York office for Chamah.

Over the years, Chamah became a successful and accomplished international organization assisting Russian Jews on three conti-nents—in the United States, Israel, and the Former Soviet Union. Rabbi Zaltzman is currently president of Chamah International. Under his leadership, Chamah expanded its activities to include social and medical services, educational programs, and a publish-ing division. In 1989, Zaltzman returned to Russia to represent Chamah's publishing department at the Moscow International Book Fair. He is also the author of a memoir, *Samarkand,* which was published in Hebrew, English, Russian, and Yiddish and upon which this abridged edition is based.

Rabbi Zaltzman was honored in the US Senate in 2016 for his humanitarian work as part of Jewish American Heritage Month. He lives in Brooklyn with his wife, Shoshana. They are parents of a daughter and a son and are blessed with many grandchildren and great-grandchildren.